Borderwork

FEMINIST ENGAGEMENTS WITH COMPARATIVE LITERATURE

EDITED BY

Margaret R. Higonnet

Cornell University Press

Copyright © 1994 by Cornell University

First published 1994 by Cornell University Press.

Printed in the United States of America

⊗ The paper in this book meets the minimum requirements of the American National Standard for Information Sciences—Permanence of Paper for Printed Library Materials, ANSI Z39.48-1984.

Library of Congress Cataloging-in-Publication Data

Borderwork: feminist engagements with comparative literature / edited
    by Margaret R. Higonnet.
        p.   cm.—(Reading women writing)
    Includes bibliographical references and index.
    ISBN 0-8014-2869-6 (cloth).—ISBN 0-8014-8107-4 (pbk.)
    1. Feminist literary criticism.   2. Literature, Comparative—
History and criticism.   I. Higonnet, Margaret R.   II. Series.
PN98.W64B67   1994
809'.89287--dc20   94-11246

For my parents,
who forgave me

when I signed my transit papers on the wrong line

Contents

Acknowledgments

Work at the border may foster creative transformations. My small daughter crayoned for each of her toys a passport, which border controllers solemnly stamped. A bear, sock-doll, and beaver followed and displaced her own travels; they helped her to recall and renegotiate disruptions, losses, and passages. By marking the borders, she acknowledged separations, differences, connections. For me, this book has been that kind of passport: after I constructed the frame, many colleagues placed their marks in it. In the process, the essays that came to my desk led me to perceptions of comparative practice which my first frame could not accommodate. I had to let go of my preconceptions in order to let other approaches in. Once on a trip to the Van Gogh museum at Arnhem, I found myself outside the country before I realized the train was traveling in the wrong direction; then as now, however, there have been many polyglot counselors to help me reach the goal.

A collection of this kind depends on contributions from countless people: teachers, colleagues, students, friends, enemies, and "frenemies." Not only did the contributors themselves exchange papers and comments, but other readers also helped tighten the threads of argument in this web of thought. Foremost were Celeste Schenck and Margaret Ferguson, whose incisive and detailed comments dramatically transformed the manuscript. I am grateful that they found time to mother this project as they were nurturing their own children. My own work has benefited from the acuity, reflective proposals, and support of Doris Sommer, Harriet Ritvo, and Regina Barreca.

A number of comparatists have selflessly given their time and labor to help this book come into being: Mary Ann Caws, Sandie Bermann, Kathleen Komar, and Rosi Braidotti. Charles Bernheimer, Michael Palencia-Roth, and Susan Suleiman generously shared their work and ideas, as did Nancy Huston, Eleni Varikas, Carla Freccero, and Susan Winnett. Encouragement and suggestions at various points and places came from Hortense Spillers, Michelle Perrot, Earl Miner, Elaine Show-alter, Catharine Stimpson, Mieke Bal, and Jane Marcus. The book has always been in my mind and often in my suitcase; it has listened in at conferences and interjected itself into conversations. My closest friends have been tolerant of my obsession, keeping their doors open and their walking shoes on. Catherine Lugar was always ready to help me track down an elusive text.

The University of Connecticut Research Foundation, the Instituto Juan March, and the National Endowment for the Humanities sup-ported travel and research for this project. I also thank my students at the University of Connecticut and the University of Munich, in partic-ular Marianne Sadowski and Katharine Rodier, who have fed me a sustaining mix of photocopies, cake, printouts, and laughter.

Early and late, often very early and very late, Patrice and Ethel have been there.

M. R. H.

Borderwork

Introduction

MARGARET R. HIGONNET

> To survive the Borderlands
> you must live *sin fronteras*
> be a crossroads.
> —Gloria Anzaldúa

Along with Gloria Anzaldúa, we all dream of living without or beyond *fronteras*.[1] Borderlands, to be sure, may feed growth and exploration or may conceal a mine field. The creative work of linguistic
hybridity takes place at these points of encounter; here, too, systems of
exclusion may lead to censorship or even death. Choices and comparisons arise at frontiers: their enigma challenges us to examine, resist,
and exploit lines of division within ourselves and to test intellectual
limits, whatever their source. This volume stands as such a point of
engagement, where concepts basic to both comparative literature and
feminist theory both intersect and pull apart.

The question of boundaries is a key to what one critic has called "the
permanent crisis of comparative literature." The fertility of the field has
depended on asking again and again, "What is to be compared with
what, by whom, to what end, and under what conditions?"[2] A flurry
of handbooks in the 1960s and early 1970s charted and chartered comparative literature as a discipline. Their signposts typically pointed to
the study of periods, themes, genres, translation, literature and the
other arts, and influence (or a bit later, reception theory and intertextuality). Historically imbued studies and institutions continue to operate within these classifications.[3] But with increasing insistence today we
hear calls to "redraw the boundaries" of national literary studies, or to

[1]The epigraph is from Gloria Anzaldúa, *Borderlands: The New Mestiza = La Frontera*
(San Francisco: Spinsters/Aunt Lute, 1987), 195.
[2]Ulrich Weisstein, "Lasciate Ogni Speranza: Comparative Literature in Search of Lost
Definitions," *Yearbook of Comparative and General Literature* 37 (1989): 99–100.
[3]In spite of his subtle critique of earlier theoretical models, for Claudio Guillén the
"basic issues" remain genres, themes, literary relations, and historiology, in *The Challenge
of Comparative Literature* (Cambridge: Harvard University Press, 1993).

"find theories' that cross borders, that blur boundaries."[4] As early as 1956, René Wellek rejected the "customshouse" model of binary comparison across national boundaries, arguing instead that a truly comparative literary history would describe transnational genres, schools, or periods, placing texts "inside a scheme of universal literature."[5] Schemes of "universal literature," however varied and expansive, may nonetheless screen particular historical interests. At successive horizons, national, continental, "cultural," and "civilizational" models require different interpretive grids. As many have noted, schemes that single out a language, a continent, or an empire all obscure the complex interweavings of cultural processes by masking the cultural and linguistic hybrids that emerge at their own limits. Indeed, all hermeneutic systems select among horizons of interpretation, in what is inevitably "a political and cultural act."[6] For this reason, many comparatists today weave together multiple disciplines in a reading practice that may be called métissage, a practice which recognizes that representation cuts across the boundaries of juridical, political, anthropological, and artistic discourses.[7]

Precisely the indeterminacy of comparative literature as a discipline has fostered its continuous retheorizing of interpretive models and their consequences. Why that has happened may be better understood by examining the metaphor of the title, Borderwork. A border is a complex construct that defines and localizes what it strives to contain or release. It is rarely a smooth seam; an edge may ravel, gape open at interstices, or leak in both directions. Borders mark sites of rupture, connection, transmission, and transformation. Rather than understand them as static lines of demarcation, margins, or impermeable walls, therefore, we might want to examine them as what anthropologists call contact zones. Since the work of cultural transmission in contact zones is im-

[4]Stephen Greenblatt and Giles Gunn, eds., Redrawing the Boundaries: The Transformation of English and American Literary Studies (New York: Modern Language Association of America, 1992), 1–11; Gloria Anzaldúa, introduction, to Making Face, Making Soul = Haciendo Caras: Creative and Critical Perspectives by Feminists of Color, ed. Gloria Anzaldúa (San Francisco: Aunt Lute, 1990), xxv.

[5]René Wellek and Austin Warren, Theory of Literature (New York: Harcourt Brace & World, 1956), 245. I borrow the term "customshouse" from Clayton Koelb and Susan Noakes, eds., The Comparative Perspective on Literature: Approaches to Theory and Practice (Ithaca: Cornell University Press, 1988), 8.

[6]Debra A. Castillo, Talking Back: Toward a Latin American Feminist Literary Criticism (Ithaca: Cornell University Press, 1992), xvii.

[7]See, for example, Françoise Lionnet, Autobiographical Voices: Race, Gender, Self-Portraiture (Ithaca: Cornell University Press, 1989), 8; an outline of pairings is provided by Jean-Pierre Barricelli and Joseph Gibaldi, eds., Interrelations of Literature (New York: Modern Language Association of America, 1982).

provisational and interactive, the literary critic who examines such processes of transmission can move beyond "one-way questions."[8]

In the late twentieth century, the violent redrawing of political frontiers around the world has complicated the comparativist's ideal of open borders in a "global" republic of letters, an ideal that itself emerged from world conflict. The crisis provoked by renewed nationalisms and by the pursuit of "ethnic purity" coincides with a sustained reconsideration of definitions of geographic and linguistic identity which have regulated the discipline of comparative literature. Differences internal and external to a culture have acquired such value that some propose renaming the field "contrastive literature," as "an antidote to certain homogenizing, westernizing, monistic tendencies of Comparative Literature as an academic discipline.[9] As the remapping of national frontiers proceeds, so does another kind of borderwork: testing the continued pertinence of concepts that institutionalize much literary scholarship. In all areas of literary study, framing concepts such as genre, national literature, the site of the critic, and literariness have come into question. For the American Comparative Literature Association (ACLA), the defining disciplinary concepts have come in such doubt that Charles Bernheimer's 1993 "report on standards" questions their very applicability. The Bernheimer report attacks the field for its restrictive Eurocentrism, exclusive focus on high literary discourse, and passive reproduction of the canon; it calls on comparatists to "theorize the nature of the boundaries to be crossed."[10]

The border has been a privileged, if hazardous, trope for feminist activity. "Border feminists," to borrow a phrase coined by Sonia Saldívar-Hull in Criticism in the Borderlands, have examined processes of marginalization that exclude texts produced by minority groups and devalue "minor" genres or movements.[11] Others call for investigation of "border cases," where hierarchic binarisms that govern symbolic economies—such as black versus white or male versus female—become

[8]See Mary Louise Pratt, Imperial Eyes: Travel Writing and Transculturation (New York: Routledge, 1992), 7; and Eugene Eoyang, "Polar Paradigms in Poetics: Chinese and Western Literary Premises," in Comparative Literature East and West: Traditions and Trends: Selected Conference Papers, ed. Cornelia Moore and Raymond Moody (Honolulu: University of Hawaii Press, 1989), 11–21.

[9]Michael Palencia-Roth, "Contrastive Literature," ACLA Bulletin 24.2 (1993): 47–60.

[10]Charles Bernheimer et al., "A Statement of Purpose: Comparative Literature at the Turn of the Century" (draft version). The final version of the report will appear with responses in Comparative Literature in the Age of Multiculturalism from Johns Hopkins University Press.

[11]Sonia Saldívar-Hull, "Feminism on the Border: From Gender Politics to Geopolitics," in Criticism in the Borderlands: Studies in Chicano Literature, Culture, and Ideology, ed. Héctor Calderón and José David Saldívar (Durham: Duke University Press, 1991), 210.

unsettled.[12] The trope can become hazardous when it conveys the claim that work on the margin brings an immunity to critique or a moral superiority; it then turns into an excuse that conceals the privileged status of most academics and the limits of individual vision.

This book works at the meeting points of comparative literature and feminist criticism, testing conceptual boundaries that constrain their practices. What might feminist engagements with comparative literature yield? A family romance or an armed conflict? The idea that feminist theories can renovate not only literary study at large but comparative literature specifically has wide currency. In an essay written for the Modern Language Association, Cary Nelson observed that feminists have shifted attention "from how to interpret literature to how the discipline of literary studies is constituted."[13] The logic of feminist scholarship, according to Lillian Robinson in a volume on "decolonizing tradition," "necessarily entails rethinking the entire literary tradition" to encompass "excluded classes, races, national groups, sexual minorities, and ideological positions. . . . What this means is a more truly comparative literature."[14] Gayatri Chakravorty Spivak has also spoken of "feminism as the movement with the greatest radical potential within literary criticism."[15] Daniel Stempel, in his introduction to *Comparative Literature East and West,* specifically contrasted the traditional focus of comparative literature on areas such as "genre study, historical periods, movements, source and influence studies, myth and themes" to "feminist literary history and criticism, whose transformation of traditional scholarship is visible in every journal."[16] In his ACLA report on standards, Charles Bernheimer suggests that the discipline develop links to feminist studies, "arguably the most influential theoretical approach of the past twenty years."[17] This volume explores those links, but it does not see the connection as simple or without tensions.

Whereas the anthologies that proliferated in the 1970s often suggested that comparative literature was "an entity with its own unmis-

[12]Valerie Smith, "Split Affinities: The Case of Interracial Rape," in *Conflicts in Feminism,* ed. Marianne Hirsch and Evelyn Fox Keller (New York: Routledge, 1990), 271–87.
[13]Cary Nelson, "Against English: Theory and the Limits of the Discipline," *Profession* 87 (1987): 46–52.
[14]Lillian Robinson, "Canon Fathers and Myth Universe," in *Decolonizing Tradition: New Views of Twentieth-Century 'British' Literary Canons,* ed. Karen R. Lawrence (Urbana: University of Illinois Press, 1992), 29.
[15]Gayatri Chakravorty Spivak, *The Postcolonial Critic: Interviews, Strategies, Dialogues,* ed. Sarah Harasym (New York: Routledge, 1990), 118.
[16]Daniel Stempel, introduction, to Moore and Moody, *Comparative Literature East and West,* ix–x.
[17]Bernheimer, "Statement of Purpose."

takable *Gestalt*,"[18] feminist critics have conspicuously used the genre of the anthology to break up monolithic concepts of feminism. Teresa de Lauretis, for example, warns, "An all-purpose feminist frame of reference does not exist, nor should it ever come prepackaged."[19] Just as there are many feminisms, so are there many comparatisms—a point made by Clayton Koelb and Susan Noakes in their collection, *The Comparative Perspective on Literature*.[20] Yet some comparative institutions lag behind the innovative range of individual practices; dedicated journals often reinforce a narrow Eurocentric canon of writers and critics, as do many departmental reading lists.[21]

This volume aims to break up perceptions not only of feminism as a singular theory or cultural politics, but of comparative criticism as an "entity" or discipline. It juxtaposes different voices, to stress not homogeneity but conflicts and discontinuities, and to do so by exploring a range of discourses—female circumcision, rape, slavery, and pedagogy, for example. If some of these voices propose a new relationship between comparative literature and feminist criticism, others engage a debate over the totalizing, psychologizing, and individualizing of literary and cultural difference. Theory figures here not in isolated splendor but as a practice that generates fresh readings. The clustering of essays around four topics—the construction of identity, genre theory, the site of the critic, and institutional engagements—should not obscure the interweaving of many of these topics within the essays.

Under the impetus of postcolonial and post–cold war politics, new theoretical approaches have facilitated and accelerated institutional change. In response to demands for a more "multicultural" curriculum, anthologies of "world literature" are adapting their contents to include texts from beyond Europe, and translations serve a burgeoning interest in "third world" literatures; studies in comparative poetics open new doors of understanding; journals have emerged to address altered conceptions of comparative practice that are more global and more inter-

---

[18]Weisstein, "Lasciate Ogni Speranza," 98. More recent collections such as *The Comparative Perspective on Literature*, edited by Clayton Koelb and Susan Noakes, reflect the trend to decenter literary study.

[19]Teresa de Lauretis, ed., *Feminist Studies, Critical Studies* (Bloomington: Indiana University Press, 1986), 14.

[20]Koelb and Noakes, *Comparative Perspective on Literature*.

[21]See Margaret Higonnet, "Feminist Criticism and Comparative Literature," in *Littérature générale/littérature comparée*, ed. Paul Chavy and György M. Vajda (Bern: Lang, 1992), 269–75; and Kathleen Komar, "Feminist/Comparatists and the Art of 'Resisting Teaching,'" in *New Visions of Creation: Feminist Innovations in Literary Theory*, ed. María Elena de Valdés and Margaret R. Higonnet (Tokyo: International Comparative Literature Association, 1993), 180–86.

disciplinary.[22] As attention shifts to popular culture and oral arts, neglected populations, including women, move to the fore. Subaltern studies have been particularly hospitable to feminist work; postcolonial studies highlight the comparative work to be done within national boundaries.[23] These innovations point to new forms of intertextuality, to "other languages and cultures, other disciplines, other races, or the other sex."[24] "Other to whom?" one might nonetheless ask. The liberating model of the critic as traveler, exile, or hobo, while drawing perspicacious and imaginative critics such as Edward Said, Jane Marcus, and Houston Baker, also carries with it a baggage of voyeurism and self-exculpation, on which Susan Sniader Lanser reflects in this volume.

The question of the female subject shapes the first section, which draws on debates that the concept of identity has sparked both in comparative literature and in feminist theory. Although the gap between an individual woman and the state may seem vast, recent work on nationalisms has examined the way that "imagined communities" inscribe and exploit gender. In the domain of comparative Latin American studies, for example, Jean Franco and Doris Sommer have traced the way that successive social meanings of national identity (for example, as pure blood or as a stable hearth) accrue around the female body.[25] These meanings are not themselves fixed. In a radical critique of the categories of identity used by many feminists, Judith Butler asks how language constructs the categories of sex. Feminist work in com-

[22]Examples include the *Longman Anthology of World Literature by Women, 1875–1975*, ed. Marian Arkin and Barbara Shollar (New York: Longman, 1989); Mary Ann Caws and Christopher Prendergast, eds., *Harper-Collins World Literature Reader* (New York: Harper-Collins, 1993); Earl Miner, *Comparative Poetics: An Intercultural Essay on Theories of Literature* (Princeton: Princeton University Press, 1990); and journals such as *Synthesis*, which, according to a 1993 flyer, planned to present "neglected" perspectives, interdisciplinary work, and topics such as "feminism, multiculturalism, . . . comparative aesthetics" (flyer).

[23]Spivak, of course, has been highly influential here. See also Rajeswari Sunder Rajan, *The Lie of the Land: English Literary Studies in India* (Delhi: Oxford University Press, 1992); Hilary Kilpatrick, "Arab Fiction in English: A Case of Dual Nationality," *New Comparison* 13 (1992): 46–55; and Reed Way Dasenbrock, "Intelligibility and Meaningfulness in Multicultural Literature in English," *PMLA* 102 (1987): 10–19. The question of women's "national" identity is clearly raised by the works in eleven languages (and spanning thirteen centuries) presented in the two volumes of Susie Tharu and K. Lalita, eds., *Women Writing in India* (New York: Feminist Press, 1991).

[24]Koelb and Noakes, *Comparative Perspective on Literature*, 17.

[25]Jean Franco, "Beyond Ethnocentrism: Gender, Power, and the Third World Intelligentsia," in *Marxism and the Interpretation of Culture*, ed. Cary Nelson and Lawrence Grossberg (Urbana: University of Illinois Press, 1988), 508; Doris Sommer, *Foundational Fictions: The National Romances of Latin America* (Berkeley: University of California Press, 1991). See also Andrew Parker, Mary Russo, Doris Sommer, and Patricia Yaeger, eds., *Nationalisms and Sexualities* (New York: Routledge, 1992).

parative literature has reopened earlier understandings of identity as national or linguistic, on the grounds that political identities simultaneously construct and erase the female subject. For feminist critics under the influence of poststructuralism, the borders of "personal" identity have come to be seen as shifting and constructed, not fixed or organic; likewise, social identities are no longer naturalized in nineteenth-century positivist terms as "racial." "Gender trouble" complicates feminist theory: What *is* a "female subject"? To what extent has the psychoanalytic dimension of much feminist study (whether of the female subject or of related genres such as the female bildungsroman) reinforced Eurocentrism? Can a comparative feminist criticism take into account the different interactions of class and race with gender? Such questions, which have come to the foreground in contemporary feminist theory, are cast up for consideration by several contributors to this volume. Françoise Lionnet, for example, asks whether gender relations differ in non-Western societies under the impact of caste and noncapitalist economies. If so, are feminist, gender-conscious approaches appropriate?[26]

A related plane on which comparative and feminist approaches intersect is that of linguistic identity. Although the idea of a linguistically unified nation-state has special force in Europe, elsewhere the exceptions outnumber examples. Is bilingualism a problem or an asset? Feminist theories of code switching and of double-voiced writing contest older notions of linguistic purity and coherence within national boundaries. Yet much cross-cultural feminist work is subject to the charge that it depends on translations and transplanted cultural concepts. An exemplary exception is Regina Harrison's interdisciplinary study of Quechua women's traditions in the Andes, to which the MLA awarded the Katherine Singer Kovacs prize in 1991.[27]

Is sex itself a language, a semiotic system, or a sociolect? If one accepts the premise that control of the female body is, in the words of Santi Rozario, "of the utmost importance in maintaining group bound-

[26]Among the many volumes that raise such questions, particularly suggestive critiques can be found in Castillo, *Talking Back*; Spivak, *Postcolonial Critic*; Anzaldúa, *Making Face*; Judith Butler, *Gender Trouble: Feminism and the Subversion of Identity* (New York: Routledge, 1990); Trinh T. Minh-Ha, *Woman, Native, Other: Writing Postcoloniality and Feminism* (Bloomington: Indiana University Press, 1989); and Fedwa Malti-Douglas, *Woman's Body, Woman's Word: Gender and Discourse in Arabo-Islamic Writing* (Princeton: Princeton University Press, 1991).

[27]In her fascinating study of popular culture and oral arts, Regina Harrison juxtaposes anthropology and textual analysis, women's laments and their love amulets: *Signs, Songs, and Memory in the Andes: Translating Quechua Language and Culture* (Austin: University of Texas Press, 1989).

aries and social hierarchy,"[28] does it follow that female sexuality is a text inscribed on the body—as essays in this volume by Françoise Lionnet and Rajeswari Sunder Rajan suggest? Do literary forms and aesthetic norms take shape around the female body as signifier? The inscription of violence as ambivalent preserver/destroyer of "feminine" integrity has triggered meditations both on the fetishization of a woman's body as text and narrative moment and on its unrepresentability.[29]

Questions about individual identity have shifted the orientation of historical study as well. In response to earlier assumptions that "national" or "cultural" traditions are coherently determined by dominant groups, a fresh interest in countertraditions and internal cultural contradictions flourishes. Until recently, for example, the discipline of comparative literature occluded the functioning of color lines as well as gender in the cultural construction of identities and literatures. A more sensitive literary history will recognize what Hortense Spillers calls in her afterword to *Conjuring* a "matrix of literary discontinuities."[30] The former blindness to racially defined traditions in literary history is no longer possible for comparatists, as pressure has been brought to bear on the discipline by specialists in African American literature who challenge the defining norms of national literary analysis. Within the framing language of comparatism, for example, Henry Louis Gates, Jr., has repeatedly interrogated "black" identity as a professional tool. Thus, in an essay first presented at the MLA, he argued that a "black" text must be cited both within the American tradition and within its particular tradition, defined not by racial biology or a mystical essence called blackness "but by the repetition and revision of shared themes, topics, and tropes, a process that binds the signal texts of the black tradition into a canon.... It is no more, or less, essentialist to make this claim the existence of French, English, German, Russian, or American literature.... For nationalism has always been the dwarf in the critical, canonical chess machine."[31] The impact of such renewed questions about

[28]Santi Rozario, "Ethno-Religious Communities and Gender Divisions in Bangladesh: Women as Boundary Markers," in *Intersexions: Gender/Class/Culture/Ethnicity*, ed. Gill Bottomley, Marie de Lepervanche, and Jeannie Martin (North Sydney: Allen and Unwin, 1991), 14–32.

[29]See Mieke Bal, *Femmes imaginaires: l'ancien testament au risque d'une narratologie critique* (Paris: Nizet, 1986); and Lynn A. Higgins and Brenda R. Silver, eds., *Rape and Representation* (New York: Columbia University Press, 1991).

[30]Hortense J. Spillers, "Cross-Currents, Discontinuities: Black Women's Fiction," in *Conjuring: Black Women, Fiction, and Literary Tradition*, ed. Marjorie Pryse and Hortense J. Spillers (Bloomington: Indiana University Press, 1985), 251.

[31]Henry Louis Gates, Jr., "On the Rhetoric of Racism in the Profession," in *Literature, Language, and Politics*, ed. Betty Jean Craige (Athens: University of Georgia Press, 1988), 26.

the intersection of national and individual identity is most visible in this volume in essays on diasporic African literatures, a concept that must include Portuguese, Spanish, French, and Creole literatures, as well as indigenous and anglicized forms. When focused on the writings of women, "diaspora" criticism can inaugurate a new practice of feminist comparative literature, represented here by VèVè Clark and Bella Brodzki.[32]

The comparative study of texts rests on assumptions about the group identities not only of authors but also of *texts*—their participation in conventions or "norms" characteristic of a culture, period, or genre. Genre theory, to which the second section of this volume is devoted, has undoubtedly been one of the strong suits of comparative literature. Feminist explorations of the construction of the individual female subject have dramatically shifted genre study by tracing the way the gender of the protagonist dictates the rules of the game. According to Lore Metzger's interpretation here of the marginal ballad genre, the taboo subject of the female vampire or lamia sustains the aesthetic transformation of the ballad form by writers such as Goethe and Coleridge. Yet the shadow side of genres, marked by various forms of cultural difference, has often eluded critical attention. The issue of violence centered on a female body as text links the essays on rape and slavery in Part I of this volume with the studies in genre theory of Part II. It can be a problem of form: if dramatic theory depends on a social process of victimization and exclusion, asks Anca Vlasopolos, does that linkage explain our inability to read certain problem texts?

One genre has received particular attention from feminists because its very center is the formation of the subject: the bildungsroman.[33] A prime example of a form first described in terms of a male protagonist as member of a social or artistic elite, this genre has been reconceived in light of the forces that "form," limit, and liberate female protagonists. Marianne Hirsch traces intertwined processes of transformation that affect men as well as women, and reconfigure family structures through

[32]See Gay Wilentz, *Binding Cultures: Black Women Writers in Africa and the Diaspora* (Bloomington: Indiana University Press, 1992); and VèVè Clark, "Developing Diaspora Literacy and *Marasa* Consciousness," in *Comparative American Identities: Race, Sex, and Nationality in the Modern Text*, ed. Hortense J. Spillers (New York: Routledge, 1991), 40–61.

[33]See, by Marianne Hirsch, "Spiritual Bildung: The Beautiful Soul as Paradigm," in *The Voyage In: Fictions of Female Development*, ed. Elizabeth Abel, Marianne Hirsch, and Elizabeth Langland (Hanover, N.H.: University Press of New England, 1983), 23–48; *The Mother-Daughter Plot: Narrative, Psychoanalysis, Feminism* (Bloomington: Indiana University Press, 1989), esp. 91–121; and her essay in this volume.

narrative displacements. She returns to the canonical text of *Jane Eyre* as a comparatist who reassesses feminist assumptions.

More contrastive approaches to genre underscore historical and cultural difference. In her cross-cultural analysis of Buchi Emecheta's *Slave Girl*, Bella Brodzki unfolds ways in which African and African American slave narratives both share common structures and differ, depending on the moment of record, as to the gender of the protagonist, and the special terms of servitude imposed on women in a given society. In my own essay, working within one fairly limited period, when most fiction about World War I was written, I question the canon shaped by literary critics who have assumed a relative homogeneity among writers and their experiences. To dispel that critical fiction I ask why women are not recognized as writers about war. How does masculine authorship become conflated with authenticity, or the "real"? How does the inclusion of women's texts from places as far-flung as Bengal or the Cameroons alter our understanding of war literature and of the complexities of national identity?

Genre and period study have tended to go hand in hand in the past because certain periods seem to favor one form or another, as Georg Lukács noted. In turn, our understanding of a period may reflect a narrow critical stress on one elite literary form and its makers. The task of rethinking the reach of group identities can help us to realign the clusters of common literary structures and to recognize how these inscribe social difference. As Chris Cullens suggests here in her study of eighteenth-century women, certain literary commonalities among a group of writers spring from their group identity within the social order: thus the German and English women whose novels she studies shared adverse material conditions of literary production—obstacles to education and publication—that shape the twists of their plots. If we turn our gaze to these neglected women writers, we can begin to recognize a broad period phenomenon, one that has eluded students of the Romantic period, traditionally understood to be an Olympus inhabited by male poets.

Other, historically defined clusters may be flung across time as well as space and language, suggesting that new literary histories need to be written. In several books and articles Annette Kolodny has broken open traditional concepts of masculine territorial conquest in American literature. She defines "frontier literature" as intrinsically multilingual, polyvocal, intertextual, and multicultural. If a frontier is not a line but a "territory or zone of interpenetration between . . . previously distinct societies," then the hybridized styles, tropes, and structures of frontier texts will demand a "radically comparativist" and interdisciplinary scholarship.[34]

The inflection of a genre may depend on class background, color, or other cultural structures. The theme of "passing" can now be recognized not only as a product of racism and homophobia but as constituting a narrative "line" in novels that dramatize attempts to construct a self that defies essentialist and determinist social regulation. Sexual practices can furthermore provide a map to concealed literary traditions: Biddy Martin has argued on behalf of grouping lesbian texts together as expressions of "a desire that transgresses the boundaries imposed by structures of race, class, ethnicity, nationality."[35]

Who cuts the border? This question posed by Hortense Spillers in *Comparative American Identities* affects our understanding of genre analysis and literary history, of authors and critics.[36] The third section of this volume investigates the position of the critic. It asks how her voice speaks, translates, or ventriloquizes. If we do not speak ourselves but "are spoken" by language and culture, what does it mean to engage in a critical activity of interpretation and explanation? Who speaks for whom? The problem is pervasive (if not intractable): if reading is a form of dialogue with an interlocutor, how can one avoid usurping the voice of the other? Does any act of criticism necessarily constitute "information retrieval"? The implied authenticity that lies behind charges of usurpation presumes that there are proximate others that one *can* represent and speak for. Where should the line of difference fall? Such difficulties thread through this volume, from Françoise Lionnet's opening response to a dialogue between an Egyptian novelist and a prostitute, through Sabine Gölz's meticulous examination of Derrida's criticism as a form of gendered mime, to Fedwa Malti-Douglas's provocative questions about the politics and proprieties of a feminist approach to Arab women's texts and Obioma Nnaemeka's proposals for a multicultural pedagogy.

For a comparatist it is particularly pertinent to acknowledge the multiplicity of sites that a critic occupies—a point that Greta Gaard speaks to eloquently in her suggestive study of bisexual theory as a form of comparatism. One way to think about this multiplicity has been to pos-

---

[34]Annette Kolodny, "Letting Go Our Grand Obsessions: Notes toward a New Literary History of the American Frontiers," *American Literature* 64 (1992): 4, 15.

[35]Biddy Martin, "Lesbian Identity and Autobiographical Difference(s)," in *Life/Lines: Theorizing Women's Autobiography*, ed. Bella Brodzki and Celeste Schenck (Ithaca: Cornell University Press, 1987), 94.

[36]Hortense J. Spillers, "Introduction: Who Cuts the Border? Some Readings on 'America,'" in *Comparative American Identities*, 16.

tulate a divided critical positioning, the critic as the "voice of the shuttle." But is that the voice of the comparatist who commutes between literatures, or of the silenced woman? Obioma Nnaemeka proposes cultural study by juxtaposition in order to defamiliarize one's own most familiar cultural practices. What might be the hazards in turn of a feminist bifocalism or "pluralism"?[37]

Identity politics bear directly on feminist poetics and criticism. Repudiations of the critical practice of "speaking for others" reflect an awareness that "where one speaks from affects the meaning and truth of what one says . . . a speaker's location is epistemically salient."[38] Much feminist criticism has assumed, in an inversion of age-old misogynist attitudes, that the woman who reads reads resistantly, and differently, from the man who reads.[39] This model implies an oedipal struggle between "young" feminists and older (male?) comparatists. Some such contestatory model probably lurks within any revisionist project, whether the stakes are the (re)definition of genres or the evaluation of a critical approach, as in Sarah Goodwin's reflections here on feminism and the "new historicism." For the purpose of responding to indiscriminate attacks, it may be useful to postulate a community of feminist critics, or even to recognize the threat of exile on an island within the seas of academe—a metaphor that Nancy Miller exploits with vivid force and subtlety, imagining herself as Philoctetes' sister.

Yet disagreement seems to have increased about how categories should be drawn, and about how membership in conflicting groups informs critical practice. It is important not to hypostasize the female or the male reader. Here the indeterminate figure of the "polysexual" critic, proposed by Greta Gaard, offers a fresh alternative to rigid positioning. Can a readerly identity be inscribed on a woman's body? Do cultural practices separate or unite women across boundaries of age, class, and legal status? Françoise Lionnet forcefully asks whether one can interpret a text about a practice such as excision without raising issues of moral evaluation and bias. And Obioma Nnaemeka likewise

---

[37]See Elizabeth Meese, *Crossing the Double Cross: The Practice of Feminist Criticism* (Chapel Hill: University of North Carolina Press, 1986).

[38]Linda Alcoff, "The Problem of Speaking for Others," *Cultural Critique* 20 (Winter 1991–92): 6–7.

[39]See Judith Fetterley, *The Resisting Reader: A Feminist Approach to America Fiction* (Bloomington: Indiana University Press, 1978); and Patrocinio P. Schweickart, "Reading Ourselves: Toward a Feminist Theory of Reading," in *Gender and Reading: Essays on Readers, Texts, and Contexts*, ed. Elizabeth A. Flynn and Patrocinio P. Schweickart (Baltimore: Johns Hopkins University Press, 1986), 31–62. Susan Noakes examines the cliché from a comparative, thematic perspective in "On the Superficiality of Women," in Koelb and Noakes, *Comparative Perspective on Literature*, 339–55.

wrestles with the possibilities of shaping a critical sisterhood across cultural difference.

In this vein, critics such as Spivak have charged their readers to reflect on comparative practice as a form of "information retrieval," or the exploitation of "native informants" as a system of literary colonization that leaves Western theories and "great traditions" (the work of Wordsworth or Woolf) in undisturbed power. Feminist comparatists such as Jean Franco, Debra Castillo, and Rey Chow have likewise noted that Western theory tends to project a non-Western material-political Other on which to operate.[40] Spivak targets totalizing interpretive acts as forms of critical violation or even rape.

Figuring comparative literature as "rape," although melodramatic, leads to broader questions about study of the Other. Do we demarcate ontological boundaries in order to project outward the negative or repressed side of our discourse? Indeed, the prevalence of rape as a topic of critical theory (to which Rajeswari Sunder Rajan here urges our attention) suggests that the violation of the female body displaces some other, unspoken critical violation. How can one work at the border without absorbing, usurping, or silencing another? Understood in this way, ethnographic or cultural study is always implicitly ethnocentric, freighted with scopophilia, and prone to view the Other as a feminized and subordinate spectacle.[41] The would-be multiculturalist becomes a critical tourist, as Fedwa Malti-Douglas and Susan Sniader Lanser argue, insulated from threat of contamination by theoretical antibiotics.

Institutionalized distinctions between scholarship and teaching, reinforced by the trend toward theoretical abstractions in comparative literature, have led comparative critics to neglect their site in the classroom. Drawing on her experience in teaching introductory courses, Obioma Nnaemeka proposes that teachers resist the one-way, Eurocentric bias of much critical interpretation by employing the critical voice as a shuttle that moves in both directions across the border. Comparative study can thus defamiliarize one's own most familiar cultural practices; to go beyond the implied hierarchies of "one-way" questions and the static rediscovery of cherished preconceptions, the comparatist can place her own culture into the field of analysis.

Comparative classwork stumbles again and again against the poverty—and incompatibility within groups—of our linguistic skills. In addition, as VèVè Clark and other contributors to this volume remind us,

---

[40]Franco, "Beyond Ethnocentrism"; Castillo, *Talking Back*; Rey Chow, *Women and Chinese Modernity: The Politics of Reading between West and East* (Minneapolis: University of Minnesota Press, 1991), xvi.

[41]See Chow, *Women and Chinese Modernity*, 5, 7, 174n.

besides language there are many other historical, economic, and religious tools that a reader must acquire before the complex cultural pattern of a diasporic literature falls into place. The last section of this volume, then, reweaves threads in the web of comparative practice in the academy. How is one to shift position and to change the opening questions when most undergraduate and many graduate courses in comparative literature or in "multicultural" studies continue to present texts either in translation or drawn from postcolonial literatures in European languages?

A common complaint about comparative literature and feminist practice today is that they both remain confined within Western critical norms. As Rey Chow points out in *Women and Chinese Modernity*, however, such a critique runs the risk of displacing ethnic individuals such as herself (born and raised in Hong Kong), whose entry into a culture historically inflected by imperialism is already "Westernized."[42] A purist "nativism" would require non-Western critics to examine only non-Western topics, thereby reinscribing an idealist opposition between the West and "the rest," or between first and third worlds. Such geographic and political dichotomies impede recognition of the complex interpenetration of cultures and of differences within "national" cultures. This volume does not, therefore, attempt to differentiate first from third world feminist theories. Rather, it works to utilize feminist insights in order to nuance comparative practice and, conversely, to nuance and render more comparative the practice of feminist criticism.

The boundary becomes problematic for feminists working on gender issues, as Diana Fuss notes, "when the central category of difference under consideration blinds us to other modes of difference and implicitly delegitimates them."[43] Borderlines police not only inclusions but exclusions, not only privilege but repression—lines inscribed on the backs of those groups who are marked as different. In *Beloved* Toni Morrison describes the physical inscription of slavery as a tree of scars on Sethe's back. Maxine Hong Kingston's warrior woman Fa Mu Lan carries scar-words of revenge for her people on her back. In *This Bridge Called My Back*, Cherríe Moraga reminds herself that a bridge gets walked over.[44] The work of the border, the burden, is differentially allocated.

---

[42]Ibid., xi.

[43]Diana Fuss, *Essentially Speaking: Feminism, Nature, and Difference* (New York: Routledge, 1989), 116.

[44]Cherríe Moraga, *This Bridge Called My Back: Writings by Radical Women of Color*, ed. Gloria Anzaldúa and Cherríe Moraga (Boston: Kitchen Table/Women of Color Press, 1983), xv.

Comparative literature needs to renew continually the questions it raises about the boundaries of its subject and its practice. Many issues call for fresh approaches. The concept of a civilization remains inflected geographically by continental units, historically by neocolonialism, and aesthetically by an assumed priority of European forms and norms. Can cross-cultural study provide a new justification for "global" literary study? Attempts to expand the curriculum by including "third world" literatures embed a linear theory of political and economic development, as well as the homogenization of the West's Other. Ancient Chinese and Indian literatures, such as a ninth-century anthology of literature by nuns, can scarcely be described as emergent or "third world." Is "global" really different from "universal"? Or must comparative study abandon its totalizing aims and refocus its energies on local practices?

The complex testimonial narrative of Rigoberta Menchú, to which several essays here refer, puts into play many of the issues raised by the border for comparative work. She reminds us that this metaphor records real political costs and gains. In order to reach an audience, Menchú had to cross two linguistic thresholds: first, she had to acquire Spanish in order to communicate with *compañeros* from other villages, and second, she had to speak through an ethnographic mediator, Elisabeth Burgos-Debray. She learned Spanish, a language of colonization and exploitation, because by contrast to the twenty-two Guatemalan Indian languages, "Spanish was a language which united us." The linguistic barriers she struggles against furthermore are not neutral facts but signs of economic, educational, and political differences maintained by a structure of institutionalized violence which must be undone.[45] Just as Spanish can become a medium of joint resistance, so can the Bible, an imported text, offer models of resistance in the stories of Jael and Judith. Menchú cites the song of Judith: "He bragged that he would burn up my borders" (Jth. 16:5). Her ironic appropriation of this text as a tool for revolutionary reflection and resistance underscores the complex exchanges at work in her testimony.

Textually, Menchú works through multiple changes in position. She borrows and usurps from the "master" language and culture the tools she needs to liberate her people; she passes from the oral work of organization to the mediated, written work of international mobilization.

[45]"We have to erase the barriers which exist between ethnic groups, between Indians and ladinos, between men and women, between intellectuals and non-intellectuals, and between all the linguistic areas." Rigoberta Menchú, *I, Rigoberta Menchú: An Indian Woman in Guatemala*, ed. Elisabeth Burgos-Debray, trans. Ann Wright (London: Verso, 1984), 162, 223.

She insists on continuously changing activist roles so that no one alone speaks for others. To foreground lines of difference can make action and change possible. Yet Rigoberta Menchú also warns us that no narrative can exhaust her readers' desires or be fully transparent, free of boundaries: "I'm still keeping my Indian identity a secret. . . . Not even anthropologists or intellectuals, no matter how many books they have, can find out all our secrets."[46]

Reading at the crossroads, reading along the borderlines of silence, is the work that confronts both comparative literature and feminist criticism today.

[46]Ibid., p. 247.

Part I

Cross-Cultural Constructions
of Female Subjects

1

Dissymmetry Embodied: Feminism, Universalism, and the Practice of Excision

FRANÇOISE LIONNET

> What is most needed is some kind of special illumination of the structural dissymmetry that runs all through and conditions the entire fabric of social and individual life.
> —Fatima Mernissi

The experience of academic feminist criticism since the 1970s has created almost insurmountable differences between "Western" modes of analysis of the concrete status of women in various non-Western cultures on the one hand, and non-Western women's subjective experience of their own position on the other. Whether it is conflict between "American" and "French" approaches, "essentialist" and "poststructuralist" epistemologies, or "first" and "third" world women, differences of ideology fuel disagreements that threaten to preclude dialogue. In such a climate it has become imperative to reexamine the ground from which such conflicts develop, and to try to modulate and nuance the conceptual frameworks that generate these oppositions. To do so, I would like to propose a truly *comparative* feminist criticism, one that is performed on the border between those disciplinary categories. Such an approach aims not at conflict resolution but rather at reframing the issues in such a way that dialogue can remain open and productive, allowing critics to map out new articulations of cultural expressions.

Some critics have suggested that feminism should not be considered a "unitary entity . . . *in* which conflicts can or should be contained," and that feminist activism cannot be subsumed "under the illusion of a

I thank Nawal El Saadawi for her interest in this essay, the friends and colleagues who made generous and careful comments on an early draft, and the participants in the 1990 Harvard English Institute, where this essay was first read. A short version was published in *Passages* 1 (1991), and is reprinted by permission. I also thank the Rockefeller Foundation for supporting my work during 1991–92. All translations are mine, unless otherwise noted. My epigraph is from Fatima Mernissi, *Beyond the Veil: Male-Female Dynamics in Modern Muslim Society* (Bloomington: Indiana University Press, 1987), ix.

unitary governing ideal," be it "woman" or "truth."[1] This argument implies that we might be ill advised to appeal to a set of "universal" (i.e., Western humanist) values which would allow feminists to come to a consensus about the possibility of sharing certain beliefs or points of view regarding both the nature and function of feminism as a global process, and the social construction of femininity within different cultural contexts. The point is well taken: ethnocentric value judgments have no place within a truly diverse, multicultural, and multiracial feminist inquiry.

Yet there is a distinction to be made between *cultural* and *moral* relativism. The question of universalism comes back to haunt us if we do not carefully examine the consequences of a cultural relativism marked by ignorance of, and indifference to, everything non-Western, and thus exemplifying what Kathleen Barry has called a form of "Western liberal particularism that says 'hands off' to anything produced in Third-World nations or cultures." Antiethnocentrism can have the unfortunate consequence of undermining feminist political solidarity, and this kind of liberalism reinforces "Third World masculinist nationalism [which] . . . attempts to isolate women in their cultures and identify western women as their enemy."[2] It is therefore important to continue speaking of community, and to attempt to find a common theoretical and ethical ground from which to argue for political solidarity without either objectifying the "other" woman or subsuming collective goals under the banner of sameness. As Gayatri Spivak stated more than a decade ago: "However unfeasible and inefficient it may sound, I see no way to avoid insisting that there is a simultaneous other focus: not merely who am I? but who is the other woman? How am I naming her? How does she name me?"[3]

I enter the debates on universalism and particularism by briefly ex-

---

[1]Marianne Hirsch and Evelyn Fox Keller, eds., *Conflicts in Feminism* (New York: Routledge, Chapman & Hall, 1990), 2.

[2]Kathleen Barry, foreword to Evelyne Accad, *Sexuality and War: Literary Masks of the Middle East* (New York: New York University Press, 1990), ix. I am emphatically suggesting not that Hirsch and Keller are guilty of this kind of liberalism but that their theoretical positions might lead to such logical consequences.

[3]Gayatri Spivak, "French Feminism in an International Frame," *Yale French Studies* 62 (1981): 179. These lines have been cited by numerous feminist critics who have used it to underscore the need for a "particularist" or "relativist" approach to the study of different cultures. See Elizabeth Abel, "Race, Class, Psychoanalysis? Opening Questions," in Hirsch and Keller, *Conflicts in Feminism*, 197–99; Jane Gallop, "The Monster in the Mirror: The Feminist Critic's Psychoanalysis," in *Feminism and Psychoanalysis*, ed. Richard Feldstein and Judith Roof (Ithaca: Cornell University Press, 1989), 13–24; and Helena Michie, "Not One of the Family: The Repression of the Other Woman in Feminist Theory," in *Discontented Discourses: Feminism/Textual Intervention/Psychoanalysis*, ed. Marleen S. Barr and Richard Feldstein (Urbana: University of Illinois Press, 1989), 15–28.

amining the discursive contexts of a concrete and specific ritual practice: the phenomenon of female excision and infibulation, which is performed in parts of Africa and the Middle East, and which constitutes an important aspect of the cultural identity of Islamic women.[4] These ritual practices, often defined as various forms of sexual mutilation, have since colonial times been denounced by missionaries, colonial administrators, Western media, feminist critics, and health service professionals. They have decried the existence of such "ethnic" customs as "barbaric" or "anachronistic," that is, in terms that often smack of racist, anti-Islamic rhetoric. In the 1970s—especially after 1975, which was declared International Women's Year by the United Nations—the issue suddenly mobilized European and American feminists, to the point that in 1979, Renée Saurel could claim that those practices "have caused much blood to be shed for thousands of years, and much ink for the past two."[5]

In contemporary Western medical and anthropological literature, and in journalistic reports, the subject of excision is often treated peremptorily, in an impassioned, reductionist, and/or ethnocentric mode which represents the peoples who practice it as backward, misogynistic, and generally lacking in humane and compassionate inclinations: in other words, as has always been the case with respect to Africa and Africans, the dominant rhetoric emphasizes lack, absence, failure, inhumanity, and greed.[6] Unfortunately, counterarguments also tend to use inflammatory language. In an interview Mamadou Kante links the recent interest shown by Europeans in the sexual lives of African women to their desire to control the birthrate in Africa: "Everyone knows that if they [i.e., the Western powers] succeed in controlling women under one pretext or another, then the birth-rate in Africa will be under control. Under the misleading pretext of excision, that is the hidden agenda. Such is the realm of occult political forces."[7]

[4]There are three main types of female circumcision. Clitoridectomy, considered to be the equivalent of male circumcision, consists in the removal of the prepuce of the clitoris. Excision is the removal of the prepuce, the clitoris itself, and the labia minora. Infibulation consists in the removal of the clitoris, "the whole of labiae minora and majora, and the stitching together (suturing) of the two sides of the vulva leaving a very small orifice to permit the flow of urine and menstrual discharge." See Olayinka Koso-Thomas, *The Circumcision of Women: A Strategy for Eradication* (London: Zed Books, 1987), 16–17.

[5]Renée Saurel, *L'enterrée vive* (Geneva: Slatkine, 1981), 20.

[6]Anne de Villeneuve, "Étude sur une coutume somali: les femmes cousues," *Journal de la société des africanistes* 7. 1 (1937): 15–32; Fran Hosken, *The Hosken Report: Genital and Sexual Mutilation of Females* (Lexington, Mass.: Women's International Network News, 1982), 201; and Françoise Lionnet, "Identity, Sexuality, Criminality: 'Universal Rights' and the Debate around the Practice of Female Excision in France," *Contemporary French Civilization* 16 (Summer 1992): 294–307.

[7]Mamadou Kante, "L'excision," *Présence africaine* 142 (1987): 180.

Kante may well be justified in questioning the Western powers' motives behind the campaign for birth control: the concern about "galloping demography" in nonwhite countries is indeed laced with racist fears and instincts for self-preservation stemming from the fact that whites are a global minority, and a wealthy one, intent on curbing growth among those generally poorer than they are. But is it really fair to link the fight against excision to the racist wish to control nonwhite women's reproductive capabilities? Or does this accusation simply blur the real issue, marginalizing the female victims while the two opposing sides trade abuse and insults? Statistics do show that excision and infibulation can have lethal side effects that contribute to increased mortality rates for mothers and infants at the moment of delivery.[8] To thus conflate the Western fears about higher birthrates in the "third world" with the human rights issue of maternal and infant health seems to be a downright contradiction. But, of course, birth control information did make its entrance into Africa with the same health care professionals who have denounced genital mutilations in moralizing terms. The attitude of suspicion exemplified by Kante is easy to understand even if one cannot agree with it.

Unfortunately, the generally offensive rhetoric leaves little room for the careful examination of two competing claims: on the one hand, the campaign for the abolition of all such ritual practices on the basis of a universal ethical imperative against the physical torture and psychological impairment of millions of women;[9] on the other hand, a claim of respect for the cultural autonomy of African societies critical of any feminist intervention as "acculturation" to Western standards.

Yet African women themselves have, in no uncertain terms, proclaimed that the issue is theirs to debate and discuss. Of several texts by African women who examine the problem with great care, three are particularly noteworthy: *The Circumcision of Women: A Strategy for Eradication* by Olayinka Koso-Thomas is a well researched document, focused on Sierra Leone, which outlines a twenty-year plan for eradication; *La parole aux négresses* by Awa Thiam is a compilation of interviews with women from francophone and anglophone West African states (Ivory Coast, Guinea, Mali, Senegal, Ghana, and Nigeria); and *The Hidden Face of Eve* by Nawal El Saadawi raises the issue as it

[8]See Michel Erlich, *La femme blessée: essai sur les mutilations sexuelles féminines* (Paris: L'Harmattan, 1986), 132–33; and Koso-Thomas, *Circumcision of Women*, 27.

[9]There are approximately 80 to 100 million excised women in the world today. Of those, about 5 million have also undergone infibulation. See Erlich, *Femme blessée*, 277, and Alice Walker, *Possessing the Secret of Joy* (New York: Harcourt Brace Jovanovich, 1992), 281.

relates to North Africa and the Middle East. Saadawi's novel *Woman at Point Zero* is, with Evelyne Accad's *L'excisée*, one of the few fictional accounts written with moving sincerity and autobiographical detail. It is a more effective and convincing denunciation than many pragmatic or political treatises because it allows the reader to enter into the subjective processes of the individual, to adopt her stance.[10]

These writers are all Western-trained feminist intellectuals or scientists (Koso-Thomas and Saadawi are physicians) who denounce the practice from the vantage point of the educated elite—hence, some have argued, from a perspective more "Western" than "African," and thus alienated from the masses, who would neither read them nor sympathize with their views. There is, in other words, a dissymmetry of class and ideology between them and the uneducated masses, a dissymmetry that is inevitable, since literacy and education remain, to a large extent, steps that favor Westernization. But there are important indications that "progress" is being made; arguments in favor of a form of cultural relativism that would excuse excision on strictly cultural grounds do not have as much currency as some vocal critics of interventionism might lead us to believe.

Indeed, a close examination of some defenses of excision tends to reveal inconsistencies. For example, although Joséphine Guidy Wandja argues in favor of the specificity of African sexuality, and stresses the deep meaning ("signification profonde") of traditional African rituals, declaring that "the African model of sexuality cannot be . . . the same as the European model," she nonetheless must conclude her essay in defense of particularism with a "universally" valid statement that grounds sexuality in the materiality of the body. She does so despite her earlier emphasis on the "optique spiritualiste" of secular African traditions, which she had previously contrasted to the mechanistic and materialist approach of the Americans Masters and Johnson. She asks: "Indeed, how is it possible to explain the age-old customs of a people on the basis of very recent discoveries (20th century)? One can read, for example, that *excision suppresses women's right to experience pleasure,* but in their research, *specialists* would have to give a unanimous definition of *pleasure.*"[11]

[10]Koso-Thomas, *The Circumcision of Women;* Awa Thiam, *La parole aux négresses* (Paris: Denoël/Gonthier, 1978); Nawal El Saadawi, *The Hidden Face of Eve: Women in the Arab World,* trans. Sherif Hetata (London: Zed, 1980), and *Woman at Point Zero,* trans. Sherif Hetata (London: Zed, 1983); Evelyne Accad, *L'excisée* (Paris: L'Harmattan, 1982). Subsequent citations of *Woman at Point Zero* and *The Hidden Face of Eve* appear in the text.
[11]Joséphine Guidy Wandja, "Excision? mutilation sexuelle? mythe ou réalité?" *Présence africaine* 142 (1987): 58, 56.

If the issue is one of defining what constitutes "pleasure," then it seems acceptable to relativize the *definition* according to sociocultural context and/or sexual preference. But Wandja never questions "le droit au plaisir," the right of women to be sensually and/or sexually fulfilled. As a matter of fact, she grounds the ethical problem in the physicality of the body, universalizing the well-being (if not the full integrity) of that body. Hence, one might argue, her position does not invalidate the search for an ethical imperative. Moreover, Wandja falls into what is perilously close to contradiction, for the other side of the coin remains the question of pain: How is it possible to reconcile the fundamental human right to pleasure with the willful infliction of pain on the body of the female child?[12] Her particularist approach fails to justify relativism.

There are, however, in all cultures many practices that aim at regulating, transforming, and "improving" the body. I would be falling into the ethnocentric trap if I did not point out that in the West, the pursuit of an elusive ideal of femininity is also mediated by *pain* (inflicted by the corset, for example). French-speaking female children grow up hearing that "il faut souffrir pour être belle" (you must suffer to be beautiful), and the pain of childbirth has generally been considered the "normal" fulfillment of a woman's destiny—a rite of passage, a difficult but necessary ritual. Similarly, excision and circumcision are considered rites of passage, initiatory practices the purpose of which is precisely to test the mettle of the individual, her endurance of pain, her ability to remain impassive and stoic in the face of severe discomfort. It is a "character-building" experience. It creates solidarity, closeness, and sisterhood among the initiates. Thus, as Wandja puts it, a successful initiation confers respect and dignity on the child now become woman. As an initiatory practice, excision serves the same purpose as other forms of ritualized violence in many different cultures (e.g., fraternity hazing and its occasionally fatal consequences). Furthermore, excision is an operation that has an aesthetic function—on a par with plastic surgery and other (Western) forms of self-denial: what Susan Bordo has called the "normalizing disciplines of diet, make-up, and dress ... [through which] we are rendered more ... focused on self-

---

[12]Need I state that all published oral testimonies of educated *and* illiterate women dwell on the painful aspect of the procedure and its sequels, even if some interviewees maintain that their sexual response (i.e., their ability to experience orgasm) is not affected? See Chantal Patterson, "Les mutilations sexuelles féminines: l'excision en question," *Présence africaine* 142 (1987): "At this stage of the debate I would like to stress the following points: 1. Different civilizations live, practice, and conceptualize eroticism and sensuality differently. 2. If there is any mutilation, a system of compensation must be set in motion by the body, this extraordinary machine" (165).

modification. . . . [These] practices of femininity may lead us to utter demoralization, debilitation, and death."[13]

That is why, I would argue, it is quite possible to link excision to the general cultural paradigm of the reproduction of femininity and its concomitant depersonalizing effects. Marie Bonaparte, who had the opportunity to examine many excised women in Egypt in the 1930s, speculated, with Freud, that the practice stemmed from a wish to maximally "feminize the female" by removing the clitoris, "this cardinal vestige of her masculinity," and to intimidate and suppress the child's sexuality. But she also noted that "the physical intimidation of the girl's sexuality by this cruel excision would not achieve the aim of feminizing, vaginalizing her, any better than the psychical intimidation of the clitoridal masturbation of European little girls."[14] Since the operation suppresses genital structures which are "phallic," the ethnopsychiatrist Michel Erlich adds, the psychological dimension of these operations are "inscribed as the specific manifestation of masculine castration anxiety in front of the "castrated" female sexual organ." In this reading of the practice, male fears of women's sexuality would be the unconscious motivation for exaggerating, and thus controlling, femininity. But, paradoxically, infibulation, which might first appear to be a "hyperfeminization" of the genitalia, can also on the contrary be interpreted as a "phallisation" of the vulva, which has been rendered smooth and convex, thus evoking "a phantasmatic phallus." These conflicting yet complementary interpretations underscore the arbitrariness with which a visually based, and apparently "objective," interpretive grid can be used. The ambiguities and indeterminacies stressed by Erlich point toward the "thickness" or polyvalent nature of all symbolic systems, as Clifford Geertz has shown.[15] It is clear that there are embedded incoherences in the signifying text of culture, and there can be no simple cause, and therefore no simple "solution," to the complex cultural phenomena known as practices of genital mutilation. As Tobe Levin declares: "Western activists must learn to enter the value system of the 'circumcised' to avoid the counter-productive approach based on ignorance and indignation alone."[16]

[13]Wandja, "Excision?" 57. Susan R. Bordo, "The Body and the Reproduction of Femininity: A Feminist Appropriation of Foucault," in *Gender/Body/Knowledge: Feminist Reconstructions of Being and Knowing,* ed. Alison M. Jaggar and Susan R. Bordo (New Brunswick: Rutgers University Press, 1989), 14. See Erlich, *Femme blessée,* 183, for a comprehensive survey of the "aesthetic" argument.
[14]Marie Bonaparte, *Female Sexuality,* trans. John Rodker (New York: International Universities Press, 1953), 207.
[15]Ehrlich, *Femme blessée,* 14. Clifford Geertz, *The Interpretation of Cultures* (New York: Basic Books, 1973).
[16]Tobe Levin, "Women as Scapegoat of Culture and Cult: An Activist's View of Female

It is by pointing out some of the incoherences in cultural practices that we can begin to make sense of them. Indeed, the "official" discourse—on both sides of the ideological fence separating abolitionists from traditionalists—tends to overemphasize coherence, in the one case by appealing to abstract humanitarian notions, in the other by claiming the importance of cultural autonomy and specificity. In 1985 the president of Senegal, Abdou Diouf, stated the position of his government:

> Female mutilation is a subject that is taboo. . . . But let us not rush into the error of condemning [genital mutilations] as uncivilized and sanguinary practices. One must beware of describing what is merely an aspect of difference in culture as barbarous. In traditional Africa, sexual mutilations evolved out of *a coherent system,* with its own values, beliefs, cultural and ritual conduct. They were a necessary ordeal in life because they completed the process incorporating the child in society.
>   These practices, however, raise a problem today because our societies are in a process of major transformation and are coming up against *new socio-cultural dynamic forces in which such practices have no place* or appear to be relics of the past. What is therefore needed are measures to quicken their demise. The main part of this struggle will be waged by education rather than by anathema and from the inside rather than from the outside. I hope that this struggle will make women free and "disalienated," personifying respect for the eminent dignity of life.[17]

President Diouf invokes a "coherent system" of traditions to which he opposes the "new socio-cultural dynamic forces in which [the old practices] have no place." In other words, two symmetrical and coherent systems seem to be opposed, the new displacing the old, the need to disalienate women taking precedence over the physical ordeal of excision. But one might contend that the so-called coherent systems are in fact already undermined by what Mieke Bal has called a "countercoherence," the coherence of dissymmetry, of unequal power relations based on and reinforced by the use of language as an instrument of control, as a weapon capable of ensuring powerlessness in the victims.[18]

Consider, for example, that in many parts of Islamic Africa, notably the Sudan and Somalia, the worst form of insult is to call someone "a gaping vulva." There, speech acts perform tradition, reinforcing the

---

Circumcision in Ngugi's *The River Between,"* in *Ngambika: Studies of Woman in African Literature,* ed. Carole Boyce Davies and Anne Adams Graves (Trenton, N.J.: Africa World Press, 1986), 208.
   [17]Quoted in Koso-Thomas, *Circumcision of Women,* appendix 5, 106; emphasis added.
   [18]Mieke Bal, *Death and Dissymmetry: The Politics of Coherence in the Book of Judges* (Chicago: University of Chicago Press, 1988), 18, 23, 138.

doxa, the meaning of age-old practices. Ideologemes contribute to ensure powerlessness before the social system so that women may take their rightful place as subjected objects of desire. Women are named and defined by men who thus shape their self-understanding. Female self-knowledge is mediated by social perceptions conditioned by patriarchal culture.

Saadawi gives us an intimate and shocking look at this predicament in *Woman at Point Zero*. The protagonist Firdaus, whose name means "paradise" in Arabic, is taught the alphabet by her sexually abusive uncle (15). Later on, when she is living the life of a prostitute, the men to whom she submits also name and define her. They call her "slut," "bitch" (50), "you street walker . . . you prostitute" (49, 62), "you are not respectable" (70), and she begins to use those words herself (50), having internalized the vision conveyed by those speech acts which help perpetuate the status quo. For Saadawi, the construction of female subjectivity is clearly a process of gradual internalization of social knowledge—an internalization that engenders a split, a *Spaltung*, such as the one analyzed by psychoanalytic critics. For Saadawi, too, the female subject is a site of conflicts between an imposed social identity and a shared feminine identification mediated by the intimate experience of physical and verbal abuse, excision, and insult.

If, as Elizabeth Abel has argued, "it is too early for feminism to foreclose on psychoanalysis," then Saadawi provides us with a powerful example of the uses to which psychoanalysis can be put when we are attempting to understand, interpret, and resist certain debilitating cultural practices. As Abel puts it: "The urgency of theorizing subjectivity within a range of social contexts has made it less productive to reiterate old oppositions within psychoanalytic feminism, or between psychoanalysis and contemporary feminism, than to imagine more fluid intersections."[19] Indeed, Saadawi's work as a psychiatrist and a novelist highlights the productive ways in which psychoanalysis, when it is not insulated from social and discursive practices, can help us make sense of, and indeed resist, those discourses that perpetuate women's oppression.

Thus, Firdaus realizes that words have a substance that is "palpable," "tangible"(70, 71), a materiality and a weight as real as that of the bodies that arouse and abuse her. As Firdaus's powerful anger makes clear, words can be means of control, abuse, and torture: "The words continued to echo in my ears . . . buried themselves in my head like some *palpable* material object, like *a body as sharp as the edge of a knife*

[19]Abel, "Race, Class, Psychoanalysis?" 199, 186.

which had cut its way through my ears, and the bones of my head to the brain inside. . . . I could almost see them as they traversed the space separating his lips from my ears, like *tangible* things with a well-defined surface, exactly like *blobs of spit*, as though he had aimed them at me from between his lips" (70–71; emphasis added). These words are sharp and cutting, instruments of contempt and disdain, ejaculations ("blobs of spit") that defile and contaminate the hearer, as in an act of rape. Words maintain the dissymmetry of power between the sexes by entering the woman's consciousness, serving as scalpel in a metaphoric lobotomy that mirrors the genital excision: "The knife . . . had cut its way through my ears . . . to the brain inside." The soft tissue of the ear with its orifice that leads to the brain has an unmistakable sexual connotation. Words rape as surely as the penis, or the knife that the groom must use on his wedding night to open his bride's vulva and consummate the marriage. Saadawi thus conflates the act of speech and the act of sex in a way that clarifies and buttresses Bal's claims about dissymmetry.

Furthermore, words—uttered or written—have the same power as money: they are akin to paper money ("a mere piece of paper" [66], "the whole ten pound note" [65], contact with which produces in Firdaus a physical sensation as violent and as sudden as the unexpected orgasms provoked by her abusive uncle and clients. The symbolic value of words and money is thus conflated in a way that underscores their respective worth as currency, as means of exchange within a system that attributes to women a similar exchange value depending on their physical conformity to patriarchal standards of sexual beauty and purity. These standards are themselves based on a distortion of the idea of cultural *symmetry* which is presumed to exist between male and female processes of acculturation of the body.

Indeed, the question of symmetry is so often raised by traditionalists (see Wandja, for example) who want to emphasize either the equivalence between circumcision and excision or the need to leave cultural interpretations of Africa to Africans (or both) that we must examine its tenets. I have already mentioned that the dissymmetry "educated" versus "illiterate" is evoked whenever feminist points of view are brought into focus, especially because feminism is considered to be a foreign—that is, Western—import.[20] The fact is that there is an obvious analogy between circumcision and excision: they both consist in the ablation of a part of the body for the ostensible purposes of hygiene and sexual attractiveness, and as a means of correcting the primal androgyny, or original bisexuality, of each being, a belief held by some Nilotic peoples

[20]See the critique of Thiam in Patterson, "Les mutilations sexuelles," 165.

and by the Mande and Kwa of Western Africa.[21] Hence for both sexes the operation is meant to *inscribe* a particular sexual identity on the body, to mark it as cultural, to give it symbolic meaning, that is, to *differentiate* it. In Foucault's terminology excision is part of a network of practices that "discipline" the body, functioning as a means of social control, and reproducing unequal relations of power along with gender identity. Mary Douglas has shown that there are symbolic relationships between the human body and the social body, that rituals can be interpreted in terms that link purity with order and impurity with disorder, the latter being a sign of danger and power.[22] Excision, like circumcision, thus "purifies" the body, renders it fit to belong to its assigned place within a social order which it no longer threatens by its impure, abject nature—that is, its undifferentiated, dangerous sexuality. The painful ordeal to which the individual is subjected becomes a sign that the body can transcend pain, can endure. It is proof that the flesh is under the control of the spirit, in other words, that the embodied self can become sufficiently detached from its physical sensations to attain the state of "pure" and heroic subjectivity.

But there ends the expected symmetry. It becomes a *dis*symmetry when the focus is once again placed on the body. From a strictly anatomical perspective, only a piece of flesh is removed from the male member, whereas in the case of the female, a sexual organ is cut off. By all accounts the infliction of pain through circumcision cannot even begin to be compared with that of excision and infibulation. In *The Hidden Face of Eve*, Saadawi graphically describes her own experience of the knife, making a confession that can be juxtaposed to the silent testimonial of Firdaus in *Woman at Point Zero:*

> I was six years old that night when I lay in my bed, warm and peaceful in that pleasurable state which lies half way between wakefulness and sleep, with the rosy dreams of childhood flitting by, like gentle fairies in quick succession. I felt something move under the blankets, something like *a huge hand, cold and rough,* fumbling over my body, as though looking for something. Almost simultaneously another hand, as cold and as rough and as big as the first one, was clapped over my mouth, to prevent me from screaming.
>
> They carried me to the bathroom. *I do not know how many of them there were*, nor do I remember their faces, or whether they were men or women.

[21]Ehrlich, *Femme blessée*, 210–18.
[22]Michel Foucault, *Discipline and Punish* (New York: Vintage, 1979); Mary Douglas, *Natural Symbols* (New York: Pantheon, 1982) and *Purity and Danger* (London: Routledge & Kegan Paul, 1966).

The world to me seemed enveloped in a dark fog which prevented me from seeing.
. . . All I remember is that I was frightened and that *there were many of them,* and that something like an *iron grasp* caught hold of my hand and my arms and my thighs, so that I became unable to resist or even to move. I also remember the icy touch of the bathroom tiles under my naked body, and *unknown voices and humming sounds interrupted now and again by a rasping metallic sound* which reminded me of the butcher when he used to sharpen his knife before slaughtering a sheep for the *Eid.*
My blood was frozen in my veins. . . .
I imagined the thing that was making the rasping sound coming closer and closer to me. Somehow it was not approaching my neck as I had expected but another part of my body. Somewhere below my belly, as though seeking something buried between my thighs. At that very moment I realized that my thighs had been pulled wide apart, and that each of my lower limbs was being held as far away from the other as possible, gripped by *steel fingers* that never relinquished their pressure. . . . Then suddenly *the sharp metallic edge* seemed to drop between my thighs and there cut off a piece of flesh from my body.
I screamed with pain despite the tight hand held over my mouth, for the pain was not just a pain, it was like a searing flame that went through my whole body. After a few moments, I saw a red pool of blood around my hips. . . .
I did not know what they had cut off from my body. . . . *I just wept, and called out to my mother for help. But the worst shock of all was when I looked around and found her standing by my side. Yes it was her, I could not be mistaken, in flesh and blood, right in the midst of these strangers, talking to them and smiling at them,* as though they had not participated in slaughtering her daughter just a few moments ago. (7–8; emphasis added)

If we follow Elaine Scarry in her argument that the pain of torture is a process that "unmakes" the world and the self, dissolving the boundary between inside and outside, conflating in an almost obscene way private and public, then the experience described by Saadawi underscores the "unmaking" of the child's environment.[23] Visual and auditory perceptions become blurred; trust is forever destroyed as the mother's smiling face denies the reality of the shock and the pain. The strangers are described as body parts: a huge hand, cold and rough, an iron grasp, unknown voices, steel fingers. The child's own body reacts to the cold bathroom floor, to the rasping sound of metal being sharpened, to the metallic edge of the knife, and to the searing flame of pain that envelops her.

[23]Elaine Scarry, *The Body in Pain: The Making and Unmaking of the World* (New York: Oxford University Press, 1985), 53.

But the disjunction and depersonalization caused by the pain is replaced by a strong sense of urgency and agency when she sees her sister being carried away in order to submit to the same fate. A mirroring effect comes into play when the sister's eyes meet and they are both united by the memory of a past and future pain: "They carried me to my bed. I saw them catch hold of my sister, who was two years younger, in exactly the same way they had caught hold of me a few minutes earlier. I cried out with all my might. No! No! I could see my sister's face held between the big rough hands. It had a deathly pallor and *her wide black eyes met mine for a split second, a glance of dark terror which I can never forget"* (8; emphasis added). The remarkable anger voiced by the six-year-old child who protests on behalf of her younger sister is an almost mythical example of the agency and autonomy manifested by the body despite its disintegrative suffering. Here symmetry exists powerfully: the excised child sees herself in her sister, and *feels with* the sister. The empathy is complete and total. Yet, in her novel *Woman at Point Zero*, it is precisely this question of empathy that will haunt the adult narrator who first resists identification with Firdaus as she struggles to understand her position vis-à-vis this "other" whose lower-class status and identity as a murderer, she initially feels, invalidates any comparison between them as symmetrical female subjects.

Woman at Point Zero is a lyrical testimonial that exemplifies the countercoherence of dissymmetry, the possibility of resistance to hegemonic pressures and to the cultural master narrative. Here the countercoherence of "the body in pain" manifests itself in a feeling of irretrievable loss which opposes sensations to language and ideology, subjective structures to cultural doxa. It is emblematic of issues raised by the work of Gayatri C. Spivak: the name of "the other woman," and the relationship between autobiography and "truth." In an interview with Sneja Gunew, Spivak has pointed out that "if one looks at the history of post-Enlightenment theory, the major problem has been the problem of autobiography: how subjective structures can, in fact, give objective truth."[24]

These issues continue to be widely debated in recent feminist theory. Saadawi's work can be used as an excellent example of the self-reflexive questioning that can make feminist criticism sensitive to the way scholarly discourse names "the other woman" and appropriates her voice, for *Woman at Point Zero* is itself the appropriation of another woman's story by a scholar whose research on female offenders brings her into

---

[24]See Mary Lynn Broe and Angela Ingram, eds., *Women's Writing in Exile* (Chapel Hill: University of North Carolina Press, 1989), 420.

close contact with the painful experiences of an extraordinary woman. This association between the educated researcher and the "(un)common criminal" changes the terms of the equation between "self" and "other" or "subjective" and "objective," enacting a transfer of values and feelings, locating the practice of writing at the intersection of multiple forms of knowledge.

Now, my own purpose here is also to make a scholarly appropriation: to scrutinize Saadawi's text, to examine the way in which it contrasts and collapses the language of patriarchy and the language of the body, bringing into focus those aspects of the narrative that might allow for its redefinition as self-portrait. By appropriating Firdaus's voice yet allowing intersubjective communication to occur, Saadawi raises the hope that it is in fact possible to come to an acceptable compromise regarding the possibility of interpretation and the role of "intervention" in the local practices of certain African societies. If autobiography is the means by which women represent themselves, then to understand their subjective experience of excision and its affective and cultural ramifications we need to look for traces of these preoccupations in their texts, and to listen to their silences.

Saadawi's work often has a hypnotic, incantatory quality which draws the reader into its world: if, as Spivak puts it, "subjective structures can, in fact, give objective truth," then Saadawi's struggle in *Woman at Point Zero* to come to terms with Firdaus, "the real woman" (1) whose story she tells, testifies to her efforts to elevate this case study to the status of an exemplary narrative of female oppression and emancipation—in other words, to give universal appeal to the story of this Cairo prostitute who is awaiting execution in Qanatir Prison for the murder of her pimp.

When, in her author's preface, Saadawi states: "Firdaus is the story of a woman driven by despair to the darkest of ends. This woman, despite her misery and despair, evoked in all those who, like me, witnessed the final moments of [her] life, a need to challenge and to overcome those forces that deprive human beings of their right to live, to love and to real freedom" (iv), she is emphasizing generally unproblematic values, but these values could hardly be taken for granted in Anwar Sadat's Egypt. What makes her story compelling, then, is the highly personal tone, the erosion of distance between the authorial self and the narrating "I" of Firdaus. Indeed, if Saadawi is first drawn to Firdaus because of her exceptional nature, the focus soon shifts to their shared experience of oppression as women in a patriarchal culture. What the text puts in motion is a strategy of displacement and identification between two women who are "objectively" very different—

from the point of view of their respective social classes, their education and profession—but whose intimate experiences as women are uncannily similar. The narrative suggests that the universal can be known only through the particular or the personal, that it is the concrete subjective experience of this "other woman" that allows the scholar to relate to her as woman and sister, and to bring her back to life through her writing.

There is, finally, an ironic parallel. Six years after the publication of her book, on September 5, 1981, Saadawi herself became a political prisoner, along with a thousand other people alleged to have committed crimes against the state, and whom President Sadat considered to be threats to the stability of his regime. The telling of Firdaus's story thus becomes a rehearsal for Saadawi's own descent into the hell of an Egyptian prison. Saadawi is, and will become, Firdaus, the double that compels her. To tell Firdaus's story is to give voice to the "other" that haunts her, to see her own face in the contours of the prostitute's narrative, and to be provided with a moving link to her own experiences as an excised woman.

Trained as a research scientist, Saadawi initially tries to distance herself from Firdaus, struggling to remain faithful to the (male) scholarly principles of "objectivity" which she has learned to value in her profession. She tries to maintain her calm, her detachment as a scientist, while stressing the disturbing and depersonalizing impact of the emotions that take hold of her: "Subjective feelings such as those that had taken hold of me were not worthy of a researcher in science. I almost smiled at myself as I opened the door of my car. The touch of its surface helped *to restore my identity, my self-esteem as a doctor*" (5; emphasis added). The researcher in her exhibits a Western and male belief in the importance of autonomy and rationality. As Jessica Benjamin has argued: "Both in theory and practice [Western] culture knows only one form of individuality: the male stance of overdifferentiation, of splitting off and denying the tendencies toward sameness, merging, and reciprocal responsiveness."[25] That is why Saadawi tries to negate the value of sensory perceptions in the acquisition of knowledge: when the prison warder tells her that she "senses" that Firdaus "knows" Saadawi, the author ponders, "Why should that indicate that Firdaus really knew me?" (5). Because Saadawi is powerfully attracted to Firdaus, she fears for her autonomy and objectivity. But her discovery of the "sameness"

[25]Jessica Benjamin, "The Bonds of Love: Rational Violence and Erotic Domination," in *The Future of Difference*, ed. Esther Eisenstein and Alice Jardine (New Brunswick: Rutgers University Press, 1985), 46.

of their experiences militates against her continued adherence to male standards of rationality. Her self-doubts signal a move toward *in*differentiation: Firdaus becomes a figure for the sister whose eyes succeeded in bringing Saadawi's disintegrative self/world back to a coherent point where agency—in the form of resistance to excision, as well as in the act of storytelling—became possible again because she identified and merged with the feelings of her sister.

Firdaus first refuses to see Saadawi, and this rejection threatens to undermine the doctor's self-confidence, her faith in her work: "Compared to her, I was nothing but a small insect crawling upon the land amidst millions of other insects" (3). But however much she may try to distance herself from Firdaus, Saadawi cannot escape the gradual but ineluctable fusion with her case study. The narrative sets this course in motion from the very beginning: both women experience feelings of self-doubt for which they compensate by expressing a need to "feel superior to everyone else" (11). Although Saadawi understands that Firdaus's refusals are directed not at her personally "but against the world and everybody in it" (5), she feels threatened by Firdaus's strength. When Firdaus finally agrees to talk, and the physician is called back, Saadawi lyrically describes her feelings of jubilation: "I walked with a rapid, effortless pace, as though my legs were no longer carrying my body. I was full of a wonderful feeling, proud, elated[,] happy. The sky was blue with a blueness I could capture in my eyes. I held the whole world in my hands; it was mine. It was a feeling I had known only once before, many years ago. I was on my way to meet the first man I loved" (6).

Saadawi's dependence on Firdaus's acceptance of her erodes all her attempts to keep her distance. A doubling occurs, and functions as a metonymic displacement between author and narrator whose voices echo each other, thus making it hard for the reader to know who speaks. Saadawi begins a journey which takes her into Firdaus's world, under Firdaus's control: when she enters the cell to talk, it is Firdaus who orders her to "sit down on the ground" (7), and who demands, "Let me speak. Do not interrupt me" (11). Saadawi loses her sense of reality, does not feel the cold and bare ground under her, becoming completely absorbed in "the voice of Firdaus" (7), as if entering a dream or a trancelike state of complete self-dissociation. The first and the last parts of the book, framing Firdaus's actual autobiographical tale, respectively end and begin with the same passages describing the author's entry into an oceanic state: "It was the cold of the sea in a dream. I swam through its waters. I was naked and knew not how to swim. But I neither felt its cold nor drowned in its waters" (7, 107).

The novel thus begins and ends by blurring the distinctions between "subject" and "object," psychiatrist and case study, author and prisoner, biography and autobiography, fiction and documentary. The narrative seems to enact a pattern which, according to Rita Felski, is common to the genre of the feminine confession, and to its authors, namely, "their overwhelming yearning for intimacy." Felski asks: "What . . . are the reasons for this blurring of the distinction between autobiography and fiction in feminist literature? Feminist confession exemplifies the intersection between the autobiographical imperative to communicate the truth of unique individuality, and the feminist concern with the representative and intersubjective elements of women's experience." She later remarks: "Feminist confession often reveals particularly clearly the contradictions between the desire for total intimacy and union, which seeks to erase all boundaries between desire and its object, and the act of writing as a continuing deferral of any such identity."[26] In *Woman at Point Zero,* the desire for intimacy is first of all the author's. Saadawi develops a strong need to be close to Firdaus, to understand her and be accepted by her. The decision to write a novel is an attempt to deal with this interest and fascination which had developed during the interviews Saadawi carried out in the prison cell: "[Firdaus] vibrated within me, or sometimes lay quiet, until the day when I put her down in ink on paper, and gave her life after she had died" (iii).

"Until I put her down on paper": by writing down and giving back the other woman's life, Saadawi assumes control over the obsession that had consumed her. But Firdaus, too, yearns for intimacy. When she meets Sharifa Salah el Dine, the madam who becomes her mentor, or when she talks of her love for Ibrahim, a co-worker, it is in terms similar to those used by Saadawi: "The sky over our heads was as blue as the bluest sky" (51); and "It was as though I held the whole world captive in my hands. It seemed to grow bigger, to expand, and the sun shone brighter than ever before. Everything around me floated in a radiant light" (82). The repetitions form a leitmotif which interweaves Saadawi's subjectivity with Firdaus's. Both voices have merged into one, both bodies experience the same feelings of loss and detachment from surrounding reality with occasional and fleeting experiences of fulfillment. Past and present, self and other mirror each other, and the narrative accentuates the interchangeability of speaker and listener as intimate

---

[26]Rita Felski, *Beyond Feminist Aesthetics: Feminist Literature and Social Change* (Cambridge: Harvard University Press, 1989), 109, 93, 108.

and private experiences point to a common sense of loss and betrayal deeply rooted in their memory.

Since the preface and the first and last parts of the narrative relate the author's personal reactions to Firdaus and situate the middle part as a retelling, in the first person, of Firdaus's oral confession, to read the novel is to be twice removed from the original story, which is, however, retold in a way that preserves the flavor of the oral exchange. The almost obsessive use of repetition as a narrative device allows the reader to enter into the consciousness of both subjects, to take part in an organic process of storytelling, in which it becomes impossible to separate the teller from the tale.[27] Saadawi/Firdaus tells a story that unmasks an ancient truth about patriarchy, namely, that women need not fear what enslaves them, that freedom and "reciprocal responsiveness" is possible. Even if the outcome is death, the story is a posthumous lesson in courage—a lesson that Saadawi also gives us as an activist and a writer of "resistance literature" whose books are banned in her own country.[28]

As she explains in her introduction to *The Hidden Face of Eve*, Saadawi sees her writing as having a social function which is bound to disturb and unsettle those in power: "It was also natural that a small minority express their fear, or even panic, at words written by *a pen sharp as a scalpel that cuts through tissue to expose the throbbing nerves* and arteries embedded deep in a body. . . . My pen will continue to lay bare the facts, clarify the issues, and identify what I believe is the truth" (3; emphasis added). Saadawi uses her pen as a scalpel, turning back on society the instrument of torture that it used on her. Like her, Firdaus was marked at a very young age by the mutilation of excision, by the intervention of the mother and of her accomplice, the woman who carries "a small knife or maybe a razor blade" (13). Firdaus mentions this initial trauma without any commentary. It is a brief parenthesis, a secret no sooner shared than buried in the enveloping silence of the text. This act is never again mentioned. But what returns is the insistent questioning of the body, of its sensations of pleasure and pain, "a pleasure [she] . . . had lived in another life . . . or in another body that was not [her] body" (48). Identical terms are used seven times (14, 22, 26, 33, 48, 56, 78) in the narrative to describe these sensuous physical impressions. Firdaus's confession uses this refrain to underline the link be-

---

[27]As Trinh T. Minh-Ha has observed: "In this chain and continuum, I am but one link. The story is me, neither me nor mine. . . . My story, no doubt is me, but it is also, no doubt, older than me." Trinh T. Minh-Ha, *Woman, Native, Other: Writing Postcoloniality and Feminism* (Bloomington: Indiana University Press, 1989), 122–23.

[28]See Barbara Harlow, *Resistance Literature* (New York: Methuen, 1987), 137–40.

tween her unfulfilled desire for intimacy and the erotic awakenings which set her body adrift toward innumerable male bodies, toward prostitution—passively at first, then freely chosen because "as a prostitute [she] had been looked upon with more respect" (75) than when she was a "respectable" (70) employee.

Firdaus's silence is in sharp contrast to Saadawi's graphic confession (cited earlier) which fills in the blanks of the novel. In both cases the mother is cast as an instrument of the patriarchy, as the means by which "femininity" is initially reproduced, thus allowing the system to perpetuate its hold on each generation of girls. For Firdaus, the betrayal of the mother and the loss of intimacy is metaphorized throughout in the use of a recurring trope: it is the image of two eyes, "two rings of intense white around two circles of intense black" (17), in which each color grows more intense, more engulfing. Firdaus is overcome by the gaze which is linked at first to her mother's enveloping, supportive presence: "Two eyes to which I clung with all my might. Two eyes that alone seemed to hold me up" (17). Later these eyes are evoked when she meets Iqbal, a schoolteacher, and the feeling is one of intense, nameless pleasure: "I held her eyes in mine, took her hand in mine. The feeling of our hands touching was strange, sudden. It was a feeling that made my body tremble with a deep distant pleasure, more distant than the age of my remembered life, deeper than the consciousness I had carried with me throughout" (29–30). This "deep distant pleasure" is articulated as a "memory," as the trace within the body of "something no sooner remembered than forgotten" (33), intangible yet real, a loss of physical being that motivates and subtends her later denunciations of the familial, social, and political structures that maintain sexual oppression.

It is particularly interesting that the pervasive and undefined sense of loss communicated by Firdaus should correspond so precisely to what object relation theorists have articulated as an archaic yearning for the mother's body, for the plenitude of indifferentiation. In her discussion of mother-infant relationships, Nancy Chodorow, for example, has argued that this early relationship, with its issues of "primary intimacy and merging" is crucial in establishing the foundation for future adult relationships.[29] Adults all have some aspect of self that wants to recreate the experience of primary love, the feeling of comfort and satisfaction derived from the sense of identification with another. As Michael Balint has suggested, "This primary tendency . . . is the final aim

[29]Nancy Chodorow, *The Reproduction of Mothering: Psychoanalysis and the Sociology of Gender* (Berkeley: University of California Press, 1978), 79.

of all erotic striving."[30] In Saadawi's narrative, the mother-daughter relationship is based on a fundamental lack—the lack of trust, the lack of physical continuity between the two—which contrasts sharply with the lateral, sisterly identification described at the scene of excision in *The Hidden Face of Eve*. This lack engenders a desire for nurturance which gets translated into an erotic longing for intimacy with Iqbal, Sharifa, or Ibrahim.

It must be noted that the death of Firdaus's mother is immediately followed by a move from the familial home and the native village to the city and her uncle's apartment, where she has her first glimpse of herself in a mirror: the scene is one of misrecognition which fills her "with a deep hatred for the mirror" (21), for the features of her face which remind her of either her father ("the big ugly rounded nose") or her mother ("this thin-lipped mouth" [20]). Fragmented by disconnections, her image of herself points to the inaugurating experience of the self-portraitist as described by Michel Beaujour: "emptiness and absence."[31] Separation from her rural home breeds self-hatred and propels Firdaus on a search for other experiences of love and closeness which will reproduce the primary intimacy of early childhood, the experience of "boundary confusion or equation of self and other."[32] Also worth noting is Saadawi's first encounter with Firdaus, an encounter that actually places Firdaus in an ambiguous position in relation to gender, thus suggesting that her sexual identity is androgynous, and therefore disruptive and disturbing to the social order.

Thus, when the prison doctor first describes her to the author-narrator, Saadawi reports his words in indirect speech: "[He] told me that this woman had been sentenced to death for killing a man. Yet she was not like the other *female* murderers held in prison" (1; emphasis added). It is through his words that the reader and the narrator first encounter Firdaus. He inscribes her as a feminine presence/absence, an enigmatic and silent figure ("She ... won't speak to anyone ... she asked for pen and paper. . . . Perhaps she was not writing anything at all"), sensual and duplicitous ("If you look into her face, her eyes, you will never believe that so gentle a woman can commit murder" [1]). But, by contrast, what the narrator *hears* is a strong, highly masculine

[30]Quoted ibid. As Abel has noted, "Feminist object relations theory . . . explicitly locates the production of gendered subjectivity in historically specific and socially variable caretaking arrangements" (185). It thus seems highly appropriate to use Chodorow to interpret Saadawi's novel.

[31]Michel Beaujour, *Miroirs d'encre* (Paris: Seuil, 1980), 9.

[32]Nancy Chodorow, "Family Structure and Feminine Personality," in *Woman, Culture, and Society*, ed. Michelle Z. Rosaldo and Louise Lamphere (Palo Alto: Stanford University Press, 1974), 57–58.

voice: "The voice was hers, steady, cutting deep down inside, cold as a knife. Not the slightest wavering in its tone" (6). This voice connotes an instrument: the knife that foreshadows the murder of the pimp. The cold-blooded murder is the ultimate act of resistance and liberation on the part of Firdaus, an act comparable in fact to the act of writing for Saadawi, since writing produces similar consequences—imprisonment, solitary confinement—and since the description of the murder echoes Saadawi's metaphors for writing: "I raised the knife and buried it deep in his neck. . . . I stuck the knife into almost every part of his body. I was astonished to find how easily my hand moved as I thrust the knife into his flesh, and pulled it out almost without effort. . . . I realized that I had been afraid, and that the fear had been within me all the time, until the fleeting moment when I read fear in his eyes"(95).

To infer a parallel between the act of writing and the act of murder allows us to further the comparison and identification between Saadawi and Firdaus. There is dissymmetry between the act of writing, which is an act of creation, and the act of murder, which is a form of suppression; but there is also symmetry of the movements of the hand which moves the pen on the paper, or the knife into the flesh. To write (for a woman) and to kill are both forms of social transgression which lead to jail. The pen, which inserts words onto the page, and the knife, which indelibly marks the body, are means of control, tools whereby power can be appropriated. Since the foundational sign of appropriation and power is, of course, the masculine gesture of sexual possession, in which the penis can be used as a weapon, as in an act of rape, it becomes clear why Firdaus is such a subversive figure. Her fundamental transgression is that she reverses the traditional social roles on a symbolic as well as a real level: she trespasses on male sexual territory by using the knife as a means of penetration. Similarly, Saadawi's inscription of a woman's text on the masculine fabric of Egyptian culture is a form of trespass which deserves punishment because it interferes with the culturally acceptable codes of femininity.

What motivates Saadawi's writing is her hope for the future, her desire to "lay bare the facts." Similarly, when Firdaus talks about exchanging secrets and sharing stories with her school friend Wafeya, it is in order to paint a picture of the future which can give them both hope and courage: "If I had something to say, therefore, it could only concern the future. For the future was still mine to paint in the colours I desired. Still mine to decide about freely, and change as I saw fit. . . . Sometimes I imagined that I would become a doctor, or an engineer. . . . I kept imagining myself as a great leader or head of state" (25). To appropriate the knife or pen is to appropriate the future: to dream of its possible configurations beyond the limitations of gender and class, and most of all beyond the limitations of mutilation. Saadawi's desire for an "objective" stance parallels Firdaus's wish for a "masculine" role. But each woman needs an interlocutor to legitimate her quest, to provide reciprocity and intersubjective exchange. This reveals each woman's preoccupation with issues central to the relational nature of female subjectivity, to what Chodorow calls "the lost feeling of one-ness."[33] Firdaus moves through the text with a physical yearning for the "paradise" of childhood, which is associated here with a time "be-fore"—that is, before the betrayal by the mother and the torture of excision.

In contrast to her feelings of having a body which she does not experience as her own, her description of male bodies gives them a materiality and a specificity which borders on caricature. There is the ostentatious piety of the village fathers as they come out of the mosque every Friday, "nodding their heads, or rubbing their hands one against the other, or coughing, or clearing their throats with a rasping noise, or constantly scratching under the armpits and between the thighs" (13). The image of the father who eats alone in front of his starving children has echoes of Ousmane Sembene's depiction of the polyga-mous husband in his movie *Mandabi:* "His mouth was like that of a camel, with a big opening and wide jaws. . . . His tongue kept rolling round and round in his mouth as though it also was chewing, darting out every now and then to lick off some particle of food that had stuck to his lips, or dropped on his chin" (19). Her old husband has a dis-gusting face with an open and smelly sore; her clients, whether clean or dirty, rich or poor, are nothing but heavy bodies under which she closes her eyes and waits.

Physically and verbally battered, Firdaus feels a rage which culmi-nates in the scene of the murder. It is a cathartic moment which helps her realize that anger sets her free to *reappropriate* language, to face "the savage, primitive truths" (102) and to be beyond fear and death. Fir-daus finally names herself: she refuses to be a victim, and is willing to be a criminal because she prefers, as she puts it, "to die for a crime I have committed rather than to die for one of the crimes *you* have com-mitted" (101). This *you* names the ultimate *other*, the one who creates *my* hell.[34]

[33]Chodorow, *Reproduction of Mothering,* 79.
[34]I allude here to Jean-Paul Sartre's famous remark, "L'enfer, c'est les autres," in his play *Huis clos* (*No Exit*).

To the question Spivak asks—"How am I naming [the other woman]? How does she name me?"—Saadawi might answer in the words of Roland Barthes and Nadine Gordimer: that a "writer's enterprise—his [sic] work—is his [sic] essential gesture as a social being," and that writers "take risks they themselves do not know if they would."[35] When Saadawi braids her identity with that of Firdaus because of their shared experience of pain and betrayal, she gives us a powerful example of feminine textuality as what I call *métissage*, as dialogical hybrid which fuses together heterogeneous elements.[36] Because Saadawi's use of the pen lands her in jail just as surely as Firdaus's use of her knife, we are in the presence of a mutual and reciprocal "naming" which effaces differences in order to point to an *essential* truth: that beyond their social differences, the two women share a *nominal essence* qua excised women.[37] Since this sexual mutilation is the most important cultural signifier of femininity, "biological" femininity becomes a culturally determined fact, linked to specific local practices. When Saadawi denounces those practices, she puts herself in jeopardy. By appealing to universal human rights, she attempts to build bridges across cultures, showing the validity of a "Western" mode of analysis (psychoanalytic object relations theory) which allows her to name her subjective experience of pain and to situate it within an *inter*subjective context. As a critic who does not belong to the Islamic Egyptian culture, I am nonetheless interpellated by this dimension of the narrative, and I must respond to it in a way that "universalizes" the integrity of the body. But, I would argue, this form of universalism does not objectify the other and subsume her into my worldview: what it does is create a relational space where intersubjectivity and reciprocity become possible.

[35]Nadine Gordimer, *The Essential Gesture: Writing, Politics, and Places* (New York: Knopf, 1988), 286–87. She is using Roland Barthes's formulation in *Writing Degree Zero*, in *Barthes, Selected Writings*, ed. and intro. Susan Sontag (London: Fontana, 1983), 31.

[36]See Françoise Lionnet, *Autobiographical Voices: Race, Gender, Self-Portraiture* (Ithaca: Cornell University Press, 1989), chap 1.

[37]See Diana Fuss, "Reading Like a Feminist," *Differences* 1.2 (Summer 1989): 78, and *Essentially Speaking: Feminism, Nature, and Difference* (New York: Routledge, Chapman & Hall, 1989).

2

"Changing Masters": Gender, Genre, and the Discourses of Slavery

BELLA BRODZKI

"He had never sold anyone before, and now he persuaded himself that what he was about to do was not selling in its actual sense."[1] What is "selling in its actual sense"? A young African man about to exchange his seven-year-old sister for money measures his action against a fixed standard, and, moved by his own rhetorical argument, concludes that his (trans)action can be distinguished from "selling in its actual sense." How he comes to that conclusion and its moral and political implications for the study of comparative literature are of paramount concern to me. Difference, it would seem, both acknowledges and dismisses a ground for comparison. Especially ironic because structured as a negative assertion—"he had never sold anyone . . . he was not selling"— the older brother's exercise in critical self-deception is an exemplary moment in Buchi Emecheta's novel *The Slave Girl,* a text that both compels comparative analysis and challenges the terms of current comparatist practice. What does slavery mean? How do different cultural narratives about national, social, and individual identity, sameness and difference, frame our "sense" of slavery? And how does a feminist approach to issues of subjective agency and possibility, power, property, and propriety ("le sens propre du terme") change the character of such an inquiry?

Slavery as an institution has persisted, indeed flourished, since ancient times across continents and empires, exceeding even those boundaries during the fifteenth to nineteenth centuries when an international slave trade made human bondage virtually a universal practice. In turn, the discourse on slavery has itself become a kind of master narrative in which reductive and restrictive categories co-opt as well as overtly

A skeletal version of this essay was read at a Modern Language Association special session (New Orleans, 1988) on the colonial subject in women's autobiography, organized and chaired by Julia Watson. I thank Margaret Higonnet for her invaluable insights throughout the preparation of this essay and Louise Yelin for her generous and incisive comments on its final form.

[1] Buchi Emecheta, *The Slave Girl* (New York: Braziller, 1977), 37; hereafter cited by page in the text.

exploit all manner of difference. Masculinist and nationalist models of slavery have dominated American critical discourse. In order to decenter these assumptions, especially as they focus on the African American slave narrative, in this essay I take up the issues of gender, race, and imperialism in a modern African novel about slavery. By reading and rereading race, gender, and genre intertextually in *The Slave Girl*, we may engage directly with the features of multiculturalism, spatial plurality, alter/nativity, hybridity, syncretism—all aspects of an inherently comparative methodology—and resist reflexively the tendency toward another universalist, internationalist, or patriarchal metropolitan paradigm.

Slavery as idea has been distinguished from slavery as social system. Comparative historians and theorists recognize a continuity between older and more modern forms of slavery while differentiating between abstract legal status and an actual set of institutions involving economic functions and interpersonal relationships. Although the ambiguous status of the slave as both property and person had been interrogated from Aristotle to Locke, it was in the eighteenth-century debates over natural law that slavery assumed a central position for American and European moral philosophers, theologians, and political theorists such as Montesquieu and Jefferson. This Enlightenment argument, often cast in terms of the conflict between the right to freedom and the will to dominate, tested the limits of humanist logic and moral codes. In "progressist" theories of racial inferiority, the near-conflation of "natural" and "law" conceived of one standard for the laws of nature and another for the laws of nations. It became strangely possible to condemn slavery in the realm of moral abstraction but continue to justify it as politically inevitable or economically necessary in the real world. In the nineteenth century the great slave controversy between abolitionists and advocates pivoted on whether American slavery, based on the total subjugation of one race by another, was essentially different from historical varieties of bondage and serfdom. Even in the late twentieth century, literary critics have been wrestling with the discourse of American slavery as much as with the institution itself, if indeed they are separable.

The debate has centered partly on the discursive construction of slavery as a key to national identity. For Deborah McDowell and Arnold Rampersad "slavery is perhaps the central intellectual challenge, other than the Constitution itself, to those who would understand the meaning of America."[2] As David Brion Davis has brilliantly shown, an un-

---

[2]Deborah McDowell and Arnold Rampersad, eds., *Slavery and the Literary Imagination* (Baltimore: Johns Hopkins University Press, 1989), viii.

reconcilable moral contradiction underlies America's mission and meaning: America—the idealized projection of European hopes for a new beginning—flourished not by liberating itself from previous structures and practices but rather by extending and perfecting the institution of slavery. The transatlantic slave trade, which was an essential aspect of colonization and an integral part of the early economic and social development of the nation, began with Columbus.

Implicitly missing in all the earlier debates was the perspective of the enslaved subject, for, as Davis puts it, until modern times "few slaves recorded their thoughts and . . . scholars did not think the subject worthy of study."[3] Yet this voice is not difficult to locate: one need but turn to slave narratives, the body of literature written or dictated by ex-slaves of African descent who were transported to the New World in the eighteenth and nineteenth centuries. Henry Louis Gates, Jr., defines slave narratives as "only those written works published before 1865, after which time *de jure* slavery ceased to exist," and asserts that by the same token, "the slave narrative proper could no longer exist after slavery was abolished." He acknowledges that using the "absolute abolition of slavery as the cut-off point for this genre" might be construed as arbitrary. But the rich generative potential of the slave narrative, its formative influence on narrative structures and strategies of subsequent African American literature, makes it possible to argue that "after 1865 the generic expectations of these autobiographies altered drastically."[4]

That alteration parallels a striking rhetorical shift in slave narratives, from the antebellum comparison of slavery to a tomb to the postbellum comparison to a school of life. Linking this change in representational strategy to the development of Afro-American literary realism, William Andrews characterizes these different portrayals of the experience of having endured and survived slavery as "existential" (antebellum) as opposed to "pragmatic" (postbellum). Elsewhere Andrews contends that the valorization of the romantic, rebellious antebellum fugitive slave narrator has skewed our notions of the history of the genre, prescriptively limiting for ideological reasons a necessarily dynamic signifying process. Contrary to orthodox critical opinion, which has fixated on one model, Andrews argues that "the image of slavery, along with the metaphor of black selfhood, undergoes revision as the nineteenth century evolves."[5]

[3]David Brion Davis, *The Problem of Slavery in Western Culture* (Ithaca: Cornell University Press, 1966), 30; hereafter cited by page in the text.

[4]Henry Louis Gates, Jr., *The Slave's Narrative*, ed. Charles T. Davis and Henry Louis Gates, Jr. (Oxford: Oxford University Press, 1985), xxii.

[5]William L. Andrews, "The Representation of Slavery and the Rise of Afro-American

Beyond the debate over nineteenth-century texts, slave narratives are widely regarded as the pretext and/or master paradigm for all African American autobiography and fiction. These first-person accounts of human bondage are necessarily generic hybrids, ingeniously combining elements of autobiographical, fictional, and historical discourse; as reflexive and symbolic performances, they enact modes and forge models of black selfhood and identity in the most challenging of contexts. Testimonials to the transplantation, brutalization, and enslavement of black people by those who endured and survived—and who, not incidentally, also managed to gain access to the crucial networks of publication—they are predicated on the capacity of an individual narrator to represent, to stand for and stand *in* for, those whose voices have been silenced but whose stories are interwoven with the narratives of others.

Thus as foundational American texts whose borders have been variously contested, slave narratives are complexly figurative cultural documents which reveal the discursive complexity of slavery as a rhetorical construct—at particular moments in American history. In putting the word "slavery" in quotation marks, Hortense Spillers offers a provocative reminder that (even) the notion of slavery belongs to a discursive field and thus is not exempt from the play of radical textuality:

> It seems to me that every generation of systematic readers is compelled to "reinvent" slavery in its elaborate and peculiar institutional ways and means.... In a very real sense, a full century or so "after the fact," "slavery" is *primarily* discursive, as we search vainly for a point of absolute and indisputable origin, for a moment of plenitude that would restore us to the real, rich "thing" itself before discourse touched it. In that regard, "slavery" becomes the great "test case" around which, for its Afro-American readers, the circle of mystery is recircumscribed time and again.
> ... It becomes increasingly clear that the cultural synthesis we call "slavery" was never homogeneous in its practices and conception, not unitary in the faces it has yielded.... To rob the subject of its dynamic character, to captivate it in a fictionalized scheme whose outcome is already inscribed by a higher, different, *other*, power, freezes it in the ahistorical.[6]

Realism," in McDowell and Rampersad, *Slavery and the Literary Imagination*, esp. 62–67; and Andrews, "Toward a Poetics of Afro-American Autobiography," in *Afro-American Literary Study in the 1990s*, ed. Houston A. Baker, Jr., and Patricia Redmond (Chicago: University of Chicago Press, 1989), 85.

[6]Hortense Spillers, "Changing the Letter: The Yokes, the Jokes of Discourse, or Mrs. Stowe, Mr. Reed," in McDowell and Rampersad, *Slavery and the Literary Imagination*, 28–29.

The dynamic literary legacy of slavery contains multiple historical and cultural discourses. Tendencies toward reifying the "cultural synthesis we call 'slavery' " are being contested and challenged today, not only by scholars but by an increasing flow of novels about slavery as well.[7] As this generation of readers and writers across national and linguistic borders "reinvents" slavery to serve the crucial and changing needs of current racial identity politics, critics and scholars must reinvent and enlarge our comparative critical frameworks to engage the issues they raise.

These successive textualizations remind us that we cannot witness slavery through a unitary prism—historical, national, cultural, ideological, racial, or sexual. The danger of doing so is glaringly apparent in *The Problem of Slavery in Western Culture,* David Brion Davis's classical account of the historical problems of defining slavery in the West. As he puts it, certain "nagging contradictions . . . originate in the simple fact that the slave is a *man*"(31). This distinction clearly belongs to the realm of metaphysics, for the sphere of operation is commodification; a "man" means *not* an animal or a thing, a generic rather than a gendered human being.

In the lines that follow, however, "man" has more specific gendered connotations, and the slippage between the universal and the gendered meaning of the terms is crucial: "In general it has been said that the slave has three defining characteristics: his person is the property of another man, his will is subject to his owner's authority, and his labor or services are obtained through coercion. Since this description could sometimes be applied to wives and children in a patriarchal family, various writers have added that slavery must be 'beyond the limits of family relations' " (31–32). Davis's formulation writes off one form of enslavement against another, privileges one version or experience over another. A reader sensitive to a more diffused collection of "nagging contradictions" notices that effacing gender as a category of analysis here has enormous long-range implications. A logical sleight of hand makes it possible to acknowledge that the practice of slavery crosses structural boundaries and intersects with other forms of patriarchal domination, and simultaneously to dismiss the real and theoretical consequences of that realization. It has obviously been easier to preserve

---

[7]Contemporary American novels about slavery, some of which use the slave narrative model, include Margaret Walker's *Jubilee* (1966), Ernest Gaines's *Autobiography of Miss Jane Pitman* (1971), Ishmael Reed's *Flight to Canada* (1976), Octavia Butler's *Kindred* (1979), Charles Johnson's *Oxherding Tale* (1982), Sherley Anne Williams's *Dessa Rose* (1984), and Toni Morrison's *Beloved* (1987). Gayl Jones's *Corregidora* (1975) is dominated by the memory of slavery.

the abstract universalist pretensions of the concept of slavery as extra-familial, nondomestic (i.e., male) oppression than to question the epistemological (in this case Eurocentric *and* sexist) bias underlying the notion of what constitutes "family relations" in a particular society (Oh, that's not enslavement, that's family!). As I have suggested, the cultural "text" of slavery, despite the rich and textured exchange that surrounds it, remains a point of convergence for exclusionary, insular, and I would say arbitrary readings. What follows is an attempt to diffuse, diversify, and displace such readings by examining a narrative that presumes neither a masculine nor an American perspective.

The frame of reference implicit in most criticism of slave narratives shifts dramatically when the context is African slavery in the early years of the twentieth century and the text is *The Slave Girl* (1977), by the Nigerian author Buchi Emecheta.[8] What does such a gesture produce? It suggests that the intertextual relations of the slave narrative novel are not only linguistic and national, as Gates suggests ("a sub-genre of American, English, French, and Spanish fiction")[9] but diasporic; these relations by necessity encompass colonial and postcolonial Caribbean and Latin American writing as well. An anglophone, postcolonial, "third world" text, *The Slave Girl* problematizes the relations between nation and race, gender and genre, which figure so strongly in African American slave narratives, including those by women: it questions the possibility of any totalizable discourse on slavery. To treat Emecheta's novel as a slave narrative involves displacing generic issues about authenticity, credibility, and truth as they are figured in the authorial "I," issues that until recently, and for understandable reasons, have plagued American studies of narratives by ex-slaves.[10] Beginning with the prem-

---

[8]*The Slave Girl* is situated between two other novels by Emecheta in which slavery is intrinsically related to the status of women as wives and mothers: *The Bride Price* (1976) and *The Joys of Motherhood* (1979).

[9]Gates, *Slave's Narrative*, xxii.

[10]Credibility is an issue not only in slave narrators' textual strategies but also in the work of earlier scholars and critics who strove to make credible and valuable by white cultural criteria the full range of black expression. On the problem of authenticity, see Jean Fagin Yellin, who changed the terrain when she documented the authenticity of Harriet Jacobs's celebrated *Incidents in the Life of a Slave Girl* (Cambridge: Harvard University Press, 1987) and situated its central importance in the slave narrative tradition. See also Hazel Carby, *Reconstructing Womanhood: The Emergence of the Afro-American Woman Novelist* (Oxford: Oxford University Press, 1987), 45–61. On the obsession with authority and authorship in the slave narrative, see Francis Smith Foster, "Harriet Jacob's *Incidents* and the 'Careless Daughters' (And Sons) Who Read It," in *The (Other) American Traditions: Nineteenth-Century Women Writers*, ed. Joyce W. Warren (New Brunswick: Rutgers University Press, 1993), 92–107. On the vexing relationship between subjective agency and critical reception in the female slave narrative, see Valerie Smith, "Loopholes

ise that all slave narratives are narratives of liberation, I focus on thematic, tropic, and structural affinities between nineteenth-century slave narratives and this modern novel about slavery, but I argue that these similarities must be read differently because of the novel's specific colonial context.

For Emecheta, slavery—as a fundamental feature of the African social and political economy—is inextricably tied to sexual oppression, a specific and traditional form of oppression that was reinforced and extended through the more generalized subjugation of African peoples by Europeans, but the terms of which must be relativized, localized, and historicized. Unlike slaves in the Occidental export trade, which valued men for their productive capacities, the great majority of slaves within the internal African market were women and children; women were in higher demand and generally more highly valued, less because of their reproductive capacities than because they have always performed a large amount of productive labor in African society. Of course, the importance of women's roles within the system did not preclude devaluation of gender and marginality of status. Women's submissive socialization and the "outsiderness" that always characterizes the slave point to the crucial and diverse function of women in real as well as symbolic slave economies. My purpose here is not to compare slavery in the Americas with the complex variety of African slavery; to do so would only implicitly reinforce the idea that African slavery was a particularly "benign" (read: deviant) version, since it did not correspond to the Western model. Instead, one concern here is the uses to which the various discourses on slavery can be put. Not surprisingly, the Eurocentric stereotypes and images of slavery (and freedom) until recently provided for Western anthropologists and historians (even literary critics) the norm against which non-Western institutions and practices were identified, named, and measured.[11]

A postcolonial novel about indigenous slavery by an African woman

---

of Retreat: Architecture and Ideology in Harriet Jacob's *Incidents in the Life of a Slave Girl,* in *Reading Black, Reading Feminist,* ed. Henry Louis Gates, Jr. (New York: Penguin, 1990), 212–26, and especially Carla Kaplan, "Narrative Contracts and Emancipatory Readers: *Incidents in the Life of a Slave Girl,*" *Yale Journal of Criticism* 6.1 (1993): 93–119.

[11]See Suzanne Miers and Igor Kopytoff, "African 'Slavery' as an Institution of Marginality," in *Slavery in Africa: Historical and Anthropological Perspectives* (Madison: University of Wisconsin Press, 1977), 3–84; also Paul Lovejoy, *Transformations in Slavery: A History of Slavery in Africa* (Cambridge: Cambridge University Press, 1983). As Claire Robertson and Martin Klein state in their groundbreaking study of women as central figures in African slavery, "Many accounts of African slavery are written as though the slaves were exclusively men." See Claire Robertson and Martin Klein, "Women's Importance in African Slave Systems," in *Women and Slavery in Africa* (Madison: University of Wisconsin Press, 1983), 3–25.

disrupts Western contemporary discourse on slavery precisely because Emecheta's enslaved heroine would seem to fulfill the requirements of what Cynthia Ward calls "a unified representation of the perfectly *other* 'Other'—black, female, colonized." Yet how this "authentic" African female subject is "othered" depends, as always, on who is doing the "othering." Emecheta criticism "available in the United States," according to Ward, interprets her novels as "feminist parables" while "appropriating the 'African woman's experience' as part of a universal liberatory discourse" without "regard for issues that concern African literary critics." By contrast, " 'African' readings of Emecheta seek to situate her work within the African literary canon . . . rejecting the imposition of neocolonial—European and North American—values and imperatives, including feminism" (that is, critical of individualist-inflected imperial feminism).[12] Such divergent attempts to press Emecheta's writing into one kind of essentialist service or another make clear that her representation of African women is neither unequivocal nor reducible to an either-or model.

Must we dichotomize the problem of subject construction in *The Slave Girl,* and might there exist ways that move beyond Africanist/feminist or African/female? Although there seems to be no way at present to constitute a politics of subjectivity and representation in which race and gender do not function as the dominant, competing, or interchangeable terms, *The Slave Girl* invites us to question whether it is advantageous or desirable to occult all other conceptual possibilities or theoretical configurations in favor of this interpretive model. It invites us to continue to trace the effects of "the politics of theory" in our reading and question our perceptual frameworks, our critical presuppositions and categories, especially as we begin to take them too much for granted. This means subverting the canon beyond merely enlarging, extending, or exchanging the set of culturally valorized and authorized texts to include a previously ignored or repressed set. For to counter the idea of "canonicity" itself is to question categorically the category and change the conditions of reading for all texts, to read differently, alongside, against, to contextualize and recontextualize.

Assuming the double critical identity on which the present volume rests, the feminist necessarily brings a perspective that challenges the field of comparative literature to contest its own disciplinary boundaries, seen as social, aesthetic, political, and linguistic. Certainly a 1988 collection of essays whose stated purpose is to "exemplif[y] what com-

---

[12]Cynthia Ward, "What They Told Buchi Emecheta: Oral Subjectivity and the Joys of Otherhood," *PMLA* 105.1 (1990): 84–85.

paratists actually do" indicates that feminist theory has made some incursions into current comparative practice, if often outside traditional institutional boundaries. The editors, Clayton Koelb and Susan Noakes, attest that comparatists "have had to learn to participate in an international community of theoretical exchange," and they acknowledge that comparative literature faces unstable categories and shifting frameworks. They find it "seems to be less a set of practices (e.g., comparing texts in different languages, comparing literary and 'nonliterary' texts, comparing literature and the other arts) and more a shared perspective that sees literary activity as involved in a complex web of cultural relations."[13]

This description, however, does not suffice to delineate the new perspective, for "cultural relations" covers an amorphous range of literary encounters and engagements. It does describe the contents of the volume, which displaces the classic Eurocentric focus on "historical and international contexts" of comparative practice toward the East-West axis: one essay addresses the theoretical implications of "emergent literature"; another laments the arbitrariness of the "comparatist's canon."[14] Precisely because the practitioners of comparative literature are by definition multilingual and their approach multicultural, heterocritical, and interdisciplinary—and because theory itself has become the arena in literary studies of greatest self-conscious politicization—the field of comparative literature might be said to encompass cultural criticism. Or perhaps, one could argue, it is even an emergent form of cultural criticism, like the literature comparatists are compelled more and more to address.

A feminist comparatist critique engages the very status of multicultural literacy as well as the gendered, multicultural, and/or multiracial subject of writing, a critique that bypasses previous comparatist formulations and definitions. Where feminist and cultural critical analysis intersect, difference reemerges. When subjectivity is understood to be

---

[13]Clayton Koelb and Susan Noakes, eds., *The Comparative Perspective on Literature: Approaches to Theory and Practice* (Ithaca: Cornell University Press, 1988), 11.

[14]Wlad Godzich's elegant and provocative analysis of the precarious and tense relationship between "the production of existing knowledge and the production of new knowledge," reveals comparative literature to be a discipline "at risk." Over and against the "petrified. . . , hegemonic, and monumentalizing view of . . . national, international, and comparative literature," he celebrates the multifarious and disunifying writings of "newly constituted subjects" in a "field" reconceptualized as "the enabling condition of cultural elaboration" ("Emergent Literature and the Field of Comparative Literature," in Koelb and Noakes, *Comparative Perspective*, 18–36). By contrast, in Frank Warnke's essay, "The Comparatist's Canon: Some Observations," his marked concern for "the neglect of Dutch letters" is counterbalanced by his contempt for literature about Colette's "characteristic subject matter and her own myth-image as the sexy Frenchwoman" (50).

less a matter of construction per se than of position, how to avoid privileging, subsuming, eliding, or conflating the categories of race and
gender becomes a paramount concern. Both sides are quick to recognize
transgressive models or insidious encoding in the discourse of the
other, especially when there is already inscribed in the profile of "feminist" a white or Eurocentric bias and in the profile of "cultural critic"
a masculinist bias.

In a 1990 essay on African women's writing and African feminist
criticism, Susan Andrade discusses what appears to be an irreconcilable
difference between the two, manifested in the tendency to read the
"valorized category allegorically" so as to "displace and replace gender
or race":

> For Eurocentric feminists, race is merely a trope for gender, another way
> to understand the larger oppression of women. For masculinist cultural
> critics, the privileged category of race subsumes all others; gender serves
> as a lens through which the greater oppression of Non-Europeans can be
> understood. Neither of the above theoretical positions offers a space from
> which an African feminist criticism can be articulated, for neither is able
> to address the hetereogeneity that analysis of African women's texts must
> foreground: to respect the cultural heterogeneity of Africa as well as that
> of African women.[15]

Indeed, lessons should be taken from Emecheta's own practice, which
"offers a space" for feminist comparatist theorizing; her text is no less
"African" because it focuses on those local traditional social structures
that continue to frame the contemporary politics of female identity.

Beginning with the prologue's function, the panoramic unfolding of
an oral and physical landscape, the narrator of *The Slave Girl* insists
rather didactically (as if assuming an audience unfamiliar with the territory) on specificity—of place, history, subject, and the forces that
connect them. Although Emecheta certainly does not mitigate the devastating effects of foreign intrusion into native traditions or the horrors
of colonial domination, she offers an ironic warning to those who
choose to forget that "slavery begins at home." The double entendre of
the word "home" figures powerfully in a narrative set against the back-
drop of colonial rule, in which an African child is sold into slavery by
her older brother in her own land after the premature death of her
parents. The novel's title, resonant with the titles of the many African
American slave narratives that precede it, suggests the divestment of

[15]Susan Z. Andrade, "Rewriting History, Motherhood, and Rebellion: Naming an African Women's Literary Tradition," *Research in African Literatures* 21.1 (1990): 94.

individual identity by the overarching category of "slave girl"; but the far-reaching implications of the protagonist's enslaved condition are not grasped by the reader until the final paragraph, when Emecheta's narrator directs her attack on the patriarchal institution of marriage and the status of women in African society.

Emecheta's novel portrays a "naive" Igbo tribal life in Ibuza at the dawn of the twentieth century, sometime after the abolition of the Euro-American slave trade. The narrator maintains a consistently ironic tone; her epic perspective situates the narrative at the privileged point of intersection of history and myth, both temporally and spatially inside and outside the system:

> The people of Ibuza—at a time when it was glorious to be an Englishman, when the reign of the great Queen Victoria's son was coming to its close, when the red of the British Empire covered almost half the map of the world, when colonisation was at its height, and Nigeria was being taken over by Great Britain—did not know that they were not still being ruled by the Portuguese. The people of Ibuza did not realize that their country, to the last village, was being amalgamated and partitioned by the British. They knew nothing of what was happening; they did not know that there were other ways of robbing people of their birthright than by war. The African of those days was very trusting. (15)

This is a classic description of what Abdul JanMohamed has delineated as the "dominant" phase, as distinguished from the "hegemonic" phase, of colonialism: the dominant phase "spans the period from the earliest European conquest to the moment at which a colony is granted 'independence.' . . . During this phase the 'consent' of the natives is primarily passive and indirect." It is precisely the "colonizer's ability to exploit preexisting power relations of hierarchy, subordination, and subjugation" within the indigenous society that makes his domination over the native so insidious. As economic and social practices, slave trafficking and female subjugation were superimposed on African structures that were already in place. By contrast, JanMohamed argues, "in the hegemonic phase (or neocolonialism) the natives accept a version of the colonizers' entire system of values, attitudes, institutions, and modes of production. . . . The natives' internalization of Western cultures begins before the end of the dominant phase." Emecheta provides many examples of the "contradictions between the covert and the overt aspects of colonialism."[16]

[16] Abdul R. JanMohamed, "The Economy of Manichean Allegory: The Function of Racial Difference in Colonialist Literature, in *"Race," Writing, and Difference,* ed. Henry Louis Gates, Jr. (Chicago: University of Chicago Press, 1985), 80–81.

Ojebeta, the first daughter in her family to have survived beyond the first few minutes of life, is born into this political context. Although girls were not "normally particularly prized creatures," Ojebeta is especially cherished by her parents, her singularity a sign of her preciousness. To ensure that "she remains in the land of the living," her father takes an extensive journey to Idu, the mythological name for the old Benin empire, "said to be situated at that point where the blue sky touched the earth, [where] the people of Idu were the last humans you would see before you came to the end of the world" (20). He returns with special charms and rattles designed for the baby girl to wear to frighten away her friends from the land of the dead who will want to spirit her back to the other world.[17] At a time when, as the narrator says, "there was little division between myth and reality," between the microcosmic world of the village and the mysterious realms which extend beyond it, Ojebeta's father's arduous but successful journey takes on fatally symbolic overtones. While the mystical powers of the charms suggest that Ojebeta's life is symbolically overdetermined, their range of influence is limited; they will not be able to protect her from the threats of the material world. The degree to which she is loved by her father represents the monetary value placed on her by her brother in the absence of protective parents.

The 1918 influenza epidemic, at first ascribed to "natural" causes, kills both parents as well as many others in the village. The narrator soon makes it clear, however, that "Felenza" is "white man's death": "They shoot it into the air, and we breathe it in and die" (25). Moving in and out of this self-contained conceptual world into the larger geopolitical sphere of events, the narrator attempts to make sense of this strange and violent incursion. Finally, she provides a concrete but no more assimilable account of chemical warfare waged by the superpowers of World War I:

> Most people living in the interior of Nigeria did not know that the whole country now belonged to the British who were ruling them indirectly through the local chiefs and elders. Now, in the year of 1916, the rumors said that the new colonial masters were at war with their neighbours the

[17]Florence Stratton argues that Emecheta's identification of Ojebeta as an *ogbanje*, the Igbo term for spirit child—"believed to be destined to die and be reborn repeatedly to the same mother unless a means can be found to break the cycle"—signifies ambiguous status on two levels. The myth functions as a way to explain infant mortality in many West African societies, and it emblematizes the limitations of female destiny. See Florence Stratton, "The Shallow Grave: Archetypes of Female Experience in African Fiction," *Research in African Literatures*, Special Issue on Women's Writing, ed. Rhonda Cobham and Chikwenye Okonjo Ogunyemi, 19.2 (1988): 148.

"Germanis"; and the latter fought the British by blowing poisonous gas into the air. . . . Many inside Ibuza were asking themselves what they had to do with the Germanis, and the Germanis with them. There was no one to answer their questions. (27)

When Ojebeta's father is stricken, her mother is "confined to her hut like a prisoner until her months of mourning were over" (29); although exempt from death herself, the child is surrounded by it. Indeed, in the scene in which her mother has died in the night, she literally sleeps in death's arms. Snuggling close to her mother's breast in the early morning hours, seeking "warmth, reassurance, and protection" (28), Ojebeta lies unaware that the maternal space is now occupied only in spirit.

While taking care not to attribute the child's subsequent enslavement to any one cause, the narrator does establish a connection between the devaluation of subjectivity within colonialism's complex and extensive representational network and the domestic devaluation of females within the patriarchal family and African society generally. If not for the attention paid to historical context and concrete detail, this narrative might begin to resemble a folk or fairy tale in which just the right confluence of circumstances creates a vacuum that only evil can fill. In Emecheta's hands the slave narrative trope of the journey is refigured and ultimately subverted, used, as it were, for different ends; it also prefigures Ojebeta's passage from childhood to womanhood. For Florence Stratton, who reads *The Slave Girl* as a female bildungsroman, an archetypal story of entrapment, the sexual suggestiveness of this particular journey marks a crucial inversion of human development. Tragically, the contours of Ojebeta's life will shrink as she moves "from autonomy and self-assertion to dependency and abnegation, from the freedom and fullness of girlhood into the slavery and self-denial of womanhood."[18] Whereas her father's arduous quest involves risking his life to save Ojebeta, her brother Okolie at his first opportunity sacrifices her for his own gain. At seven years of age, Ojebeta is deceived into believing that she and her brother are taking a day trip to Onitsha, one of Africa's central markets, to visit a relative who was married out of her tribe. Instead, after hiking for miles "through various kinds of forests, wading streams, and being ferried in a canoe" (46), they reach crowds of gaily covered stalls. In a painfully protracted scene in which the "small, helpless, and terrified child" serves as a commodity in the human bazaar—sold for the few pounds her brother needs for his coming-of-age celebration—Emecheta plays the pathos of the child's situation against the brother's despicable weakness.

[18]Ibid., 148–50.

Throughout the transaction Okolie is coolly observed through the eyes of the cosmopolitan female merchant, who understands the "true" value of things and people. Depicted as a greedy and foolish village farmer whose social pretensions and crude manners merit ridicule, Okolie provides an afternoon's entertainment for all. The implication that his personality defects transcend the limitations of his rural background and are not circumstantial but essential is later borne out when neither his marriage nor his business dealings proves fruitful. It seems important that his moral failure be contrasted with the strength of Ojebeta's character and intelligence, so that even as a slave she surpasses him. The irony has a double twist, however, because although Okolie never achieves anything, his failures could be realized only at Ojebeta's expense, so to speak; in the end, gender overwrites subjective possibility anyway. When Ojebeta's charms are cut off, signifying to her and the outside world that she has lost her connection to her dead parents and her previous identity, the reader knows that her brother's betrayal of her is complete. His characterization as a pathetic but not malicious human being is crucially tied to Emecheta's general portrayal of colonized men as self-centered, vain, and childish, sometimes even well-intentioned, but crucially susceptible to delusions of power and the lures of immediate gratification, be they sensual or material. Ultimately, men are weak people, propped up by a system that reinforces their self-delusions. Only Ojebeta's father is exempt from such categorical derision.

Using the technique of free and indirect speech ("He had never sold anyone before and now he persuaded himself that what he was about to do was not selling in its actual sense"[37]), the narrator outlines the differences between the buying and selling of human beings for foreign white markets and an internal commercial system which depended on thriving labor and a class system based on acquired wealth, but not without reminding the reader of the links between them. Hours after Okolie sells his sister into slavery, his attitude and bearing recall "those days when it was easy for the European to urge the chief of a powerful village to wage war on a weaker one in order to obtain slaves for the New World" (73). Domestic slavery is justified by one wealthy female trader as a social service as well as an economic necessity: "Where would we be without slave labour, and where would some of these unwanted children be without us?" The narrator's response is short, the tone sharp: "It might be evil, but it was a necessary evil" (64). Hence the reader is apprised that it was within the brother's power and right to sell his younger sister into slavery, that it was neither illegal nor culturally unsanctioned, but that the act was to be understood, nonetheless, as an emotional betrayal or a familial transgression. Indeed, it appears that when certain kinds of kinship relations are overdetermined, kinlessness and exploitation go hand in hand; Emecheta indicates that it is precisely the slippage between kinship and abuse that enabled indigenous slavery to exist.

For Ojebeta the transition from security to slavery, though in no way comparable to the horrific descriptions of the Middle Passage in African American slave narratives, is psychologically wrenching. Unlike African American narratives in which slavery fuels a rural agricultural economy and emancipation means escaping the terrors of the southern plantation for the perils of the northern city, here an immediate opposition is established between the poor tribal ways to which Ojebeta is accustomed and the busy, sophisticated urban life to which she must adapt. As a slave, Ojebeta sleeps in special quarters and works with other slave girls as a seamstress. Her wealthy black mistress is represented as cunning and complicitous with the powers that be and have been; formerly the concubine of a Portuguese man, she owns one of the largest textile stalls at the Onitsha market which serves as the commercial center for the entire region. She traffics in human labor, but is portrayed as a kind of benign despot: she cares about her slaves. The cruelties of slavery are not mitigated in this portrait of an African slave girl's existence, but slavery has a human face—that of the harsh but caring surrogate mother, Ma Palagada, who strives to create a version of an extended family, supported somewhat by her husband, Pa Palagada.

Emecheta's detailed and carefully drawn depiction of slavery discloses its structural and functional aspects, but she seems concerned ultimately with the ways in which women have internalized their sexual subjugation. She represents slavery not only as a signifier of social status or position, or even a particular historical destiny, but as a psychic condition, a way of being. Thus, there are no rhetorical indications here that the narrator knows more than she chooses to tell, that she is protecting the reader from worse, or that she is negotiating the limits or boundaries of the representable, as is often the case in African American slave narratives, most notably in Harriet Jacobs's *Incidents in the Life of a Slave Girl*. It is surely a fundamental aspect of Emecheta's agenda in this third-person narration to show that there is no gap between the slave's lack of subjective agency and her capacity to express it. Under this system the limitations of female experience and slave consciousness are synonomous.

Ojebeta's initial sense of estrangement gives way to a sense of belonging to a community: the sororal relations she enjoys with the other slave girls help to compensate for the childhood she has lost. During her years of servitude, Ojebeta is exposed to the "civilizing" effects of education, etiquette, and Christianity. In contrast to the paradigmatic scene of instruction in African American slave narratives, in which the slave is both symbolically and actually empowered by her ascent to literacy, in *The Slave Girl* not only is literacy not seen as dangerous knowledge, but its effects benefit all the participants in the system. The fact that Ma Palagada's slaves know how to read permits her to charge more for the dresses the girls make; her profit and prestige increase. Not only do her slave seamstresses copy the fashions of white European women for the wealthy women in the region, but on Sundays they themselves wear silk to church for all to see. The irony is that instead of providing the slave girl with the means to conceptualize her own freedom, education here signals socialization into a colonially inflected cultural system of values.

By highlighting the development of her slave heroine's social and intellectual abilities, Emecheta introduces new variants into what seemed to be a closed system, including the relative exercise of choice in a world where none would have seemed possible. When Ma Palagada dies, chaos ensues, and Ojebeta has the chance to run away home to her people.[19] Ojebeta suffers the death of her mistress "as if she had been her real mother," weighs alternatives, and decides that "she would rather go back to Ibuza and eat the mushrooms of freedom than stay in this house, and eat meat in slavery" (146–47). Deviating sharply from African American slave narratives and defying the expectations of readers familiar with them, the escape itself is described in a few lines, and no special significance is accorded this symbolic passage beyond the expected emotional stress Ojebeta experiences.

Ojebeta is welcomed warmly when she returns to her village, and is celebrated for the polish and sophistication she has acquired; she carries herself differently from Ibuza women and speaks like a girl born in Onitsha, "with rounded 'Rs' and a slowness of delivery, each word drawn out" (107). Others refer to her nine years of slavery as if she had spent them at finishing school—an attitude that recalls William Andrews's characterization of the accommodation strategies of the African American postbellum slave narrator. Although her brother is criticized

---

[19] Andrade, "Rewriting History," reads the central drama of Ma Palagada's mysterious "sudden illness" and subsequent death, in which the 1929 Igbo Women's War is marginally inscribed, as an example of Emecheta's "dialogizing of oppositional behavior." This strategy provides a historical context for interpreting women's complicity and resistance or rebellion in which the latter is represented so marginally as to be constructed as "un-inscribable" (108).

severely for his greedy act by the people of her village, in their perception a malevolent cause has resulted ultimately in a positive effect. But
as Ojebeta's practices and beliefs begin to diverge sharply from those
of the community, she feels a strange ambivalence: great affection
slightly undermined by a sense of her own cultural superiority. As
Emecheta notes: "So afraid was Ojebeta that all she had learned at Ma
Palagada's would be wasted that she prayed to God to send her an
Ibuza man who had experience of the white man's work and would
know the value of what she had learned" (154). Now enthusiastically
involved in the Church of England, she finds a group of friends who
deem it stylish to take European names; soon Ogbanje Ojebeta becomes
Ogbanje Alice, an ironic invocation of the act of renaming so central to
African American slave narratives. Ogbanje Alice is too naive to understand how deeply susceptible she is to competing and contradictory
ideologies of power.

The narrative moves rather abruptly to its next stage. When Ojebeta
(now Ogbanje Alice) meets Jacob—a gentle, educated man who lives
and works in Lagos (that is to say, he does white man's work) and has
returned to his village to look for a girl to marry—the reader knows a
match is imminent. In order for them to marry, however, Ojebeta's two
older brothers (who also live and work in Lagos) must give their permission. More crucially, they must determine Ojebeta's bride price. After some negotiations, the marriage takes place, and the couple's
conjugal life begins happily enough. The narrator's well-placed comments about "the eternal bond between husband and wife being produced by centuries of traditions, taboos, and latterly Christian dogma"
(173), however, cause the reader to suspect that this is not a marriage
of equals, in spite of their mutual intelligence and cultivation. And
Ojebeta has other problems, one outstanding: she begins to "lose her
babies," her miscarriages a sign from the spirits that she has not escaped the destiny of an unredeemed slave. She must be bought back
from Clifford, Ma Palagada's son, who after the death of his mother
became Ojebeta's legal owner.

In the penultimate scene, where Jacob pays Clifford eight pounds—
the exact sum paid for the child Ojebeta twenty-eight years earlier—
Emecheta moves sharply between the characters' thoughts and the
words they actually say to one another. Handsome, uniformed Clifford
(serving in the British army in the big war in Europe) is astonished by
the sight of Ojebeta, now "the ghost of the girl he had known so many
years ago." No longer the energetic, laughing girl with the straight
carriage and jet black skin, she looks thinner and incomparably older
than he could ever have imagined. "Momentarily he wondered what

had happened to change her so much?" (176). The implicit response is that she had been eating "the mushroom of freedom." She passes these same moments engaged in self-justification: looking around at her one-room home and her untidy, well-intentioned husband with the red eyes, she confirms that "she would rather have this than be a slave in a big house in Onitsha." After an exchange of superficial niceties, Jacob sends Ojebeta back to the kitchen to finish her cooking so that the men can "finalize the arrangements for her permanent ownership" (177). The transaction completed, Ojebeta's two brothers, husband, and former owner sit down to a meal of steaming rice and hot chicken stew. Since Ojebeta's own position seems to preclude the possibility of self-irony, Emecheta leaves the final commentary on slavery to the narrator: "So as Britain was emerging from war once more victorious, and claiming to have stopped the slavery which she had helped to spread in all her black colonies, Ojebeta, now a woman of thirty-five, was changing masters" (179).

These scathing words indissolubly inscribe Ojebeta's status as a female subject into the larger colonialist narrative, but a narrative in which the structure of patriarchy subsumes all others. Using both the fictional conventions of slave narratives and the autobiographical interventions of slave novels, this postcolonial African author, whose mother's name was Alice Ogbanje Ojebeta, reads the politics of domination from the position of the (daughter of the) twice-mastered native woman. Ojebeta figures metonymically in this narrative *as* the colonized nation whose status and destiny are ultimately determined by the precolonial meanings attributed to class and gender differences rather than by any specific colonialist configuration of exploitation or opening up of those differences.[20] When Ojebeta is enslaved, her special charms are cut off, breaking the links to her past identity and enabling her master to constitute a new one for her: slave girl. When Ojebeta becomes a married woman, the sign that she is still a slave and not quite a wife—the link to her previous identity—is her childlessness. Her debased status is therefore unrelated to her actual enslavement, only to the unfulfilled terms of its contract. Once the exchange value of her body as the site of both productive and reproductive labor is

[20]In "Cracking the Code: Strategies in African Women's Writing" (unpublished manuscript, 1990), Chikwenye Ogunyemi identifies such a figurative strategy in many postcolonial texts by African women: "The continuing independence struggles underscored the need to obtain genuine freedom for all including the nations, who, like women, were still subjugated. The writers see woman's destiny and the motherland's as intertwined, a crucial point realized in some texts allegorically and symbolically" (1). I am grateful for her helpful suggestions on this essay.

recontextualized, though never questioned, she can assume her social identity as wife, properly understood. So much, says Emecheta's narrative, for liberation.

The Slave Girl's acerbic ending provides yet another twist on the oft-cited line from the conclusion of Harriet Jacobs's *Incidents in the Life of a Slave Girl:* "Reader, my story ends with freedom, not in the usual way, with marriage." For as Jacobs apologizes for not having met the traditional requirements of the domestic novel by achieving "only" freedom and not romance (i.e., marriage), she subverts her readers' expectations of how the plots of both domestic fiction and slave narratives are resolved. By recalling Jacobs's claim for understanding that different conditions produce different conventions, Emecheta makes her point all the more painful to consider. What if the story ends with marriage but not with freedom? What might link the destinies of a nineteenth-century romantic heroine ("Reader, I married him") and Ojebeta, the twentieth-century slave girl? Reading *The Slave Girl* from the position of the comparatist-feminist means assuming from the outset an extensive play of textual relations and intersections: between African and New World women's writing, between nineteenth- and twentieth-century postbellum and postcolonial slave narratives, between texts by men and those by women. As comparatists, we must read this text not only against different cultural grains but across critical categories of analysis and value. We would reconfigure a traditional question such as "How might a modern Nigerian novel about slavery have been influenced by slave narratives?" as "How might a modern Nigerian novel about slavery affect a contemporary reading of slave narratives?" When the discourses of slavery that are constructed and reflected in nationalist mythologies of literary history are opened up to more diverse interpretations, the limitations of national readings stand out in stark relief. To set up an equation between sexual subjugation and slavery, as Emecheta has done in all of her novels, perforce changes "our" view of slavery. It also changes "our" view of patriarchy as a global as well as a particular phenomenon. Emecheta's poignant and sobering text militates against any temptation to totalize the discourse on slavery by rendering in assimilable terms the insidiousness of all systems of bondage and the recuperation, indeed the domestication, of history.

3
Life after Rape:
Narrative, Theory, and Feminism

RAJESWARI SUNDER RAJAN

Texts do not lie outside the circuit of sexual politics but are implicated in them. It is this mode of implication, particularly as it results
in the constitution of the sexed subject, that the feminist critical method
uncovers. Rape is a term central to the poetics of narrative as well as
a crucial area of feminist politics: the raped woman functions as the
subject both *of* narrative and *in* feminism. How are rape, narrative structure, and feminist politics imbricated? How may we contest the claims
of universal or global validity advanced by feminists and narrative theorists on the grounds of rape or of desire? By indicating the historical
and specifically contextual limits within which the terms operate in
their mutually constitutive roles, a comparative approach offers an empirical check and a reference point.

"Sirai" ("Prison," 1980), a short story in Tamil by Anuradha Ramanan which quickly and ironically plots the narrative of a raped Brahmin (upper-caste) woman, serves as an exemplary "third world"
woman's text against which two master texts of "first world" literature
and their criticism can be measured: *Clarissa* (1748) and *A Passage to
India* (1924), works whose central episodes turn on the rape of their
female protagonists. In addition, Maya Angelou's *I Know Why the Caged
Bird Sings* (1971), Alice Walker's novel *The Color Purple* (1982), and Jonathan Kaplan's film *The Accused* (1988) may serve as representative contemporary American "feminist" narratives of rape. Because these texts
occupy heterogeneous historical, cultural, racial, and gendered locations, they foster an exploration of different ways in which rape and
the raped woman enter representation as the subject of narrative, as
well as of the different politics they engender within feminism.

Anuradha Ramanan is a prolific writer of fiction, both short stories
and novels, for popular mass-circulation Tamil magazines (published
mainly in the state of Tamil Nadu in south India). "Prison" first ap-

A version of this essay also appears in my book *Real and Imagined Women: Gender,
Culture, and Postcolonialism* (London: Routledge, 1993), © 1993 by Rajeswari Sunder Rajan.

peared in one of these magazines as the prizewinning entry in a short
story competition; it was subsequently filmed and included in an anthology of Ramanan's short stories bearing the same title.[1]

"Prison" is a post-rape narrative concerned with showing how the
female protagonist, Bhagirathi, survives the fear and humiliation of her
rape by a stranger and her subsequent abandonment by her husband.
Bhagirathi comes to a small village in Tamil Nadu as the eighteen-year-
old bride of the temple priest Raghupathy. She catches the eye of Anthony, the rich and rakish village landlord, who immediately plots to
catch her alone. The story begins with his easy, insolent rape of Bhagirathi, in broad daylight, at a time when the priest is offering prayers
at the temple.

Bhagirathi, shocked and frightened, seeks her husband's protection.
He spurns her in anger and walks out of the house, never to return.
Bhagirathi wanders the streets, becoming a byword as a fallen woman.
Then she reaches a decision: she goes to Anthony's house, announces
she is going to live there, and forbids him to touch her again even
though he has already ruined her. Anthony is stunned and remorseful.
At her insistence he arranges for Bhagirathi to have her own living
quarters and her own cooking utensils. After some years he remon-
strates with her at her confined existence and offers to find her husband
for her. She mocks his naïveté, and insists that he too must share her
punishment: her continued presence in his house will be his bane. They
spend thirty years in this fashion, living in the same house, hardly
talking to each other. She proudly goes every day to the river to fetch
her own water, braving the villagers' taunts. Anthony leaves more and
more of the management of his lands to her, and she is meticulous in
her dealings. He is a Christian and she a Brahmin, but she places flowers every day at his shrine to the Virgin Mary. Her presence in his
house inhibits his drinking and womanizing.

Finally, Anthony lies ill. When he goes into a fit of coughing and
gropes for a basin to spit into—there is no attendant—Bhagirathi hears
him and offers him the basin, speaking her first direct words to him in
all their years together. He is moved at her offer of service but considers
himself unworthy of her attentions. Anthony dies shortly after, leaving
her his house and enough money to live on comfortably. The rest of
his wealth goes to orphanages. At his death Bhagirathi realizes that he
has cared more for her than the husband who made his marriage vows
to her. She takes off her *thali* (the symbol of marriage worn around the

[1]Anuradha Ramanan, "Sirai" (Prison), *Kunguman,* June 15, 1980; rpt. in Anuradha Ramanan, *Sirai* (Madras: Kanimuthu Pathippagam, 1984); all translations are my own.

neck) and places it on the butt of Anthony's gun. Better to live as the widow of Anthony than the wife of Raghupathy, she decides. She lies down weeping to mourn him.

The question that irresistibly offers itself is: What impels Bhagirathi's social and sexual rebellion? If I choose to read "Prison" as a feminist text, I do so in spite of a complete absence in the story of any feminist "solution" to the issue of rape. Among the possibilities that the story presents on behalf of Bhagirathi—vagrancy, suicide, return to her rapist, or reclamation by her husband—there is not even a suggestion of recourse to women's groups and their strategies of resistance. Ramanan does not consider that an activist women's group might provide Bhagirathi with legal aid to prosecute her rapist or seek out her husband and claim maintenance from him.[2] Nevertheless, a certain "feminism" (here, Western liberalism and a "liberated" sexual code) is implied in any attack on religious orthodoxy in the Indian social context. In this situation Ramanan leaves the initiative and resources for coping entirely to Bhagirathi, though she is a product of a culture that largely negates any meritocratic individualism and envisages an entirely subordinate role for women. Needless to add, Bhagirathi's rebellious celibacy has little to do with modern sexual liberation. But destitute and socially outcast though she is, Bhagirathi still retains her identity as a superior caste subject, and she deploys it to intimidate her rapist, first into accepting her in his house, and then into leading a life of chastity with her.

There are two ironies here. The first is that a Brahmin is male by definition; a Brahmin woman is not formally initiated into the rites of castehood, nor does she follow any separate practices of Brahminhood except as they relate to her connection with the male Brahmin. A Brahmin is born into his caste, a Brahmin woman is born his daughter. "Brahmin woman" is a derived identity. The second irony is that in today's Tamil Nadu, Brahminism has been stripped of virtually all its traditional material and political claims to power—the religious supremacy of the priesthood and its monopoly over learning—in large part as a result of a vigorous Dravidian (non-Aryan) political and cultural movement in this century.[3]

---

[2]Ramanan revealed to me in conversation that her covert purpose in the story was reformist: she hoped to establish the need for the rehabilitation of "fallen women."

[3]Two political parties, the Dravida Munnetra Kazhagam (DMK) and the All-India Anna Dravida Munnetra Kazhagam (AIADMK), have emerged from this movement, opposed by the Brahmin Association. The anti-Brahmin movement has made its consequences felt largely in the related spheres of education and employment, where massive reservation of places for "backward" classes and tribes by the Dravidian parties in power has kept Brahmins out of prestigious state-run educational institutions, bureaucratic jobs,

Yet it is through laying claim to one of the standard practices of Brahminism—ritual purity—that Bhagirathi secures her safety. On the grounds that she would otherwise be contaminated, she demands her own living quarters and her own cooking utensils, and fetches her own water. She ideologically dominates Anthony, more powerful than her in every other way, by asserting her superior caste status. The semiotics of purity bear further scrutiny. Bhagirathi invokes one standard of purity (caste) to modify or displace another (female sexuality) by claiming for the former a greater validity and broader social import. Taking into account the complexity of the social procedures by which both caste and female chastity are invested with power, Bhagirathi plays off one against the other.

Why and how does her strategy work? The most important of the reasons is the supremacy that "Brahminism" as a cultural and ideological value still retains in contemporary Tamil Nadu. In spite of successfully curbing institutional Brahmin influence in the region, the Dravidian political parties have failed to forge a counterculture. Their early ideological struggles for atheistic rationalism and a reformist language policy aimed at de-Sanskritizing the Tamil language have largely lost their force. The upward class and caste mobility of non-Brahmin groups has instead been directed toward, precisely, Sanskritization.[4]

But where is the locus of these superior values? Not in the Brahmin male, marginalized in the economic and political spheres: it is precisely *his* emasculation that the rape of his wife emphasizes. Instead the Brahmin *woman* now assumes and deploys "Brahmin" values in the context of an identity crisis. The separation in "Prison" of ideological value from political and economic power, analogous to the separation of the Brahmin woman from the Brahmin man, dramatizes a crucial historical warp.[5] A realignment of gender positions is inscribed through the crisis in caste identity.

---

and political appointments. A significant diaspora of Brahmins has occurred to other states in India as well as to countries in the West. Since education and administration had been the traditional preserves of the Brahmin community, its social role and function have been severely diminished. At the same time, the Brahmin priesthood is no longer attended with divine sanction or political influence; Brahmin priests are now merely poorly paid performers of temple rituals and private worship in a few households. In response to decreased demand, fewer traditional Sanskrit institutions teach the Vedas, or religious texts.

[4]Sanskritization is the process of evolution among caste groups toward adopting upper-caste customs in areas such as dowry, religious ritual, and temple worship.

[5]This argument is reinforced by a popular and controversial Tamil film, *Vedam Puthidu* (The new Veda), which articulately and intelligently attacks the caste system. But here, too, Brahmin values (vegetarianism, ritual purity, Sanskrit learning, nonviolence) are val-

It is only the confluence of Brahminism and femininity at this specific historical juncture that allows Ramanan to grant Bhagirathi access to the power of asserting caste status. Nothing in the traditional content of Brahminism—or Hinduism more broadly—would encourage Bhagirathi's negotiation with her sexual violator in this way. She ironically recalls the legendary figures of Ahalya and Sita from Hindu mythology, women raped or abducted who are forced to establish their chastity through miraculous tests or prolonged ordeals.[6] As traditional narrative models, these legends propose purification for the violated woman through symbolic death (transformation into a stone, passage through fire) to resolve the crisis of rape or attempted rape. These tests and ordeals through which women must pass in order to qualify for reentry into "society" give Bhagirathi no reason to suppose that she can defy sexual mores with impunity.

Nevertheless, the "rewards" of these processes of sexual violation, test or ordeal, and survival are great for the women who undergo them. Ahalya and Sita become triumphant and enduring cultural symbols of *pativrata,* or husband worship; their legendary and heroic chastity retains a powerful ideological hold on the Hindu imagination. Thus, in a narrative that is structured as a series of escalating shocks aimed at the Hindu bourgeoisie—first the victim's return to her rapist, then the Brahmin woman's cohabitation with a lower-caste Christian—the greatest blow lies in the story's ending, when Bhagirathi blasphemes *pativrata* by casting off her *thali* and draping it over the butt of Anthony's gun (an equally transparent symbol of physical and sexual power).[7] Confounding marriage and rape, she sees marriage as a prolonged sexual domination by the male and rape as a momentary violent aberration; but each is compensated by and entails the man's responsibility for the woman. The familiar and somewhat clichéd polemic against sexual double standards also involves Bhagirathi in a more complex judgment of the two men: "The man who lived with me for six months cast me off in an instant. And here is this man who com-

---

orized and shown to exert ideological influence; here the embodiment of such values is the Brahmin (male) child.

[6]Ahalya, wife of the sage Gautama, is raped by the god Indra, who comes to her in the night in the form of her husband. Turned to stone by her husband's curse, she is restored to human form only years later when the god Rama steps on the stone. In the epic *Ramayana,* Rama's wife, Sita, is abducted by the evil king Ravana and held captive until Rama rescues her. Before she can be restored to him, public opinion must be satisfied; she undergoes an ordeal by fire to prove that she has remained chaste.

[7]Ramanan's story and the film based on it created an uproar. The Brahmin Association launched a protest both at the "dishonor" of a Brahmin woman's rape and at the notion of her repudiating the *thali,* invested with a profound mystique.

mitted a moment's folly, and has cherished me ever since without any expectation of return!" So long as the identity of "wife" allows Bhagirathi to maintain as well the identity of "Brahmin woman" and thus create a zone of safety, she holds on to it. But with Anthony's death she can repudiate that identity and become "Anthony's widow," a woman without a man. Wife/widow, Brahmin/not-Brahmin, protection/autonomy are alternating and opposed states and identities which Bhagirathi adopts as circumstances warrant, with the goal at one level of mere survival but at another of social interrogation and critique.

Bhagirathi's foregrounding and deployment of her caste and marital identities are not, however, built on a transcendence or obliteration of Anthony's sexual violation. Instead, Bhagirathi presents herself to Anthony as the woman he has raped: "The woman who stood before him gazing so fiercely ... Was that a woman's gaze ... How was it he hadn't fallen before it earlier? ... No woman he had raped had ever come to stand at his door like this before, with a gaze that pierced like a spear." Within Ramanan's frame, the female victim of rape narrative becomes the subject of a second narrative, scripted by her, one that escapes past models offered by male narratives ("no woman ... had ever ... "). Bhagirathi never allows Anthony to forget that the defining act of their relationship is his rape of her. Her insistent thrusting of her fallen status upon Anthony results in that foregrounding of the "sexual differential" that Gayatri Spivak has emphasized in her discussion of the raped woman, the protagonist of "Draupadi," an act that turns her for her enemy into "a powerful 'subject,' " "a terrifying superobject."[8]

The identity of a raped woman which Bhagirathi embraces is not based, it must be emphasized, on a conventional acceptance of the *loss* of chastity, and thereby the diminution of "full" womanhood. Ramanan allows Bhagirathi to make an appropriative, revisionary reading of the religious texts of Hinduism to apply to her situation. As Raghupathy, the priest, returns home from the temple, he is murmuring the opening invocation from the Upanishads: "Purnam adah, Purnam idam, purnat purnam udacyate / Purnasya purnam adaya purnam evavasisyate" (That is full and this is full. Out of that eternal whole springs forth this eternal whole, and when the whole is taken from the whole, there still remains the complete whole.)[9] This description of godhead as a metaphysical plentitude is transferred by Ramanan to a description of human, including female, selfhood; she finds sanction in it to repudiate

[8]Gayatri Spivak, trans., "Draupadi," by Mahasweta Devi, in *Writing and Sexual Difference*, ed. Elizabeth Abel (Chicago: University of Chicago Press, 1982), 387.
[9]*The Upanishads*, trans. Chitrita Devi (New Delhi: S. Chand, 1973), 1.

the metonymic social definition of chastity (as women's precarious "possession" which can be lost or as a "component" of sexual integrity).[10]

Although the identity that Bhagirathi retains or adopts after her rape—as superior caste subject, as another man's wife, as raped woman—is constituted within the boundaries of her religion and culture, there is room for her to grow, improvise, and assert herself within her "prison." For instance, she daily places flowers at the feet of Anthony's statue of the Virgin Mary: whether construed as an act of worship, a gesture of female solidarity, or a dignified concession to and recognition of Anthony's god, it is deliberately and freely performed. Another space of development is her growth into the role of manager of his property. As Anthony delegates power to her, she comes to handle all the produce and sale of his land, and when he dies she inherits part of his wealth. This inheritance ultimately prevents Anthony's death from becoming a second abandonment. She is compensated for her loss of social and caste status by acquiring economic power, as "Anthony's widow."

Anthony's role in the "charade" is in part a response to rules set by Bhagirathi; in part the model for his active reformation comes from his own religion. A strong if sentimental sense of sin leads him to piety, penance, and charity. His celibacy is dictated by his characteristic conversion of the woman he has raped into a sexless maternal figure, the type of the Virgin Mary. Bhagirathi's relationship to the Virgin is not, of course, one of identity. The Hindu models of female chastity available to her are not sexless figures but heroic and "innocent" married women. The dialectic between two sets of religious values, Hindu and Christian, as mediated by their norms of female purity is complex. Anthony's Christianity, we must note, is also encoded by Ramanan in social, as opposed to merely religious, terms. Indian Christians, especially in rural south India, are for the most part converts from lower-caste Hindu groups. Ramanan tacitly reinforces the stereotype of rapacity associated with their "original" caste identity as non-Brahmin men, even as she grants them the "redeeming" values of their new religious identity as Christians.[11]

It is clear that the ideological structures that the story both operates within and strains against in its construction of the raped woman as subject are shaped by the realities of its social, religious, and cultural limits; but included in these realities is a certain liberalizing, modern-

[10]Personal communication from Ramanan.
[11]I am grateful to Ania Loomba for pointing this out to me.

izing discourse of "feminism." There is a danger in both story and criticism of idealizing Bhagirathi's feminist individualism.[12] Her choices cannot themselves be valorized as feminist: as a destitute woman, she seeks not independence but male protection; she repudiates her identity as Raghupathy's wife only to take on that of "Anthony's widow"; she enforces Anthony's chaste behavior toward her at the cost of laying waste her own sexual life;[13] above all, she succeeds in securing her safety and purity only by entering a "prison," as Anthony ruefully points out.

Ramanan explores the concept of the "prison" creatively. Sociologists have observed that Indian women experience social space "in such binary oppositions as private/public, danger/safety, pure/polluted."[14] Ramanan deconstructs these oppositions by blurring spatial designations. Bhagirathi is raped in a "safe" place, her home (paradoxically, no place is considered more safe than a house whose doors stay open), which Anthony enters "as if he owned it." Bhagirathi herself is caught napping, "her head pillowed on the threshold" where Anthony "looms." The threshold, of course, is the open space that confounds the inside of the house with the outside. After her rape, Bhagirathi is literally errant, a homeless woman forced to spend the nights in the porch of her husband's locked house or the temple courtyard, spaces that are both within and without enclosures, marking her own indeterminate subject status. The people of the village pronounce her a woman "of the streets," that terrifying, ejected, antisocial female element, a bogey for "good" girls.

The discourse of crime and punishment invariably foregrounds the concept of the "prison" as incarcerating the individual wrongdoer in the interests of the larger social good. But Bhagirathi's entry into purdah does not fit this moral schema; her reentry into the domestic sphere is performed as an act of violent intrusion, not one of discreet disappearance. Her occupation of the woman's inner rooms designated as purdah is a form of territorial conquest. Purdah in certain Western feminist analyses has been equated with "rape, forced prostitution, polyg-

[12]Some feminist essays on texts by cultural "others" idealize feminist individualism as a solution to women's predicament. See, for instance, King-Kok Cheung, " 'Don't Tell': Imposed Silences in *The Color Purple* and *The Woman Warrior*," *PMLA* 103 (1988): 162–74.

[13]Ramanan emphasizes Bhagirathi's passionate nature. The cool porcelain statue of the Virgin contrasts with Bhagirathi's turbulence as she stands before the mirror applying her *kumkum* (the dot on her forehead): "The sweet memories . . . of her married life . . . dissolve in her heart like syrup."

[14]Rashmi Bhatnagar, "Genre and Gender: A Reading of Tagore's *The Broken Nest* and R. K. Narayan's *The Dark Room*," in *Woman/Image/Text: Feminist Readings of Literary Texts*, ed. Lola Chatterjee (New Delhi: Trianka, 1986), 173.

amy, genital mutilation, pornography, the beating of girls and women,"
as instances of "violations of basic human rights."[15] But in such analyses, as Chandra Mohanty has argued, "the institution of purdah is . . .
denied any cultural and historical specificity, and contradictions and
potentially subversive aspects of the institution are totally ruled out."[16]
In "Prison" the experience of purdah is precisely rewritten in terms of
its contradictions and subversive aspects. Segregation works both ways:
Bhagirathi's occupation of the inner rooms confines Anthony to the
hall—for her only a passage of transit—just as her expulsion from her
husband's house has resulted in his disappearance into a perpetual diaspora. Bhagirathi's entry into Anthony's house is a parody of his entry
into hers.

Furthermore, Bhagirathi refuses literal imprisonment, risking public
exposure every day by going to the river to fetch water. Here Ramanan inserts the private-public opposition into areas constitutive of
narrative and subjecthood as well. Bhagirathi becomes a public figure
in the small village community, ironically referred to as Anthony's
"woman," and the subject of ribald speculation and rumor. What remains private is the truth: their chaste relationship as man and
woman. In the modern female bildungsroman the development of an
individualistic female selfhood builds on such a polarity of private integrity and public opprobium. When a woman's consciousness of individualistic identity is forced into existence through social isolation
brought on by the stigma of sexual impropriety—as is Bhagirathi's—
this development stands in contrast to the politics of feminism. Terry
Eagleton has confidently asserted, for instance, that "a modern Clarissa would not need to die" because of the access she would have to
help from women's groups.[17]

Victimhood in such an argument provides the female subject access
to a sense of collective gendered identity based on shared oppression.
In the absence of such organized resistance—an absence naturalized by
the narrative's setting in a small rural community in an unspecified
recent past—a tenuous individualism shapes the female subject's resistance. Ideally this selfhood constitutes for the female subject existential
freedom, space for growth and change, a full "inner life," and some
access to power, even if the venture ends as a costly one. The exercise

[15]Fran Hosken, "Female Genital Mutilation and Human Rights," *Feminist Issues* 1
(1981): 15. Hosken's position is discussed in Chandra Talpade Mohanty, "Under Western
Eyes: Feminist Scholarship and Colonial Discourse," *Boundary* 2 (1984): 333–58.

[16]Mohanty, "Under Western Eyes," 347.

[17]Terry Eagleton, *The Rape of Clarissa: Writing, Sexuality, and Class Struggle in Samuel
Richardson* (Oxford: Basil Blackwell, 1982), 94.

of choice clearly cannot be a sufficient condition for a woman's freedom when her choices are few and severely determined.

I have tried to show how the female protagonist of this Tamil short story must deploy her "superior" identity as Brahmin woman and also foreground her abject destiny as raped woman; how she is complicitous in a politics of caste as well as isolated by the brute reality of rape; how she *chooses* her prison as well as chooses a *prison*. The claims of a certain "realism" do not permit more than this evenhanded distribution of gains and losses for the oppressed female subject within the short story's narrative mode. Nevertheless, the politics of the story—its ironic polemic against sexual morality, its overt purpose to *épater les bourgeois*—results inevitably in a valorization of Bhagirathi's individualistic, even antisocial, will to survive. A feminist critical enterprise is therefore obliged, even as it is constantly aware of the story's balance of forces, to privilege strategically its incipient utopian gesture toward the reclamation of the raped female subject.

In Samuel Richardson's *Clarissa* (1748) and E. M. Forster's *Passage to India* (1924), as in "Prison," rape serves as an allegory for other political encounters. In *Clarissa* the main characters are also antagonists in a deadly class struggle; in *A Passage to India* they are racial opponents in the colonial conflict. The female protagonist becomes the victim of rape as much because of her membership in her caste, class, or race as because of her sexual identity; one might even say that she is less the object of sexual desire than the scapegoat in a struggle of larger forces.

In the two novels, however, the complex identity that is constructed for the female subject undergoes a curious transformation at the point of rape. Clarissa's cry "I am but a cypher" expresses a raped woman's perception of total annihilation of self following on physical subjugation, coercion of will, and psychological humiliation. Questions of volition, so central to the constitution of the individualist humanistic subject of the novel, are significantly in abeyance.[18]

Clarissa Harlowe's self-extinction is compensated by her spectacular absorption into her author's sympathies after her rape, figured within the text by the solicitude of her lover's friend Belford, and replicated in critical practice by the partisanship of a host of critics. A heroine so totally taken over by authorial and critical sympathy has no scope or need to develop any self-assertive dimension. In contrast to Richardson's takeover of Clarissa there is Forster's fastidious repudiation of

[18]Eagleton considers her choice of illness only "a tragic option for self-extinction" (ibid., 87).

Adela Quested after she produces her account of the supposed attack on her. She drops out of the narrative after the event, only to reappear much later as a reduced and disoriented witness for the prosecution. Forster's limited interest in Adela Quested is replicated by most critics of the book.

For Forster, it is the feminine sensibility of Mrs. Moore that has the best chance for developing interpersonal relations in the colonial situation; but because of female *sexuality* (Adela Quested's) these relations can also be jeopardized. The split in femininity between sensibility and sexuality results in the surrogacy of Mrs. Moore's function after the Marabar Caves episode. She suffers a trauma in the caves very similar to Adela's, falls ill, is infected by a cynical misogyny, dies, and is apotheosized in a series of developments more appropriate to the raped Adela.

The reification of female victimhood is a familiar procedure in the fiction of male novelists (one has only to think of Hardy's *Tess* or Galsworthy's Irene Forsythe in *The Man of Property*). All that is really left for the raped woman to do is to fade away: Adela, doing the decent thing, retracts her charge and returns to England; Clarissa, transcending her body's humiliation, falls ill and dies.

Paradoxically, at the same time that she becomes an existential "cypher," the raped woman also turns into a symbolic cause. She becomes the representative of her social group, the very embodiment of its collective identity. The assumption of embattled positions around a raped woman's cause often marks an identity crisis for a group, as historical examples amply prove.[19] The woman's newly recognized identity— which may be more properly described as her function in an economy of sexual propriety and property—becomes an emotional war cry and the prelude to the virtual disappearance of the concerns of the woman herself. Although Clarissa has been alienated from her family for much of the novel, once she dies her cousin rushes to avenge her in defense of the family's honor. In *A Passage to India* Forster shows British officialdom and its wives gathering around Adela Quested in an upsurge of sentimental patriotism (which is trivially shifted to the more appropriately symbolic railway official's wife: "This evening, with her abundant figure and masses of corn-gold hair, she symbolised all that is worth fighting and dying for").[20] Ironically, Adela's project *not* to be an Anglo-Indian results only in the confirmation of her colonial identity,

[19]See the connections traced by Hazel Carby between "lynching, empire and sexuality," in "On the Threshold of Women's Era: Lynching, Empire and Sexuality in Black Feminist Theory," *Critical Inquiry* 12 (1985): 262–77.

[20]E. M. Forster, *A Passage to India* (New York: Harcourt Brace, 1924), 181.

sentimentally acclaimed by her fellow Anglo-Indians and savagely asserted by Forster.

I intend these observations on the subjectification of the raped woman in the two novels to serve as a contrast to the consolidation of the female self in "Prison." The successive assumption, deployment, and repudiation of superior castehood by Bhagirathi herself, her thrusting of her raped condition upon her rapist, and her determined self-fashioning, indicate the birth and development of feminist individualism in circumstances of necessity and survival. Although Bhagirathi seeks her solution in terms of what I call for convenience feminist individualism, this "liberation" bears no resemblance historically to the individualism of the humanist subject at the center of Western literary genres such as tragedy or the novel (consider King Lear, or Hardy's Michael Henchard). This subject position, when offered to *female* protagonists such as Clarissa Harlowe or Adela Quested, breaks down under the assault of rape. Bhagirathi's "selfhood" is instead a "palimpsest of identities,"[21] both constituted and erased by history, so that in the gendered subject, religious, caste, class, and sexual attributes are foregrounded in succession according to the exigencies of the situation. Choice and necessity become indistinguishable in such identities in flux.

A feminist "thematics of liberation," as Teresa de Lauretis has cautioned us, is insufficient to counter the force of masculine desire which invests all narrative.[22] This is why feminist texts of rape must also engage in textual strategies to counter narrative determinism. Such negotiations are achieved by and result in *alternative* structures of narrative. One means to this end is the structural location of the rape incident at the beginning of a woman's story. Narrative beginnings differentiate closures. In "Prison" the positioning of the scene of rape at the beginning preempts expectation of its late(r) occurrence. Not only is the scene of rape diminished by this positioning, but it is also granted a more purely functional purpose in the narrative economy, and narrative interest becomes displaced onto what follows. Ramanan is not alone in designating the narrative function of rape as the initiating moment of women's "knowledge." In both *The Color Purple* by Alice Walker and Maya Angelou's *I Know Why the Caged Bird Sings*, the de-

---

[21]For an elaboration of this notion of female subjectivity, see Zakia Pathak and Rajeswari Sunder Rajan, "Shahbano," *Signs* 14 (1989): 573.

[22]See Teresa de Lauretis, *Alice Doesn't: Feminism, Semiotics, Cinema* (Bloomington: Indiana University Press, 1982), 103–57. De Lauretis endorses Roland Barthes's position that narrative is "international, transhistorical, transcultural"; but she specifies that "subjectivity is engaged in the cogs of narrative, meaning, and desire," and further that "the relation of narrative and desire must be sought in the specificity of a textual practice" (106).

velopment of the female subject's "self" begins *after* the rape and occupies the entire length of the narrative.

Furthermore, "Prison" is marked by a laconic narrative mode which abbreviates an account of thirty years into a few pages, alternating between a terse past-tense narrative of representative quotidian events and a present-tense account of only four exchanges between different pairs of characters. The brevity of the story subverts the narrative model of desire built on the prolongation of suspense and the postponement of climax. *The Color Purple* is similarly innovative in its narrative devices: it creates generic instability by mixing history with utopian romance, causality, and wish fulfillment. As a result, Celie's story, which begins with her rape by the man she thinks is her father, ends with the restoration of her family, her economic independence, and her creation of a community of equals. These endings, as Christine Froula points out, are "all the more powerful in that they emerge from Celie's seemingly hopeless beginnings": "Celie's beginning could have been a silent end," but instead "her ending continues the proliferating beginnings that the novel captures in its epistolary form, its characters' histories, and the daily revelations that Shug names 'God.' "[23] Angelou achieves a similar liberation in *I Know Why the Caged Bird Sings* by framing a narrative within narrative: the fantasy of the raped child is enclosed within, and her silence "rescued" by, the memoir of the adult writer.

Clarissa, in contrast to "Prison," develops the action over a relatively short period of time—a matter of a few weeks—into one of the longest novels in the language, through an excruciatingly realistic transcription of events. In *Clarissa,* as in *A Passage to India,* the moment of rape is virtually the exact structural center of the narrative, so that the plots describe a graph of climax and anticlimax around that point. Having made the scene of rape central to their structures, the novels cannot altogether avoid on the one hand a certain tension, not unlike sexual titillation, and on the other a certain relaxation of tension, resembling postcoital boredom, around that point. The additional implication of a narrative structure which finds its center in the representation of rape is that it must then seek a further (postcoital) erotic goal: this, as we shall see, is offered in the "trials"—the death or disappearance—of the raped woman.

But, famously, at the center of these narratives lies only absence. Nei-

---

[23]Christine Froula, "The Daughter's Seduction: Sexual Violence and Literary History," in *Feminist Theory in Practice and Process,* ed. Micheline R. Malson et al. (Chicago: University of Chicago Press, 1989), 156, 161, 155.

ther novel actually represents the scene of rape, and this only partially for reasons of delicacy or sexual prudery. In his investigation of *Clarissa,* Terry Eagleton argues that rape itself is unrepresentable because "the 'real' of the woman's body" marks "the outer limit of all language."[24] This claim is part of the male mystique built around rape (as around childbirth); such narrative theory fetishizes rape as a limit of narrative to be tested over and over. Eagleton implicitly opposes woman as "real" or "nature" to man and language. Richardson offers an ostensibly simpler explanation: neither actor in his epistolary drama, Lovelace or Clarissa, wishes to record the event of rape, a reluctance that is natural enough, given the novel's commitment to psychological verisimilitude. Wishing to guarantee female purity and absolve male responsibility, Richardson represents Clarissa as drugged and Lovelace as in a frenzy, "not himself," when the act is perpetrated. For these "reasons" the act is "unrepresentable" in *this* text. But so suggestive is this mimetic absence that ingenious critics have asked whether Clarissa Harlowe was "really" raped.[25]

In *A Passage to India* the authorial reticence about the rape is part of the indeterminacy of meaning, the blur of events by means of which Forster hopes to convey the "mystery" and "muddle" of India. So while he accompanies the accused doctor Aziz on his itinerary to the caves closely enough to provide him with an alibi, Adela is left to wander the caves alone. At the end of the "Caves" section Aziz's friend Fielding makes a weak attempt to ascertain the "truth," only to be met with Adela's indifferent: "Let us call it the guide. . . . It will never be known. It's as if I ran my finger along that polished wall in the dark, and cannot get further."[26] The omniscient author, so much in evidence elsewhere in the novel to explain matters and settle issues, never tells us what "really" happened. *A Passage to India* pronounces, virtually and legally at least, that no rape was attempted on Adela Quested.

What are the implications of this silence at the heart of the text? *Clarissa* is a great proto-feminist novel, and *A Passage to India* is a major testament of liberal humanism; both, therefore, are works that might be expected to be unequivocal about an act of male sexual aggression against a woman. But their reliance on, and doubts about, the woman's

[24]Eagleton, *The Rape of Clarissa,* 61.

[25]See Judith Wilt, "He Could Go No Farther: A Modest Proposal about Lovelace and Clarissa," *PMLA* 92 (1977): 19–32, cited in Eagleton, *Rape of Clarissa,* 61.

[26]Forster, *Passage to India,* 263. Oliver Stallybrass states that in Forster's early drafts there was, in fact, an assault; see his essay "Forster's 'Wobblings': The Manuscripts of *A Passage to India,*" in *Aspects of E. M. Forster,* ed. Oliver Stallybrass (London: Edward Arnold, 1969), 153–54.

"unsupported word" as to her ordeal suggest a deep underlying male fear that rape could be a female lie or fiction. How a "normative narrative" may subvert even a feminist "thematics of liberation"[27] is illustrated by the implications present in Jonathan Kaplan's film *The Accused*, the powerful true story of Sarah Tobias's attempt to indict her rapists legally. In an effort to replicate the court's search to discover whether the rape "really" happened, the film succumbs to the device of the flashback, a device available only to narrative, and never to any court of law, however sedulously it may try to recreate the scene of crime. By replaying the scene of rape, the film once again makes it central to the narrative, the "climax" of the graph of its linear structure. If the absence of the scene of rape at the heart of a narrative (as in *Clarissa* or *A Passage to India*) serves to *mystify* its actual occurrence, the brutal naturalism of its cinematic representation in *The Accused* provides a *confirmation* that enforces the same conclusion: the "unsupported word" of a raped woman cannot represent rape.

Rape is often treated as a female fiction or fabrication in another sense as well, one that suggests the complicity of the woman, particularly in social and cultural situations that permit "free" man-woman relationships based on "romantic" love. Historically *Clarissa* reflects a period marked by changes in family structures, when marriage based on the partners' choice was beginning to prevail. *A Passage to India* is the product of a postwar period that witnessed the first major movement in women's sexual liberation and the emergence of the "emancipated" woman (of whom Adela Quested is the type). Additionally, Clarissa and Adela are involved with men outside their social spheres; the situations are fraught with possibilities of misknowing, mixed signals, wrong timing, false interpretations, and projections of desire. In such changing and historical phases of sexual relationships, sexual consummation may convincingly be represented as an event that is premature and skewed rather than gratuitous, and therefore not "really" rape.

Female choice itself is debased by association in hypocritical confusion about involuntary desire. Clarissa's self-blame is also based on the construction of an immutable "male" nature (the "brute") and a "female" nature (the "lady"). Thus, when a woman is raped, "who was most to blame, I pray? The brute, or the lady? The lady, surely! for what she did was *out* of nature, *out* of character, at least: what it did was *in* its own nature."[28] It is not surprising either, to find that in *A Passage to India*—in which Aziz indisputably did not rape Adela—

[27]The phrases are from de Lauretis, *Alice Doesn't*, 156.
[28]Samuel Richardson, *Clarissa* (London: Everyman, 1968), 3:206.

Adela should feel an obscure guilt, endorsed by Forster, for a certain sexual laxness on her part toward Aziz, based on no more than her preoccupation with her impending marriage to Ronny: holding hands with Aziz while climbing the rocks, a tactless question to him regarding the number of his wives, and a passing mental admiration of his physical beauty.

In contrast, "Prison," set in contemporary India, still records a society where marriages are arranged, and where all extramarital relationships between the sexes are inhibited, if not entirely prohibited. Anthony's rape of Bhagirathi is a routine exercise of droit du seigneur, not the index of a relationship gone awry. Bhagirathi's "responsibility" lies in allowing herself to have been seen by Anthony, in making a "spectacle" of herself: "Foolish Bhagirathi on the first two days had walked to the river four times to fetch water where Anthony was sitting alone on his porch." The victims of familial rape in *The Color Purple* and *I Know Why the Caged Bird Sings* are children, initiated into sexual knowledge by these early encounters, and though they internalize guilt in a complex way, they are unequivocally "innocent." In both these novels, as in "Prison," the fact of rape—even if not its graphic representation—is acknowledged in stark, brutal terms as the very *premise* on which the narrative is built.

If the suggestive desire and guilt of the raped women in *Clarissa* and *A Passage to India* turn them into more complex subjects, after the rape they are nevertheless reduced to unproblematic victimhood. Questions of (female) desire and guilt, intertwined in the explanation for rape in these texts, are reproduced in the self-confessed experience of the (male) reader or critic, as articulated by William Beatty Warner: "The 'rape of Clarissa' as an imagined event which is cruel and uncalled for drifts toward, and becomes entangled with 'the rape of Clarissa' that we enjoy in reading, and repeat in our interpretations." Here Warner equates rape and reading: since reading *Clarissa* is an entry into private correspondence, it involves, like rape, both the guilt and pleasure of "violating a taboo." In both activities there is "guilt at using others for our pleasure."[29]

These literary representations of rape also have difficulty avoiding the mimetic replication of the act. The fact that the enactment of rape takes place in private and secret places requires the author to conduct

[29]William Beatty Warner, "Reading Rape: Marxist-Feminist Figurations of the Literal," *Diacritics* 13.4 (1983): 31–32. But even in *Clarissa*—where the subject position offered the reader is that of Lovelace, the secret reader/rapist—an overt alignment between author and female protagonist injects pain as an element into the passive process of being read and being raped, and may conceivably dilute the aggressive pleasures of reading/raping.

his readers into the innermost recesses of physical space. Richardson leads us into the bedchamber of Clarissa Harlowe, Forster into the dark and claustrophobic Caves of Marabar. Or as readers we may be located in the space of the "truth"-seeking spectators in a courtroom, as in *A Passage to India*. The countermovement of novelistic narrative is precisely this emergence into the public light. Having probed the private, the narrative then seeks to *make public* the privileged knowledge gained in the incursion. The female subject is caught up in this trajectory. It is her transgressive wandering (her "error" in both senses of the word) that led in the first place to her confinement or imprisonment, the necessary condition of rape. The incarceration is followed by her reemergence into the public sphere. Richardson narrates the long and elaborate public spectacle of Clarissa's dying and Forster the public trial of Aziz, which is equally, of course, the trial of Adela. The succession of private ordeal by public display could not be more pronounced, nor—as raped women have again and again testified—more traumatic. These too are ordeals, trials like those of Ahalya and Sita, which absolve the raped subject of "guilt" and thereby mark her fitness for reentry into the social or moral domain.

The structuring of private and public fictional spaces; the intrusive, voyeuristic aspect of novel reading; the pleasure of mastery over and possession of the "passive" text in reading; narrative's very trajectory, its movement toward closure which traverses the feminine as object, obstacle, or space[30]: it is these inscriptions of desire and guilt in narrativity itself which are negotiated in a feminist reconstitution of the female subject of rape. Feminist texts of rape counter narrative determinism, as I have tried to show, in a number of ways: by representing the raped woman as one who becomes a subject *through* rape rather than merely one subjected *to* its violation; by structuring a *post-rape* narrative that traces her strategies of survival instead of a *rape-centered* narrative that privileges chastity and leads inexorably to "trials" to establish it; by locating the raped woman in structures of oppression other than heterosexual "romantic" relationships; by literalizing instead of mystifying the representation of rape; and, finally, by counting the cost of rape for its victims in terms more complex than the extinction of female selfhood in death or silence. Although a feminist "thematics of liberation" may not be a *sufficient* condition for rewriting the female subject and female reader of narrative, it may nevertheless generate the tensions and contradictions that allow the decentering of male desire, and with it the sexual thematics that structure much narrative. There-

---

[30]De Lauretis, *Alice Doesn't*, 143.

fore, the structural motors of narrativity are interrupted and significantly deflected by the forms of feminist individualism dictated by a text's history, ideology, and cultural models.

The introduction of a "third world woman's" text into a collection of American feminist critical essays is not exempt from problems even when the comparative method sanctions such heterogeneity. The critic who brings her own "native" text, not available within the canon or even in translation, to such an enterprise appears to be a "native informant" contributing to the "master discourse." She runs the danger of exoticizing her wares, implicitly privileging the text as more "authentic" or more "real" in content than Western texts, idealizing it as an alternative to Western cultural aporias, or offering it as a textual enigma that challenges Western critical theory and its cognitive structures. I have tried to sidestep some of these temptations by my choice of a representative and popular contemporary magazine story rather than a literary "classic." The text's contradictions—its invocation of "universal" concepts, themes, and structures of narrative—rape, and feminism—as well as its implication in specific historical conditions of production (contemporary caste politics, the women's movement in India, religious ideologies)—may allow it to be viewed simply as a demystified cultural product. The comparative method must not seek to relativize difference at the expense of denying a commonality of politics and cognitive structures.[31] The "extreme relativist position," Satya Mohanty has argued, "is in no way a feasible theoretical basis of politically motivated criticism." If, on the one hand, I have relativized the different "contexts of production of cultural ideas" through the comparative method, I have, on the other, sought to promote the "genuine dialogue" among the feminist positions on rape and the theories of rape and narrative that these different contexts throw up, thus hoping to retain the force of a "political" criticism.[32]

[31]In the words of Aijaz Ahmad, "Many of the questions that one would ask about [the third world] text may turn out to be rather similar to the questions one has asked previously about English/American texts." "Jameson's Rhetoric of Otherness and the 'National Allegory,' " Social Text 17 (1986): 9.

[32]Satya Mohanty, "Us and Them: On the Political Bases of Political Criticism," The Yale Journal of Criticism 2,2 (Spring 1989): 15. Since I wrote this essay several works have come to my attention which have provided welcome reinforcement and elaboration of my arguments. See Brenda R. Silver, "Periphrasis, Power, and Rape in A Passage to India," Novel 22 (Fall 1988): 86–105; Elliot Butler-Evans, "Beyond Essentialism: Rethinking Afro-American Cultural Theory," Inscriptions 5 (1988): 121–34, which discusses Alice Walker's story about interracial rape, "Advancing Luna—and Ida B. Wells"; Sharon Marcus, "Fighting Bodies, Fighting Words: A Theory and Politics of Rape Prevention," in Feminists Theorize the Political, ed. Judith Butler and Joan W. Scott (London: Routledge, 1992).

Part II
Genre Theory

4

Modifications of Genre:
A Feminist Critique of "Christabel"
and "Die Braut von Korinth"

LORE METZGER

Criticism indeed consists of analyzing and reflecting upon limits.
—Michel Foucault

The study of genre has been a driving force in literary theory and criticism from Plato and Aristotle to Todorov and Genette. Locating itself at the intersection of description and prescription, theory and empirical observation, genre criticism has functioned to conserve literary kinds along with the value system of canonical models. The concept of genre, as Claudio Guillén has pointed out, "looks forward and backward at the same time. Backward, toward the literary works that already exist. Forward, in the direction of the apprentice, the future writer, the informed critic."[1] The system of genres thus functions as a code of transmission, a law of inheritance that discriminates between legitimate and illegitimate heirs.

It is no accident that in the revolutionary decades of the later eighteenth century, Edmund Burke grounded his antirevolutionary position in the concept of inheritance: "We wish to derive all we possess as *an inheritance from our forefathers.*" Thus, according to Burke, even rights, freedom, reform, and power are to be regarded as kinds of property; the idea of "entailed inheritance" "furnishes a sure principle of conservation, and a sure principle of transmission; without at all excluding

Versions of this essay were presented at the convention of the Midwest American Society for Eighteenth-Century Studies, October 1990, and at the International Comparative Literature Association Congress in Tokyo, August 1991; one also appears as "Modifications of Genre: A Feminist Critique of 'Christabel' and 'Die Braut von Korinth' " in Patricia B. Craddock and Carla Hay, eds., *Studies in Eighteenth-Century Culture*, vol. 22 (East Lansing: Colleagues' Press for the American Society for Eighteenth-Century Studies, 1992), reprinted by permission.
    [1] Claudio Guillén, *Literature as System* (Princeton: Princeton University Press, 1971), 109.

a principle of improvement. It leaves acquisition free; but it secures what it acquires."[2]

Such a principle of well-regulated transmission of social, cultural, and political patrimony includes the codes that govern genre and gender. Just as *property* and *propriety* derive from the same root, so do *genre* and *gender*. It is remarkable that this connection has been ignored by most critics writing on genre, from René Wellek and Northrop Frye to Paul Hernadi and Gérard Genette—with the notable exception of Jacques Derrida—when it seemed perfectly obvious early in this century to the German humorist Roda-Roda, who summed up genre distinctions as follows: "A man alone: a lyric poem; two men: a ballad; one man and one woman: a novella; one man and two women: a novel; one woman and two men: a tragedy; two women and two men: a comedy."[3] Even this playful bit of categorization reveals that genre articulates gender roles. Attention to the way gender roles are represented by literary genres in different cultures raises questions about the part literature plays in generating, disseminating, enforcing, or subverting the rules of social relationships by which individuals acquire gendered identities. Genre thus forms a crucial point of articulation between feminist and comparatist interdisciplinary criticism.

If leading comparatists have notably disregarded the intersection of genre and gender, feminist critics have rarely addressed issues of genre when theorizing gender while also slighting the resources of a comparatist perspective. The masculinist discourse of genre theory, from Aristotle to the present, has been grounded in and has served to legitimate the Western canon while occluding the politics of its theoretical foundation. Even when genre theory includes the dialectics of genre and of countergenre, as Claudio Guillén's does, it ignores the role of gender in focusing on generic continuities and discontinuities from a structural-historical perspective. And even when Alastair Fowler's influential *Kinds of Literature* proposes the concept of family resemblances as the key to generic relations, it disregards gender just as it dismisses contemporary theory, as Mary Jacobus astutely observes, "in the interests of conserving an ultimately dynastic view of literary history." Moreover, women's texts on genre theory participate in this masculinist discourse, as Adena Rosmarin's pragmatic theory, grounded in the interaction of difference and similitude, remarkably demonstrates. For her

---

[2]Edmund Burke, *Reflections on the Revolution in France* [published with Thomas Paine, *The Rights of Man*] (Garden City, N.Y.: Doubleday, 1981), 43, 45.

[3]Cited in Rosalie L. Colie, *Resources of Kind: Genre-Theory in the Renaissance*, ed. Barbara K. Lewalski (Berkeley: University of California Press, 1973), 30.

the power of genre empowers (masculinist) criticism to constitute and valorize the (canonical) literary works of art.[4]

Although feminist criticism has challenged the foundations of gender-less critical judgments, its intense interest in genres converges on those previously considered marginal or feminized (e.g., domestic novel, romance, gothic) rather than on genres valorized as universal and exemplary (e.g., epic, tragedy, dramatic monologue).[5] Furthermore, when feminist criticism does focus on canonical genres, it rarely contests their underlying regulatory power but instead creates female subgenres—the female bildungsroman, autobiography, utopia, or fantasy—which reinforce the gender boundaries of genres.[6] (Interestingly, a comprehensive 1991 collection of essays on feminist theory and practice subsumes both gender and genre under other categories such as body, discourse, desire, autobiography, and so on.)[7] Yet important theoretical work on gender like Judith Butler's could be productively extended to analyze how in literary as in other social texts gender interacts performatively with genre, how genre/gender identity "is performatively constituted by the very 'expressions' that are said to be its results."[8] This emphasis on the performative possibilities of genre/gender formations and transformations would begin to address the task Celeste Schenck posed for feminist theory: "to question the hypostasizing and . . . limiting of genre to a designation of *form* or *norm*."[9] Surely the time has come to interrogate the

---

[4]Mary Jacobus, *Romanticism, Writing, and Sexual Difference* (Oxford: Clarendon, 1989), 188. Adena Rosmarin, *The Power of Genre* (Minneapolis: University of Minnesota Press, 1985), 49–50. Along with Rosmarin's example of women's participation in genderless genre theory, I should here include Rosalie Colie's otherwise splendid *Resources of Kind* and my own speculations on genre in *One Foot in Eden: Modes of Pastoral in Romantic Poetry* (Chapel Hill: University of North Carolina Press, 1986).

[5]From the vast array of important recent studies, let me cite a few key examples dealing with fiction or nonfictional prose: Nancy Armstrong, *Desire and Domestic Fiction: A Political History of the Novel* (New York: Oxford University Press, 1987); Laurie Langbauer, *Women and Romance: The Consolations of Gender in the English Novel* (Ithaca: Cornell University Press, 1990); Felicity A. Nussbaum, *The Autobiographical Subject: Gender and Ideology in Eighteenth-Century England* (Baltimore: Johns Hopkins University Press, 1989); and Bella Brodzki and Celeste Schenck, eds., *Life/Lines: Theorizing Women's Autobiography* (Ithaca: Cornell University Press, 1988).

[6]See, for example, Anne Cranny-Francis, *Feminist Fiction: Feminist Uses of Generic Fiction* (New York: St. Martin's Press, 1990); Patricia Waugh, *Feminist Fictions: Revisiting the Post-modern* (London: Routledge, 1989); Elizabeth Abel, Marianne Hirsch, and Elizabeth Langland, eds., *The Voyage In: Fictions of Female Development* (Hanover, N.H.: University Press of New England, 1983); Marleen Barr, ed., *Future Females: A Critical Anthology* (Bowling Green, Ohio: Bowling Green State University Press, 1981).

[7]See Robyn R. Warhol and Diane Price Herndl, eds., *Feminisms: An Anthology of Literary Theory and Criticism* (New Brunswick: Rutgers University Press, 1991).

[8]Judith Butler, *Gender Trouble: Feminism and the Subversion of Identity* (New York: Routledge, Chapman and Hall, 1990), 25.

[9]Celeste Schenck, "All of a Piece," in Brodzki and Schenck, *Life/Lines*, 286.

complex regulatory transactions as well as the aesthetics of genres as ideologically informed.

It should always be borne in mind not only that genre and gender are etymologically linked but also that they engender a semantic repertory, as Philippe Lacoue-Labarthe and Jacques Derrida have reminded us, which is much larger and more expansive in French than in English, genre always including gender within its scope. Similarly, in German, *Gattung* (genre) connects with *Gatte/Gattin* (husband/wife) and establishes generic connections as an act of begetting or coupling (*gatten*).[10] Thus gender is genre's double and diffuses, refocuses, and problematizes the codes, laws, norms, and boundaries of genre.

Significantly, this semantic field links genre and gender with property through the criterion of propriety that governs normative judgments and establishes the legitimate members of proper families. The rules regulating the decorum of literary works and the proper behavior of women recall the fact that classical rhetoric from Aristotle on was dominated, as Patricia Parker has so convincingly argued, "by the notion of 'place'—of territory already staked out, of the tropological as inseparable from the topological—and thus also of 'property,' or of place where a word properly belongs." In the eighteenth century, Hugh Blair, like Edmund Burke, was concerned with establishing rules for language according to the dictates of propriety that would arrest the instability engendered by improper tropes.[11] Rhetorical "property," words in their proper place, is a form of "entailed inheritance," confirming the Burkean principle of the stable, patrilineal transmission of landed property which "leaves acquisition free" but "secures what it acquires";[12] and rhetorical "property" also entails the dictates of propriety governing genre and gender.

Even violations and transgressions of the dominant codes of genre and gender, like transgressions of other laws, do not negate but rather validate the laws' legitimacy. Tzvetan Todorov has argued that transgression indeed requires a law to be transgressed, and that, furthermore, "the norm becomes visible—lives—only by its transgressions." And he supports his argument by citing Maurice Blanchot's claim that James Joyce's exceptional works "establish a law and at the same time

---

[10]Philippe Lacoue-Labarthe and Jean-Luc Nancy, *The Literary Absolute*, trans. Philip Barnard and Cheryl Chester (Albany: State University of New York Press, 1988), 91, 144 n.26; Jacques Derrida, "The Law of Genre," trans. Avital Ronell, *Critical Inquiry* 7 (Autumn 1980): 74.

[11]Patricia Parker, *Literary Fat Ladies: Rhetoric, Gender, Property* (London: Methuen, 1987), 36, 156.

[12]Burke, *Reflections*, 45.

suppress it. . . . Each time, in these exceptional works where a limit is reached, it is the exception alone that reveals to us this 'law' whose uncommon and necessary deviation it also constitutes."[13] It follows that acts of transgression, transformation, displacement, or inversion of proper generic codes make visible and recognizable the codes that they abrogate.

I choose Goethe's "Braut von Korinth" (1796) and Coleridge's "Christabel" (written 1797; published 1816) as my exemplary texts to problematize the normative and regulative function of genre. At the end of the eighteenth century, Goethe's and Coleridge's claiming the ballad form for serious poetry involved them in transgressing boundaries that separated high from low art as well as proper from improper gender roles. These transgressions reveal the frequently occluded dominant codes that kept literary as well as social hierarchies in their proper places.

I take my clue from Derrida's "Law of Genre," which, exploiting the enigma of the "two genres of genre," reminds us that "the genre has always in all genres been able to play order's principle." Derrida elaborates this principle into the hyperbolic command that "as soon as genre announces itself, one must respect a norm, one must not cross a line of demarcation, one must not risk impurity, anomaly, or monstrosity." This monstrous rule serves as the lever for Derrida's counterlaw "lodged within the heart of the law itself": "It is precisely a principle of contamination, a law of impurity, a parasitical economy."[14] I cannot do justice here to Derrida's brilliant argument that proceeds through an ingenious reading of Blanchot's *Folie du jour* and reveals that in fact the law of genre is madness. This ironic conclusion of course disrupts both the classic law and the Derridean antilaw of genre; the madness encompasses the mixing of sexual as well as literary genres and subverts all possibility of order, boundary, or authority.

Less subversive but nevertheless exemplifying the Derridean counterlaw of genre, the principle of contamination and impurity, the lowly subgenre of ballads, from Bishop Percy's influential collection of "ancient reliques" in 1765 to Goethe's and Schiller's, Wordsworth's and Coleridge's famous productions of the 1790s, defies yet also defines the boundaries between popular art and canonical poetry. Gothic ballads especially heighten the contamination of romance with realism, culture with barbarism, the human with the inhuman, the natural with the

[13]Tzvetan Todorov, "The Origin of Genres," *New Literary History* 8 (Autumn 1976): 160.

[14]Derrida, "Law of Genre," 56–57, 59.

supernatural, the carnal with the spiritual. The poets were involved in a process one modern critic describes as "the translation of the ballad from an active life on the popular level to a 'museum life' on a higher level."[15] Broadside and minstrel ballads began to appreciate in value with academic collections such as Percy's, a favorite hunting ground not only for English but also for German poets, assembling as folk poetry anything that deviated from the Latin-French tradition and was regarded as exotic, including specimens of "Moorish" romances, translations from Chinese, and a paraphrase of the Song of Songs, along with other "reliques of ancient poetry"—all of which Percy freely emended.[16]

The most influential ballads in Percy's collection were those like "The Childe of Elle" and "Sir Cauline," for which he fabricated missing sections of narrative by borrowing from romances.[17] It is worth noting that Wordsworth praised Percy's "reliques" as exhibiting "true simplicity and genuine pathos," while he also sought to distance his own *Lyrical Ballads* as serious poetry from popular works written for mass appeal.[18] His praise for Gottfried August Bürger's enormously popular "Lenore," which was based on a Percy ballad, stressed precisely the difference between popular folk poetry and art for the masses: "Bürger is always the poet; he is never the mobbist, one of those dim drivellers with which our island has teemed for so many years."[19]

This simultaneous admiration and distrust for popular works was in fact part of an ongoing eighteenth-century paradox in which Percy, like Samuel Johnson, played a significant role. In his preface and editorial comments in the *Reliques*, Percy sought to adjudicate for his public living "in a polished age" between the rudeness and artlessness of "old rhapsodists" and contemporary poetry "of a higher class." He deliberately intermingled some "little elegant pieces of the lyric kind" to gain acceptance for the traditional ballads. He set up a contest between "those who had all the advantages of learning," writing for "fame and posterity," on the one hand, and, on the other, "the old strolling min-

---

[15]Albert B. Friedman, *The Ballad Revival* (Chicago: University of Chicago Press, 1961), 79.

[16]Thomas Percy, ed., *Reliques of Ancient English Poetry* (1765), 6th ed., 4 vols. (London: Samuel Richards, 1823).

[17]Friedman, *Ballad Revival*, 297–98.

[18]William Wordsworth, "Essay, Supplementary to the Preface (1815)," in *Literary Criticism of William Wordsworth*, ed. Paul M. Zall (Lincoln: University of Nebraska Press, 1966), 176.

[19]These are Wordsworth's words as quoted by Samuel Taylor Coleridge in a letter to William Taylor, translator of Bürger's "Lenore," drawing on an exchange of letters about Bürger while Wordsworth and Coleridge were in Germany. See *Collected Letters of Samuel Taylor Coleridge*, ed. Earl Leslie Griggs, 6 vols. (Oxford: Clarendon, 1956–71), 1:566.

strels," who "looked no farther than for present applause, and present subsistence." Yet frequently, Percy observed, the palm is awarded to the minstrels.[20]

Such cautious praise for popular poetry turned into revolutionary enthusiasm by the German *Sturm-und-Drang* writers, among whom the young Goethe was a leading figure. In his autobiography he recalled how Herder's influential tutelage led him to discover a new perspective on poetry: "Hebrew poetry, which, following the example of Lowth, [Herder] treated perceptively, popular poetry [*die Volkspoesie*] . . . and the oldest poetic records [*Urkunden*]—all bore witness that the art of poetry was indeed a universal and popular-national gift [*eine Welt- und Völkergabe*] and not a private legacy of a few refined, cultivated [*gebildeten*] men."[21] Thus, at the end of the eighteenth century, leading poets in England and Germany found in popular poetry ammunition against neoclassical elitism while at the same time they sought to authenticate their experiments and smuggle them into the canons of high art.

When Coleridge borrowed some motifs for his vampiric narrative "Christabel" from Percy's *Reliques,* he turned to the lower class of minstrel ballads, whose simplicity Wordsworth declared to have "absolutely redeemed" English poetry.[22] Goethe, who had found inspiration for his popular "Erlkönig" in Herder's influential collection of folksongs, *Volkslieder* (1777–78), turned, by contrast, to a classical source, Phlegon of Tralles, for his thoroughly unclassical production "Die Braut von Korinth."[23] It is most likely that Coleridge knew Goethe's daring ballad, first published in Schiller's *Musen-Almanach* for 1798 (the volume actually appeared in the fall of 1797). It was the first literary depiction of a female vampire who was not monstrous but beautiful and irresistible.[24]

Both Goethe's and Coleridge's ballad-romances feature as their central event an erotic encounter with an attractive vampire, an act of moral transgression that is also a transgression of genre. In both poems the vampire represents the ambiguous status of a woman who is neither

[20]Percy, *Reliques*, 10–11.
[21]Johann Wolfgang Goethe, *Gedenkausgabe der Werke, Briefe und Gespräche*, ed. Ernst Beutler, 27 vols. (Zurich: Artemis, 1948–71), 10:448; hereafter cited as *GA*. All translations are my own.
[22]Wordsworth, *Literary Criticism*, 180.
[23]Emil Staiger, *Goethe*, 3 vols. (Zurich: Atlantis, 1952–59), 2:308. Goethe himself denied that Phlegon of Tralles was his source, according to his friend Friedrich von Müller, but gave no specifics about any other except that the bride's name was Philinnion (*GA*, 23: 348).
[24]Peter D. Grudin, *The Demon-Lover: The Theme of Demoniality in English and Continental Fiction of the Late Eighteenth and Early Nineteenth Centuries* (New York: Garland, 1987), 64.

quite human nor inhuman, neither mistress of her life nor slave of her master, who is both victim and victimizer. Both poems clearly violated contemporary moral and aesthetic norms and were received as scandalous, licentious, and obscene. In Goethe's case, public opinion was severely divided about his "Braut von Korinth": whereas some readers were affronted by its "most disgusting of all bordello scenes" and its "desecration of Christianity," others considered it "the most perfect of all of Goethe's shorter works."[25] In Coleridge's case, though sixteen years elapsed between the intended publication of "Christabel" in *Lyrical Ballads* (1800) and its actual publication in 1816, critics similarly found a good deal to praise and to blame. They granted it originality but frequently found it unintelligible, senseless, or absurd. An anonymous pamphlet, "Hypocrisy Unveiled, and Calumny Detected," referred to Byron's "Parisina" and Coleridge's "Christabel" as "poems which sin as heinously against purity and decency as it is well possible to imagine."[26]

Goethe's "Braut von Korinth" was particularly scandalous for its foregrounding of a "bride" whose virginal appearance masks a lascivious vampire. Dramatizing this "low" subject matter in a ballad whose literary artistry and authorship by a world-renowned poet gave it a claim to generic legitimacy was bound to intensify the contemporary readers' shocked recognition that it transgressed all bounds of moral and literary propriety. Since Goethe wrote "Die Braut von Korinth" during a time of intensive occupation with classical models, with the problem of selecting and matching themes and forms proper for different poetic kinds, the work appears as a deliberate affront. It exploits the demonic sphere of the vampire to mask a bourgeois psychodrama, the conflict between the impulse toward unrestrained sexual desire and the restraints of social codes and conventions.

The poem's opening signals a traditional popular ballad, offering no hint of its being, as Goethe dubbed it in his journal, "the vampiric poem" (*GA, Tagebücher*, supplemental vol. 2:209). It begins in medias res; the setting consists of place names (Athens and Corinth) without any descriptive details; time is not mentioned at all; and characters are introduced generically, without proper names. The narrator speaks soberly of a young man (*Jüngling*) from Athens, a pagan who comes to Corinth as stranger and guest (*Gast*); the recurring term "guest" ety-

[25]For these opinions, see the letter from the gossipy Weimar philologist and archaeologist Karl August Böttiger to the poet Friedrich von Matthison, October 18, 1797, in *Goethe in vertraulichen Briefen seiner Zeitgenossen*, ed. Wilhelm Bode, 3 vols. (Munich: Beck, 1982), 2:116.
[26]Coleridge, *Collected Letters*, 4:917n.

mologically links and blurs the relations of guest, host, and stranger. The youth is defined by his future kinship to his Christian host's younger daughter. Their fathers, related through mutual hospitality— Goethe's economically coined word is *gastverwandt*—had early betrothed them:

> Beide Väter waren gastverwandt,
> Hatten frühe schon
> Töchterchen und Sohn
> Braut und Bräutigam voraus genannt.[27]

These relational roles, whether marital or hospitable, replace proper names in defining family and social status. The poem exploits the ballad convention of minimizing individual identity as it focuses on a culture that contains the individual's aspirations within generic codes. The text early establishes the principal characters' belonging to discordant cultural, religious, and political spheres (Athens and Corinth, pagan and Christian), which are tenuously bridged by their fathers' (the law's) oath to perpetuate their own kinship through their offspring.

These marks of lawful relations, like the codes of ballad conventions, simultaneously enforce lines of authority and mask the tensions of change. They mark the "bridegroom" as an outsider in Corinth who nonetheless feels entitled to an honored place in his host's house, ignoring their political and religious disparity. The public sphere of Athens and Corinth quickly recedes as we follow the "bridegroom" into his lavish private chamber (*Prunkgemach*). Subtly the cool, distanced narrative tone modulates into increasingly lyrical intimacy as the pagan guest is visited in turn by "a strange guest" (*ein seltner Gast*), a seemingly proper (*sittsam*) young woman in a white veil, who is so estranged in her own house that she is unaware of the guest's presence: "Bin ich, rief sie aus, so fremd im Hause, / Daß ich von dem Gaste nichts vernahm?" In words that mysteriously veil her ontological status, she warns the youth, who seeks to interest her in the gifts of Ceres, Bacchus, and Amor, that she does not belong to the realm of joy, that she has already taken "the last step": "Schon der letzte Schritt ist, ach! geschehen." It is striking that whereas the potential bridegroom is indeed culturally an outsider, he has received an honored place in the household in which the bride, the host's daughter, who should be an insider, is a displaced person, alienated, marginalized, without the right to her

---

[27]"The fathers were related through mutual hospitality and early preordained daughter and son as bride and bridegroom."

proper place. As she has already hinted, she is nowhere at home, having uncannily returned from the grave. She is an unrecognized revenant. Her vampiric presence is indeed *unheimlich*, though neither the narrator nor the bridegroom nor the mother shudders at or even notes her grave hints.

The text follows ballad convention in limiting the narrator's role to formulaic reporting of the features of the young woman's appearance that strike the guest—white veil, a black and orange fillet—and then shifting to her own words without any intrusive moral judgments. Observing this ballad tradition, however, underscores the text's and invites the reader's complicit acceptance of the woman's dispossessed status, (she is relegated to her "cell"), which contrasts dramatically with the bridegroom's secure and privileged place in the same household. But we are no sooner led to expect adherence to ballad convention, with its formulaic sparsity of details reported in impersonal language, when the poem disdains this constraint and establishes an emotionally involved tone in dramatizing the turbulent love scene between the two "guests."

Here Goethe decisively parts company with ballad tradition, not only as it is known from inherited models but also as it was established in his own previous contributions, such as the immensely popular "Heidenröslein." Schiller's close friend Christian Gottfried Körner, who shared their *Balladenstudien* of 1797—what Goethe inimitably called their playing around with the nature and perversion of balladry ("im Balladenwesen und Unwesen herumtreiben" [*GA*, 19:286])—advised that a small dose of love would enliven ballads as long as it was kept in the background and sensed only through its effect, as in Schiller's ballad "Der Taucher" and Goethe's "Es war ein König von Thule."[28] Goethe himself stated in July 1797 that Schiller's and his efforts were directed toward maintaining the traditional tone and mood of ballads while choosing more elevated (*würdiger*) and manifold subject matter (*GA*, 19:287).

Transgressing the boundaries set by these precepts, "Die Braut von Korinth" distills the most passionate excitement into brief exclamations of verbal magic, like *Liebesüberfluß*. Seamlessly intermingling narrative, dialogue, and lyric, the text violates generic norms as readily as social proprieties, preferring aesthetic impurities and moral ambiguities. Thus, at the witching hour (*Geisterstunde*) the seeming virgin turns first into a voracious maenad ("Gierig schlürfte sie mit blassem Munde /

---

[28]Christian Gottfried Körner, *Briefwechsel zwischen Schiller und Körner*, ed. Klaus L. Berghahn (Munich: Winkler, 1973), 268.

Nun den dunkel blutgefärbten Wein'') and then into a femme fatale who lusts for her lover's fiery mouth (''Gierig saugt sie seines Mundes Flammen'') and finally into the gothic vampire who longs to suck her lover's blood (''zu saugen seines Herzens Blut''). The incremental repetition, with its variations within a structural formula, recalls the ballad convention even as it violates its restraint through its powerful language of sexual passion, producing an unprecedented lyric-narrative-dialogical form to represent the shared excess of the moment of love: *Liebesüberfluß*. This surplus overflows all boundaries demarcating one speaker from the other, indirect from direct discourse, joyful desire from passionate fury (*Liebeswut*), youthful love from demonic possession:

> Heftig faßt er sie mit starken Armen,
> Von der Liebe Jugendkraft durchmannt:
> Hoffe doch, bei mir noch zu erwarmen,
> Wärst du selbst mir aus dem Grab gesandt!
> Wechselhauch und Kuß!
> Liebesüberfluß!
> Brennst du nicht und fühlest mich entbrannt?[29]

Dionysian rapture joins vampiric desire in an unprecedented erotic lexicon. Goethe forges a style that achieves its striking vividness and concentrated intensity by calling attention to its verbal medium, its lyric magic, rather than by approaching visual precision. Indeed, only a few months after completing the ballad Goethe complained to Schiller of the public's childish and barbaric lack of taste that caused it to prefer the illustrations of key scenes over employing the imagination. He saw this corrupt tendency as leading to the intermingling of art forms, without mentioning the fact that he himself had contributed to compromising the purity of genre, that in an unclassical impulse he had fearlessly violated the ''impenetrable magic circles'' within which he had insisted each work of art should be properly bound by its own properties (*Eigenheiten*) (*GA*, 20:473).

The ballad's lyric intensity is broken by the return of the narrator's cool voice reporting the mother's stealthy voyeuristic eavesdropping at the door, where she overhears ''des Liebestammelns Raserei'' (love's stammering frenzy). Once more the text breaks with ballad convention

---

[29]''Impetuously he seizes her with powerful arms, shot through with youthful strength of love: Still hope to warm you at my side, even if you were sent to me from the grave itself! Exchange of breath and kiss! Love's overflowing! Aren't you in flames, and don't you feel me set afire?''

as, in response to the mother's moralistic intervention, the bride usurps the narrator's role in the entire final section—six stanzas, constituting nearly one fourth of the whole ballad—and addresses a passionate monologue to the intruder, delivering an indictment of Christian morality and its mortification of the flesh. The mother emerges in the daughter's discourse as representing an excess of religious zeal that has transformed her betrothal under Venus' aegis into a marriage to Christ. The mother's oath was taken in a moment of delirium, which is also a moment of madness; it was thus both an act of gratitude for her recovery from sickness and an act of sick fanaticism. In a reversal of the oedipal triangle, the mother envies the daughter's active sexuality. As Franco Moretti points out in a different context, "The repressed returns, then, but disguised as a monster."[30] The daughter represents herself as a human sacrifice, denied by her ascetic and repressive mother even the enjoyment of a single night's passion. She suggests not only that her mother is responsible for her death and her return as a vampire but also that her religion is a kind of vampirism demanding human sacrifice. Should we, however, see the mother too as a victim of Pauline Christianity, since the poem is set at the time of Corinth's conversion? And if so, what does this pagan-Christian historical moment signify to the reader of Schiller's *Musen-Almanach* in 1797? Merely a moment in Goethe's psychobiography, his nostalgia for the freer moral climate of Rome after his return to the narrower bourgeois-aristocratic dukedom of Weimar?[31]

The only psychic life this poem explores is that of the vampiric revenant, whose freedom of choice is minimal. She has escaped repression only through death. She clearly represents herself as one more sinned against than sinning, more victimized than victimizing. Just as her father had the power to settle her marriage and her mother the power to betroth her to the church against her will, an unnamed mysterious power controls her even as vampire, driving her to fulfill her undesired destiny in a way that seals her lover's fate and the fate of those who must succeed him. Powerless to put an end to the cycle of victimization, she implores her mother to immolate her with her lover in a pagan rite. Her desire to escape from her death-in-life into a love-death destabilizes

---

[30]Franco Moretti, *Signs Taken for Wonders* (London: Verso, 1983), 103.

[31]Goethe was frequently accused of pagan immorality both in Germany and abroad, especially in England. On one occasion he defended himself by ironically citing all the heroines, among whom he might have included the "bride" in this ballad, who pay for their transgressions with death. What could possibly be more Christian? ("Ich heidnisch? Nun habe ich doch Gretchen hinrichten und Ottilie verhungern lassen; ist denn das den Leuten nicht christlich genug? Was wollen sie noch Christlicheres?" [*GA*, 22:579]).

the authority of father and mother, church and fate. The poem leaves it an open question whether the mother grants her daughter's death wish, whether Eros and Thanatos vanquish Christ. The final words are the daughter's passionate plea for the transgression of Christian doctrine through a return to the ancient gods:

> Höre, Mutter, nun die letzte Bitte:
> Einen Scheiterhaufen schichte du;
> Öffne meine bange kleine Hütte,
> Bring in Flammen Liebende zu Ruh!
> Wenn der Funke sprüht,
> Wenn die Asche glüht,
> Eilen wir den alten Göttern zu.[32]

There is no reply.

The ending of "Die Braut von Korinth" is unsettling because it refuses to provide a comforting closure with the return to the world from which the demonic has been expelled and banished, the kind of reassuring closure that became a dominant convention in all later vampiric literature, especially in the Dracula versions.[33] Goethe's ending refuses equally to validate the stable, existing order and to authorize the vampire's subversive challenge to social institutions. As Silvia Volckmann has persuasively argued, such ambiguous vampiric symbolization banishes woman—and not only woman as vampire—to the site of death and of the Other. The Romantic poets' recourse to the concept of the feminine as subversive of oppressive authority becomes an "ideological trap."[34] Trust in the eternal feminine may not necessarily lead upward.

In "Christabel" the role of woman as vampire and vampire as woman is ideologically complicated by the doubling of female protagonists. The poem's polymorphous complexity exceeds ballad convention, as is clear by a cursory glance at its prototype in Bishop Percy's collection, "Sir Cauline." Christabel, whose proper name is one of Percy's emendations, the daughter of a nameless king, chaste object of

[32]"Hear, Mother, my final request: raise a funeral pyre, release me from my fearful, narrow dwelling, grant the lovers their rest in flames; the scattering sparks, the glowing ashes will speed us toward the ancient gods."

[33]For an incisive discussion of the thematic structure and psychosexual implications of the Dracula versions, see Christopher Craft, " 'Kiss Me with Those Red Lips': Gender and Inversion in Bram Stoker's *Dracula*," in *Speaking of Gender*, ed. Elaine Showalter (New York: Routledge, 1989), 216–24.

[34]Silvia Volckmann, " 'Gierig saugt sie seines Mundes Flammen.' Anmerkungen zum Funktionswandel des weiblichen Vampirs in der Literatur des 19. Jahrhunderts," in *Weiblichkeit und Tod in der Literatur*, ed. Renate Berger and Inge Stephan (Cologne: Böhlau, 1987), 166.

many suitors, is loved by Sir Cauline, who, not being her peer, is rejected and banished by the king. Christabel secretly loves the banished
knight but is of course powerless. She can do nothing but wring her
lily-white hands, moan, shriek, swoon, and expire "with a deepe-fette
sighe," when her devoted knight is killed in a joust with a giant.

Coleridge borrows from Percy only the material for an opening tab-
leau: Christabel in the castle woods late at night praying for her distant
lover's well-being. Coleridge then immediately enlivens the received
formulaic narrative through a counterplot focused on the more complicated, disruptive, demonic female character, the vampiric Geraldine,
who probably owes her beautiful looks and seductive demeanor to
Goethe's "bride." In the incomplete "Christabel" generic codes are difficult to decipher since the narrative never clearly establishes a dominant mode, changing focus as it does from characters' psychological
complexities to dramatic dialogue, to lyric evocation, to incremental
repetition, to sentimental romance, to erotic initiation, to chivalric rules,
and to gothic bathos.[35] These divergent strands contaminate ballad simplicity while blurring the implicit boundaries between high and low
art, between social propriety and poetic license. The vampire-as-woman
is the parasitic agent that appropriates the proprieties and undermines
the stability of the social as well as the aesthetic text.

Let me focus here on only one episode, the scandalous homoerotic
encounter between the saintly Christabel and the mysterious "weary
woman scarce alive" whom she rescues. Invoking her father's chivalric
service, the proper daughter offers the hospitality of her chamber to
the homeless and uncanny (unheimliche) Geraldine, whose ambiguous
virtue is revealed in the momentary glittering of her eyes. As the narrative unfolds, it well exemplifies Franco Moretti's observation that
"vampirism is an excellent example of the identity of desire and fear."[36]

Insofar as Coleridge's narrator presents himself as a rather artless
minstrel reciting a received narrative, he casts the reader in the role of
fascinated listener and prurient onlooker. Like the narrator, the implied
reader is male.[37] The narrator's presence in the bedroom functions to
turn both women into objects exhibited for the pleasure of the male
viewer-listener. Borrowing Jerome Christensen's term, we might call

[35]Karen Swann discusses the generic complexities and disturbances in " 'Christabel':
The Wandering Mother and the Enigma of Form," *Studies in Romanticism* 23 (Winter
1984): 533–53.
[36]Moretti, *Signs Taken for Wonders*, 100.
[37]The "masculinization" of the spectator position is fully discussed in relation to film
in Laura Mulvey's influential *Visual and Other Pleasures* (Bloomington: Indiana University
Press, 1989), 14–38.

this moment a "Scene of Fascination," as distinguished from Harold Bloom's "Scene of Instruction": whereas the scene of Instruction takes Raphael's discourse in book 5 of *Paradise Lost* as its prototype, the "pattern of the scene of fascination is that where, transfixed, Satan gazes at the nakedly veiled Eve, tempted to become the tempter."[38] Although the narrator in "Christabel" is no satanic tempter, his interest in the virgin's disrobing and lying down "in her loveliness" is both voyeuristic and moralistic. He gives no details about Christabel's body beyond stating that she undressed her "gentle limbs," but he presents the naked Christabel as raising herself on her elbow to look at Geraldine. He then appropriates her gaze to display Geraldine in the process of undressing. Coleridge expunged the line describing half her bosom as "lean and old and foul of hue," but he gave the narrator enough license to evoke gothic sexual fantasies that entice the reader into imaginative collaboration:

> Then drawing in her breath aloud,
> Like one that shuddered, she unbound
> The cincture from beneath her breast:
> Her silken robe, and inner vest,
> Dropt to her feet, and full in view,
> Behold! her bosom and half her side—
> A sight to dream of, not to tell!
>
> (1.247–53)

It is the sight of woman as a gothic object on display. Ironically, in his preface to the poem the author apologizes for the irregularities in his meter, which he assures his reader were "not introduced wantonly,"[39] but he does not apologize for the erotic irregularities.

If in this scene the narrator controls the text, at other times Geraldine's disruptive presence seems to escape his mastery. He resorts to stereotypical roles from gothic romance to contain her: beautiful damsel in distress; noble lady abducted by violent barbarians; seductress of both the innocent heroine and her father; usurper of power over the dead mother. Her duplicity engenders a total disruption of law and order, striking at the family, the core of bourgeois stability. She generates her own narrative explaining her entrance into the baron's house-

---

[38]Jerome Christensen, "Setting Byron Straight: Class, Sexuality, and the Poet," in *Literature and the Body*, ed. Elaine Scarry (Baltimore: Johns Hopkins University Press, 1988), 126.

[39]Samuel Taylor Coleridge, *The Complete Poetical Works*, ed. Ernest Hartley Coleridge, 2 vols. (Oxford: Clarendon, 1912), 1:215.

hold, which she enforces as the operative truth. Skillful purveyor of carefully manipulated facts that she is, she effectively spellbinds Christabel into reproducing her version:

> ... in the dim forest
> Thou heard'st a low moaning,
> And found'st a bright lady, surpassingly fair;
> And didst bring her home with thee in love and in charity.
>
> (1. 274–77)

Moreover, even without prompting, Sir Leoline later produces her narrative for her when the bard displaces the minstrel narrator and relates his dream of the struggle of a gentle dove whose wings and neck are caught in a snake's coils. Ignoring the bard's identification of dove and Christabel, Sir Leoline rationalizes his attraction to Geraldine by identifying her as "Lord Roland's beauteous dove" (2.569). Masking sexual desire with chivalric duty, he dismisses the poet's ineffectual, feminized words and promises more manly action on Geraldine's behalf: "With arms more strong than harp or song, / Thy sire and I will crush the snake" (2.570–71). Geraldine's unlawful intrusion thus crushes all potential counternarratives, ensnares patriarchal authority, and leaves the legitimate daughter marginalized and without a voice.

Geraldine, who can be seen as "an evil substitute mother,"[40] disrupts the father-daughter relationship but is instrumental in restoring the boyhood friendship between the two patriarchs, Sir Leoline and Sir Roland. The narrator's paean to male friendship was the only section of this capacious narrative of which reviewers approved. Hazlitt, whom Coleridge suspected of maliciously spreading the story that Geraldine was a man in drag,[41] admired the passage as the only "genuine burst of humanity" in the poem, the only place where "no dream oppresses" the author, "no spell binds him."[42] "Constancy," Coleridge's narrator asserts, "lives in realms above" (2.410); the youths' idyllic friendship ends as each insults "his heart's best brother" (2.417), but though they part, neither ever again finds another "to free the hollow heart from paining" (2.420).

Geraldine's capacity to enthrall, to captivate and spellbind her chosen

[40]Margery Durham, "The Mother Tongue: *Christabel* and the Language of Love," in *The (M)other Tongue: Essays in Feminist Psychoanalytic Interpretation*, ed. Shirley Nelson Garner, Claire Kahane, and Madelon Sprengnether (Ithaca: Cornell University Press, 1985), 181.

[41]Coleridge, *Collected Letters*, 4:917.

[42]Quoted in Swann, "Christabel," 544.

subject, suggests that she is an artist figure. The mesmerizing power of her large blue eyes that "glitter bright" (1.221). links her to Coleridge's Ancient Mariner, who was created at roughly the same time, in the fall of 1797. The vampire's art and art's vampirism engage in a morally ambiguous transaction with an empathic Other, who is powerfully transported into an imaginary realm, which, as Plato so sternly warned, can through its mimetic effect make the recipient participate as readily in evil as in good.

In their theoretical writings the Romantic poets unambiguously extolled the virtues of the imagination, as in Shelley's paradigmatic formulation:

> The great secret of morals is love; or a going out of our own nature, and an identification of ourselves with the beautiful which exists in thought, action, or person, not our own. . . . The great instrument of moral good is the imagination; and poetry administers to the effects by acting upon the cause. Poetry enlarges the circumference of the imagination by replenishing it with thoughts of ever new delight, which have the power of attracting and assimilating to their own nature all other thoughts, and which form new intervals and interstices whose void for ever craves fresh food.[43]

While thus expunging the Platonic doubt about the imagination's potentially immoral identification with evil, Romantic authors in their poetry, most notably Goethe in *Faust*, nevertheless displayed the vampiric capacity for "attracting and assimilating . . . all other thoughts," leaving the vampiric reader forever craving "fresh food." The post-Romantic locus classicus of this amoral complicity between the artist and his reader, Charles Baudelaire's *Fleurs du mal*, exquisitely articulates the vampiric imagination as both an external power and part of the poet's and reader's psyche, as both the enslaver and the enslaved. Neither the poet nor the reader, his double ("mon semblable"), can escape the demonic entrapment, driven as they are to forge the irresistible Faustian pact.

We might ask why Coleridge chose to name his vampire-artist Geraldine rather than Gerald.[44] Does the female visage of the vampire, like the female features of the snake tempting Eve in Renaissance paintings, deflect the seductive power of evil away from patriarchy and suggest

---

[43]Percy Bysshe Shelley, *Critical Prose*, ed. Bruce R. McElderry, Jr. (Lincoln: University of Nebraska Press, 1967), 12–13.

[44]Moretti offers the ingenious claim that works featuring women as vampires represent elite culture whereas those featuring men are part of mass culture (*Signs Taken for Wonders*, 103–4).

that women's narcissism is at the root of all evil? That when women command the poet's strange power of speech, they draw others into their own ambiguous sphere, controlling both subconscious and conscious mind? Having experienced the spell of art, the victim returns to her own familiar world, able to recall only traces of her vampiric experience, like the aura of a forgotten dream. Although both the Mariner and Geraldine are types of the *poète maudit*, the male figure's curse empowers him and enlightens his spellbound male listener, whereas the female's demonism paralyzes her captivated female subject, who mimes her gestures (rolling eyes, hissing tongue) without gaining access to either wisdom or power.

Thus, in key moments Christabel unwittingly functions as Geraldine's double, a doubling that allows us "to see 'feminine' genre and gender alike as cultural fantasy."[45] The fantasy takes on multiple benevolent and malevolent perspectives of meek maiden and cunning vampire, chivalric poet and imperious baron, which can be articulated only through generic mixtures, impurities, contaminations; they subvert the sense communicated by the formulaic repertory of the ballad that hierarchical social relations are universal and unchanging. Yet even as the text destabilizes the rules of genre and gender it makes visible the limits it transgresses. Christabel, that paragon of maidenly innocence and meek obedience, cannot finally confirm the triumph of feminine virtue, combining smiles with tears in her first experience of sin. And Geraldine, the humanly inhuman vampire, cannot unambiguously confirm the subversion of patriarchal law, but neither can she be bound by the domestic sphere. Needlework is not her favorite occupation. Instead of being trapped in a single social role or single narrative genre, Geraldine lures her listeners through desire and fear into her sphere of influence. The woman as vampire thus signals a way of escaping (not transforming) cultural codes but without generating a utopian counternarrative.

Neither "Christabel" nor "Die Braut von Korinth" provides the closure that in the gothic fiction of their time contained or expelled the violent forces it so thrillingly entertained. Driven by figures risen from the grave to prey on the living, their narratives suggest the virulent danger of unresolved conflicts from the past threatening to undermine the stability of the present.[46] This threat is more clearly social as well

[45]Swann, "Christabel," 541.

[46]See David Punter's perceptive comment that the gothic "occupied a borderguard position, forever on the lookout for threats from without, whether from the un-dead aristocracy or simply from the past, or even from within the bourgeois order itself, from

as psychological in the completed "Braut von Korinth" than in the fragmentary "Christabel," since Goethe explicitly situates his narrative in a historical moment of change from pagan to Christian morality, a "progress" that he depicts as harshly repressive. The reader of 1797 would easily recall the revolutionary work of *la guillotine*, which could hardly be said to have replaced the ancien régime with a gentler and kinder new order. Yet we cannot simply equate Goethe's and Coleridge's vampires with revolutionary bloodletting. They are far more ambiguous: they are both attractive and disruptive, both desirable and terrifying, leading the reader both to empathize with their subversive energy and to fear their demonic entrapment.

In the microstructure of Goethe's and Coleridge's vampiric ballads, in which the threats from past social systems are encoded as undead female demons, we can view and review far more clearly than in macrostructures like Romanticism the interplay between genre and gender, between authors' unpredictable creativity and predictable codes and conventions, between individual neologisms and inherited cultural systems. Such reviews are needed in order to arrive at theoretically more precise articulations of genre and gender in literary and cultural history.

---

those aspects of reality, psychological and social, which threatened to break through the thin web of ideological conformism and disrupt conservative synthesis." David Punter, "Social Relations of Gothic Fiction," in *Romanticism and Ideology*, ed. David Aers, Jonathan Cook, and David Punter (London: Routledge & Kegan Paul, 1981), 117.

5
Female Difficulties, Comparativist Challenge: Novels by English and German Women, 1752–1814

CHRIS CULLENS

Comparative literature is an academic field which, in spite of its interdisciplinary structure, still tends to reinforce traditional literary-
historical schemas of periodization, canon formation, and genre. What
comparativists define themselves as "doing" in their dissertations,
books, and course descriptions still often seems to receive its institutional legitimation by reference to one of those traditional categories,
to a collection of major figures, or to a recognized pattern of cross-
national literary influence or "history of ideas" paradigm.

This can make it difficult to find a niche for cross-national approaches
to women's social history, noncanonical women writers, or indeed to
any type of literature labeled "popular" or "mass." It may have become
possible now to write or teach on comparative topics such as George
Eliot *and* George Sand, or on major twentieth-century women writers
from Virginia Woolf to Christa Wolf; it is even possible, for instance,
to work on a whole group of "minor" female authors writing within
one genre and one national literature. But if one wants to devote time
to a field such as the letters, journals, and household accounts of sev-
enteenth- and eighteenth-century German, French, and English women,
or North and South American women's magazine fiction, the institutional framework and audience for such an undertaking remains more
limited. This type of research is necessary if feminist literary studies
within the university are to fulfill their potential for questioning the
very definition of "literature," and are not to end up revolving around
yet another (female) "major works by major authors" canon. Yet such
feminist comparative studies are further impeded by the sheer mass of
background and historical material relating to two or more national

A version of this essay appears in my book *"Female Difficulties": Novels by English and
German Women, 1752–1814* forthcoming from Stanford University Press and is reprinted
here by permission.

cultures which must be mastered, and by the problems of rare or un-translated sources.

My examination of the work of English and German female novelists writing between approximately 1750 and 1810 has led me to conclude that standard paradigms of literary periodization, canonization, and form do not always offer helpful guidelines for defining the special characteristics and role of this fiction within the framework of a comparative analysis. In the last decades of the eighteenth century the novel did undeniably consolidate its hold on the literary market; in turn, the form's popularity, and specifically the subgenre of the epistolary novel, gave writing women their best opportunity so far to gain some modicum of authorial credibility within the English and German publishing industries.[1] But how does one account for the contributions of these female novelists to the novel's "rise" and dominance within an inter-European or cross-national context?

A starting point is provided by the basic fact that women novelists writing in these two languages during this era used much the same range of subgenres and plots, and produced structurally and tonally similar works. This similarity cannot, however, be conveniently explained by direct contact (few German women ever had the chance to visit England, or vice versa). Biographical evidence rarely permits generalizations about what English and German women could have been absorbing from translations, or sources such as review journals, correspondence, or personal acquaintance, of one anothers' literature. In addition, these commonalities among women writers are not accounted for by the standard demarcations of literary periods or schools, such as neoclassicism, the Age of Johnson, the Enlightenment, *Sturm und Drang*, and various Romanticisms. In England, between the death of Smollett in 1771 and the 1790s, fictional subgenres became so fluid and syncretic that even traditional literary scholarship has approached those two decades as a kind of canonical interregnum, to which designations such as the Age of Sensibility do limited justice. By contrast, in German studies, literature of these decades tends to get measured against the two big categories of classicism and Romanticism. But, as Jeannine Blackwell summarizes the resulting "methodological hindrances": "At a time of unique and prolific novel publication and salon activity, women's lit-

---

[1]See Jane Spencer, *The Rise of the Woman Novelist: From Aphra Behn to Jane Austen* (Oxford: Basil Blackwell, 1986); Silvia Bovenschen, *Die imaginierte Weiblichkeit: Exemplarische Untersuchungen zur kulturgeschichtlichen und literarischen Präsentationsformen des Weiblichen* (Frankfurt am Main: Fischer, 1979); and Nancy Miller, *The Heroine's Text: Readings in the French and English Novel, 1722–1782* (New York: Columbia University Press, 1980).

erary lives fit into neither frame. Women did not write Romantic novels or poetry—they wrote Gesellschaftsromane, Erziehungsromane, described Frauenideale, and organized literary intercourse in the semi-public sphere of the salon. . . . Women, with a different literary tradition and different cultural role expectations, were simply marching to a different drummer."[2]

Indeed, Romanticism's "high argument" manifested itself as an aesthetic ideology steered by an overtly masculinized image of the artist. This tended to exclude female writers of narrative fiction from the sphere of "high art," and hence exercised little pull on them, at least until the Brontës.[3] (The one major exception was probably Madame de Staël.) As a result, women publishing novels in the late eighteenth century by and large did not court identification with, or advertise a polemical adherence to, contemporary literary movements. Writing at the level of popular rather than pointedly innovative fiction, the majority of these female novelists based their appeal and their claim to authorial credibility on their depictions of the ubiquitous dilemmas of domestic life, their flexible reworkings of tried-and-true plot paradigms and character constellations, and a narratorial stance that combined "sympathetic" portrayal with purportedly conservative moral guidance. Consequently, no simple rubic (even "sentimentalism," capacious as that term is) can cover the works of these female novelists.

Instead of trying to slot such authors into existing paradigms of period and influence, it is more valuable to examine their works in terms of the conditions of production within which they operated. First, similar social-historical conditions governed the whole sphere of education, *Bildung,* and literacy for English and German women, dictating their approach to writing and reading fiction. Second, similar market conditions in England and Germany enabled women to claim a limited writerly authority as popular novelists, as they drew on an inter-European literary subtradition of popular fiction which continued to flourish apart from "high culture" aesthetic innovations. Third, female novelists were to a large extent shut out from participating in the institutions, public opportunities, and collective undertakings that shaped and bonded the sensibilities of male novelists (the university years, especially important in Germany; the "Grand Tour" and possibility of

---

[2]Jeannine Blackwell, "Anonym, verschollen, trivial: Methodological Hindrances in Researching German Women's Literature," *Women in German Yearbook* 1 (1985): 39–59, 46–47.

[3]See M. H. Abrams, *Natural Supernaturalism: Tradition and Revolution in Romantic Literature* (New York: Norton, 1971), 17–70; and Margaret Homans, *Women Writers and Poetic Identity* (Princeton: Princeton University Press, 1980).

extended, unsupervised travel; the editorship of literary periodicals; and so on). Women instead found their training ground in the related activities of letter writing and journal keeping, benefiting from an unsystematic "home" education in which (as pedagogical moralists ceaselessly warned) the reading of novels and romances themselves seemed to have played a suspiciously large role. Indeed, when female novelists in both languages write about female characters, they recur to the issue of how textual consumption and production by women can both discipline and destabilize proper notions of femininity and domesticity.

The English writer Frances Burney titled her last novel, published in 1814, *The Wanderer, or Female Difficulties*. Burney's novel represents a culmination of an eighteenth-century tradition of feminocentric fiction; hence, it is logical that its subtitle should announce the work's intention to deal programmatically with the wide spectrum of complications attendant on female existence, when it is defined in terms of a rather narrow range of socially acceptable options. The fictions of Burney and her less well known English and German female contemporaries all reflect on specifically *female* difficulties, the omnipresent limitations imposed by eighteenth-century standards of correct feminine behavior and self-presentation. Likewise, this fiction reflects structurally the efforts of female writers to cope with the difficulties of assuming literary authority under conditions of production which subjected them to a special set of external and internalized constraints. Women who wrote during this period knew they had to "watch themselves," in every sense: they focused intensely on the specular and psychological dynamics of being an object of monitory surveillance. These writers made the imperative to "watch yourself" into a byword, as their heroines also ceaselessly watch themselves textually—in interpolated journals, letters, and confessional accounts—even as they watch themselves being watched by others around them. The torment unleashed by this internalized mandate is one of the difficulties that leave their mark on eighteenth-century novels by women, while the pleasures and the narcissistic gratification that imperative legitimates, however deviously, constitute a productive side effect of the same set of difficulties.

The resulting self-conscious, ambivalent awareness of their own crucial and vulnerable role in the "encouragement" of proper female readers and their oblique, partial assumption of full aesthetic authority thus shaped the works of female novelists during this era *regardless* of the language and novelistic subgenre (gothic novel, historical novel, *Tendenzroman*, courtship or marriage plot) they were employing, whether they were writing in 1770 or 1814, or under the ostensible influence of Richardson, Rousseau, Goethe, rationalism, sentimentalism, or Romanticism. What makes this particular body of novels so interesting is precisely that *all* these subgenres, influences, and modes became amalgamated within that matrix of popular fiction which female novelists claimed as their own territory. This amalgamation calls for some qualification of the suggestion that female writers of the era were marching to a *single* different drummer, however ubiquitous the female difficulties they confronted may have been, and productively complicates any monolithic conceptualization of both "tradition" and "countertradition." If that, in turn, makes it difficult to approach fiction produced by women in both languages during this period in terms of the linear, isolated national evolution of one genre, period, or school, then maybe we should view this as an encouragement to look at what defines the cross-national continuity of late eighteenth-century women's fiction first and foremost in terms of the singularities of the works themselves, and the social-historical conditions and transformations that made them possible.

In late 1796 literary Germany was abuzz with curiosity about the author of a new novel, which had appeared in installments in Schiller's periodical *Der Horen*. The work, *Agnes von Lilien*, appeared anonymously, and Schiller zealously guarded the secret of its authorship, leading some people to suspect that he was the author. Other readers credited it to Goethe, since the new novel bore some resemblance to *Wilhelm Meister*, even though its eponymous protagonist was female. Neither Schiller nor Goethe was flattered by this attribution, in spite of the novel's popularity, although Schiller at least derived a malicious pleasure from watching the Schlegel circle lead the way in proclaiming Goethe's authorship; Caroline Schlegel reportedly even praised Goethe for achieving a new height in the representation of female character. By mid-1797, however, the name behind this overnight literary success was out: it belonged to Schiller's sister-in-law, Caroline von Wolzogen, a lady known up to this point less for her literary efforts than for her divorce. After three editions between 1798 and 1800, the novel and its author largely disappeared from the public eye, *Agnes von Lilien* being remembered as a charming minor work and Wolzogen for her relation to, and memoir of, her eminent brother-in-law. Nonetheless, German literary historians, inasmuch as they have accorded the novel any attention, generally persisted in identifying it with Goethe by categorizing it as a *Wilhelm Meister* imitation, albeit a failed one.

Yet the only full-length study of the novel—a Berlin dissertation from 1914—concludes (I think correctly) that the novel has less to do with *Wilhelm Meister* than with Richardson, and specifically with *Sir Charles*

Grandison, from which several features appear to have been imported. As Wolzogen later recalled, Schiller often joked that people would always be able to guess she and her sister were of the generation that had grown up with Grandison. (Indeed, Richardson's last novel, often still regarded critically as his weakest, may well have exercised a more lasting influence than the feminocentric plots of his first two works on Continental female authors.) Even more suggestive is the fact that *Agnes von Lilien* also displays a striking similarity to the English novelist Frances Burney's *Evelina*, published twenty years earlier.[4] Whether Wolzogen had actually read *Evelina* is not ascertainable—and perhaps not the main issue. But what points of reference literary historians select to establish the framework within which they position a work, whether those focal points consist of another text (*Wilhelm Meister*), authors (Goethe and Schiller), genre (the bildungsroman), "school" (Weimar classicism), or a single dominant language (German), is of crucial importance. The application of these categories to figures who, like Wolzogen, are doubly marginalized as female and as producers of "ephemeral" popular literature makes it all too easy to assign them a place as imitators, trivializers, or at best popularizers of a hegemonic national literary tradition.

Currently Wolzogen, like many of her English and a few of her German female contemporaries, is receiving renewed attention; a planned edition of her complete works has already yielded a reprint of *Agnes*, and will eventually encompass her second novel, uncollected *Nachlaß*, and journals. Such editorial undertakings make research and teaching substantially easier; but they do not guarantee that the same old critical categories will not be applied to the newly available text. In his Afterword, for instance, the editor of the recent *Agnes* reprint recurs to an old lament, proclaiming regretfully that Wolzogen's novel is indeed "no *Wilhelm Meister*. Whereas there all parts of the work enter into a connection with each other, here [in *Agnes*] clear discrepancies exist." Two intervening centuries of German literary criticism have not loosened the hold of the classicist aesthetics by which a work is judged, and in this case inevitably found wanting, according to the effect it produces of internal coherence and closure. The editor is also bothered

---

[4]Stephan Brock, *Caroline von Wolzogens "Agnes von Lilien" (1798): Ein Beitrag zur Geschichte des Frauenromans* (Berlin: H. Blanke's Buckdruckerei, 1914). As Brock notes, both *Agnes von Lilien* and *Evelina* feature supposedly orphaned heroines, raised by kindly pastors in the country, who are abruptly moved into an unsettling urban milieu where, in the course of successfully undergoing a string of compromising personal embarrassments, they are reunited with their parents and emerge vindicated under the enamored but critical scrutiny of the older noblemen who finally become their husbands.

by how the destiny of Wolzogen's female protagonist "is constantly being forced in new directions by external, often insignificant circumstances"; he caps his critique by approvingly citing Goethe's own expressed irritation with the jumpiness and the abrupt rhythm of the novel's exposition, "which don't allow one a moment to arrive at a feeling of ease" ("lassen einen nicht einen Augenblick zur Behaglichkeit kommen").[5]

Goethe's dissatisfaction with the lack of readerly *Behaglichkeit*—literally, "comfort" or "coziness"—the novel generates may ring familiar to readers of Frances Burney, Charlotte Smith, Ann Radcliffe, Benedikte Naubert, and other gothic-influenced female novelists of the 1790s. Compared to Burney's later female protagonists, or the spectacularly persecuted medieval heroines of Naubert's historical fiction, Wolzogen's Agnes leads an idyllic life. But the "female difficulties" of all these protagonists, reflected in the dis-ease, discrepancies, and tension generated by their stories, originate precisely in their female vulnerability to the power of "insignificant circumstances" and misleading appearances to determine the structure and rhythm of their existence. Agnes's horror-struck exclamation when she must "cloak the truth in silence, must become the victim of the unfortunate conjunction of circumstances which sully the purity of my character in *his* eyes!" (1:292) could be taken, almost word for word, from countless novels by Wolzogen's female contemporaries, both English and German.

Likewise, if these feminocentric novels do display the surfeit of abrupt, even "unbelievable" plot turns for which they are criticized, these features represent a structural embodiment of the young, dependent single woman's subservient positioning vis-à-vis all the people in her world who *are* able to assert authority over her and who *can* accordingly subject her to peremptory impositions and transitions. Female protagonists simply cannot extricate themselves from the nexus of the nuclear family as easily as the picaro and the roaming protagonists of the male bildungsroman. Even the many heroines supposedly orphaned in infancy find their dead parents exercising a baleful influence beyond the grave, or, if long-lost mothers and fathers should miraculously pop back up, they bring with them a new set of conflicting claims of affection and authority. For instance, Wolzogen's Agnes, like the later protagonist of Burney's *Female Difficulties*, is faced with having to purchase the freedom of an imprisoned, politically persecuted father with an unwanted marriage. Thus, her father's apparently disinterested

<hr />

[5]Caroline von Wolzogen, *Agnes von Lilien*, in *Gesammelte Schriften I*, ed. Peter Boerner (Hildesheim: Georg Olms, 1988), 2:402–3; all further references are cited in the text.

decision to have Agnes's education concentrate on the inculcation of a stoically self-reliant inner serenity ultimately serves his needs as much as her own. "My daughter should be able to achieve through her self all that constitutes the true worth of life, and neither the enjoyment nor the want of the uncertain endowments of happiness should be capable of destroying the balance of her finer being" (2:132). *Gleichgewicht, Gleichmuth, Harmonie*—balance, equanimity, harmony: the frequency with which such words are invoked like a mantra by Wolzogen's own protagonist and other beset heroines created by her fellow female novelists leaves it unclear whether these all-encompassing terms encode a feminine ideal of obedient docility or one of resolute independence—or the psychological double bind of living up to both ideals simultaneously.[6]

The questions Wolzogen's *Agnes von Lilien* raises, as well as the reception her novel encountered, make it an unusually apt example of the issues involved in a comparativist analysis of eighteenth-century women's fiction. Viewing the novel in a comparativist context does not merely widen the traditional interpretive parameters, but, more important, it focuses analytic attention on exactly what the text does, in its own terms, rather than on what it fails to do. By the same token, structural and stylistic "discrepancies" and readerly "discomfort," rather than being summarily condemned or explained away, need to be employed as valuable clues to the desires as well as the anxieties women novelists of the era were activating and assuaging. After all, the enthusiastic consumption and production of fiction by women has been a constant factor of the European literary market for almost three centuries. As Lillian S. Robinson observes: "Feminists are not in agreement as to whether domestic and sentimental fiction, the female Gothic, the women's sensational novel functioned as instruments of expression, repression, or subversion, but they have successfully revived interest in the question as a legitimate cultural issue. It is no longer automatically assumed that literature addressed to the mass female audience is necessarily bad because it is sentimental, or for that matter sentimental because it is addressed to that audience."[7]

---

[6]For other approaches to Wolzogen's novels, see Christa Bürger, *Leben Schreiben: Die Klassik, die Romantik, und der Ort der Frauen* (Stuttgart: Metzler, 1990), 161–63; and Antonie Schweitzer and Simone Sitte, "Tugend-Opfer-Rebellion: Zum Bild der Frau im weiblichen Erzeihungs-und Bildungsroman," in *Frauen Literatur Geschichte: Schreibende Frauen vom Mittelalter bis zur Gegenwart,* ed. Hiltrud Gnüg und Renate Möhrmann (Stuttgart: Metzler, 1985), 144–65. For a superb consideration of why more German women of Wolzogen's generation did not write, see Ulrike Prokop, "Die Einsamkeit der Imagination. Geschlechterkonflikt und literarische Produktion um 1770," in *Deutsche Literatur von Frauen,* ed. Gisela Brinkler-Gabler (Munich: C. H. Beck, 1988), 1:325–65.

[7]Lillian S. Robinson, "Treason Our Text: Feminist Challenges to the Literary Canon,"

The impact of feminist criticism has by now become undeniable within German as well as English eighteenth-century studies, although it infiltrated the former field more slowly, and more through the efforts of marginalized scholars. When attention is paid to the German women writing during the "Goethezeit" it still tends to be directed to traditionally recognized figures such as Rahel Varnhagen, Caroline Schlegel-Schelling, and Bettina von Arnim, whose oeuvres are to a large extent epistolary or outside the category of popular fiction. German literature also had its Sarah Fieldings, its Ann Radcliffes, its Frances Burneys and Mrs. Inchbalds.[8] Their oeuvres, however, have received much less attention than those of their English female contemporaries, to the extent that they have been critically relegated to what, in German terminology, is labeled, with telling severity, *Trivialliteratur*—literally, "trivial literature," although the word would more likely be translated as "mass literature" in English. Indeed, it is increasingly apparent that the "high-low" dichotomization of literature itself has a strong gendered component and that the female producers and consumers of "mass" or "middle-brow" culture have played a major role during the last two centuries in constituting the often unnamed abjected "Other" of neoclassicist, Romantic, and modernist aesthetic practice.[9]

The sociology of literature, and especially the examination of critical categories applicable to mass literature, popular culture, and even "kitsch," has been one of the strong points of postwar German literary studies influenced by the Frankfurt school, the reader-response theory of Wolfgang Iser, and the Konstanz school's reception theory. Yet, paradoxically, even as such scholarship served to legitimate the study of

in *The New Feminist Criticism: Essays on Women, Literature, and Theory,* ed. Elaine Showalter (New York: Pantheon, 1985), 116.

[8]See the introduction to Ruth-Ellen B. Joeres and Mary Jo Maynes, eds., *German Women in the Eighteenth and Nineteenth Centuries: New Studies in Social and Literary History* (Bloomington: Indiana University Press, 1985), ix–x; and also Katherine Goodman and Edith Waldstein, eds., *In the Shadow of Olympus: German Women Writers around 1800* (Albany: SUNY Press, 1992), 1–29. The two major studies of German eighteenth-century women's novels are Christine Touaillon, *Der deutsche Frauenroman im 18. Jahrhundert* (1979; rpt. Vienna: Wilhelm Braumüller, 1919); and Helga Meise's indispensable *Die Unschuld und die Schrift: Deutsche Frauenromane im 18. Jahrhundert* (Berlin: Guttandin & Hoppe, 1983). See also Eva Walter *"Schrieb oft, von Mägde Arbeit müde": Lebenszusammenhänge deutscher Schriftstellerinnen um 1800—Schritte zur bürgerlichen Weiblichkeit* (Düsseldorf: Schwann-Bagel, 1985); and Jeannine Blackwell and Susanne Zantop, eds., *Bitter Healing: German Women Writers from 1700 to 1830* (Lincoln: University of Nebraska Press, 1990).

[9]Andreas Huyssen, "Mass Culture as Woman: Modernism's Other," in *Studies in Entertainment: Critical Approaches to Mass Culture,* ed. Tania Modleski (Bloomington: Indiana University Press, 1986), 188–207. See also Marion Beaujean, *Der Trivialroman in der zweiten Hälfte des 18. Jahrhunderts: Die Ursprünge der modernen Unterhaltungsliteratur* (Bonn: Bouvier, 1964); and Christa Bürger, Peter Bürger, and Jochen Schulte-Sasse, eds., *Zur Dichotimisierung von hoher und niederer Literatur* (Frankfurt am Main: Suhrkamp, 1982).

popular literature and culture, at the same time the key concept of the Culture Industry discouraged an examination of the artifacts of popular culture on their own terms, and for their own aesthetic merits.[10] As Tania Modleski states: "It is one of the great ironies in the development of mass-culture theory that the people who were first responsible for pointing out the importance of mass art simultaneously provided the justification for slighting it."[11] This situation has contributed to the occlusion of women's writing as an object of scholarly interest, especially in German studies, since within the canonical outlines of German literature such writing is even more likely to be located outside the boundaries of the high or "autonomous" art which has proved so influential in propagating and institutionalizing the ideology of the *ewig Weiblich*, the Eternal Feminine.

But, whatever culturally specific version of the *ewig Weiblich* German and English women lived with, the conflict between the overwhelming public presence of a feminine ideal and the typical quotidian female difficulties left an indelible mark on the novels they produced. For even when they turned to a species of fiction that claimed (and was accorded) limited literary authority, female novelists were necessarily confronted with the contradiction inherent in their own "unfeminine" entry into a masculine public sphere, and driven to acknowledge, however delicately or deviously, the gap thus opened up between public ideal and personal conduct.

The last decades of the eighteenth century, together with the first twenty years of the nineteenth, witnessed not only the emergence of a new liberal discourse of gender, but also the intersection of this discourse with other debates shaping the public sphere of politics. The 1790s mark the high point of the theoretical discussion of what role, if any, women might play in the ongoing production of communal history; essays published during the decade by Talleyrand and Condorcet in France, by Mary Wollstonecraft and Catherine Macaulay in England, and by Theodor von Hippel in Prussia all argue for an extension of certain male prerogatives to select females.[12] The same period also witnessed the consolidation of the ideology of idealized femininity, a de-

---

[10]See Lillian S. Robinson, *Sex, Class, and Culture* (Bloomington: Indiana University Press, 1978), 69–94; Fredric Jameson, "Verdinglichung und Utopie in der Massenkultur," in Bürger et al., *Zur Dichotimisierung von hoher und niederer Literatur*, 108–41; and Tania Modleski, *Loving with a Vengeance: Mass-Produced Fantasies for Women* (New York: Methuen, 1984).

[11]Modleski, *Loving with a Vengeance*, 26.

[12]See Susan Bell and Karen M. Offen, eds., *Women, the Family, and Freedom: The Debate in Documents*, vol. 1, *1750–1880* (Stanford: Stanford University Press, 1983).

110   Chris Cullens

velopment that served to recontain the nascent emancipatory impulses
unleashed by the Enlightenment and the French Revolution, and to
push public reconsideration of "the woman question" back by over half
a century. During the roughly forty years in which the "proper lady"
worked her way up to the "Angel of the House" and the "perfektes
Frauenzimmerchen" of mid–eighteenth-century conduct manuals was
apotheosized into the "Priesterin und Lichtbringerin" of the German
Romantics, the various discourses on gender within medicine, law, psychology, and aesthetics managed to restabilize the potentially threatening force of the feminine by conceding it the privileged roles of
domestic organizer and cultural consumer within the private sphere.
As Mary Poovey has summarized: "The ultimate effect of the revolutionary decades was to intensify the paradoxes already inherent in propriety. . . . As a consequence, the women who grew up during these
decades, or who immediately inherited their ideological legacy, experienced a particularly intense version of the contradictions we have
been examining."[13]

Nevertheless, in spite of this abandonment of overt emancipatory
agitation, it was also between roughly 1760 and 1810 that women in
both Germany and England started entering the public realm of publishing to an unheard-of extent—as poets, polemicists, dramatists, and
above all novelists. J. M. S. Tompkins estimates that a third to a half of
the novels that stocked the English circulating libraries during this era
were written by women—although that is difficult to verify, given that
precisely this class of ephemeral production was most quickly consigned to historical oblivion, and that female authors seem to have been

[13]Mary Poovey, *The Proper Lady and the Woman Writer: Ideology as Style in the Works of
Mary Wollstonecraft, Mary Shelley, and Jane Austen* (Chicago: University of Chicago Press,
1984), 30. Two other considerations of changing conceptualizations of gender roles at the
end of the century in relation to literature are Barbara Becker-Cantarino, "Priesterin und
Lichtbringerin: Zur Ideologie des weiblichen Charakters in der Frühromantik," in *Die
Frau als Heldin und Autorin*, ed. Wolfgang Paulsen (Munich: Fink, 1979), 111–24; and
Volker Hoffmann, "Elisa und Robert oder das Weib und der Mann, wie sie sein sollten:
Anmerkungen zur Geschlechtercharakteristik der Goethezeit," in *Klassik und Moderne: Die
Weimarer Klassik als historisches Ereignis und Herausforderung im kulturgeschichtlichen Prozeß*,
ed. Jörg Schönert and Karl Richter (Stuttgart: Metzler, 1983), 80–97. Relevant secondary
sources on social history include Lawrence Stone, *The Family, Sex, and Marriage in England,
1500–1800* (London: Weidenfeld & Nicolson, 1977); Roy Porter, *English Society in the Eighteenth Century* (Harmondsworth: Penguin, 1982); Heidi Rosenbaum, *Formen der Familie:
Untersuchungen zum Zusammenhang von Familienverhältnissen, Sozialstruktur und sozialem
Wandel in der deutschen Gesellschaft des 19. Jahrhunderts* (Frankfurt am Main: Suhrkamp,
1982); Barbara Becker-Cantorino, *Der lange Weg zur Mündigkeit: Frau und Literatur, 1500–
1800* (Stuttgart: Metzler, 1987); and Karin Hausen, "Die Polarisierung der 'Geschlechts-
charaktere'—Eine Spiegelung der Dissoziation von Erwerbs-und Familienleben," in *Seminar: Familie und Gesellschaftsstruktur*, ed. Heidi Rosenbaum (Franfurt am Main: Suhrkamp,
1983), 165–92.

especially inclined to anonymous publication. Elizabeth Friedrichs lists over two hundred female authors writing in German during the century, but again, many of their works have apparently disappeared, known only by their titles.[14]

The novels by English and German women, of course, still must represent a limited percentage of the total novelistic output between 1770 and 1810, a period in which the rate of production jumped astronomically. But, even while reviewers sneered at yet another febrile product of a female pen, or damned it with faint praise, the public at large still voted with their pocketbooks, encouraging publishers to worry less about the sex of a work's author than its salability, and encouraging even more women to venture into this field. Hence, despite the dictates of an internally contradictory and increasingly rigorous ideology of femininity, on the most basic economic level the market was undeniably granting to select women precisely what the moralists admonished them to renounce: the license to indulge in their own powers of imagination, and a taste for financial self-sufficiency. Even as polemicists on both sides of the Channel were recurring ad nauseam to Rousseau's observation that the best woman is exactly the one who is not talked about at all, who consists of a kind of public tabula rasa, a historical nonentity, publishers and readers were implicitly encouraging the "talk" of and about women in print, rewarding female authors as never before for their personal histories or fabulated accounts of spectacular female lives for the delectation of the public.

This development ensured that the female novelist, together with other varieties of the Lady of Letters, would become an increasingly visible, if not always approved, type in the course of the century. Female authors were not, of course, a totally unknown phenomenon before the onset of the era. In England prior to 1730 Aphra Behn, Delariviere Manley, and the novelist and journalist Eliza Haywood had all supported themselves by writing—but at the price of literary and personal notoriety. And no German woman produced a first-class fictional hit until 1771, when Sophie von La Roche's *Geschichte des Fräuleins von Sternheim*, which was edited by Wieland and praised by Goethe, ushered in a new era of fictional production in German by women.[15]

[14]J. M. S. Tompkins, *The Popular Novel in England, 1770–1800* (London: Methuen, 1932), 119–20; and Elizabeth Friedrichs, *Lexikon der deutschsprachigen Schriftstellerinnen des 18. und 19. Jahrhunderts* (Stuttgart: Metzler, 1983). See also Katherine M. Rogers, *Feminism in Eighteenth-Century England* (Urbana: University of Illinois Press, 1982), esp. appendix, and Meise, *Die Unschuld und die Schrift*, 253–59.

[15]See Monika Nenon, *Autorschaft und Frauenbildung: Das Beispiel Sophie von La Roche* (Würzburg: Königshausen & Neumann, 1988).

Several German women who published fiction during the three decades that followed had some personal connection with one or more prominent literary men: Caroline von Wolzogen; Sophie Mereau (later Brentano's wife); Georg Forster's former wife, Therese Huber; the dramatist Kotzebue's sister, Amalie Ludecus; Friedrich Schlegel's wife, Dorothea (the daughter of Moses Mendelssohn); Friederike Helene Unger, the wife of the influential Berlin publisher and friend of Nicolai and Jacobi; and the poet August Bürger's wife, Elisa Hahn (whose scandalous divorce from him made a bigger impression on the German public than her subsequent novels). Others broke into publishing without the benefit of well-placed male connections and, in some cases, abandoned it just as unobtrusively. Karoline von Wobeser, for example, having produced one of the sensational successes of the 1790s, *Elisa, oder das Weib wie es sein soll* (Elisa, or woman as she should be), a didactic novel which insists that the truly good woman lives for home and family, at least had the grace to take her own advice; resisting the temptations of success, she disappeared back into anonymity, never to be heard from again. And Benedikte Naubert, who turned out an average of two full-length works a year between 1787 and 1802, thus managing to dominate the market for historical fiction in Germany by virtue of not only the quality but also the quantity of her production, was able to preserve her anonymity until 1815.

Although some women writers were free from the financial pressure to write, many others found themselves motivated to write for profit only during certain intervals of their lives. In both German-speaking Europe and England, a certain pattern of women who looked to their pens to support themselves and their dependents in the wake of marital abandonment, separation, or widowhood is evident (Charlotte Smith and Mary Ann Radcliffe, left with ten and eight children, respectively, to support; Anne Masterman Skinn, Eliza Fenwick, Elisa Hahn, Isabella Wallenrodt, Caroline Augusta Fischer). During the late eighteenth century, after all, the field of economic options for female self-support actually narrowed; likewise, there is evidence that, at least in England, the wealth accessible to women in the forms of property settlements, inheritances, and jointures also decreased. For some, such as Frances Burney, Dorothea Schlegel, and the older Sophie von La Roche, the income generated by their writing, while it did not spell the difference between destitution and comfort, was still a welcome addition. Others, such as Huber and Mereau Brentano, became full-time, self-supporting literary professionals, eking out a precarious but independent living from the combined activities of novel writing, journalism, editing, and translating. (Translating poses a particularly interesting case, since it provided women with a way into the literary market that offered them training in their craft, as well as exposure to another national literature.)

In England the professional involvement of women such as Huber and Mereau Brentano is paralleled by the industriousness of novel-writing journalists such as Mary Wollstonecraft and Mary Hays, and the inexhaustible Charlotte Smith. Of course, in England female nov-elists made their mark earlier than in German-speaking Europe; the 1760s had been punctuated by the appearance of works by women writers, some patterned on Richardsonian precedents, and sometimes written by women personally acquainted with Richardson, such as Eliz-abeth Griffith and Charlotte Lennox. Sophia and Harriet Lee, as well as Clara Reeve, were all writing in the 1780s; Charlotte Smith's career actually began in that decade; and Frances Burney's had been inau-gurated in the 1770s, with the runaway success of *Evelina*.

But it was the 1790s, a decade marked in England by social unrest and political agitation, which was dominated by the spectacular success of the gothic novelist Ann Radcliffe and by the literary and publicistic activities of the Jacobin writers, including a remarkable number of women—not only Wollstonecraft and Hays, who were to bear the brunt of the public malice directed toward such radicals in petticoats, but also Elizabeth Inchbald, Mary Robinson, Eliza Fenwick, and Amelia Opie. Some of these women, such as Opie, were later to disassociate them-selves from the politics and personalities of the Jacobin circle, while yet other women writing around the turn of the century, including the satirist Elizabeth Hamilton and the ever-formidable Hannah More, strove to combat what they viewed as the especially noxious influence of their liberal literary contemporaries.

And yet, despite the frenetic political agitation and sometimes rabid personal animosities that characterized English literary life during this decade, dichotomous categories such as "freethinker" versus "didactic moralist" or "liberal" versus "conservative" really say less about the position of these English women novelists than the fact that all of them, whatever their overt political stance, were resorting to the medium of the published word to articulate their perspectives on events taking place in the realm of public history. Nothing illustrates the importance of this factor more clearly than the writings of Hannah More. Author-ship was certainly not one of the attributes included in More's concep-tion of the ideal female, and yet she apparently did not dwell on the ironic contradiction evident between her rigorous strictures and the ex-ample of her own successful, thoroughly professional career. More was not unique in this respect, for she provides just one illustration of what Jane Spencer views as "a trend very general in the later years of the century: women novelists were carving a public niche for themselves by recommending a private, domestic life for their heroines."[16]

This disjunction between market-generated opportunities and gendered roles and expectations was only one of the components of female authorship in England and German-speaking Europe during the late eighteenth century. Women were caught in other, homologous contradictions in almost every sphere of their experience—on the levels of education, of marriage, of domestic organization and child rearing, of social interaction outside the home, of their cultural positioning vis-à-vis literary tradition, and of political involvement and affiliation. These conflicts are reflected in the works (as well as the careers) of English and German female novelists of the era, but in the highly mediated form that the novel permits. On the one hand, the genre of the novel may have granted eighteenth-century authors an unprecedented license to examine and represent the conditions and the unfolding panorama of contemporary life. On the other hand, the fascination this newly opened up literary territory exercised on the popular imagination still by no means legitimated unsupervised narrative and thematic free play within its boundaries. It is indeed possible to view the novel as a form fundamentally connected to the tropes and themes of transgression, the transgression that ensues on a variety of levels when the modern self of Western subjectivity, in encountering communal forces that threaten its prerogatives, discovers its autonomy and alienation.[17] But visions of the novel as a literary carrier of ideologically destabilizing energy have to be balanced by the admission that the attention paid within the novel to the phenomenon of the self contemplating itself is overdetermined by the limited repertoire of narrative models available in the late eighteenth century for the fictional inscription of individual destiny. This in turn ensured that the novel, by its very popularity if nothing else, itself functioned as a vehicle for the recontainment, the proper socialization— in short, the supervisory policing—of the reading and writing subject. Indeed, as Friedrich Kittler has shown, a semiotechnology of reading and writing which emerged in the eighteenth century in tandem with the addictive habit of novel consumption served to anchor the interiority of the literate individual precisely in his or her ability to overlook

---

[16]On More, see Rogers, *Feminism in Eighteenth-Century England*, 209–13; and Mitzi Myers, "Reform or Ruin: 'A Revolution in Female Manners,'" in *Studies in Eighteenth-Century Culture*, ed. Roseann Runte (Madison: University of Wisconsin Press, 1979). Spencer, *Rise of the Woman Novelist*, 20.

[17]See Tony Tanner, *Adultery in the Novel: Contract and Transgression* (Baltimore: Johns Hopkins University Press, 1979); also Peter Stallybrass and Allon White, *The Politics and Poetics of Transgression* (Ithaca: Cornell University Press, 1986).

the materiality of the "letter's" inscriptive medium in order to internalize and personalize the "spirit" of its message all the more thoroughly. Likewise, Nancy Armstrong has linked the eighteenth-century novel of conjugality and domesticity to the related form of the conduct manual, positing that such fiction carried on, in its own terms, the more overtly didactic handbooks' mission of redefining and reorganizing middle-class private life around gender differentiations.[18]

Furthermore, it seems logical that the fate of the female self, which was arousing so much novelistic interest from the middle of the eighteenth century onward, would be particularly affected by the conflict between self-exploration and self-discipline played out in the novel—on the levels of individual female authors, female readers, and fictional female protagonists. The weaker sex was, after all, supposed to be more in need of helpful supervision, far more vulnerable to being hastily judged on appearance, however unjustly. This emphasis on the vigilant monitoring of female behavior in turn not only intensified the self-consciousness of women writers, heightening the conflict foregrounded in the novel between the development of a certain self-conception and others' possible misconceptions, but also loaded the dice in favor of conventionally admonitory representations of female fate.

Most English and German women novelists seem to have worked with the generic resources at hand, utilizing the fictional tools they found to highlight certain pragmatic difficulties inherent in contemporary female existence, to delineate the contours of an acceptably self-conscious female subject, and to gesture toward experiences not depicted in detail on account of decorum, conventions, or lack of exposure. This description may run the risk of appearing to domesticate or diminish the achievements of these writers by presenting them as examples of the art of the miniature, a matter of unobtrusive permutations. But then Walter Benjamin has noted how dangerous "the domesticated passions"—of the collector, the copyist, the obsessional correspondent, and other artists of the appropriated detail—can be.[19] And, by extension, perhaps most literary genres, like other discourses, are in actuality transformed not by abrupt, dramatic epistemological breaks, as effected by the experiments of a handful of radical aesthetic innovators, but rather by means of the gradual, micro-level widening

[18]Friedrich Kittler, *Discourse Networks, 1800–1900* (Stanford: Stanford University Press, 1990). Nancy Armstrong, *Desire and Domestic Fiction: A Political History of the Novel* (Oxford: Oxford University Press, 1987).

[19]Walter Benjamin, "Eduard Fuchs: Collector and Historian," in *The Essential Frankfurt School Reader*, ed. Andrew Arato and Eike Gebhardt (New York: Urizen, 1978), 241.

or shifting of the total range of "enunciatory possibilities."[20] As Dana Polan suggests: "Rather than understanding formal innovation to be a deconstruction of dominant ideology, we might want to deconstruct the whole underlying philosophy of a critical practice that places innovation and dominance in opposition, that understands mass culture to be an ideological form that is most effective when it is formally and thematically most simple."[21]

Furthermore, to categorize these writers in terms of an either/or schema—either formally conservative or pointedly experimental, either docile imitators of given "masculine" fictional constructs or exponents of a consciously "female" tradition or *Frauenliteratur*—entails ignoring complexities that arise when members of a culturally marginal group encounter a dominant literary heritage, particularly at a historical juncture where a recognizably feminist or proto-feminist political discourse is just beginning to emerge. For this situation another interactive model is required, one that acknowledges the fact that women writing "are not, then, inside and outside of the male tradition; they are inside two traditions simultaneously, 'undercurrents,' in Ellen Moers's metaphor, of the mainstream."[22] Or, to use Sigrid Weigel's favored specular metaphor of "der schielende Blick" (which denotes either an oblique sidelong gaze or, simply, a cross-eyed gaze), feminist scholars must proceed on the assumption that female writers since the end of the eighteenth century have viewed themselves and their female readers through the prescribed lens of internalized phallocentric cultural constructions of "the feminine," producing a necessarily split, doubled, or wavering focus.[23] At any rate, whether the conceptual model is to be specular or hydraulic (crossed eyes or cross-currents), both suggest that a constant factor of women's literary culture, whatever the language, will consist of an inconsistency that results from a constitutive ambivalence.

This brief outline of the conditions and contradictions pertaining to female authorship in the late eighteenth century suggests that an investigation of novels written during that period by women could be enriched not just by crossing the demarcated disciplinary boundaries of various national literatures, but also by drawing simultaneously on

[20]See Michel Foucault, *"The Archaeology of Knowledge" and "The Discourse on Language,"* trans. A. M. Sheridan Smith (New York: Harper & Row, 1972), 166–77.

[21]See Dana Polan, "Brief Encounters: Mass Culture and the Evacuation of Sense," in Modleski, *Studies in Entertainment,* 170.

[22]Elaine Showalter, "Feminist Criticism in the Wilderness," in *Writing and Sexual Difference,* ed. Elizabeth Abel (Chicago: University of Chicago Press, 1983), 32.

[23]Sigrid Weigel, "Der schielende Blick: Thesen zur Geschichte weiblicher Schreibpraxis," in Inge Stephan and Sigrid Weigel, *Die verborgene Frau: Sechs Beiträge zu einer feministischen Literaturwissenschaft* (Berlin: Argument, 1983), 83–137.

several other relevant fields of inquiry: the sociology of publication and reading practices; pedagogy; philosophy; personal biography (when possible); the social history of family, childhood, and adolescence; and the development of the scientific, medical, and proto-psychiatric discourses which, as Thomas Laqueur has shown, have constructed gender and steered representation in the process of "making sex." Comparative literature, after all, in spite of its traditional methodologies and sometimes circumscribed self-definition, currently appears to offer one site within the institution of the university humanities where this kind of boundary-crossing borderwork is more likely to be greeted with tacit toleration, if not open encouragement. But whatever approach is deployed, and however pluralistic it may be, it is absolutely indispensable, in this case, that it be articulated with the detailed close textual analysis of the novels themselves. For in the late eighteenth century the novel form was, in spite of the formal precedents furnished by Richardson and Fielding in England and Gellert in Germany, in an amorphous phase and able to encompass a looseness, digressiveness, and (in spite of the bounds of decorum) expansiveness of both scope and tone. In this respect the tight formal symmetry of Jane Austen's novels is not necessarily representative of the work the majority of her female contemporaries were producing, for whom discursiveness itself seems to be one noticeable side effect of the complex discursive conjuncture to which they are responding. It is therefore all the more necessary to approach these texts, often cursorily dealt with or accorded a brief plot and thematic summary in the secondary literature, as complete, complicated artifacts. Episodes, subplots, and individual characters need to be viewed within the structure of the work as a whole, for it is only in the context of the whole that the significance, indeterminacies, and revealing "discrepancies" embedded in discrete narrative elements may become fully visible.

In fact, many of the texts themselves are riddled with structural oddities, narrative blind spots and dead ends, and ideological inconsistencies—notably the inconsistency of a "happy ending" (usually matrimony) hastily or limply appended to a narrative to smooth out belatedly the rocky stretches of resentment, rebellion, apprehension, and misapprehension that have impeded the heroine's recognition and assumption of her proper, preordained "female destiny." As Helga Meise has noted: "The 'chaos' of writing, the attempt to anchor ironies and irritations in writing itself, pulls the 'literarization of female destiny' . . . into visibility, even when it is considered as an aberration. Writing is therefore a particularly dangerous means of propagating 'female destiny,' simultaneously miming it and unmasking it, not taking it seriously and, at the same time, seeking out yet other adventures in its name."[24] Janet Todd, too, has noted how the very act of writing could function to widen, if not completely spring, the limits of the eighteenth-century "sentimental female image": "In sentimental literature women could complain obliquely, refashion the structures of power they inhabited, recreate their own images, and reform men. Through writing, repression turned into expression, and the passivity of the ideal was modified by a creative act of literature that could not be passive."[25]

Given such significatory cross-currents, it is essential to admit once again that these texts, precisely inasmuch as they encode the contradictions operating between material conditions, ideological formations, and what Raymond Williams has called the mediating "structures of feeling," simultaneously reinforce and resist the era's assumptions about the role of women and the woman writer. For most of these novels are neither brazenly rebellious nor merely smugly sanctimonious. Instead, they can be both by turns, since many are played out within a shifting, unstable interpretational terrain in which small acts take on troublingly double-edged connotations, where "resignation" may be a cipher for resentment, where properly feminine submission becomes, in hindsight, blind gullibility, and where silence can provide either a shield for duplicity or the only way of remaining honest. These textual half-tones make such works especially appropriate objects of the type of "grey, meticulous, and patiently documentary" analysis Michel Foucault called "genealogical," which "operates on a field of entangled and confused parchments, on documents that have been scratched over and recopied many times."[26]

As Foucault emphasizes elsewhere: "We must not imagine a world of discourse divided between the dominant discourse and the dominated one; but as a multiplicity of discursive elements that can come into play in various strategies. . . . Discourses are not once and for all subservient to power or raised up against it, any more than silences are."[27] Furthermore, as Biddy Martin has commented: "It is neither an

[24]Meise, *Die Unschuld und die Schrift,* 206.
[25]Janet Todd, ed., *The Dictionary of British and American Women Writers, 1660–1800* (Totowa, N.J.: Rowman & Allanheld, 1985), 19–20.
[26]Michel Foucault, "Nietzsche, Genealogy, History," in *Language, Counter-Memory, Practice: Selected Essays and Interviews by Michel Foucault,* ed. Donald F. Bouchard (Ithaca: Cornell University Press, 1977), 139. For a useful application of Foucault, see the introduction to Katherine Goodman, *Dis/Closures: Women's Autobiography in Germany between 1790 and 1914* (New York: Lang, 1986).
[27]Michel Foucault, *The History of Sexuality* (New York: Random House, 1980), 1:100–101.

absolute silence nor an absolute exclusion which characterizes women's situation in western culture and perpetuates our oppression, but rather a constitutive silence and an assimilated speech."[28] This makes it almost impossible to describe their social positioning in any context in terms of unrelieved oppression or total exclusion. But the last four decades of the eighteenth century can at least be identified as a turning point, if in a limited sense, inasmuch as a group of English and German women—admittedly almost all middle to upper class and relatively well educated—exploited a particular cross-national conjuncture of economic, aesthetic, and discursive developments to appropriate one field of literary articulation, the novel. If many of these writers' works are marked by the unresolved triangular tension between a traditionally enjoined female silence, a decorously assimilated speech, and a certain privilege of expression, then that ambivalence should not be taken as an indication of such novels' triviality or timidity, or used to reinforce criteria by which they become, at best, the evolutionary forerunners of more overtly critical "feminist" texts, or of a unidirectionally plotted Female Great Tradition.

The comparative analysis of the late eighteenth-century women's novel can serve, in fact, as a test case to demonstrate how individual works by women writers can be productively approached not only vis-à-vis their adherence to or divergence from discrete literary traditions (whether defined by language, school, or linear development), but also as part of the formative yet fluid matrix provided by a cross-national continuum of shared female experiences and productive "difficulties." If this, in turn, seems to call for simultaneously negotiating a dangerous number of critical acts of mediation and translation—between two languages, two literatures, two bodies of critical commentary, between social history and literary history, between "popular" and "high" art— such mediation has been the traditionally accorded task, risk, and, above all, pleasure of comparative literature within the institution of literary studies.

[28]Biddy Martin, "Feminism, Criticism, and Foucault" in *New German Critique* 27 (Fall 1982): 18.

6

Emotions Unpurged: Antigeneric Theater and the Politics of Violence

ANCA VLASOPOLOS

> The slaughter of the child Dionysus is an exemplary tale, whose persistence throughout multiple retellings may lead one to wonder whether . . . in the final analysis it does not appeal to some inclination within ourselves.
>
> —Marcel Detienne

Recent developments in dramatic theory and in commentaries on specific authors and plays increasingly point to issues of violence and of violent exclusion. At a time in history when, on the one hand, we have been allowed a glimpse of possibilities for large-scale rearrangements of social contracts in the absence of violence, and, on the other hand, we experience rising familial and intrasocial violence, the link between drama and crisis cries out for reexamination. In 1989 central Europe underwent a revolution unprecedented in human history, and one unforeseen by most analysts of social crises. What was extraordinary about the events symbolized by the taking down of the Berlin Wall was the absence of violence. For once, collective action did not manifest itself in bloody revenge or victimization, not even, with very few exceptions, in the jailing of former leaders. (I am forced to distinguish here between events in central Europe and the unfinished—some say not yet begun—revolutions taking place in eastern Europe, most notably in Romania, Albania, and the former Yugoslavia.) In the former Czechoslovakia, particularly, the overthrow of the regime was linked with the creators of and participants in the experimental drama known as the Magic Lantern.

Yet while against all predictions violence seemed briefly to recede at the national political level for at least one region of the globe, at the "domestic" level violence continues unabated, or is on the rise.[1] In a

---

[1] A graph released by the Senate Judiciary Committee, published in the *Detroit Free Press*, August 1, 1990, 8A, showed a projected increase in homicides from 9,110 in 1960 to 23,200 for 1990. According to *Statistical Abstracts* for 1990 the actual rate rose to approximately 24,871, or 10 homicides per 100,000 U.S. citizens.

single two-year period these news items (some of which were reported nationally and even internationally) made the headlines of the local papers of the sixth largest metropolitan area and eighth largest city in the United States, namely, Detroit: A woman kills her only child, a four-year-old daughter, in an attempt to punish her for "soiling herself," by placing her inside a washing machine and turning on the wash cycle. A man diagnosed as schizophrenic refuses to take his medication, brings his two small sons to his place of employment, a foundry, places them in a ladle, and burns them in the furnace. Encumbered by debts, a twenty-eight-year-old man drives his wife and four children into the Detroit River; the children all drown. A woman and her lover demand custody of her child from the child's foster parents, then proceed to beat the child to death with an extension cord. A man served divorce papers in the morning by his wife shoots her and their two sons dead on the afternoon of the same day. Two girls find a runaway girl's skinned head in a friend's freezer and bring it to the police station; the rest of her body is found buried in the backyard of a suburban home. The coroner calls it a ritual slaying. The number of children shot annually in Detroit exceeds the number of days in the year.

This summary of gruesome news should not be interpreted as an attempt on my part to provide corroborating evidence in support of the epigraph, which naturalizes myth as infanticide and makes narratives of infanticide complicit with either action or desire. Rather, it suggests that as feminists we need to reexamine the obsession with domesticity in nineteenth-century art and our late twentieth-century preoccupation with local knowledge. This shift of interest from the global to the particular can be attributed not so much to the feminization of discourse or the valorization of the underclass as to the bourgeois myth of individualism, which, by presuming that all *men* are created equal, moves the arena of class struggle into the family, into the minute particulars of everyday domestic life. It is here, in the familial sphere, that hierarchy in regard to women, children, and servants (we see the gradual disappearance of the male servant) still holds sway in the same unquestioned and dramatically explosive way as under absolute monarchy or totalitarian regimes. We need to scrutinize both the familial and the political stage in order to uncover societal complicity with the victimization of the powerless.

The explanation that power relations engender a "trickle-down" effect of violence—the master beats the wife, who beats the child, who kicks the servant, who kicks the dog—need not be written off as a simplistic cliché. We live in an era in which the family intrigues of the royal house, the kind that propel the plots of classical tragedies and impinge on the welfare of the entire community, are displaced in favor of ethnic groups and individual families, which gain importance as symptomatic indexes of the community's welfare. As Teresa de Lauretis notes: "Social science research on wife beating . . . is altogether recent; and incest, though long labeled a crime, was thought to be rare and, in any event, not related to (family) violence. In other words, the concept of a form of violence institutionally inherent—if not quite institutionalized—in the family, did not exist as long as the expression 'family violence' did not."[2] We perceive social disorder not merely in terms of a familial microcosm that has replaced the palace macrocosm as a reflection of the health or illness of a society, but as a lateral process, as violence among equals rather than violence spreading *de haut en bas*. A feminist scrutiny of the "domestic" in both its social and its theatrical manifestations is urgently needed, since this vision of society as represented by the family hides the hierarchic nature of both state and family, and it throws responsibility for disorder onto the personal or family unit in a perpetuation of the myth of individuality and equality.

Because of my family's and my personal history, which encompasses extermination, imprisonment, and exile—a history unfortunately all too common—I became interested in theater as the art form that is predicated on the representation of agon, a performance during which someone always loses, and we as spectators are expected to sympathize with the loser in a tragedy and laugh the loser off the stage in a comedy. My history has rendered me more attentive to the process of selecting a loser in drama than to the emotions traditionally elicited by the genres of comedy and tragedy. As a comparatist I am fascinated by the flexibility of theater as it exists in the West. Unlike written texts, which only sporadically become performances and which underwent drastic changes of form as the focus of representation moved from the court to the parlor, theater has retained its performative function, namely, as a collective exchange between actor(s) and spectators, whose terms to be sure are subject to the flux of cultural negotiations, but which has remained more unvaried and formalized than the readerly experience. As a woman who felt best defined politically by a UN refugee identity card stamped "Stateless," I am interested in the way in which theater accustoms us to societally decreed exile or death, especially as the home becomes the stage, and in theater itself as a more disseminated, more translatable commodity than other writings. More important, my aim

[2]Teresa de Lauretis, *Technologies of Gender: Essays on Theory, Film, and Fiction* (Bloomington: Indiana University Press, 1987), 33.

is to discover why theater against the grain, the theater that discloses our complicity with the process of victimage, has been seen by critics—and, if we can believe the testimony of observers, by audiences—as theater that "does not work," as antitheater, as problem plays.

From its earliest connections to ritual, as well as from the literal and figurative space that theater occupied in the ancient world, we can glean its role as both reflection and reinvention of sociopolitical consensus. It is no accident that the first theoretician of theater was also the source of classical culture's most authoritative texts on the physical world and on politics, as well as the tutor to the royal scion who grew up to rule much of the known world. The stage is the world, the theater is the globe, as the Renaissance playwrights never tired of reminding their audience. When the neoclassicists used Aristotle's *Poetics* as a manual of theatrical good behavior, they were not misinterpreting; rather, they were reinventing theater in the context of absolute or gloriously restored monarchies. Similarly, the battle of *Hernani* and the experiments in England with closet drama replicated the polarization of revolutionaries and reactionaries as well as the retreat from urban public art which characterized Romanticism. Theater in the West did not begin to bridge the gap between high culture and popular culture in the nineteenth century until playwrights started to adopt the discourse developed in novels under the rubric of realism and naturalism. In other words, late nineteenth-century theater became aligned with attacks against bourgeois individualism which ironically recall ancient Delphic determinism, and as a basis for their authority playwrights borrowed the prestige of the newly ascendant scientific discourse of medicine on genetics and of natural science on evolution, particularly natural selection. In the collusion between theater and the social sciences, we see the subversion of the rationalist ideal of individualism by the new determinism, which receives its most powerful and, until recently, least examined formulation from psychoanalysis.

What interests me, however, is less the ways in which theater is complicit with the dominant interests of its time than the creation of new borders that goes on in so-called antitheater or problem plays. In order to articulate the resistance of plays such as *Coriolanus, Le misanthrope,* and *Hedda Gabler* to what I regard as our customary acculturation as spectators to the process of victimage, I need first of all to establish the link between clearly defined generic theater and the spectacle of victimization. From my point of view, such a link appears as we move from the classicist view of genre boundaries to the challenge to classicism posed by anthropological applications of the sacrificial ritual, and especially to recent feminist redefinitions of the stage-audience contract that is negotiated through performance.

One need not, as Richard Levin insists, read theatrical texts from the parti pris of irony in order to arrive at the view that drama is par excellence a spectacle about violence.[3] In *Playboys and Killjoys* Harry Levin summarizes the exemplary classicist position: "Conflict is inherent in all drama, and its manner of resolution—whether it favors the protagonists or the antagonistic forces, whether we exult with the victors or condole with the losers—is another distinction between comedy and tragedy."[4] The two principal mainstays of the classical position appear in this admirably terse summary: first, drama is inherently about conflict; and second, drama is divided into two genres, comedy and tragedy, which elicit opposite audience responses to the winners and, implicitly, the losers of the conflict. Tomes have been written to elaborate on these two principles, and, as I shall discuss, critical approaches to individual plays generally begin with considerations of genre, that is, with arguments about the success of the play in creating the ideal generic response of cheering the victor(s) in comedy and lamenting the loser(s) in tragedy. Moreover, arguments about audience response generate critics' analyses of characters in light of these two genres. Again, Harry Levin summarizes the classicist assumptions about genre and its heroes: "If tragedy elicits our compassion, comedy appeals to our self-interest. The former confronts life's failures with noble fortitude, the latter seeks to circumvent them with shrewd nonchalance. . . . The uniqueness of the tragic protagonist is marked by superlatives," whereas comedy neutralizes "tragic potentialities" (14–15).

One unstated assumption of classicists becomes apparent in Levin's statement about audience response to comedy: "Instinctively we sympathize with pleasure-seeking youth, looking through *his* eyes at crabbed age, feeling *his* distrust at whatever stands in the way of fulfilled desire" (96; emphasis added). That assumption is of course glaringly evident in a desire that Levin takes to be universal both in its manifestation and in the sympathy it elicits from the audience, namely, male desire. As feminist critics have noted, the introduction of female desire on stage finds acceptance only if it is represented as male desire in drag; otherwise it leads to problems of genre classification for critics and

---

[3]See Richard Levin, *New Readings versus Old Plays: Recent Trends in the Interpretation of English Renaissance Drama* (Chicago: University of Chicago Press, 1979).

[4]Harry Levin, *Playboys and Killjoys: An Essay on the Theory and Practice of Comedy* (New York: Oxford University Press, 1987), 32; subsequent citations appear in the text.

audience confusion as to where to confer its sympathy, at least according to the critics who record audience reactions. As for tragedy, Aristotle's requirements for the hero in *Poetics* exclude women from that category entirely, although not from being portrayed as characters other than the hero, such as "wives, cousins, friends, slaves," in Gerald Else's witty elucidation of the Greek text.[5] Even when they acknowledge the relation of theater to ritual, classicists see theater as transcending ritual, and consequently they invest it with civilizing power. William Gruber observes that "there is no acting without violence . . . nor drama without some mode of punishment," and he ruefully admits to a willed blindness about the very issue he has raised: "Trying, therefore, to be as cheerful as possible, . . . we might distinguish between virtual and actual victimage." Typically, he discusses audience response as identification and declares that, once identification occurs, "aesthetics suddenly becomes ethics" and "theater offers renewed possibilities for understanding the relationship between the life of a society and the strategies of its art."[6] If the whole notion of unanimous identification becomes suspect not just from a Brechtian but from a feminist perspective, theater may indeed offer possibilities for scrutinizing the relationship between society and the strategies of its spectacles.

Whereas classicists defend the transcending power of theatrical catharsis despite its problematic applicability to gender and class, critics who use anthropology to investigate ritual practices or to analyze the uses of theater emphasize the inextricable connection between theatrical violence and the sacrificial function of the ritual underlying drama. In exploring the dynamics of the narrative opposition between the Orphic account of sacrificial ritual and that of the Aristotelian school of the fourth century, Marcel Detienne concludes about Greek practice: "Political power cannot be exercised without sacrificial practice. Any military or political undertaking . . . must begin with a sacrifice."[7]

Similarly, in tracing the secularization of Greek thought and the political transition from the absolute monarchy of Mycene to the Athenian polis, Jean-Pierre Vernant writes: "Politics, too, had the form of *agon*: an oratorical contest . . . all rivalry, all *eris* presupposes a relationship

[5]Gerald F. Else, *Aristotle's Poetics: The Argument* (Cambridge: Harvard University Press, 1967), 457.

[6]William E. Gruber, *Cosmic Theaters: Studies in Performance and Audience Response* (Athens: University of Georgia Press, 1986), 167, 168.

[7]Marcel Detienne, "Culinary Practices and the Spirit of Sacrifice," in *The Cuisine of Sacrifice among the Greeks*, ed. Marcel Detienne and Jean-Pierre Vernant, trans. Paula Wissing (Chicago: University of Chicago Press, 1989), 3; subsequent citations appear in the text.

of equality: competition can take place only among peers."[8] Without
dwelling on societal crisis per se, both Vernant and Detienne make it
clear that the illusion of equality underlying the political agon and
the sense of unanimity about the sacrificial ritual were intended to
avert large-scale violence by means of the contained and regulated violence of competition and sacrifice. In the first case, Vernant explains,
practices that accentuated social inequality became prohibited: "What
was now extolled was an austere ideal of reserve and restraint, a severe, almost ascetic way of life that obscured differences of manner
and rank between citizens in order to bring them closer together"
(65). In effect, social practices sustained an elaborate system of decep-
tion about the real inequality of the citizens—the male citizens, that
is—precisely so as to avoid violence: "Blood revenge, which had been
limited to a narrow circle but had been obligatory for the relatives of
the dead *man*, and thus could set in motion a disastrous cycle of
murder and reprisal, was supplanted by repression organized by the
city . . . and involving the community as a *whole*" (75; emphasis
added). A passage from Aristotle's *Politics* obliquely hints at the dangers of exceptionality by damning with excessive praise: "When a
family, or some individual, happens to be so pre-eminent in virtue as
to surpass all others, then it is just that they should be the royal family and supreme over all, or that this one citizen should be king of
the whole nation. . . . For surely it would not be right to kill, or ostra-
cize, or exile such a person."[9] It is clear that the question of inequality with regard to gender and class arises only to be repressed in
Greek thought and, as we shall see, arises only recently and sporadically in contemporary thought.

Even if the seeming unanimity of the community were granted, the
ritual designed to mask the victimage was itself fraught with dangers,
since if not rigorously contained the lesser violence could easily have
erupted in social violence. In the case of the sacrificial ritual, Detienne
writes: "There is a desire to play down the violence in the sacrificial
ceremony, as if from the very outset it were necessary to disclaim any
guilt of murder" (9). But, more significant for the performative aspect
is his description: "On a linguistic level it is impossible to separate the
one who is both sacrifier and sacrificer from the one who delegates the
killing to a subordinate. . . . The blurring of distinctions here is fundamental. For what is hidden in this way is the naked act of violence,

[8]Jean-Pierre Vernant, *The Origins of Greek Thought* (Ithaca: Cornell University Press,
1982), 47; subsequent citations appear in the text.
[9]*Politics*, in *Introduction to Aristotle*, ed. and trans. Richard McKeon, 2d rev. ed. (New
York: Random House, 1973), 658.

as if the features, the distinct face of the one who strikes and kills with the ax or knife were best left shrouded in darkness" (12).

Whereas Detienne concentrates on the role of presiding over and/or actually performing the ritual killing—a role that like a mask, covers up individual identity and personal responsibility—Claude Gandelman interprets the tragic mask as a coverup of the victim, "the totemic shape," "the obscene snout of the goat," which he argues is very much the same as the scapegoat of the Hebrew purification ceremony.[10] There seems to be a need to disguise or leave to darkness both those who practice and those upon whom are practiced the contained violence of ritual or of theater as homeotherapy for communal violence.

Two theoreticians who combine Detienne's and Gandelman's interests and who stand Janus-like on opposite sides of the same terrain are René Girard and Victor Turner. Both accept the relation of theater to ritual, and both examine ritual and theater as moments of crisis capable of rending the social fabric. Girard, the literary critic whose passion for anthropology has transformed him into a cultural-religious sage, sees the ritual of victimage as a narrative or performance that disguises itself under a point of view that is always that of the sacrificing crowd; the only text that goes against this master narrative and undermines the unanimous point of view is the New Testament.[11] Girard argues passionately for the truth of victimage narratives. He refuses them the pure invention of fantasy, since he finds that persecutors, by taking their righteousness for granted, are too naive to dissimulate. A text such as *Oedipus Rex*, however, needs to be stripped of its illusory logic in order to be made to disclose its sacrificial narrative. Thus we may conclude that Girard views theater as a more complicated and ambivalent setting for sacrifice than historical narratives.

By contrast, Turner begins as an anthropologist with a passion for literature, and in his cultural critique presents a much more optimistic, less Eurocentric view of ritual and theater. By examining the phases of social crisis, which in his description seem to share features of the classical-theater plots, Turner arrives at the conclusion that crisis and its resolution do not necessarily result in murderous unanimity nor in the restoration of the status quo.[12] His pattern, which seemed naively sunny

[10]Claude Gandelman, "The Semitic Catharsis, Greek Tragedy, Christian Missa," *Stand* 21.4 (1977): 43.

[11]See René Girad, *Violence and the Sacred*, trans. Patrick Gregory (Baltimore: Johns Hopkins University Press, 1977), and *The Scapegoat*, trans. Yvonne Freccero (Baltimore: Johns Hopkins University Press, 1986).

[12]See Victor Turner, *Dramas, Fields, and Metaphors: Symbolic Action in Human Society* (Ithaca: Cornell University Press, 1974).

a decade ago, seems to have prophesied the central European revolution of 1989–90 much more accurately than Girard's insistence on Judaeo-Christian revelation as the only path to abjuring violence. The contrast that I find significant in Turner's and Girard's expositions of societal crisis is that for Turner the crisis can move a group in a given society to a transitory utopian plane, where experimentation and creative disorder crystallize into new forms of social order, so that when the inevitable return to everyday social intercourse is reestablished, the radical changes experienced by those partaking of the utopian *communitas* are partially incorporated in the new order; whereas for Girard the return after the sacrificial crisis is always to the status quo, to a community dominated by fear of mimetic violence and periodically united in a murderous determination to avoid it by means of the contained violence of sacrificial ritual.

Despite these fundamental differences, Turner and Girard remain committed to a belief in unanimity, whether in the case of *communitas* or victimizing community, and they represent crises ultimately as the unifying agents of society in a monolithic, unproblematized way very similar to the classicists' views of audience response to genre. In effect, the unanimity they describe often consists of decisions made by leaders and followed by their dependents or prisoners, the two latter categories having no choice but to seem to go along, since their dissent either could not be articulated or remains unrecorded. In other words, the history of a crisis is always the after-the-fact inscription or remembrance of the sacrificer, not the victim. As an intended victim whose recollections are heard because his rescuers won, Primo Levi recounts the historical foresight of his would-be butchers:

> However this war may end, we have won the war against you; none of you will be left to bear witness, but even if someone were to survive, the world will not believe him. There will perhaps be suspicions, discussions, research by historians, but there will be no certainties, because we will destroy the evidence together with you. And even if some proof should remain and some of you survive, people will say that the events you describe are too monstrous to be believed: they will say that they are the exaggerations of Allied propaganda and will believe us, who will deny everything, and not you. We will be the ones to dictate the history of the Lagers.[13]

Thus, for someone like me, Girard's seeming exception, the New Testament, represents not the scapegoat story told from the point of view

[13]Primo Levi, *The Drowned and the Saved*, trans. Raymond Rosenthal (New York: Simon & Schuster, 1988), 11.

of the victim, but the victory of Judaeo-Christian religion over older or concurrent forms of worship, such as Wicce or the Gnostic Gospels, whose practitioners were systematically victimized and whose alternative narratives were silenced by the Church Triumphant.

If we examine the operations of ritual and theater from the angle not of the silenced victims but of those excluded from participation, we discern the hierarchy that dominates both performances and hides under the mask of unanimity. In regard to ritual, Detienne's examination of Thesmophoria reveals both the exclusivity of sacrificial rituals in the Greek city and Greek men's fearful imaginings about the single festival celebrated only by women. First, the ritual within the city: "With respect to sacrifice, it is the female population that forms the most important category of marginals. . . . They are kept apart from the altars, meat, and blood . . . they are admitted into the larger circle of commensals only by the intermediary of someone having the right to obtain for them this favored treatment. At a sacrifice, particularly a blood sacrifice, women cannot function as full adults." Yet, despite the clear separation between the category "woman" and blood sacrifice, which extends to a linguistic barrier—"the word [mageiros] has no feminine form . . . the Greek system does not allow any thought of women as butchers and sacrificers"—narratives about Thesmophoria indicate not only a preoccupation on the part of men to identify "woman" but a deeply ingrained fear of what women may do when they escape from under the control of male hierarchy. As Detienne relates:

> This fear, which attributes homicidal—or "androcidal"—projects to the most domestic of women is . . . reborn in the contradiction manifest in a festival in which women among themselves are assuredly the exemplary "lawful wives" of citizens but in which a city, now the exclusive property of women, at last possesses the weapons of sacrifice and thereby threatens the "other" city—all the more so because the strictly male prerogative to kill and slaughter has fallen into the hands of the best of the race of women.[14]

Significantly, this feared group of marginals comprises only the protected, respectable women of the polis. Nothing is said on the subject of those who, in addition to being women, also threaten the hierarchy by remaining unassigned, so to speak, to the ownership of any one male and who therefore have no legal right to representation or to sacrificial meat. May not these undifferentiating, anarchic agents, who,

[14]Marcel Detienne, "The Violence of Well-Born Ladies: Women in the Thesmophoria," in Detienne and Vernant, *Cuisine of Sacrifice*, 131–32, 143, 147.

despite their imaginary power, are forbidden access to weapons, become themselves the ideal target of victimage? And since Detienne himself depends for his investigation of Thesmophoria on narratives of the imaginary, may we not see theater as the meeting place of hierarchical order and the hallucinatory fear of the "other"?

Detienne's suggestive speculations receive ample support from Page duBois's *Centaurs and Amazons,* an extensive study of the link between gender and hierarchy in Greek thought and in classical-theater representation. DuBois posits a shift in discourse from Aeschylus to Aristotle that can be briefly, and I hope not reductively, summarized as constructing difference through analogy versus constructing difference by hierarchy. She dubs these modes literary/poetic and philosophic, respectively, and she reads in both an obsession with boundaries, which changes focus from seeing the world divided into enemies without versus Greeks within to an attempt to discover the enemies within the polis and even within the sacred space itself. Occupying the category "enemies," centaurs, Amazons, and foreigners were seen to hold in common a disregard for "ordered festivity." But this necessity of identifying the enemy within, which, as we shall see, is the driving motive for the process of victimage, may work in the same way as the imaginary narratives surrounding Thesmophoria, that is, those most likely to find themselves as victims on the altar and those excluded from contact with the weapons of sacrifice become the ones charged with disrupting or inverting the sacrificial economy. DuBois writes: "If, in the changed social and economic situation, the enemy was discovered within, a new rationalization of internal political control was necessary; the theory of natural hierarchy is that rationalization." Her conclusion serves to bring to the fore some of the reasons why issues of gender, class, and foreignness (which includes race) have so often not entered classicists' considerations of the unanimity of audience response and social crisis interpreters' views of societal consensus: "The project of this philosophy, from its earliest expression in Plato and Aristotle, was from its beginnings centered on questions of hierarchy, of mind over body, man over woman, "human" over foreigner, over slave. The model of dominance, with its concomitant dualism, as a description of natural relationships in all cases, survived as a defining structure in post-Platonic and post-Aristotelian discourse."[15]

Indeed, this model of dominance, as Sander Gilman shows, survives in the dominant scientific and medical discourses of the nineteenth and

---

[15]Page duBois, *Centaurs and Amazons* (Ann Arbor: University of Michigan Press, 1982), 29, 145, 152.

twentieth centuries, in which difference is defined as pathology and is exemplified by sex, race, and class. A merging of the three as a marker of pathology appears in law courts, fiction, and the visual arts, as well as in late nineteenth-century theater.[16]

The complicity between theater and patriarchal order has not escaped feminist critics of drama. The dominance of the Aristotelian discourse in dramatic theory has, however, led to an attempt by many simply to write off all theater except for feminist-written or improvised and feminist-produced all-female performances. Although this rather separatist move (I use the qualifying "rather" because some feminist theater critics do preserve vestiges of Marx and Brecht in their prescriptions for a new theater) does raise issues of audience division and performative subversion, it nevertheless remains caught in the problematics of essentialism. Both Sue-Ellen Case and Jill Dolan, for instance, examine the myth of audience unanimity succinctly. On the basis of Aristotle's definition of women and slaves in *Poetics* and *Politics*, Case declares: "Denied tragic qualities, cleverness, authority of deliberation and the right to speak, women seem to be excluded from the dramatic experience." She sees a parallel between theater and society: "Along with the suppression of the public appearance of the female gender, its metaphorical appearance in cultural productions became suppressed as well: the absence of women's voices in literature, philosophy, theology and other branches of learning was the counterpart of their absence from [church] choirs and the stage." There is, however, a danger in equating the world with the stage: archival studies by feminist scholars have unearthed abundant evidence of women's voices in fields previously regarded as the exclusive preserve of men. The question of interrupted transmission, of course, remains. For Case, the emergence of women on stage does not mitigate what she calls "the alliance of theatre with patriarchal prejudice," since when women do make their appearance, they fulfill the "fiction of the female gender," representing the gendered female body rather than a genuine female point of view.[17]

Dolan goes even farther in denying not only the idea of audience unanimity but the very notion of identification being possible for the feminist spectator, who "sees in the performance frame representatives of her gender class with whom she might identify—if women are represented at all—acting passively before the specter of male authority."

[16]Sander Gilman, *Difference and Pathology: Stereotypes of Sexuality, Race, and Madness* (Ithaca: Cornell University Press, 1985).

[17]Sue-Ellen Case, *Feminism and Theatre* (London: Macmillan, 1988), 18, 21, 19, 27.

The only position Dolan envisions for the feminist spectator is one of critical distance, a female Brechtian alienation: "A materialist feminist critique can recuperate some of [Brecht's] theories to focus on representation's perpetuation of social relations of gender, race, and sexuality, as well as class."[18]

My own difficulty with this position is twofold. First, a categorical rejection of empathy that speaks for all feminist spectators silences dissent in the same way as the classicists' assertions about audience identification with male desire. I am not willing to relinquish my viewpoint as feminist spectator because at certain performance times I have identified with a female character in a play. I think that Dolan and Case deny the subversive power of a great actor, director, or ensemble, which can undermine and explode any designs that patriarchal intent may have had in the construction of the play. Second, if the position of the feminist spectator is always that of the outsider able to deconstruct the culture, just where is that privileged "outside" which allows the feminist spectator to remain immune to the influence of her own culture in the construction of her own gendered, racial, class-bound self? I believe these acts of transcendence are easier to theorize than to practice. Perhaps more useful to my own recuperative project is Barbara Freedman's more problematized approach to genre and to the tension between what she calls "narrative drama," the male plot, and " 'theatricality' or 'performance,' " which can function so as to disrupt the former. Initially, she too gives us a classicist position à rebours in regard to genre: "As with our political party system and our gender system, traditional Western theatre offers us only two stages, comic and tragic, upon which are always playing some version of Oedipus or its sister play, The Taming of the Shrew." Yet Freedman recognizes that while agonistic theater needs the mask of gender and class, it also "points to the masquerade." Moreover, she concludes that theater through spectacle manages a space not strictly bound by language, where surprising reversals can occur: "Theatre is the place where a male ruling class has been able to play at being the excluded other. . . . If theatre has offered men a chance to identify with the place of a mother's look, to imitate the mother's desire, and to control the woman's looking back, theatre also offers the opportunity to reframe that moment from a point of view alien to it."[19]

---

[18]Jill Dolan, The Feminist Spectator as Critic (Ann Arbor: UMI Research Press, 1988), 2, 107.

[19]Barbara Freedman, "Frame-up: Feminism, Psychoanalysis, Theatre," in Performing Feminisms, ed. Sue-Ellen Case (Baltimore: Johns Hopkins University Press, 1990), 58, 60, 74.

We can see the moments of unease, of generic slippage, in theater as the cracking of the mask that reveals the masquerade beneath it and with that revelation puts into question the stability of assumptions about genre, which after all are assumptions about unanimity on issues such as gender, class, and race. Once put in question, this illusory unanimity, which represents the required first step toward the process of victimage, can be shattered, and the effect that Brecht much after the fact describes as alienation can break up the audience's unity of emotion, can transform the audience from mob to uneasy individuals aware of their differing, ambivalent, complex reactions to the spectacle before them. In transgressing the boundaries of genre, and implicitly of the social hierarchy supported by genre, antigeneric theater serves as the limen, that unstable and undefined border that offers both a critique of the status quo and a provisional glimpse of what a different social arrangement might be. In the twentieth century, in which the antigenre becomes normative, we see at least one instance of the victimized becoming .president of a republic. But before we can rejoice in the transformative power of the critique and of the practice of nonviolence, we must remember that political revolutions have remained for the most part all-male affairs, as the theater (with few, but more and more visible, exceptions) remains a predominantly male art form.

Where, why, and how do those moments of generic blurring, which question hierarchic arrangements based on victimage, occur? In attempting to arrive at answers, will I be defining a third theatrical genre or redefining the hybrid that we encounter in theater history as tragicomedy, mixed-genre play, dark comedy, problem play, bourgeois tragedy? Like any contemporary critic I am beset by a sense of belatedness in undertaking a discussion of genre. Jean-Marie Schaeffer argues that "a radical change in conception [about genre] occurred toward the end of the eighteenth century; henceforth literary theory would no longer be conceived as a descriptive and/or normative activity but as a speculative, interpretive undertaking. . . . The objective of the generic theory was to interpret the existence and intrinsic organization of this new object: why and how does literature exist?" Though I would disagree with his interpretation of the classical era as one in which a "hierarchy [among genres] is purely axiological and does not lead to a global logical structuration or to a system," the question with which I began this section places me squarely in the wake of the "radical change" that Schaeffer detects at the end of the eighteenth century. Nevertheless, in speaking of antigeneric theater as a genre, I am in complete agreement with Schaeffer's analysis of the relation of genre and individual text:

"Every text, inasmuch as it is grasped in its genesis, is always logically either posterior or anterior to a given generic classification. . . . Far from being definable with the aid of genre, it is the individual text that decides, in part, what a contingent ulterior generic definition will be."[20] He concludes that, being inevitably retrospective, generic classification cannot be interpretive; yet in the history of dramatic criticism, generic classification has always had not only an interpretive value but the power to lend legitimacy and respectability to individual texts.[21] Schaeffer's argument about text and genre, however, can be usefully applied to moments in the history of theater such as the almost universal declaration in the twentieth century of "the death of tragedy," which represents a break in twentieth-century theater from retrospective generic norms toward a norm whose very plethora of names (theater of cruelty, theater of the absurd, street theater, guerrilla theater, living theater) shows the undecidability and multiplicity of its generic conventions. I would, however, argue for antecedents to this twentieth-century antinorm, plays that anticipate the slipperiness of genre by breaking the generic codes that they themselves summon only to betray, with the effect of producing the unease that begins to crack the ideology of classical genre.

The plays I have chosen as representative are firmly entrenched in the canon of theater. It may seem peculiar for a feminist critic to devote herself exclusively to a comparative analysis of drama written solely by male authors, and canonized male authors at that. Yet as a feminist and comparatist I hope always to labor in the shadow of my obsolescence as critic. The issues that unite, divide, and continue to consume us, issues eminently present in these plays, will, I hope, be superseded by future generations, and the forms of their theater be as incomprehensible to us as our preoccupations will be to them. On that utopian note, let me turn to the specific topos of the three plays I have selected: *Coriolanus, Le misanthrope,* and *Hedda Gabler.*[22]

In the context of a generic breakdown and the resultant confrontation

---

[20]Jean-Marie Schaeffer, "Literary Genres and Textual Genericity," in *The Future of Literary Theory,* ed. Ralph Cohen (London: Routledge, 1989), 168, 169, 175.

[21]See Dolan, *Feminist Spectator as Critic,* 22, on the Aristotelian pedigree that Robert Brustein felt compelled to give Marsha Norman's play *'night, Mother* so that it might be considered serious theater.

[22]I am at work on a study of antigeneric drama which will include the three plays mentioned here and two twentieth-century plays, discussed extensively in my essays, "Authorizing History: Victimization in *A Streetcar Named Desire,*" *Theatre Journal* 38.3 (1986): 322–34, rpt. in *Feminist Rereadings of Modern American Drama,* ed. June Schlueter (London: Associated University Presses, 1989), 149–70; and "The Perils of Authorship in *Le voyageur sans bagage,*" *Modern Drama* 29 (1986): 601–12.

of the audience with an imperfectly masked process of victimage, these three plays present continuities in terms of resistance to genre while at the same time they are discontinuous in regard to culture-specific features. I do not wish to argue that these plays are exemplary of anti-generic theater, since I hope that if my methods and aims in this investigation gain credence, a reader may come up with equally representative selections of plays that have resisted genre and, implicitly, the unanimity of response ideally elicited by classical tragedy and comedy. In addition, I hope that we might gain enough wisdom from history so that as active participants in performance—actors, director, audience—we may deconstruct such "exemplary" texts as *The Merchant of Venice,* as has, in fact, been the case in post–World War II productions of the play.[23] In other words, despite valiant efforts by Richard Levin and Northrop Frye to make us accept Shylock as the traditional Renaissance vice and thus quiet our unease, it has become increasingly difficult not to hear echoes of the contemporary meaning of ghetto and not to see in the black-clad figure the concentration camp scapegoat of European civilization. We can only hope that other exemplary texts such as *The Tempest* and *The Taming of the Shrew* will produce, and be produced with, the same representational unease.

The plays that I have selected have in common a number of salient points that prove particularly fruitful for a comparative analysis. First, in each the focus directs itself relentlessly to the hero; there are few if any scenes in which the hero is absent, and there are virtually no subplots. Despite this intense concentration of plot on the hero's actions and presence, she/he never rises to tragic stature or descends to the status of comic vice. Thus, in traditional generic terms there is no tragic fall or comic expulsion. Second, the hero lives in a period of sociopolitical and economic crisis that she/he exemplifies or embodies. Third, the hero insists on sociopolitical and ethical distinctions in a historical moment when society is on the brink of dissolving or altering those very distinctions. Ultimately, what these plays have in common is the place they hold in my consciousness as "sore thumbs" of canon and repertory. It is not surprising that three plays written before the twentieth century have enjoyed more of a vogue in contemporary late twen-

---

[23]For instance, a 1974 television production of *Merchant,* with Laurence Olivier in the role of Shylock, ends with a cantor's voice singing the kaddish, the traditional Jewish prayer for the dead. This superimposition not only suggests Shylock's death and his daughter's remorse, but turns the traditional golden comedy reconciliation into a view of assimilation, for both Jessica and Shylock a kind of death, figurative in her case and literal in his.

tieth-century repertory, in which generic breakdown is far less startling, than in their own time.

I do not want the solidus in she/he to obscure the fact of gender, which becomes more self-consciously complicated as we move into the nineteenth and twentieth centuries. I have deliberately chosen to refer to the main character in each play as the hero, regardless of gender, because the word *protagonist* should be used sparingly in the case of these problematized heroes, and the word *heroine* connotes passivity: the heroine is the figure the hero sets out to rescue. In fact, the question of gender, which is explicitly raised in *Hedda Gabler*, is intricately tied to the critique of genre ideology posed by these plays. Whereas in *Coriolanus* and *Le misanthrope* Shakespeare and Molière use gender differences and the collapse of these differences to opposite ends but without offering a direct critique of the very notion of gender differentiation, in *Hedda Gabler* victimage is represented in ways that are further problematized by the questioning of gender identity which cuts across class differences.

Both *Coriolanus* and *Le misanthrope* bring up issues of hierarchy, differentiation, and lack thereof, and treat the problem of disposing of individuals who, as Aristotle puts it, are "pre-eminent in virtue." It is no use arguing that Coriolanus and Alceste are unpleasant persons; that characteristic, decidedly, is a component of exceptional virtue, and should not be, as Aristotle seems to tell us, a criterion for exile in a just society. Yet their very unpleasantness, especially that of Coriolanus, provokes a desire on the part of the audience to approve of the victimage inexorably taking shape in the plot. Coriolanus is not an Oedipus or an Othello or a Lear whose fate we can lament as a means of reconciling ourselves to the inevitability of making scapegoats of outsiders or of dispossessed old people.[24] The play confronts us with our own intolerance by presenting us both with the spectacle of a country putting itself in jeopardy because it cannot tolerate the very *virtù* it extols, and with our own desire to comply with the sacrifice of so unlikable a hero. We are allowed to lament Othello's fall from power through Iago's manipulations without acknowledging that Othello is never more

[24]In *Totem and Taboo*, trans. James Strachey (New York: Norton, 1950), Freud postulates that tragedy reenacts the primal horde of brothers killing the father and sees the tragic spectacle as a "systemic distortion," as "the product of a refined hypocrisy" in which the victim is responsible for its victimage and the killers console themselves with laments for their victim (156). Although I agree with his deconstruction of tragic guilt, his fantasy of the primal horde is a projection of adult males fearful of losing power onto the children they would forestall from growing up to supplant them. The tragic hero combines features of the father with the status of orphan child, the latter being the chief figure of the dispossessed in Western literature.

than a pawn, used by the Christian Venetian Republic to hold his own people at bay or to help conquer them; his susceptibility to Iago stems from his already marginal position as exotic monster. *King Lear* allows us to lament the fate of dispossessed old men when in reality it is daughters and bastard sons who are dispossessed and sacrificed by powerful old men; thus the sacrifice we lament obtains our acquiescence to the further oppression of daughters and bastard sons, which in the universe of *King Lear* seems merited.

In *Le misanthrope* Alceste defeats comic expectations, as much as Coriolanus deviates from tragic expectations in Shakespeare's play. Alceste is neither the *jeune premier*, exemplary of youthful male desire, whom Harry Levin's audience presumably wishes to see triumph over elderly blocking agents, as if romance were an agon between young and old men, not the coming together of sexually attracted partners; nor is Alceste a Malvolio, easily relegated to his dark prison and then ruthlessly exiled from the joyous new order. The ambivalence we feel toward these heroes cracks the mask and allows us to perceive the plots of tragedy and comedy as the oft-repeated tales that make us acquiesce to selective slaughter, so long as we, as the Greek chorus iterates, lie low, pretend to equality, take refuge in mediocrity, and thus escape notice.

In *Coriolanus* the societal crisis with which the play opens requires a victim, and from the very first scene we are witness to the connection already established in the mob's mind between Coriolanus, commensal equality ("Let us kill him, and we'll have corn at our own price"), and excessive virtue ("What he hath done famously he did it to that end"), that is, the kind of grating, explicit excellence that disturbs the illusion of equality to the point of negating it. Much has been written about the class struggle in *Coriolanus*, but no commentator has noted the unity of purpose of patricians and plebeians, the near-unanimity about the victim, which is expressed in united attempts by patricians and plebeians to point to Coriolanus' eccentricity and exceptionality.[25] In fact, it is the patricians, not the plebeians, who "monsterize" Coriolanus in order to render him fit for the sacrifice. But in what sense is the first warrior of the nation a marginal character whose sacrifice contains rather than spreads the violence of the crisis? The most interesting, because least expected, among the general accusations brought against the potential victim is the accusation that Coriolanus' virtue is not manly: "What he

[25]See Kenneth Burke, *Language as Symbolic Action: Essays on Life, Literature, and Method* (Berkeley: University of California Press, 1966), 86–87; Paul A. Cantor, *Shakespeare's Rome: Republic and Empire* (Ithaca: Cornell University Press, 1976), 57; and Norman Rabkin, *Shakespeare and the Problem of Meaning* (Chicago: University of Chicago Press, 1981), 111.

hath done famously . . . he did it to please his mother." It becomes clear that Coriolanus, like Oedipus, is a young man without patriarchal relations. The figure of Volumnia as the unhoused wrath of "the best of the race of women," as Detienne describes lawful wives, becomes the focus of the greatest unease in the play. Her son is her power, her right to virtue and to commensals, and his link to her rather than to surrogate fathers in a society personified through Menenius' tale of the belly as a body without a head disrupts hierarchic arrangements more strongly than the plebeians' demands for representation. We never see Volumnia in her own house; in the only domestic setting, with Virgilia, she tries to tempt the young woman out of her womanly occupation. When she engages Virgilia on her side in the brawl of words with the two tribunes, they are in the street, and their public anger makes Sicinius ask, "Are you mankind?"—a question that will shortly be asked about Coriolanus in his role as Volscian general. The Amazon, the beastly, the nonhuman, and the foreign have combined into the enemy that attacks from both within and without. Only when Volumnia acknowledges her rightful habitation and name, that is, when she describes herself as the womb of *patria*, does she regain her status as Roman matron and participant in her son's sacrifice.

Coriolanus suffers first exile and then death through metaphorical emasculation, which implicitly restores social balance by a proper redefinition of gender roles. Just as the "altitude of his virtue" is interpreted by the Roman populace as part unmanly attachment to his mother and part self-serving gesture, so his exile is interpreted by the patricians and by Aufidius as lack of control. Before his death he is accused again of unmanly regard for "his nurse's tears" and is verbally reduced to a "boy of tears." His overt emasculation, combined with his having severed his ties to his *patria*, qualifies him for the role of sacrificial victim whom no one will avenge. His murder restores the illusion of equality in both Roman and Volscian societies, since neither side now possesses an invincible warrior whose singularity provokes envy and fear; it also more subtly but significantly restores the proper hierarchy of the sexes with the apotheosis of Volumnia and Virgilia as the matrons whose womanly appeals saved the state and deprived the widowed mother of her too powerful champion.

Conversely, in *Le misanthrope*, which depicts a society in which the desideratum is the metaphoric and economic emasculation of the nobility, traditionally "male" values create a potential for violence that must be contained; throughout the play the means of control is a ritualized choreography of social *bienséances*. I use the dance metaphor deliberately, taking my cue from the court dances that emphasized the interchangeability of partners and the necessity of not fixing on any one partner. The person who refuses to dance in step is literally expulsed. The sublimation of violence in a code of rigidly structured social constructions has its parallel in instances of extreme violence of language (interestingly, less on Alceste's part than on the other characters') contained in the formal and stately alexandrines. Perhaps the most explicit moment of rivaling discourses that the play exposes is the contest between Oronte's generic sonnet and Alceste's much more culturally specific ballad. Critics have regarded the affair of the sonnet as an example of Molière's genius at creating an absurd farcical situation.

The matter of the sonnet, however, becomes the subject, on the one hand, of a serious critique of the language of sentiment at and around the court of Louis XIV and, on the other, of a satire of the legal system, a satire that is sustained in the rest of the play as well and that has received little critical attention. The trials of Alceste, in both senses of the word, seem marginal to the romantic plot, but they determine the sacrificial character of Alceste's exile. In the first instance, Oronte presents Alceste with an unexceptionable love sonnet that captures every convention of the times. The classical names themselves, like those in Molière's comedy, are interchangeable, identified only by gender. The sentiments expressed strike the proper balance of a desire nicely contained by wordplay. When Alceste counters with his ballad, he names names (of king, of city) and invokes an aesthetic of excessive passion that not only is disinterested—it refuses the exchange of the city of Paris for one's love—but that putatively defies the king, albeit Henry IV and not the present one. Typically, Alceste resists and even combats the principle of interchangeability which keeps court hierarchy strictly dependent on the king's notice rather than on personal merit. He places private passion and loyalty above the public necessity of *bienséance,* of an undifferentiation that reminds us of the Greek polis and the ideal of *sophrosyne.*

Similarly, in the matter of his *procès,* Alceste again places himself in opposition to the forms required by his social milieu. He refuses to solicit the judges, letting his case stand on its individual merit. When he loses this trial, a loss foreshadowed by his loss of the earlier trial about Oronte's sonnet, he is forced to flee so as not to be thoroughly dispossessed and imprisoned. This outcome of the legal system is often overlooked by critics, who feel that Alceste's decision to retire from society is purely personal, based on his failure to impose his ways on everyone, including Célimène.[26] But if Molière intended a critique of

[26]See J. D. Hubert, *Molière and the Comedy of Intellect* (New York: Russell & Russell,

court society and of the legal system, he could hardly have made it central to his play. The only way he could introduce it would be through oblique references to Alceste as a man pursued by the law. Instead, the central discovery in the plot of *Le misanthrope* is Célimène's betrayal. This centerpiece is an extraordinary tour de force in Molière's play since it exposes precisely the kind of interchangeability to which Alceste has been objecting throughout; the lovers become in turn an excuse for Célimène's exercise of wit. She uses differentiation only to ridicule them, thus in effect to level them again into a heap of equally hopeless aspirants to her hand. The speed with which all the lovers but Alceste turn on her indicates the submerged craving for the kind of personal differentiation forbidden them by their society and underlines the collective desire for victimizing the rule breaker. Neither Célimène nor Alceste is chosen at random as victim; the first is an unprotected woman who, unlike Arsinoë, seems not to have powerful connections, and the second is a man who is on the wrong side of law and who declines to seek influence at court. Unlike the woman, whose breach, though spectacular, is confined to a single detected instance, the man, who reminds this assembly of petty aristocrats of their loss of personal distinction, is continually both sought after and reviled, and ultimately he serves as scapegoat, taking into the desert the unpardonable vice of unmasking everyone's forbidden desire for individuality.

There are critics who regard any defense of Alceste as a Rousseau-like romanticizing of a farcical hero, yet whose very insistence that we should have no sympathy for Alceste points to the fact that Alceste elicits divided responses as *honnête homme* and as object of desire.[27] Unless we are prepared to accept every other character in *Le misanthrope* as a type of humor or a clown, we have to account for Alceste's attractiveness insofar as the other characters are concerned. He is perpetually being courted by men and women who seek to be distinguished, individualized, by his regard. Ironically, their very pursuit of Alceste makes them less individuated, since the foolish and obnoxious Arsinoë and Oronte, as well as the *honnêtes* Philinte and Eliante, strive to obtain or maintain his esteem. The only way in which Alceste makes himself ridiculous is in his role as lover of a woman who refuses as adamantly

1962); and James F. Gaines, *Social Structures in Molière's Theater* (Columbus: Ohio State University Press, 1984).

[27]For the opinion that Alceste is purely comic, see Lionel Grossman, "Molière's *Misanthrope:* Melancholy and Society in the Age of the Counterreformation," *Theatre Journal* 34.3 (1982): 323–43; Nathan Gross, *From Gesture to Idea: Esthetics and Ethics in Molière's Comedy* (New York: Columbia University Press, 1982); Roger Ikor, *Molière double* (Vendôme: Presses Universitaires de France, 1977); and Robert McBride, *The Skeptical Vision of Molière: A Study in Paradox* (New York: Barnes & Noble, 1977).

to distinguish between him and her other lovers as he adamantly refuses to accept the *bienséance* of interchangeability. But, unlike Malvolio,
Alceste is not laughed off the stage as the unsuitable lover. He is chased
away by the law, and our last glimpse of him is of his being in turn
chased after by the two most typically reasonable characters in the play,
Philinte and Eliante, who hope to persuade him to return.

With *Hedda Gabler* we arrive at a late nineteenth-century variation on
Molière's critique of a society in which individual differences are reduced to the frequency of one's attendance on the king's bodily functions. Ibsen presents us with a virulent portrayal of a bourgeois
invention, the romantic triangle, a situation that presumably heightens
individuation and desire, but in Ibsen's play is exposed as a suffocating,
self-perpetuating domestic arrangement in which individuals merely
take their places and are at best able to change positions, but which
they cannot escape without being victimized. In his choice of an upper-
class hero who chafes not only at middle-class values but at gender
expectations, Ibsen takes up the class and sex issues that preoccupied
nineteenth-century society. By choosing the unconventional woman as
an aristocratic leftover soon to be disposed of, many writers of the
period were able to remain politically pure in their allegiance to the
bourgeoisie and at the same time to deal a blow to the notion of female
enfranchisement. Ibsen, however, evades this mode of stereotyping. Instead of presenting class and sex as weak-willed, morally corrupt, and
parasitic upon the energetic nouveaux bourgeois, Ibsen reduces the
characters in *Hedda Gabler*, regardless of their sex, age, and class, to
rivals and objects of desire.

The play makes clear that Hedda's suicide has nothing to do with
either of the popular bourgeois themes of late nineteenth-century art:
aristocratic degeneracy and/or lack of true womanliness. The interchangeability of participants in the triangular mobile of desire which
Ibsen constructs levels any claims to superiority that the middle class
might make and subtly undermines the sex-role differentiation imposed
by the bourgeois division of public and private spheres. By removing
or eliminating one member of the triangle, obsessive rivalries produce
victims, so that the balance of the binary arrangement, be it the romantic, the mother-son, or father-daughter couple, may be temporarily restored. We see the process of victimage in full force in *Hedda Gabler*. In
fact, we see little else. First, Ibsen prepares us for the bourgeois tragedy
of a man in love who is brought to financial ruin by a ruthless woman.
Then we see Hedda being victimized by her husband and his aunt, and
we see her in turn victimizing the aunt and the servant. The arrival of
Thea provides us with another, more likely possibility for victimage—

the unprotected woman who has left her home to be with her lover, who requires her protection rather than offering her any shelter against opprobrium. Discussed both as victim, "the black sheep of the family," and as victimizer, Lövborg, like Tesman, is another candidate for a more and more frenzied search for victimage. The Dionysian imagery, despite the seemingly commonplace circumstances, provides an apt reminder of the shift that has taken place in theater from classicism to realism in terms of the spaces in which violence occurs: the street, the marketplace, the Senate in *Coriolanus;* the street and exceedingly public salon of *Le misanthrope;* and finally the drawing room and "inner" space of *Hedda Gabler.*

We also see a domestication of violence that directs itself against children, symbolic or unborn though they may be, both as obstacles to romance and as inextricable ties between parents. The Oedipus complex may prove to be the ultimate bourgeois expression of male and female jealousy of the intrusive third party, who conveniently is the most easily victimized intruder as well. In its critique of domesticity and class pretentions to moral superiority, *Hedda Gabler* makes nonsense of the bourgeois ideal of the hearth as refuge from the cruel world of agonistic competition and of the then-current scientific theories of evolutionary superiority and eugenics.

Ultimately, then, what antigeneric drama does is refuse us the easy consolation of a resolved sacrificial crisis. In the sacrificial ritual "the animal selected as victim is led without apparent constraint in a procession to the altar. . . . The ritual takes care to obtain the animal's consent by a sign of the head . . . of its assent at the moment of libation in order to believe that no injustice had indeed been committed."[28] The tragic heroes as well as the comic vices accommodate the audience in assenting to their own sacrifice either by recognizing that their fate is their own fault or by being so unyielding as to demand their expulsion and defeat. The heroes in antigeneric drama are an uneasy bunch to live with. They act in ways that implicate them in the process of victimage; they expose themselves as unprotected characters must not do, but they resist victimage. Even when they go to a willed death, like Hedda, they do so on their own terms and to frustrate the sacrificial fate prepared for them, that is, to turn sacrifice into what it rightly is— murder. The plots of these plays, tending toward indeterminacy of genre and thus theatrical improbability, give the game away by swaying audiences in various directions at various times, making audiences uncertain about their own responses, their own ability to detect the

---

[28]Detienne, "Culinary Practices," 9–10.

truth. This is the ultimate gift of antigeneric drama: destabilizing our certainties, making us uneasy, giving us a glimpse of the violent processes in which we participate daily without recognizing them for what they are so long as violence is kept from affecting us directly. A split vision forbids mob gatherings; our own desire to do away with unpleasant people, coupled with our consciousness of a process in which victims are chosen for reasons other than their deserving to be victims, makes for a reflexivity without catharsis. We carry the bitterness of this spectacle with us.

It is perhaps all too easy to detect the power and designs of theatrical genre in a century in which theater has become normatively nongeneric and altogether borderline as an art form. I suspect that the forms that acculturate us to accept the horrors of our world and our implicit participation in them remain hidden to us, in their artistic imaginings as well as in their daily manifestations. But my hope is that we will continue to remain skeptical of victorious truths, that we will resist the power of too unanimous a persuasion, from whatever quarter it may come. And thus I argue against too vast a success for my own argument. What is at stake in such resistance, literally, is our lives.

7

Cassandra's Question: Do Women Write War Novels?

MARGARET R. HIGONNET

> I do not wish to close the frontiers of life upon my own self. I do not wish to deny myself the expansion of seeking into individual capabilities and depths by living in a space whose boundaries are race and nation.
>
> —Zora Neale Hurston

The "woman's war novel" has ordinarily seemed "a contradiction in terms."[1] There has always been a heroic male literature of war—an *Iliad* or a *Ramayana*. No other genre is so highly gendered. The exploits of men in the formation and defense of a people or nation, though they may provoke the "tears of women," do not justify their tales.[2] The Great War intensified this exclusion of women from the canon of war literature. The way the "dying lines" of war have been drawn exposes the operation of sex and race in the construction of nation.

Canonical interpretation has held that mass conscription created a new kind of artist: a "soldier-poet" who recorded his "direct experience" of a new and barbarous technology. With a typical stress on composition at the front, Patrick Bridgwater asserts, "From winter 1914 onwards most war poetry worth the title has been anti-war poetry written by poets in the line of death."[3] Critics have focused on the writer, understood to be a gifted veteran who responded to the test of his masculinity by shaping realist texts about the trenches, blood brother-

[1] Cyril Falls, *War Books: An Annotated Bibliography of Books about the Great War*, intro. R. J. Wyatt (1930; rpt. London: Greenhill, 1989), 268.

[2] See Nancy Huston, "Tales of War and Tears of Women," *Women Studies International Forum* 5 (1982): 271–82.

My thanks to Claire Tylee, Jane Marcus, Gisela Brinker-Gabler, Marie-France Doray, and Françoise Thébaud for sharing titles, texts, and ideas with me.

[3] Patrick Bridgwater, *The German Poets of the First World War* (New York: St. Martin's, 1985), 1. Despite this simplification, Bridgwater offers deft readings of German soldiers' poetry. The conventional view is reproduced in countless anthologies and critical works. See, for example, Bernard Bergonzi, *Heroes' Twilight: A Study of the Literature of the Great War*, 2d ed. (London: Macmillan, 1980).

hood, and political disillusionment. An "event" became identified with a genre and with the construction of a sexed subject; the "reality" of the war and its authoritative representation were pinned to concepts of masculinity.

This generic complex in turn helped define notions of modernity and modern national literatures, from which women would be implicitly excluded. In his 1990 study of the period Samuel Hynes generalizes, "A nation at war *is* a male nation." The art of this particular war was, it seems, also male: "The artist is not separable from the soldier." Men's direct experience of the Battle of the Somme made it necessary and possible for them to find, Hynes argues, "a new style for a new reality."[4] Indeed, when the war broke out, conservative and avant-garde thinkers alike expected that it would purge nations and literatures of fin-de-siècle effeminacy. In the event, the encoding of the war and its representation as supremely masculine was undercut by the complexity and range of men's self-gendering in wartime, traced by Paul Fussell and Eric Leed.[5]

One of the problems in defining war fiction as a genre turns on the vague central term, *war,* itself a highly gendered concept. An identification of war with the trenches precludes literature about the home front, about the economic impact of war during hostilities and after the armistice, or about rape and prostitution as seen from the perspective of women. Just as epithalamia written by men may embed different narratives of union and loss from those written by women, so may narratives by men and women about war examine different aspects of social violence.

To oppose the "battlefront" to the "home front" erases our knowledge that where the front is, there often are also homes and women. The military, according to Cynthia Enloe, must "constantly redefine 'the front' and 'combat' as wherever 'women' are not." As the nurse Ellen La Motte ironically explains in her sketch "Women and Wives," "the words home and wife were interchangeable," by contrast to any "women" at the front, who (like the homes) were "all ruined." Commonplace definitions of war draw a gendered boundary "dividing the

[4]Samuel Hynes, *A War Imagined: The First World War and English Culture* (London: Bodley Head, 1990), 88, 199, 167, 191. On the masculinist definition of modernism, see Shari Benstock, "Expatriate Modernism: Writing on the Cultural Rim," in *Women's Writing in Exile,* ed. Mary Lynn Broe and Angela Ingram (Chapel Hill: University of North Carolina Press, 1988), 20–22; and Bonnie Kime Scott, ed., *The Gender of Modernism: A Critical Anthology* (Bloomington: Indiana University Press, 1990).

[5]Paul Fussell, *The Great War and Modern Memory* (New York: Oxford University Press, 1975); Eric Leed, *No Man's Land: Combat and Identity in World War I* (New York: Cambridge University Press, 1979).

protector from the protected."[6] This ideological system reinforces women's traditional roles; it does not readily account for women's multiple wartime activities or their firsthand experiences at the front.

This conceptual frame has filtered histories of the material and symbolic impact of the war on women. During 1914–18 "manpower" shortages forced several warring states, albeit reluctantly, to coordinate women's industrial work and to establish military auxiliaries for medical, clerical, and relief work.[7] To this end official propaganda called on women to assume "for the duration" public roles previously played by men. Yet propaganda from both the right and the left simultaneously thrust women back into stereotypical roles centered on maternity and the hearth. Thus, sexual boundaries were both blurred and reinforced.

Social territory in turn affects the hierarchy of genres within which male and female artists are supposed to operate. Lines from the "front" take precedence over those from "behind." As Virginia Woolf puts it: "The values of women differ very often from the values which have been made by the other sex. . . . Yet it is the masculine values that prevail. . . . This is an important book, the critic assumes, because it deals with war. This is an insignificant book because it deals with the feelings of women in a drawing-room. A scene in a battlefield is more important than a scene in a shop."[8] Since women are symbolically barred from those wartime arenas designated as historically significant, it follows that a second boundary is drawn that relegates women to lesser genres. Although Cyril Falls grudgingly includes a few women in his bibliography of World War I books, he maintains: "Really, it is not the place of women to talk of mud, they may leave that to men, who knew more about it and have not hesitated to tell us of it."[9]

Nonetheless, women did write about the war, and in great variety.

[6]Cynthia Enloe, *Does Khaki Become You? The Militarization of Women's Lives* (London: Pluto, 1983), 15; Ellen La Motte, *Backwash of War: The Human Wreckage of the Battlefield as Witnessed by an American Nurse* (1916; rpt. New York: Putnam, 1934). See also Sara Ruddick, "Pacifying the Forces: Drafting Women in the Interests of Peace," *Signs* 8 (Spring 1983): 472; Jean Bethke Elshtain, *Women and War* (New York: Basic Books, 1987); and Margaret Higonnet, "Not So Quiet in No Woman's Land," in *Gendering War Talk*, ed. Miriam Cooke and Angela Woollacott (Princeton: Princeton University Press, 1993), 205–26. The coalescence of battlefront and home under enemy occupation is described in painful detail in Marguerite Yerta, *Les six femmes et l'invasion, 1914–1916* (Paris: Plon, 1917).

[7]There is no comparative history of women's mobilization in World War I, but see Arthur Marwick, *Women at War, 1914–1918* (London: Fontana, 1977); Françoise Thébaud, *La femme au temps de la guerre de 14* (Paris: Stock, 1986); and Margaret Higonnet, Jane Jensen, Sonya Michel, and Margaret Weitz, eds., *Behind the Lines: Gender and the Two World Wars* (New Haven: Yale University Press, 1987).

[8]Virginia Woolf, *A Room of One's Own* (1929; rpt. New York: Harvest, 1957), 77.

[9]Falls, *War Books*, 282.

They corresponded to contradictory ideological messages and to a diversity of material experiences that spanned domestic comfort far from the front as well as the ravages of life in occupied zones of Europe and Africa, where some women were deported for forced labor and prostitution, others driven into exile from homes that had been reduced to rubble. Some, such as Emmeline Pankhurst, became nationalist propagandists in 1914; many embraced the nation's need for their services with the kind of enthusiasm or pride recorded by Vera Brittain, Gertrud Baümer, and Colette.

Other distinguished women artists, including Annette Kolb, Käthe Kollwitz, Virginia Woolf, and Anna Akhmatova, were led by varied motives such as divided national allegiances, war work, personal losses, socialist activism, or pervasive cognitive dissonance to record critical reflections on wartime representation. The civic disabilities of women are, of course, underscored in wartime by the symbolic linkage of nationalism to sexuality. The contradictory wartime discourse on gender, which could at need distinguish a "motherland" from a "male nation," afforded special ironies for writers concerned to locate a voice as "women" in the male-identified genre of war fiction.[10]

To date there has been little critical work on European women's contribution to the literature of war, almost none of it comparative. Indeed, the Great War has attracted few comparative literary studies even of men's literature. Most simply juxtapose interpretations of canonized texts from countries that fought on the Western Front, or they coordinate descriptive summaries around stock motifs such as the description of the trenches, attacks on civilian profiteers, pilgrimage, or martyrdom.[11] Yet this "World" War engulfed Europe, as well as many client states and colonies around the globe, thirty-eight nations in all; it touched every class and many races; in its very diversity it serves as a hinge among literatures.

Women remain outside the scope of critics working on male writers. George Parfitt notes that "a number of novels about the war . . . were written by women, and these also have been largely ignored." He concludes: "A woman should . . . make a study of these and other war

[10]See Andrew Parker, Mary Russo, Doris Sommer, and Patricia Yaeger, eds., *Nationalisms and Sexualities* (New York: Routledge, 1992), 1–18; and Margaret Higonnet and Patrice Higonnet, "The Double Helix," in Higonnet et al., *Behind the Lines*, 31–47.
[11]See Holger Klein, *The First World War in Fiction* (London: Macmillan, 1976); Bernd Hüppauf, ed., *Ansichten vom Krieg: Vergleichende Studien zum Ersten Weltkrieg in Literatur und Gesellschaft* (Königstein: Forum Academicum, 1984); Frank Field, *British and French Writers of the First World War* (Cambridge: Cambridge University Press, 1991); and Elizabeth Marsland, *The Nation's Cause: French, English, and German Poetry of the First World War* (London: Routledge, 1991).

novels by women."[12] Paul Fussell sums up the widely shared view that women were victims, not writers: "Why haven't more women written good "war poems"? From Homer's Andromache to Vera Brittain . . . bereaved women, next to the permanently disabled, are the main victims in war, their dead having been removed beyond suffering and memory. . . . Yet the elegies are written by men, and it's not women who seem the custodians of the subtlest sorts of antiwar irony. That seems odd, and it awaits interpretation."[13]

In her introduction to the first international volume on women writers and World War I, Dorothy Goldman surprisingly concurs with Fussell and Hynes. Like them, she offers a narrow, materialist, and historically simplistic reason for excluding the work of women: "If most women's war poetry is poor," it is because as noncombatants they lacked "the catalyst which the experience of the War provided in forcing more shocking and brutal forms of expression." She observes that women novelists as a rule do not describe warfare, and concludes that this "admission of women's inexperience . . . carries the clear implication that war is not a sphere which women writers can inhabit imaginatively."[14] Even so acute a feminist critic as Sandra Gilbert is made uneasy by women's accession to protected positions of power during the war; she treats Willa Cather and Edith Wharton as custodians of patriotism and self-interest, and implies that nurses question the war because of survivor's guilt.[15] We may ask whether it is not only women's voices but also their subtle "antiwar ironies" that have been lost.

From the 1920s to the 1980s women's writing about the war was generally deprecated. The plot of Wharton's novel *A Son at the Front* "is never really able to grapple with the realities of war, in an authentic manner," according to Philip Hager and Desmond Taylor likewise, Marcelle Capy's description of the disintegration of a French village is "plotless." Cyril Falls finds Clara Viebig's story of women in wartime Berlin, *The Daughters of Hekuba*, "sordid" and its characterization "neu-

[12]George Parfitt, *Fiction of the First World War: A Study* (London: Faber & Faber, 1988), 136.

[13]Paul Fussell, *Thank God for the Atomic Bomb and Other Essays* (New York: Ballantine, 1988), 137. Susan Schweik has responded to Fussell in *A Gulf So Deeply Cut: American Women Poets and the Second World War* (Lincoln: University of Nebraska Press, 1991), 293–94.

[14]Dorothy Goldman, introduction to *Women and World War I: The Written Response* (New York: St Martin's, 1993), 7, and " 'Eagles of the West'? American Women Writers and World War I," ibid., 195.

[15]Sandra Gilbert, "Soldier's Heart: Literary Men, Literary Women, and the Great War," *Signs* 8 (1983): 422–59.

rotic."[16] Although he devotes several pages to Rose Macaulay's *Non-combatants and Others,* Samuel Hynes slights it as "not a 'war novel' " but "more like an ironic essay than a novel," and quotes a review in the *Nation:* "What surprises us is that a woman and not a man should have written 'Non-Combatants,' because the 'ethos,' the stamp and tone of 'Non-Combatants' is not feminine, but masculine. Most thoughtful people would, we think, acknowledge that the spectatorial point of view, with its concomitants of irony, detachment and critical analysis, is more often discovered in the authors than the authoress." Hynes thinks that the particularized details provided by Macaulay, who worked in 1915 in a military hospital as a nursing aid for the V.A.D. (Voluntary Aid Detachment), "confine" her imagination.[17] Whereas critics praise the "terribly realistic" scenes and bitter humor of men such as Henri Barbusse and the surgeon Georges Duhamel, Mary Borden's powerful sketches of work in a French mobile hospital are dismissed as "almost inconceivably horrible," inferior in charm and philosophy to the "gallant" mockery of Paul Alverdes's *Whistling Room.*[18] Not only must the woman writer always be measured against a male analogue, but her very right to realism is questioned. With surprising unanimity critics have dismissed women's writings about the war as inauthentic, neurotic, or unfeminine.

At the same time, the reviews provide inadvertent clues to women's experimental play with war fiction (plotlessness, sordid realism, ironic detachment). Some of the best feminist critics have begun to study English and American women's writing about the war, especially that of prominent figures such as Woolf, Wharton, Brittain, and H.D.[19] By and large, however, women from the Continent, Africa, or Asia who wrote about the war remain unknown and out of print. For a depressing explanation we may turn to Agnès Cardinal, who writes in her study of French women: "As far as I am able to ascertain, these novels are now unknown in France; and since it is unlikely that they were widely

---

[16]Philip E. Hager and Desmond Taylor, *The Novels of World War I: An Annotated Bibliography* (New York: Garland, 1981), 166, 230; Falls, *War Books,* 300.

[17]Hynes, *War Imagined,* 126, 130.

[18]Falls, *War Books,* 267.

[19]In addition to Gilbert, "Soldier's Heart," see Claire Tylee, *The Great War and Women's Consciousness* (London: Macmillan, 1990); Jane Marcus, "Corpus/Corps/Corpse: Writing the Body in/at War," in *Arms and the Woman: War, Gender, and Literary Representation,* ed. Helen M. Cooper et al. (Chapel Hill: University of North Carolina Press, 1989), 124–67; Nosheen Khan, *Women's Poetry of the First World War* (London: Harvester, 1988); and Janet Montefiore, " 'Shining Pins and Wailing Shells': Women Poets and the Great War," in Goldman, *Women and World War I,* 51–72. Two important anthologies are Catherine Reilly, ed., *Scars upon My Heart: Women's Poetry and Verse of the First World War* (London: Virago, 1982); and Gisela Brinker-Gabler, *Frauen gegen Krieg* (Frankfurt am Main: Fischer, 1980).

read at the time of their publication, I have not taken them into consideration in my argument."[20] Many women simply disappear behind the men in their lives: Claire Studer Goll's poet-husband, Yvan, is far better known; Dr. Tatiana Alexinsky's husband, Grigori, continues to be remembered for his political roles; Svarnakumari Devi's younger brother Rabindranath Tagore attempted to suppress her writing: "I have given her no encouragement but have not been successful in making her see things in the proper light."[21]

One problem in searching for the "lost voices" of such women writers is to locate a touchstone that will define a genre without imposing an artificial unity specific to one class or culture. It is important to cast a net widely, in order to recognize disparate ways of representing war. Some of the most interesting fictions engage in "sorties": they cross literary and ideological boundaries. Not all these sorties are as dramatic as those of Radclyffe Hall's heroines Stephen Gordon and Miss Ogilvie, who both leave England to drive an ambulance on the French front, and leave the constraints of heterosexuality for lesbian relationships. But a number of texts develop common narrative strategies to test the sharp social lines drawn by war. They split up the narrative structure in order to resist a unitary value system and monolithic representation of women's lives.

A second, more difficult problem is to explore comparative questions raised by women's writings. A preliminary composite of the platitudes generated in propagandistic writing on all sides would not be difficult to compile, but the existing historical evidence does not permit a contrastive analysis that fully distinguishes one writer from another, or one cultural image of the war from another (indeed, this undertaking is not yet fulfilled for men's writing). The war catalyzed expressions of nationalism by women of very different political positions. Writing strategies are intimately related to the institutional mechanisms for eliciting or silencing responses to the Great War; those mechanisms depend on the geopolitical context, as well as the gendered rules of genre.

Not until the 1970s, for example, were conditions ripe for a Nigerian woman to write a narrative about the impact of this conflict on a colony. Buchi Emecheta's *Slave Girl* has escaped the net of conventional study

---

[20]Agnès Cardinal, "Women and the Language of War in France," in Goldman, *Women and World War I*, 166. Cardinal focuses primarily on Colette. In the same collection the historian Jan Bassett presents the fiction of an Australian jingoist (" 'Untravelled Minds': The War Novels of Mabel Brookes," 113–27).

[21]Quoted in Susie Tharu and K. Lalita, eds., *Women Writing in India, 600 B.C. to the Present* (New York: Feminist Press, 1991), 1:238.

because it encodes a vision of the war from the other end of the imperial telescope: the deadly transmission of influenza by British troops is perceived as a poison gas like that used by the "Germanis"; the economic ripple of the war touches off a women's market strike after a postwar poll tax has been levied to pay off British war debts. Such calamities do not fit the model of a war defined through death at "the front." The economic gamble of the war and its costs to the colonies do not qualify as the text of a war novel.

In oral form, however, such calamities already figured in a dramatic song composed by Beti women from Cameroon about their experience of the war—a form that is even less likely to enter histories of literature about the Great War than Emecheta's novel. The Beti had been faced with the choice of staying in Yaoundé, besieged by the British in December 1915, or of fleeing to the island of Fernando Po with the Germans and Atangana Ntsama, the wealthy principal chief who orchestrated an exodus of fourteen thousand Beti soldiers and members of their families. The women sing in a dialogue, "Hé, Atangana Ntsama, the war is over! the cannon are broken." But why should they leave possessions behind? One group sees as many goods as in a market: "Such riches. I should take some!" The other group responds, "You others, move off, what are you doing there?" and boasts that they have marched through, loyal to the Germans, "without taking anything." Cast as a dramatic debate over the impossible loyalty of the colonized, this poetic commentary on the women's search for stability and survival in a wartime economy continuously shifts in meaning. The war is "over," yet divisions within the people continue; the riches of the community are abandoned or plundered, while the military's promises of future rewards are unreliable, or indeed unfounded.[22] The divided structure of the song reinforces a sense of individual difference and dignity without resolving the political issues.

Even though it is isolated in the repertoire of war texts, this song and other texts previously left at the margins of history can help readers to negotiate past limited, stock conceptions of war in order to unsettle representations of women and of this event. Textual "sorties" engage the boundaries drawn between battlefront and home front, war and peace, public and private, white and black, nation and people, men and women. By mining such boundaries, these texts explode the narrow conceptions of war on which their own exclusion from the literature of

[22]Cited by Frederick Quinn, "The Impact of the First World War and Its Aftermath on the Beti of Cameroun," in *Africa and the First World War,* ed. Melvin E. Page (Houndmills, Basingstoke: Macmillan, 1987), 176.

war has rested. Their displacement of stock conceptions becomes apparent both in the transposition of motifs and in narrative structures.

When writers such as Richard Aldington, D. H. Lawrence, Ernst Jünger, or Henri de Montherlant drew a line between the "front" and civilian life, they often attacked the "enemy" at home: parasitical women such as the notorious jingoist poet Jessie Pope or white-haired male capitalists profiteering from the blood sacrifices of soldiers. A number of women pick up this contrast but give it a particular twist.[23] They echo their assignment to the domestic front, but they also undercut this distinction by reconsidering the locus of destructive forces and the hierarchy of gendered wartime values.

One of the most conspicuous examples is Woolf's *To the Lighthouse* (1927), of which Hynes writes that it "did not try to imagine war itself."[24] In order to represent the rupture wrought by the war, Woolf presents two days at the Ramsay family's summer house, separated by several years; they bracket a brief section titled "Time Passes," during which the house falls into decay, and a cleaning woman prepares for their return. On the margins of these material transformations the war takes place, and Mrs. Ramsay and her daughter Prue both die.

We catch sight of these deaths and of the war in literal brackets: while the phallic charwoman struggles against dust and decay, the "cleansing" sacrifice of life is made (an ironic allusion to Edmund Gosse), and Andrew Ramsay is killed. The apparent arbitrariness of these parenthetical references challenges us to seek a connection to details such as Mr. Ramsay's obsessive recitation of "The Charge of the Light Brigade." Paradoxically, by calling attention to the superficial lack of continuity in her plot, Woolf points to underlying systemic manifestations of a patriarchy that kills, not only in the public but also in the private realm. When Mrs. Ramsay wards off her husband's pessimistic weather forecast, gives her child the Army and Navy Stores catalogue to cut up, or drapes her shawl over the horns that threaten her daughter Cam's sleep, she symbolically challenges a phallic cult of death. The juxtaposition of Andrew's and Prue's deaths blurs the sharp gender lines of canonical war literature. In the profusion of darkness that engulfs the house, the night, and all of Europe, it is too dark to see the future; one cannot tell sea from land or distinguish "This is he" from "This is she."[25]

[23]Here my readings often differ from those of Sandra Gilbert, whose landmark study "Soldier's Heart," confined to British and American women, stresses their sense of empowerment by the war and guilt at survival.
[24]Hynes, *War Imagined*, 345.
[25]Virginia Woolf, *To the Lighthouse* (New York: Harcourt Brace & World, 1955), 194,

Continental women's texts also interpret the war through an analysis of its operation at the homefront and its impact on a community of women. The striking structural feature of Clara Viebig's *Töchter der Hekuba* (1918), however, is not a binary contrast but its mosaic of character portraits, a technique also used by the Italian novelist Matilde Serao in *Mors Tua* (1917, published in English as *The Harvest*) and the French journalist Marcelle Capy in *Des hommes passèrent* (1930, *Men Pass*). Whereas sexual hunger in men's novels about the war is often taken to indicate the protagonist's manliness and the writer's realism, Viebig's portrayal of "the hunger of women not only for food but for men" was condemned by a reviewer as "sordid."[26] In fact, Viebig does portray six women's growing realization of their hunger for a freedom of expression both sexual and social, in a world where they are left on the margins. She weaves a tale of shifting relations among women from different classes under the economic impact of the war. The facade of normalcy cracks, and with it the unified narrative breaks up. Thrust by the war into increasingly "sordid" economic conditions, two of the women go mad, and one commits suicide. In Viebig's militarized Germany, to believe in the return of the men—that is, in the end of the war—is a sign of dementia.

Female hunger for meaningful work is the theme of a sharply etched 1930 socialist novel by Meta Scheele, which satirizes the hypocrisy of a warmongering and nationalist German middle class. Scheele follows two sisters in *Frauen im Krieg* (Women in war), a technique that allows her to contrast women's conservative and radical reactions to the upheavals and deprivations of war. Her primary focus is the wartime development and alienation of Johanna, who becomes a nurse, awakens to a lesbian encounter, and joins the suffragist movement; her fiancé, Klaus, unable to make the transition from the realm of death to postwar society, commits suicide (a theme in Cather's *One of Ours* and in Woolf's *Mrs. Dalloway* as well). Johanna's elder sister, Elise, by contrast, is seduced both literally and politically by a "foxy" opportunist who at war's end abandons the propaganda unit he had led to become head of a workers' group and local government. Through her split narrative structure Scheele explicitly confronts us with women's multiple political choices and makes it clear that women "act" in wartime, even though they may not have the vote or the right to serve in the military.

One form of action—and an instance of antimilitarist body speech—

199, 201, 189–90. Woolf's strategic ruptures may help us to understand Willa Cather's *One of Ours* (1922), which has often been thought to fall apart at the middle.

[26]Cited in Falls, *War Books,* 300; Clara Viebig, *Töchter der Hekuba, ein Roman aus unserer Zeit* (Berlin: Fleischel, 1918).

is the women's strike, which takes women workers and working-class wives emphatically into the public. Wartime strikes, as Marc Ferro notes, are a little-studied phenomenon, and women's involvement in strikes remains a particularly blank page.[27] One of the few traces of that involvement is Berta Lask's brief 1929 story "Frauen im Kampf: Eine Erzählung aus dem Weltkrieg" (Women in battle: a story of the World War), which recounts the virtually silent alignment of a group of women against strikebreakers. In a play on militarist vocabulary, Lask describes these wives of striking harbor workers as gathering in "troops," and alludes to a soft call, a brief greeting, a piece of bread shared, while they "keep their word." As the strikebreakers approach, the women form a chain, a "front" aligned against the "Front," without speaking a word, until a curse ignites the women's anger. They shout: "You cabbage heads, you jamshitters, we'll teach you to put us out. Everywhere they are on strike. The war must stop. The men must come back. We want bread." Even when the police appear, the women do not yield. Struck in the mouth by a saber, their leader rouses herself to cry "Strike!" Lask's narratorial reticence contributes to the effect of her concluding line: "It took a long time, before the police were through with them."[28]

With its forceful puns, Lask's story addresses one of the most censored kinds of battle within the war, the battle on the home front of socialist workers, many of them women, against the war. Repressed as they happened, these strikes have also been omitted from the canonized literature of the Great War, with its cult of the battlefront. Lask reminds us that working-class women have not enjoyed the luxury of the private sphere, and their mouths have been bloodied to prevent their entry into the public sphere of politics. She shows us that political unanimity in support of the war was built, in Germany and elsewhere, on the violent suppression of dissent.

When they set their novels at the home front, Viebig, Scheele, and Lask, like Woolf or Cather, deliberately remind us that war is a national activity that destroys behind the lines as well as at the front. Men die in combat, of course, often significantly at the unseen margins of these texts. But men *and women* also conspicuously die away from the front—of the flu, of hunger, or in childbirth. They may die because profiteers create shortfalls of medicines and rations, stockpile food, provide in-

[27]Marc Ferro writes about the militancy of women workers, which catalyzed the revolution in Petrograd in March 1917, in *The Great War, 1914–1918*, trans. Nicole Stone (London: Routledge & Kegan Paul, 1973), 171.
[28]Berta Lask, "Frauen im Kampf: Eine Erzählung aus dem Weltkrieg," in Brinker-Gabler, *Frauen gegen Krieg*, 230–32.

adequate equipment. Through the motif of suicide Scheele, like Cather and Woolf, challenges the identification of violence with virility. Suicide and self-wounding began to appear in the latter half of the war in men's novels, where they usually figure either martyrdom or personal incapacity. Given an emphatic position in certain women's texts, often in a penultimate scene that demystifies the heroic closure of war rituals, suicide can figure war as a mechanism of castration and autodestruction.[29]

By drawing group portraits Viebig and Scheele deliberately complicate our vision of women's relation to the wartime economy and ideology, as exploiters and exploited. They show women who defend the social rules that confine women and send young men off to kill, as well as those who evade the social script. By dividing their narrative focus and multiplying "plots," they suggest that war is about neither individual heroism nor communal suffering in combat but about the erosion of individual rights for the many and the assumption of political or economic power by the few. To rewrite the scene of war in this way necessarily entails rewriting the genre of the war novel. Through their political analysis of the boundary between battlefront and home front, such texts interrogate the more enduring boundaries drawn between public and private, between men's world and women's world.

In order to confront the censorship of critiques of the war, many women appear to have turned to another genre, the semifictional, semitestimonial sketch, whose broad dissemination calls for closer scholarly study than is possible here. One cliché of literary history is that men write epics while women keep diaries; men in the academy have painted large historical frescoes, while women amateurs have created intimate watercolors and family portraits. Women's sketches of a world-historical event break down such oppositions. A large body of fragmented narratives cast as feminine journalism or as professional records of work in mobile hospitals or casualty clearing stations appeared during and after the war in England, France, Germany, Hungary, even Russia. These texts contest the assumption that women cannot "see" war. In their testimonial form as well as in their signatures (Dr., Sister, V.A.D.), they claim the authority of the real. Their fragmentation assimilates them to the context of newsmagazines, where some of them first appeared, such as the reportorial sketches by Rebecca

---

[29]I develop issues raised by the territorialization of death in wartime in my essay "Women in the Forbidden Zone," in *Death and Representation*, ed. Sarah Goodwin and Elisabeth Bronfen (Baltimore: Johns Hopkins University Press, 1993), 192–210.

West, Colette, Claire Studer (Goll), and the socialist journalist Marcelle Capy. At the same time, compression may also inscribe the interruptive routines of work punctuated by the arrivals of wounded men. The aim of many sketches was to convey the truth about war to a civilian public; ironically, their very concern for truth has led to their disparagement and disappearance as occasional literature. By contrast, Barbusse's *Under Fire,* an autobiographical work composed out of fractured bits drawn from his diary, has been acclaimed as a "novel."

When a woman enters a field hospital, she enters an in-between zone, both of the war and not of it. Wartime nursing is an ambiguous domain, quasi-domestic and maternal but in the public service. It is a role that calls on women to care for men as well as to cure them. Should a nurse restore a man's ability to fight and wound others, or should she as a nurse-writer try to cure society of the disease of war? A feminist-socialist vision was recorded by Dr. Tatiana Alexinsky, who described her hospital train staffed by women and running between various cities and the front as "a truly feminist train."[30] Alexinsky criticizes czarist elitism and medical hierarchies of power that impede scientific objectivity and proper care of the wounded. Her pared style catches the intonations of peasants, cross-dressed female volunteers, and aristocratic relief workers. Her low-key irony conveys the contradictions of her own position, caught between socialism and nationalism, between medicine and a military operation.

The finest exposition of such contradictions can be found in Mary Borden's *Forbidden Zone* (1929), named for the shifting location right behind the troops where no civilians (and certainly no women, except nurses or prostitutes) were supposed to be found. Borden exploits the irony of her position in a militarized zone, in violation of gender dichotomies. As a nurse with the French medical corps, she transgresses the boundary between women's domestic roles and their wartime occupations. Borden translates the whole machinery of war into the language of the housewife. Stretchers are pulled out of ambulances "as loaves of bread are pulled out of the oven." Borden writes about "mending" men's bodies so that they can be returned to the trenches. "Just as you send your clothes to the laundry and mend them when they come back, so we send our men to the trenches and mend them when they come back again." The sinister note lies in the prearrangement; housekeepers do not prearrange rips. "It is all carefully arranged. Everything is arranged. It is arranged that men should be broken and

---

[30]Tatiana Alexinsky, *With the Russian Wounded* (London: T. Fisher Unwin, 1916), 11.

that they should be mended."[31] To domesticate war this way is a "conspiracy." In a closed economy of injury and cure there is no escape except death. Far more dramatically than Woolf, who ironically juxtaposes the "cleansing" of a decaying house with the propagandists' motif of "cleansing sacrifices" required to put Europe back "in order," Borden here transposes normalizing metaphors of domesticity in order to mine the concepts of normalcy and non-war in which war itself is anchored. Her sortie across the linguistic boundary segregating men's world from women's world exposes not only the complicity of women propagandists who domesticate war, but also the false political distinction between war and peace.

If one way to recognize the magnitude of women's implication in the First World War is to examine texts that sprang from women's experiences in occupied villages or medical facilities "at the front," another approach is to recognize that "home" does not always mean Surrey, Lower Saxony, or Kansas. In recent years an effort has been made by historians to acknowledge the impact of the war on Africa and ANZAC nations and to explore its interweaving of nationalism and racism. Unfortunately, this effort has borne little fruit in literary criticism, which remains firmly Eurocentric, white, and predominantly male in its focus.

One little-noticed feature in those women's writings that deliberately decenter the war is the suggestion that the European war and colonialist violence are interlocking systems. In several of the texts cited here—Woolf's *To the Lighthouse*, Scheele's *Women in War*, and Capy's *Men Pass*, for example—the theme of imperialism is a red thread tracing awareness of a political displacement that women share with people from the colonies. The irony of colonials fighting under strange skies for their oppressors was not lost on women such as Capy or Alice Dunbar-Nelson, who helped organize Negro women's war work in the face of color bars to service in white Red Cross units. In Dunbar-Nelson's play *Mine Eyes Have Seen*, the question is asked why an orphaned young black man should serve a "nation that let my father's murder go unpunished."[32] The problems of "making a man" of oneself, of maintaining family loyalties, of resisting leaders who carelessly throw men's lives away all dissolve in the face of the irresistible call to prove that the race is equal to its demands for citizenship. For Dunbar-Nelson that ambiguous position in this era of nationalisms is complicated by both race and gender.

---

[31]Mary Borden, *The Forbidden Zone* (New York: Doubleday, Doran, 1930), 125, 124. See also Marcus, "Corpus/Corps/Corpse."

[32]Alice Dunbar-Nelson, *Mine Eyes Have Seen*, in *Crisis* 15 (1918): 271.

In order to address the intersection of nationalism and imperialism even more directly, we may turn to "The Mutiny" (1919), by a Bengali woman, Svarnakumari Devi. Svarnakumari, a politically active re- former and sister of Rabindranath Tagore, was a delegate to the Indian National Congress in 1889–90 and for thirty years editor of *Bharati*, a Bengali literary journal. She juxtaposes the 1857 War of Indian Inde- pendence ("the Mutiny") with the Great War in a witty response to British nationalism from the perspective of a colonial ally whose war efforts are exacted without political reward and whose own nationalism must be firmly repressed.

Amid after-dinner chitchat among a group of Englishwomen, the nameless Bengali narrator reflects on history and the present war. Her dark reflections frame a lighthearted tale told by her English hostess about fears of native atrocities in the decades following "the Mutiny." As a young woman, Mrs. A had once been frightened by the racket of firearms going off at midnight, only to discover the next morning that a conflict had arisen between police and domestic sepoys sent to guard her—a case of overzealous guards (rival lovers of her ayah) whose outburst was "exaggerated a hundredfold by my wild imagination and fears."[33] Mrs. A's self-mocking tale-within-the-tale underscores the mis- reading of "dreadful" natives by implanted colonists.

The theme of one culture misreading another dominates the Bengali narrator's thoughts about Indian history, as she looks out from the ve- randa at the harbor. In the distance lie the island forts of the famous "pirate" Angray, who terrorized English, Portuguese, and Moguls alike. Responding to the label "pirate," she asks, "In the days when might was right, what chief, or ruler, or founder of a dynasty was not a robber or a pirate?" (227). How one reads Angray's actions or the 1857 War of Independence (when the Rani of Jhansi cross-dressed to lead her soldiers on the field of battle) depends on one's own political site.

When the other women chat about "the great war" and boast of military superiority to the French and Germans, the narrator feels si- lenced. Silence and self-division are the lot of a colonial, who has no nation of her own. She may feel pride at the victories of British troops including sepoy regiments (whose devotion to their British leaders is the focus of another story by Svarnakumari). But a wartime atmosphere makes any Indian boast of military accomplishment suspect: "If I dressed my views would they be appreciated? Most probably not. Now

[33]Mrs. Ghosal (Srimati Svarna Kumari Devi), "The Mutiny (A True Story)," in *Short Stories* (Madras: Ganesh, 1919), 337; subsequent references are cited in the text.

is a time of misunderstanding and is not mere suspicion positive proof against lifelong loyalty? Then who knows what next—indictment or internment?" (229).

Svarnakumari expands the political import of her double story in two ways, as a story of race and a story of gender. Thinking to herself, the narrator ponders the irony of her situation as a colonial, deprived of "the simple rights which loyal citizens expect" (229). "We are not treated as equals," she reflects (230). That inequality has been driven home precisely by the nationalist feelings aroused by the war, to which she as a subaltern has no right or access. "Never before had I been made to feel my racial inequality in my intercourse with English people. . . . Today, these expressions of a woman belonging to a free nation made me feel myself an utter stranger" (231). As an Indian, she feels that Occidentals interpret "our loyalty and self-sacrifice as cringing, dog-like virtues" (230).

Her fears are confirmed by the cultural imperialism of another guest, Mrs. B., who mocks the two sati pillars in memory of Angray's wives. Sati had been banned by the British in 1829. When the narrator praises the divine courage and love of suicidal women, Mrs. B's curled lip speaks eloquently: "To allow oneself to be burnt alive and not to have the power to utter a word! That is your courage! To be trodden under the heel of subjugation and feel it to be the happiness of virtue" (231). Oblivious to her own exclusion as a woman from masculine company by the British after-dinner ritual, Mrs B. identifies the culturally alien woman with the political impotence of a colonized people. In these very years Gandhi would seek political power by linking the nationalist movement of passive resistance to the "natural" female virtue of "silent suffering."[34]

As the narrator continual reminds us, and as the nested frame structure of the story underscores, cultural values are contextually bound. Sati may horrify an Englishwoman, but the fearless acceptance of death by sepoy volunteers gratifies her. The closing lines of the story announce the arrival of Indian troops in France who have "thrown themselves into the thick of the fight." Not only the French but the English government "has been touched by this enthusiastic self-sacrifice."

Svarnakumari's story points to a parallel between women's politically extorted contributions to the war effort and those of colonials. Her own political dislocation, which places Indians at a mythic "no place," enables her to interrogate nationalism without renouncing pride in her

[34]See Ketu Katrak, "Indian Nationalism, Gandhian 'Satyagraha,' and Representations of Female Sexuality," in Parker et al., *Nationalisms and Sexualities*, 398.

people. By contrast to the European texts under review here, the blurring of gender lines in this text throws into primary relief racial and imperialist boundaries. With remarkable intricacy the story dignifies self-sacrifice as an attribute of women as well as soldiers which may acquire the power to define a culture. By stressing the constant process of cultural translation and redefinition, the story raises the possibility that the sepoys' sacrifices may be absurd: they may go unrecognized. India will not be granted autonomy in reward for its sacrifices. We will forget that the Great War reached all the way to Bengal.

National memories and literary histories alike are tools of cultural construction that serve, however inadvertently, political goals and reinforce assumptions about gender and citizenship, in the republic of letters as well as in the nation. For Woolf the point may be precisely the failures of memory, the gulf cut between the official text of war and the broken cups and lives that record war's manifold shocks. For Svarnakumari Devi the dialogue between national memory and nationalist military history brings into play all the hypocrisy of European imperialism; tacitly understood behind the occluded contribution of Indian sepoys is the cultural imperialism that denigrates all Indians as self-sacrificing, effeminate subalterns. A nationalist Bengali woman has no secure site within such cultural discourses.

In retrospect, we may understand better the erasure of women from the history of war literature, even by so astute a critic as Paul Fussell. Perhaps the most obvious explanation is that many of these forgotten texts are about *women*. The a priori identification of war with masculinity symbolically exiles women from war fiction. One way to respond to this exile is to fold war back inside a domestic frame, at the risk of creating a text unrecognizable as a "war novel." Thus, in several of these texts a split narrative structure juxtaposes the lives and deaths of women with the lives and deaths of men. Matilde Serao alerts us to the possibilities of writing against the grain by dedicating *The Harvest* "to the unknown mother." Many texts by Continental women depict violence against women as part of the official war. Mosaic structures permit some writers to differentiate among women's modes of implication in war. They may draw ironic strength from responding to the overdetermined yet highly contradictory, obscurantist wartime discourses on femininity.

Similarly, texts that deal with male protagonists, but at the home front, have been occluded by literary history. Although the very term *home front* was used to foster the belief that "battles" had to be won by civilians as war became "total," in a hierarchy of fronts home remains at the bottom. In texts written as early as 1916, some women began to invert that hierarchy and to ask whether men sacrificed by the thousands are not at the bottom of a system in which the real decisions are being made by protected politicians. Ellen La Motte and Svarnakumari Devi satirize a "juggernaut" of war requiring human sacrifices that must be at once mystified and emptied of political power. Displaced from the "center" of the trenches to the "margin" of the domestic economy, the violent deaths of soldiers are assimilated to other kinds of institutionally ratified death.

The contradictory discourses of war invite ironic structures: bracketed war scenes, divided narratives, and multiple protagonists offer narrative "sorties" to escape ideological confines that are hallmarks of the genre. Precisely when women writers undercut the stock binary gender representations of war, their work became illegible as "war fiction." For to erode the borders between the realms of men and women, between public and private, is to erode the distinction between war and peace. Although grounded in actual experiences of medical "horror" in some cases, and focused on the *Realpolitik* that sends men to slaughter, the texts discussed here have seemed "unrealistic" and "sordid" to readers who expected to find a primary focus on the filth and terror of the trenches, set off from the realm of women.

Comparative study can begin to reveal how women's war fictions both participate in and resist the discursive gendering of war. It reveals the different ideological obstacles that confront women from Britain, Germany, or India. Once critics recognize inflections by race, class, and political condition, they can recuperate savage ironies in voices (of men and women, of Ibo and Bengali) that custodians of a narrowly defined male record could not hear.

8

Jane's Family Romances

MARIANNE HIRSCH

Narrative is, in sum, the most elaborate kind of attempt, on the
part of the speaking subject, after syntactic competence, to situate
his or her self among his or her desires and their taboos, that is,
at the interior of the oedipal triangle.
—Julia Kristeva

The urge to intellectual and artistic creation and the productivity
of motherhood spring from common sources, and it seems very
natural that one should be capable of replacing the other.
—Helene Deutsch

Although most mothers have been and are women, mothering is
potentially work for men and women.... There is no reason to
believe that one sex rather than the other is more capable of doing
maternal work.
—Sara Ruddick

"When his first-born was put into his arms, he could see that the boy
had inherited his own eyes, as they once were—large, brilliant and
black."[1] Paradoxically, the novel's only hint of Jane Eyre's maternity
actually serves to affirm the paternity of Edward Rochester: his gaze at
his son, and the male line of transmission by which the son inherits his
father's eyes and therefore this same gaze. This affirmation of paternity
is all the more incongruous in a paragraph that seems to challenge
masculine dominance. In revealing Rochester's regained eyesight, the
novel still reserves access and control of the symbolic for Jane and
grants her husband the discernment of nature, not of books: "He cannot
read or write much; but he can find his way without being led by the
hand: the sky is no longer a blank to him—the earth no longer a void"
(397).

Exploring this incongruity and looking, in particular, at how mater-

Part of this essay is based on my discussion of the family romance in the introduction
and chap. 2 of *The Mother-Daughter Plot: Narrative, Psychoanalysis, Feminism* (Bloomington:
Indiana University Press, 1989). The essay was written in 1991.

[1]Charlotte Brontë, *Jane Eyre* (New York: Norton, 1971), p. 397; subsequent references
are cited in the text.

nal and paternal functions are deployed in Brontë's novel provides an opportunity for a new look at a novel that has become a classic, if not a cult text, in the women's studies canon. It is possible to trace, through readings of *Jane Eyre*, the evolution of feminist literary interpretation: all the major trends are clearly represented. For feminist comparatists, however, *Jane Eyre* is more than such a touchstone. In reading the novel through the perspective of the family romance, I hope to bring together the formalist, generic, and cultural interests of the comparatist with the psychoanalytic focus of the feminist literary critic, and to bring them to bear on a text which, set at the moment of European imperial expansion, in itself raises questions about any comparatist, cross-cultural venture. As I teach this novel—and I have taught it in both comparative literature and women's studies courses—and as I write about it, I still feel as though I were shuttling back and forth between my two identities, my comparatist and my feminist selves. I hope that this reading will show some of that discursive disjointedness even as it helps to bridge it. I also hope that it will allow me to write into it my personal as well as my theoretical commitments.

Jane Eyre offers an especially radical elaboration of a *female* family romance model present in a number of Victorian novels by women writers: Brontë gives Jane the possibility not only of becoming a mother, but also of combining maternity with a different, and in the ideology of the period a contradictory, labor—the imaginative and self-engendering act of writing her own story. What makes it possible for Jane to become a mother, a condition that most nineteenth-century women writers will do anything to avoid for their heroines, is connected to the ways in which maternity is defined and deployed in the text. One key factor in this deployment is the distribution of a parental role to Edward Rochester, which enables us to read the father-son dyad described in the quoted passage as a sign not of Rochester's *paternity* but of what we might think of as his *male maternity*. Other factors include the particular class structure that underlies the novel and the specific definitions of what constitutes the labor of mothering in the first place. These definitions, however, raise certain literary questions as well; for example, one might ask whether Jane's maternity allows her to adopt a maternal voice in the text and to develop a maternal textuality, or whether, in spite of her motherhood, she continues to write her childhood fantasies and experiences.

In bringing *Jane Eyre* into the comparatist canon, and in reading it through the generic lens of the family romance, I hope also to bring it *back* to women's studies, transformed. Why the family romance? One genre where comparatist and feminist concerns have intersected frequently and fruitfully for me and for others is the bildungsroman, and one might wonder what a shift from the bildungsroman to the family romance might open up for comparatist readers of this text and of other realist novels. This shift is meant to venture a response to recent revisions in feminist readings of *Jane Eyre*, for in the late 1980s and 1990s earlier celebrations of the novel's feminist rebelliousness have been seriously challenged and reformulated. Jane Lazarre's reading of Jane as the "rebel girl," Sandra Gilbert and Susan Gubar's use of Brontë's representation of the woman writer as the "madwoman in the attic," Sandra Gilbert's reading of Jane as a female "pilgrim's progress," Adrienne Rich's demonstration of how successfully Jane overcomes the "temptations of a motherless daughter" all represent a specific moment in the practice of feminist reading, a moment that highlights individual achievement and psychological growth and development as unquestioned values for women.[2] More recently the novel has been cast instead as a portrait of a feminist individualist heroine whose marginality allows her to develop an oppositional discourse which *seem* to challenge but which actually *participates* in hegemonic ideology—Western, imperialist, racist, middle class, heterosexist, familial, psychological. Readings by Gayatri Spivak, Nancy Armstrong, and Mary Childers, among others, brilliantly explore the novel's blindnesses to its own collusions and "otherings."[3] Spivak's essay is especially pertinent in a comparatist framework, not only because it reads *Jane Eyre* against the background of European imperial expansion, but also because it confronts the nineteenth-century feminist individualism of the "marginal" Jane with the persona of the other, native, female subject. Spivak demands a comparatist reading that is fully cognizant of imperialism as the background for academic comparatism, and a feminist reading that reveals the problematic relationship between the feminist heroine and the "other" woman, her double or her victim.

Although I have found these essays illuminating, I am also concerned about how quickly they dismiss the novel's radical aspects, and with

---

[2]Jane Lazarre, "Charlotte's Web: Reading *Jane Eyre* over Time," in *Between Women*, ed. Carol Ascher, Louise de Salvo, and Sara Ruddick (Boston: Beacon, 1984); Sandra Gilbert and Susan Gubar, *The Madwoman in the Attic: The Woman Writer and the Nineteenth-Century Literary Imagination* (New Haven: Yale University Press, 1979); Adrienne Rich, "The Temptations of a Motherless Daughter," in *On Lies, Secrets, and Silence: Selected Prose, 1966–1978* (New York: Norton, 1979).

[3]Gayatri Spivak, "Three Women's Texts and a Critique of Imperialism," *Critical Inquiry* 12.1 (Autumn 1985): 243–61; Nancy Armstrong and Leonard Tennenhouse, "Introduction: Representing Violence, or 'How the West Was Won,' " in *The Violence of Representation: Literature and the History of Violence* (New York: Routledge, 1989); Mary Childers, "Lady Monsters and Woman Servants," unpublished manuscript.

them the feminism of the 1970s for which *Jane Eyre* has come to stand. Here I agree with Cora Kaplan's suggestion that "Jane Eyre is in danger of displacing Bertha Mason as a new 'monstrous feminine'—the antitext of what eighties and nineties feminism should be."[4] Kaplan's strategy—reading the novel as a thematization of contemporary British politics, firmly rooted in its 1840s context, which reveals it to be anti-imperialist, though still racist and nationalist—is very different from Spivak's, and the two together can illustrate the distance between English department new historicism and a comparatist approach informed by the cultural critique of the 1980s. In what follows I confront the more recent revisionist critical readings of *Jane Eyre* with earlier approaches highlighting the novel's subversive strategies. I do this neither in order to reinscribe *Jane Eyre* into an unquestioned feminist or comparatist canon, nor so as to claim that *Jane Eyre* is unquestionably "radical," a term that, in itself, needs reflection and contextualization. My aim is to see how some "new" comparatist questions in feminist theory concerning race, class, and empire can relocate and redefine without totally displacing "older" concerns with family, identity, and authority. It is precisely a comparatist perspective that may be able to bring out points of connection between what has come to appear as two separate moves and two separate moments in feminist criticism and theory. *Family*, in my reading, functions as a nexus organizing a variety of issues in this family romance. In responding to both older and more recent feminist concerns (maternity/paternity and class issues in relation to work and authorship), such a reading tries to envision a mother-inclusive and class-conscious feminism as well as a gender, class, and race–conscious comparatist genre theory.

Family Romances

The "female family romance" model I have identified in nineteenth-century novels by women writers is based on Freud's notion of the *Familienroman* and the strange ways in which it echoes, by both repeating and distorting, the texts of nineteenth-century realism. In making this connection I assert my belief that Freud's analysis responds to the same cultural plots as nineteenth-century fiction, and that in a number of his essays he clarifies and elucidates not only those underlying cultural plots but also the very structures of the realist novel's presentation of individual development and familial fantasies. Predictably,

[4]Cora Kaplan, "Fostering 'Chartism and Rebellion': Race, Class, and Feminism in *Jane Eyre*," unpublished manuscript.

however, Freud is clearer on spelling out a male model, one that fits Balzac's Rastignac, Dickens's Pip, or Keller's Heinrich much more readily than Brontë's Jane; a female model has to be extrapolated from his essays and read back into and against the work of women writers. My analysis does not aim to privilege Freud's insights into female psychology. I read him as a reader of fictional plots which he brings out, elaborates, and reformulates into theory, or into theoretical fiction.

In spite of its Freudian source, the notion of the family romance, more than the notion of the bildungsroman, facilitates a consciousness of the intersections of textuality with gender, class, and race. The bildungsroman is concerned with the growth and development of the individual; its source is the bourgeois culture of eighteenth-century Germany, with its idealist belief in the perfectibility of the human spirit. Its focus, as critics have charged, is indeed individualist. Even though it places individual development in the context of familial and social structures, its goal is the formation of an integrated psychological and social subject. The critic who approaches a novel through the generic rubric of bildungsroman does risk psychologizing social, political, and economic issues. Not only have feminist redefinitions of the bildungsroman raised questions about the individualist goals of *Bildung* as the traditional genre defines them, but they have looked critically at the very notion of "individual." Feminist revisionist criticism, much of it comparatist in nature, has indeed redefined *Bildung* in ways that make it more attuned to women's lives and more congruent with female-authored texts. *Bildung*, in the eyes of feminist critics, is less child-centered, less aimed toward autonomy, more affiliative and relational. It needs to be contextualized and historicized; it needs to be confronted with the insights of feminist psychology. Even a redefined individuality, however, even an individuality that is inflected by the differences that gender makes in the social, cannot easily respond to the critiques of class, race, and imperial bias; it remains privileged and informed by first world middle-class values. In continuing to be a narrative of emancipation, it fosters certain relationships and certain aspects of individuality over others. We can see these values in the readings of *Jane Eyre* that were published in the 1970s and early 1980s, although not all of those readings were informed by generic criticism and the bildungsroman. They stressed friendship and sisterhood, nurturance and affiliation, care for others and care for self. But they also stressed individuality, self-reliance, self-preservation, choice, and self-expression.[5]

---

[5]For feminist studies of the bildungsroman, see Elizabeth Abel, Marianne Hirsch, and Elizabeth Langland, eds., *The Voyage In: Fictions of Female Development* (Hanover, N.H.: University Press of New England, 1983); Rita Felski, *Beyond Feminist Aesthetics: Feminist*

It may seem paradoxical that the notion of family romance, adapted from Freud and from feminist revisions of Freud, should offer a more satisfactory alternative to the bildungsroman as a generic lens through which to read women's fiction, yet I believe that for the nineteenth-century European novel it does. In Freud's terms, the *Familienroman* is still an individual interrogation of origins, one that embeds the engenderment of narrative within the structure of family. The family romance thus combines and reveals as indistinguishable the experience of family and the process of narrative. Precisely because the family romance is the *fantasied story* of the individual place within the family unit, it is alterable and manipulable, adaptable to varied circumstances. In fact, the individual ability to shift familial circumstance, to dream of alternatives, is the essence of the family romance. The narrating subject is but a member of the unit of family, and all of the relations within that unit impinge on his or her activity of fabulation. And, as those relations shift, so can the family romance: each life story is shaped by more than one familial fantasy. Fantasies might begin in childhood and be characteristic of childhood, but they can mature to adulthood; they can even concern aging and adult development. Objecting to the family romance construct from a feminist or Marxist perspective, one might argue that family is a unit that is inherently bourgeois and conservative; that it is the agent of the transmission of property and the safeguarding of values. One might argue as well that family, at least in the psychoanalytic narrative, is still first and foremost a psychological unit. Yet, even in the Freudian schema, family is what the individual wants to manipulate, to transform, and to escape. The constraints of family are precisely what motivates the desire for liberation, social transformation, even revolution. Thus, the generic rubric of family romance shows both the power that family holds as a hegemonic mythos in the period of nineteenth-century realism and the pain, even the violence, that any transformation of its traditional oedipal and patriarchal shapes can cause.

The fantasy of family is a fantasy of relationship; it can be a collective rather than a uniquely individual fantasy. Family, moreover, is a larger unit than the nuclear one; it includes extended kin relations, and even for Freud it included servants and governesses. The narrative of family is embedded in a narrative of class aspiration and economic fantasies of enrichment. And the character of patriarchal family relations is, in the family romance, applicable to other relations, whether they be in-

Literature and Social Change (Cambridge: Harvard University Press, 1989), chap. 4; and Susan Fraiman, *Unbecoming Women: British Women Writers and the Novel of Development* (New York: Columbia University Press, 1993).

tergroup, international, or intercultural. Family structures can therefore be used as metaphors of colonial relations. I realize, however, as I adopt and adapt this model, that it remains problematic in a number of ways: it forces us to begin with Freud; it does continue to promote familial values even as it transforms and critiques them; it does weight the analysis toward the psychological even as it allows an expansion to the social and political. What is more, it reinforces the family as model and metaphor, whether positive or negative, for other forms of relation. Yet in doing so it merely reveals something that is indeed central to European realism. In spite of its problems, I believe that the generic rubric of family romance opens up certain aspects of nineteenth-century novels by women writers to scrutiny and to critique. It permits us to ask, for example, how Jane can combine the act of writing with the labor of maternity, and it permits us to see what desires shape Brontë's representation of her heroine's developmental course. It also permits us to see in a new light the transformations that Rochester undergoes in the novel. Tangentially, it permits us to evaluate anew the role of Bertha Mason and the novel's position on St. John's imperialist project. Yet I would propose this model not as transhistorically or cross-culturally valid but as applicable specifically to nineteenth-century European and American realism.

The nineteenth-century heroine's female family romance, as extrapolated from Freud, comprises three principal elements: (1) the condition of motherlessness and therefore the freedom to develop beyond the limitations of the maternal story and maternal transmission; (2) the replacement of maternal nurturance with a paternal/fraternal bond, which turns into a quasi-incestuous heterosexual romance/marriage, affording the heroine access to plot and to the symbolic; and (3) the avoidance of maternity, most often made possible by this conflation of husband with brother/father, and thereby the possibility of remaining in the plot.

For most nineteenth-century heroines maternal absence actually engenders feminine fictions. Plot demands the separation of heroines from the messages of powerlessness and disinheritance which mothers tend to transmit. Maternal stories are stories not to be repeated: from the perspective of fictional plot, mothers can only be examples not to be emulated. The somewhat unconventional though severely truncated story of Jane's mother provides an apt example. Adored by her brother, disowned by her family for making a "low" marriage to a penniless clergyman, she dies of the typhus fever he caught from the poor he visited in a large manufacturing town, leaving her daughter Jane to the care of her more conventional brother, Mr. Reed. In Mrs. Eyre's case the break with her home and family embeds her in the economically based institution of marriage and motherhood, which proves to be fatal. She is the victim of the social constraints that delimit women's lives; but, from a different perspective, she has to die so that her daughter might have a story. The benefits of Jane's motherlessness are only confirmed by the other disastrous portraits of mothers the novel presents. Mrs. Reed, Céline Varens, Antoinetta Mason, even Mrs. Ingram turn out to be debilitating obstacles to their daughters' successful development. The earlier they are eliminated, the better chance their daughters have; the deeper the mother-daughter bond, the more devastating it proves to be. From contact with their mothers, daughters inherit madness, intemperance, and savagery at worst, incompetence and flightiness at best.

Freud's analysis in "Family Romances," however, implies that mothers need to be eliminated from feminine fictions for deeper reasons.[6] The family romance, as Freud describes it, provides for the developing individual a necessary escape from the "authority of his parents," and it is this conflict over authority and legitimacy which becomes the basis for fantasy and mythmaking. Read in conjunction with Marthe Robert's gloss, *Origins of the Novel*, Freud's essay becomes the paradigm for a more extensive theory of fiction making.[7] "Indeed, the whole process of society rests upon the opposition between successive generations," Freud asserts. Two stages define this process of liberation. First, the child, feeling slighted and in competition with siblings, and seeing that his parents are not unique and incomparable as he had at first supposed, imagines that he might be a stepchild or adopted. He frees himself from his parents by imaginatively replacing them with richer, more noble, aristocratic ones. Robert calls this the "foundling plot" and discusses it as the basis for the fantastic narratives and romances of Chrétien de Troyes, Cervantes, Hoffmann, Novalis, Melville, and Kafka. At this stage in his explanation of the "foundling fantasy," Freud introduces a gender distinction, arguing that "a boy is far more inclined to feel hostile impulses toward his father than toward his mother and has a far more intense desire to get free from *him* than from *her*. In this

[6]Sigmund Freud, "Family Romances" ("Der Familienroman der Neurotiker" [1908]), in *The Standard Edition of the Complete Works of Sigmund Freud*, ed. James Strachey, 24 vols. (London: Hogarth, 1953), 9:237–41.

[7]Marthe Robert, *Origins of the Novel*, trans. Sacha Rabinowitch (Bloomington: Indiana University Press, 1980). For another extensive discussion of the family romance as fictional genre, see Christine van Boheemen, *The Novel as Family Romance: Language, Gender, and Authority from Fielding to Joyce* (Ithaca: Cornell University Press, 1987). Robert does not consider gender as a category; van Boheemen includes a brief discussion on gender in her introduction.

respect the imagination of girls is apt to show itself much weaker."[8] For Freud, the fantasies surrounding the child's relation to his or her origin, and the rebellious refusal of parental authority, processes intimately connected to the creation of fiction, are more available to the boy because they are embedded in the conflicts over authority between father and son. Because the girl fails to participate in the struggle over authority, or in the anxiety over legitimacy, she evinces, in Freud's terms, a weaker imagination.

At the second stage of the family romance a beginning awareness of "the difference in the parts played by fathers and mothers in their sexual relations" begins to inform fantasy. When the child realizes that "*pater semper incertus est,* while the mother is *certissima,* the family romance undergoes a curious curtailment: it contents itself with exalting the child's father, but no longer casts any doubts on his maternal origin, which is regarded as something unalterable." The child's fantasies, Freud insists, become sexual at this stage and take the mother as sexual object. Freud suggests that they have "two principal aims, an erotic and an ambitious one."[9] Robert classifies this plot as the "bastard" plot—the origins of the realist fiction of Balzac, Dostoyevski, Tolstoy, Proust, Faulkner, Dickens. But because of the different roles mothers and fathers play in the process of reproduction, the father alone enters into the realm of fantasy while the mother remains firmly and certainly planted in reality, excluded from the process of "fictionalization." While imagination can alter her *status* and explore her *sexuality,* it cannot replace her *identity.* This "real" mother does become the object of the child's manipulative fantasy, which turns her into an adulteress, the agent of his own social elevation. Typically the mother falls in status while the father is elevated to royalty. Ultimately, the mother is no more than an instrument in the central drama between father and son. Men thus participate more directly in the plot of class aspiration, which is an inherent aspect of the family romance, while women have only a mediated access to class mobility.

Freud and Robert do not explore the gender asymmetry of this second model. If these daydreams and fantasies are the bases for creativity, what are the implications of this shift in the family romance for the girl, especially for the girl who also wants to develop her imagination and wants to write? If the mother's identity is certain, then the girl lacks the important opportunity to replace imaginatively the same-sex parent, a process on which, Freud's model insists, imagination and cre-

[8]Freud, "Family Romances," 238.
[9]Ibid., 239, 238.

ativity depend. The father's presence, since his identity is uncertain, does not preclude fantasies of illegitimacy which can constitute a new self, free from familial and class constraints. The mother's presence, however, makes such fantasies impossible; therefore, we might extrapolate, in order to make possible the "opposition between successive generations" and to free the girl's imaginative play, the mother must be eliminated from the fiction. Yet even eliminating the mother from her plots cannot offer the girl a story that is parallel to the boy's: the drama of father and son, so fundamentally a conflict about authority and economic success in the public world, could never translate into a drama between mother and daughter. The girl's plot, if it is to have any import, must, like the boy's, revolve around the males in the family, who hold the keys to the power and ambition where plot resides.

Whereas the boy uses the mother as an instrument in the conflict with his father, however, and ultimately replaces his erotic fantasies with ambitious ones, the girl's fantasies revolve around the father in at once a more direct and a more conflicted manner. Since the father is *semper incertus,* the girl's heterosexual erotic relationships, unlike the boy's, are always potentially incestuous. *All* men are possible brothers, uncles, or fathers. Thus Freud's model implies that the danger of incest is more pronounced for the girl; the conditions for it lie at the basis of Freud's familial construction, making any marriage potentially incestuous, and, conversely, any father or brother a potentially safe erotic and sexual partner. In the female plot the father and his power *are* the object; what is more, fathers, brothers, uncles, and husbands are, in this particular psychic economy, interchangeable. Their precise *identity* is *semper incertus,* even as their *position* is forever desirable. Unlike the boy, who dreams of gaining authority by taking the father's place, the girl hopes to gain access to it by marrying him.

Thus, the "female family romance" implied in Freud's essay is founded on the elimination of the mother and the attachment to a husband/father. The feminine fiction then revolves not around the drama of same-sex parent-child relations but around marriage, which alone can place women's stories in a position of participating in the dynamics of power, authority, success, and legitimacy which constitute the plots of realist fiction. And in the marriage plot fathers, brothers, uncles, and husbands are conflated in complicated ways, and masculine representations often combine and modulate these roles.

Predictably, however, women writers do not simply hand over their heroines from mother to father/husband; they attempt to compensate for the loss of maternal nurturance by replacing the father with another man who offers an alternative to patriarchal power and dominance.

Here is where women writers, to varying degrees, challenge the model implied in Freud's essay. I have understood the female fantasy that emerges from this will to difference in Adrienne Rich's terms as the fantasy of "the-man-who-would-understand,"[10] the man who, unlike a distant and authoritarian father, would combine maternal nurturance with paternal power. The male object, in this transformation of the marriage plot, takes the form of a "brother" or "uncle" who can be nurturing even as he provides access to the issues of legitimacy and authority central to plotting. Most important, perhaps, his fraternal, incestuous status can protect the heroine from becoming a mother and thereby can help her, in spite of the closure of marriage, to remain a subject, not to disappear from plot as the object of her child's fantasy. It is thus that women writers, in a gesture of resistance, attempt to revise a cultural plot leading, with certainty and inevitability, not only to marriage but most especially to maternity, a developmental plot Freud traces in his later essays, "Female Sexuality" and "Femininity." Here Freud asserts, of course, that mature femininity means not only the replacement of the mother with the father as libidinal object, but the replacement of the wish for a penis with a wish for a child. In resisting this developmental course, women writers offer their heroines an alternative direction—and the possibility of remaining in the plot.

Yet, whereas the male foundling and bastard fantasies revolve around the self and guarantee the hero's agency, the revisionary fantasy of the-man-who-would-understand revolves around the attachment to another person, and can at best promise only a mediated access to plotting. Moreover, the fraternal lover or husband ultimately offers the heroine a limited alternative to the father's patriarchal power. The fraternal marriage, even when it comes about, is at best a qualified solution to the heroine's desire for a continuing plot. In fact, although the fraternal man-who-would-understand cannot literally become the husband of the heroine's children, he most often eventually assumes a patriarchal power that may have been veiled but that certainly was not absent during the courtship plot.[11] He frequently has to be eliminated from the heroine's life so that she will be forced to determine her own course.[12] And although the heroine's childlessness does not necessarily offer a solution that ensures her survival and imaginative creativity,

[10]See Adrienne Rich, "Natural Resources," in *The Dream of a Common Language: Poems, 1974–1977* (New York: Norton, 1978).
[11]Jane Austen's *Emma* provides a good example; see my discussion of Mr. Knightley in *Mother-Daughter Plot*, 60–61.
[12]See, for example, Charlotte Brontë's *Villette*.

her course, we assume, would be insurmountably impeded by maternity.[13]

"My Seared Vision! My Crippled Strength!"

Jane Eyre appears to be the epitome of the family romance: the orphan child, raised in a hostile counterfamily, freed imaginatively to dream of alternative familial contexts, to transform those dreams into fictions and those fictions into autobiography. As she sits in her window seat, Jane dreams her way into the family, only to realize that she is "less than a servant," brutally and unfairly cast out of their midst. Yet her healthy sense of injustice, coupled with her firm knowledge of her legitimacy, with her class affiliation, and with her education—a security that appears to be unshakable, resistant even to abuse and confinement—enhances Jane's freedom to imagine as well as her ability to analyze her situation and to speak out assertively against it. With father and mother dead, then, and with this combination of class security, clear-cut mistreatment, and, later, her education, Jane can fantasize various family romances. Her fantastic analysis of her situation appears most vividly in the dream-paintings Rochester later so admires, paintings that give us an insight into her "inward eye" and the familial landscapes it can dream up (109–11). The first, a drowned female corpse whose arm sticks out of the water below a powerful cormorant who holds her gold bracelet is perhaps her dead mother, marked by the sign of economic security representing female victimization and masculine dominance. The second, a soft pastel female bust with stars in her hair and dark, wild eyes, is clearly an alternative maternal figure of her imagination, an angry mother-goddess perhaps. The third, a colossal diademed head with hollow, despairing eyes, draped in a dark turban, could represents a patriarchal specter whose power she challenges and whose vitality she removes: his ring is of white flame, and his sparkles have a lurid tinge.

Jane is motherless, and indeed Brontë replaces the mother with other parental figures. Jane is not unnurtured: Bessie, Miss Temple, Helen Burns, the memory of Mr. Reed all contribute to her relative psychic security, although none assumes an importance she cannot fantasize herself away from. She even enjoys the spiritual nurture of the moon, which appears to her on a number of occasions as an alternative pres-

---

[13]Kate Chopin's *Awakening*, ed. Margo Culley (New York: Norton, 1976), movingly illustrates this point.

ence to the Christian spirituality represented in the novel by St. John. Until we get to Rochester, the novel conforms perfectly to the female family romance pattern: Jane is an orphan; her father's family's economic status is uncertain, but her mother's identity and position is *certissima*. Even though she is told that she is less than a servant, she knows to assert her right to be treated as an individual, and her individuality is firmly upheld by the class allegiance she can claim through maternal certainty. In the Reed household, as well as later at school, at Thornfield, and at Marsh's End, Jane has the opportunity to fantasize various familial configurations that would improve her condition. Through those fantasies Jane develops the imagination that so characterizes her.

But in Brontë's novel Edward Rochester is not the fraternal man-who-would-understand. Although at their first encounter Rochester falls off his horse and relies on Jane's assistance, although he appeals for her help on other occasions, although he cross-dresses as the Gypsy, although he "understands" Jane down to her deepest spirit and she can assert that they are "equals" as her spirit addresses his spirit, although, in other words, the novel works hard to establish their mutual understanding and in some sense their equality, Rochester never for a moment relinquishes his masculine patriarchal power, never surrenders his sexual otherness. And even though his economic, experiential, sexual, and generational power is unambiguously established early in the novel, even though it is accepted by Jane, who calls herself his dependent and calls him "master," he uses every opportunity to bolster it even further. The Gypsy scene and his charade about the impending marriage to Miss Ingram are good examples of Rochester's shameless abuse of power and status and his distance from the persona of the fraternal lover. Rochester's secrecy, his insistence about dressing Jane, about transforming her as quickly as possible into Mrs. Rochester, the "iron grip" with which he hurries her to church all leave no doubt as to his distant and powerful masculinity and to Jane's "mistake" in her choice of partner, a mistake which his violent "marital" struggle with Bertha and his hubristic attempts to defy religious and state law only serve to underscore.

Whereas in other novels the fraternal lover eventually turns into the patriarchal husband, however, veiling his phallic power only then to display it with surprising force, Rochester actually travels an opposite course: with the loss of his eyesight and his limb, he also definitively loses the dominance which made him unworthy of marrying Jane. The physical disabilities caused by the fire at Thornfield are metaphors for the harsh and painful psychological and spiritual transformations he

undergoes. At Ferndean he again and again reminds Jane of his dependence, his weakness, his "seared vision and crippled strength"
(391). Jane rewards him by insisting: "I love you better now, when I
can really be useful to you, than I did in your state of proud independence when you disdained every part but that of the giver and
protector" (392). As she becomes the intermediary by which Rochester
sees, feels, and interprets the world in and around him, Jane gains the
power Rochester has lost: "He saw nature—he saw books through me;
and never did I weary of gazing on his behalf, and of putting into
words the effect of field, tree, town, river, cloud, sunbeam: never did I
weary of reading to him" (397). They reverse roles, as she now teases
him and makes him jealous of St. John. And she maintains full control
of her story, to the point of keeping to herself, and to her reader, a
crucial moment in her tale: her own participation in the supernatural
between them reported by Rochester: "I listened to Mr. Rochester's narrative; but made no disclosure in return. The coincidence struck me as
too awful and inexplicable to be communicated or discussed. If I told
anything, my tale would be such as must necessarily make a profound
impression on the mind of my hearer: and that mind . . . needed not
the deeper shade of the supernatural. I kept these things then and pondered them in my heart" (394). Through these reversals, through Jane's
increased control and authority, Rochester becomes the twin man-who-
would-understand. "No woman was ever nearer to her mate than I am;
ever more absolutely bone of his bone and flesh of his flesh" (396, 397).[14]

But unlike other fraternal husbands or lovers who become quasi-
incestuous and thereby protect the heroine from maternity,[15] Rochester
maintains enough distance and enough masculine potency literally to
become the father of Jane's child. "His form was of the same strong
and stalwart contour as ever: his port was still erect, his hair was still
raven-black, nor were his features altered or sunk: not in one year's
space, by any sorrow, could his athletic strength be quelled, or his vigorous prime blighted" (387). Rochester is a "caged eagle," a "royal
eagle chained to a perch." And when he expresses openly his anxieties
about his potency, Jane explicitly reassures him: "You are green and
vigorous. Plants will grow about your roots, whether you ask them or

[14]For a different reading of Rochester's masculinity, see Jean Wyatt, *Reconstructing Desire: The Role of the Unconscious in Women's Reading and Writing* (Chapel Hill: University
of North Carolina Press, 1990). Wyatt sees Rochester as providing for Jane a chance
actually to marry the father and to experience a paternal nurturance that most women
desire but cannot get.
[15]For example, Mr. Knightley, Heathcliff in Emily Brontë's *Wuthering Heights,* and Ben-
edict in George Sand's *Valentine.*

not, because they take delight in your bountiful shadow; and as they grow they will lean towards you, and wind around you, because your strength offers them so safe a prop" (391). This, we might say, is the ultimate fantasy of the man-who-would-understand. Characterizing the penis and not the phallus, Rochester's is a potency without oppressive patriarchal privilege. Whereas at Thornfield Rochester had to drag Jane to be married with an "iron grip," here at Ferndean he can humbly wait for "plants" to "wind around him" gladly and voluntarily, seeking his "safe prop" on their own.

Such potency is clearly dangerous, however. For Jane that danger lies in the fact that it arouses her sexuality, a condition which, as the representation of the sensual and sexual Bertha demonstrates, is frought with pitfalls. Its only possible redemption, maternity, is also a condition that cannot, in the context of this novel, or of Victorian fiction more generally, be either a welcome or a safe one. In order to confront this double danger and to find a course allowing its heroine's survival, *Jane Eyre* needs to reshape further the female family romance fantasy.

Dreaming of Children

"To dream of children was a sure sign of trouble, either to oneself or one's kin," Jane assures us as her obsessive dreams begin (193). She has learned this, like many other things, from Bessie and Miss Abbott, the servants at Gateshead, and, as much as the novel works hard at establishing Jane's difference from servant women, she does share with them this fear of birth and maternity. Jane dreams of children on two separate occasions: first, there is a week-long series of dreams preceding the call for a return to the Reed household. Next there are two dreams preceding her planned marriage, dreamt on the same night during which Rochester is away on a trip. These dreams are usually read as delayed expressions of Jane's unprocessed childhood anger and rage. Directed at her mistreatment and her dependency, the rage of the red room stays with her as an internal barrier separating her from the possibility of marriage and adulthood. It can be argued, however, that in these dreams of children Jane plays both the role of the child and the role of the caretaker, that she sees herself not only as the helpless child but also as its mother. And in the role of mother Jane is also helpless and alone. She associates her dreams with scenes of violence and death, all familial scenes such as Richard Mason's injury at the hands of his sister, and John Reed's suicide and his mother's illness. These scenes clarify the violence that resides within familial structures, exposing the mother, in particular, to danger. The second two dreams, preceding Jane's "marriage," associate adult femininity and especially maternity with solitude, weariness, and peril. Jane feels the child to be a barrier between herself and Rochester. In both dreams she chases Rochester, but is impeded from catching up to him by the burden of the child. In both dreams he is free to leave for distant countries, or just to walk down the road, while she remains in charge of the wailing infant. And in the second dream she fails to protect the child; the wall on which she perches crumbles, and the child rolls off her knee. Her solitary maternity beomes lethal, for both mother and child.

It is at this point, as she awakens from this dream, or while still dreaming, that Jane encounters the mysterious monster Bertha, though the association of Bertha with the child dream was already established earlier. In previous readings Bertha was seen to represent a warning to Jane that she must overcome and repress her childhood rage lest she should wish to turn into the monstrous and uncontained bundle of passions which Bertha embodies, and which is reinforced by Bertha's Jamaican and Creole origins. If we read the dream as representing Jane's maternity and not her childhood anger, however, then what does the connection to Bertha mean? In this reading Bertha becomes for Jane an image of the reproduction of mothering. First, Bertha is, of course, the "infamous daughter of an infamous mother." She is also, by oedipal association, Rochester's wife, and therefore a maternal figure to Jane, a figure Jane must displace. Thus for Jane, as she imagines herself married to Rochester, and either a sexual adult woman or a mother, the rage of the red room comes back in the figure of Bertha, the married woman abandoned by her husband for her uncontrolled appetite, the woman who is doomed to repeat the mad life of her own mother. Jane's rage, then, is not the rage of the abandoned child but the rage of the abandoned adult woman who could never imagine combining sexuality and maternity, and for whom either course appears potentially ruinous. If we look at Grace Poole, Bertha's alternate persona, this association is borne out: Grace, the lone caretaker of her wailing, heavy, unpredictable charge, is the figure Jane invokes in her dream as she falls off the roof. Jane is both, of course, the neglectful caretaker and the neglected infant, both Grace and Bertha. Her unconscious anxiety and fear are aimed at the position of lone caretaker, at her sole responsibility for her own life and for the life of another who is dependent on her as she has been dependent on others.

These dreams of children are the underside of Jane's other familial fantasies, both the orphan fantasy and the fantasy of the man-who-would-understand. Whereas these are fantasies of freedom and result in creativity, the other is a fantasy of confinement and destructiveness, a fantasy of both destroying and being destroyed. And yet, at the end of the novel Jane describes her firstborn. How does she circumvent the threats and dangers of motherhood? How does she combine maternity, sexuality, and creativity? I would suggest that the novel offsets the dreams of children and the disastrous maternal portraits they paint with more reassuring visions of what maternal work might entail. If she thinks back on her history, Jane will note that if she were to have children as Mrs. Rochester, she would not in fact be the one to care for them. She herself and her cousins are raised not by Mrs. Reed but by Bessie and Miss Abbott, who feed them, dress them, tell them stories, sing to them, and even administer moral lessons to them. Mrs. Reed might bear the reponsibility for overseeing their work and training them, but, like many Victorian fictional mothers, she acts overwhelmed and helpless, and she does not do the actual caretaking work. As in the Reed household, maternal functions are scattered throughout the novel, and, except in the case of the young Bessie charged with the infant Jane, and that of Grace Poole, women with whom Jane only very partially identifies, they never rest too firmly or burdensomely on a single woman.

Jane herself is cleverly protected from the worst parts of her own "maternal" work as a teacher or governess. When she teaches at Lowood, she has the leisure to paint her watercolors and do a lot of dreaming. When she is engaged as Adele's governess, she can always send her off to her nurse, or ask Mrs. Fairfax to take her. When Adele models her new dresses, for example, Jane, even while pretending to be present, does not pay attention. Rochester describes the scene thus: "I observed you . . . for half an hour, while you played with Adele in the gallery. . . . Adele claimed your outward attention for a while; yet I fancied your thoughts were elsewhere: but you were patient with her, my little Jane; you talked to her and amused her a long time. When at last she left you you lapsed at once into deep reverie . . . you paced gently on and dreamed" (275). Teaching Adele and playing with her need not interfere with Jane's dreaming, with her imaginative and creative activities. The same is true of her work as a schoolteacher at Marsh's End: Jane teaches but has the time and leisure to study with St. John. The duties of the governess or the teacher are not represented in the novel as a form of work that invades or threatens one's identity or interferes with one's creativity. Brontë uses Jane's roles as governess and teacher effectively to establish her dependence and marginality, but she also protects Jane from any deeper contamination by the world of work: her functions and investments remain as vague, diffused, and scattered throughout the novel as possible. And, surprisingly, this remains true as Jane moves up the class and economic ladder from pupil to governess, to teacher, and eventually to mother.

Brontë exploits the liminal position of the governess within the family, so brilliantly analyzed by Mary Poovey, and also what that liminality implies—the actual caretaking functions of servants.[16] Poovey distinguishes between the mother (the idealized unemployed) and the governess (who does for wages what the mother should be doing for free and who thereby destabilizes and threatens familial boundaries). We need to see, however, that the mother is after all employed: she supervises the household, including often very young servants and governesses. Although that work is different from the actual caretaking function of servants, it is work nevertheless.[17] We also need to distinguish the governess (who in this novel can move into the role of the "underemployed" mother, whose boundary from her is tenuous and can be crossed) from the servant (who cannot because she is separated by class). In this novel, then, as in other novels of the period, maternity is a threat not because of the work middle-class mothers do, for in fact the work of middle-class mothering is only tangentially related to the physical and emotional care of children. Maternity is a threat for other, deeper reasons of identity, and those reasons interestingly and subversively connect women of different classes and backgrounds. In fact, we best see the danger of maternity in the person of Grace Poole, the caretaker contaminated by her charge. Through most of the novel Grace *is* the insane woman on the third floor, who laughs, haunts, and stabs people. We see the danger of maternity in the Creole woman, Antoinetta Mason, who transmits her insanity to her daughter, and in the French woman, Céline Varens, who abandons her child to poverty rather than raise her. We see to what lengths Mrs. Reed goes to protect herself from these dangers of maternal contamination, by hiring servants and by adopting rigid principles of patriarchal Christian education, and ultimately how devastating and lethal her maternity proves to be nonetheless.

The dangers of maternity for Jane are most clearly manifested in her relation to St. John and in her response to his demands. Although he appears in the novel primarily as the fraternal patriarch, St. John's demands on Jane resemble a child's demands. Jane nearly loses herself in

---

[16]Mary Poovey, *Uneven Developments: The Ideological Work of Gender in Mid-Victorian England* (Chicago: University of Chicago Press, 1990), esp. 126–63.

[17]I am indebted to Mary Childers for allowing me to read her unpublished analysis of the structure of work in Brontë's novel, which constitutes a fundamental disagreement with Poovey's reading.

a relation which is dictated by convention, which involves the bodily threat of contamination in the East, and which attracts her with a nearly irresistible compulsion. In all three respects this relationship resembles maternity. Opposed to her caretaking relation to Rochester, which is adult, mutual, and self-enriching rather than self-diminishing, her connection to St. John is profoundly endangering. The investment in maternity as identity is akin to Jane's investment in St. John, threatening the loss of the self Jane so firmly knows she has to take care of herself. But in this novel Brontë begins to redefine the shapes of maternal work and identity in such a way as to propose it as a viable possibility for Jane.

The Reproduction of Fathering

"He would send for the baby; though I entreated him rather to put it out to nurse and pay for its maintenance. I hated it the first time I set my eyes on it—a sickly, whining, pining thing! It would wail in its cradle all night long—not screaming heartily like any other child, but whimpering and moaning. Reed pitied it; and he used to nurse it and notice it as if it had been his own: more, indeed, than he ever noticed his own at that age. . . . In his last illness, he had it brought continually to his bedside" (203, 204). This account of Jane's infancy by the dying Mrs. Reed clarifies aspects of the family romance plot and Brontë's transformations of it. As Mr. Reed adopts Jane, and attempts to get his wife to promise to take care of her, the illegitimate family is made legitimate, thereby restoring his incestuous bond with his sister, broken by her marriage. The account is especially striking, however, because, except for Jane's dream, it is the novel's only account of actual nurturing behavior. Consoling a wailing child, in waking life, is left to a man, an uncle. This differs from but is related to other paternal and avuncular acts in the novel: Rochester's adoption of Adele, whom he does not like but pities enough to provide for her and raise her in his house; Mr. Eyre's intervention on behalf of Jane, also financial and moral, though not directly physical; to a much lesser degree the nurturing presence and moral intervention of Mr. Lloyd on behalf of Jane; and St. John's intervention to rescue Jane from the threshold of death on the moors.

These acts of paternal nurturance are powerful enough in the novel to threaten Mrs. Reed utterly. She fails to keep her promise to Mr. Reed, a promise that would extend his protection of his niece beyond his death. She cannot bear to help Mr. Eyre establish a connection with

Jane and reports her dead. What does she have to gain from this lie, which follows her to her grave? Nothing but to circumvent a form of relation she perceives as more powerful than any other: the connection between uncle and niece, a connection that can "lift [Jane] to prosperity" (210) and legitimacy within the family, and can move her firmly into the space of plot.

In sending Jane to Lowood, Mrs. Reed substitutes a different, a dominant, authoritarian and patriarchal form of paternity, Mr. Brocklehurst's domineering and oppressive child rearing practices, for Mr. Reed's nurturing care. Lowood is designed to control and contain all aspects of feminine desire, all female appetite, whether it be for food, material possessions, pleasure, imaginative play, or even knowledge exceeding the conventional canon of acceptability. Body, intellect, soul, and will have to be regimented and regulated to become smooth instruments of the reproduction of traditional values and norms. All passion needs painfully to be eliminated through humiliation and correction. Brocklehurst's authoritarian power is echoed later in the novel by St. John and his mission, associated in the novel with institutionalized Christianity. St. John functions both as Jane's demanding child and as an exacting father, much more than as the brother, as she and he want to define their relation:

> By degrees, he acquired a certain influence over me that took away my liberty of mind: his praise and notice were more restraining than his indifference. I could no longer talk or laugh freely when he was by, because a tiresomely importunate instinct reminded me that vivacity . . . was distasteful to him. I was so fully aware that only serious moods and occupations were acceptable, that in his presence every effort to sustain or follow any other became vain: I fell under a freezing spell. When he said "go," I went; "come," I came; "do this," I did it. But I did not love my servitude. (354)

Marriage to such a man is lethal: "If I were to marry you, you would kill me. You are killing me now" (363), Jane insists, realizing that St. John represents the opposite of sensual desire or sexual passion and that marital relation should not be based on such thorough repression of desire and the body.

St. John's protective and repressive paternal functions extend not only over Jane and the rest of his family but also over "his race." The manner in which St. John works for humanity is distinctly paternal and patriarchal: "Firm, faithful, and devoted; full of energy, and zeal, and truth, he labors for his race: he clears their painful way to improvement:

he hews down like a giant the prejudices of creed and caste that encumber it. He may be stern; he may be exacting: he may be ambitious yet; . . . but his is the ambition of the high master-spirit, which aims to fill a place in the first rank of those who are redeemed from the earth" (398). As "master" and father, St. John inserts himself in an apostolic line of sons and fathers, beginning with Jesus and God. This is St. John's authoritarian paternity, a paternity the novel sharply and definitively contrasts to another form of refigured paternity—that of Mr. Reed, Mr. Lloyd, Mr. Eyre, and Edward Rochester. As it reshapes paternity, the novel also distances itself from the patriarchal and imperialist civilizing mission St. John undertakes on behalf of "his race." With the critique of Brocklehurst's and St. John's paternity, the novel wants to imagine a different form of spiritual content and relation, one that is perhaps best approximated by the communication Jane achieves with the moon, or the supernatural "conversation" she has with Rochester. These are both based on a deep empathy rather than on the need to improve or correct.

Rochester is the agent of the novel's refigured paternity. From the protector of Adele who does not like children, Rochester turns into the father who hold his child in his arms and stares into his eyes. With his vulnerability Rochester gains in nurturance, and as we have seen, his nurturance is enriched by his potency. This male nurturance, built up in the novel through the figures of Reed, Lloyd, and Eyre, makes it possible for Jane to become a mother and not to claim her child but to hand it over, instead, directly to its father. In developing, ever so suggestively, Rochester's redeemed paternity, Brontë adds another dimension to the female family romance. For Rochester is a different paternal figure from the other fathers in the novel. He has money like Mr. Eyre and Mr. Reed, but he lacks the moral authority of Mr. Lloyd, and, most important, he lacks the relation to the symbolic that all three share. That contact the novel reserves for Jane: "He cannot read or write much; but he can find his way without being led by the hand: the sky is no longer a blank to him—the earth no longer a void." Whereas the other three nurturing paternal figures remain distant, disembodied, benevolent, Rochester is definitively embodied in his disability. He describes himself as a "sightless block," insisting: " 'On this arm I have neither hand nor nails,' he said drawing the mutilated limb from his breast, and showing it to me. 'It is a mere stump and ghastly sight' " (384). Thus embodied, thus responsible for earth and sky and not for books, holding his child in his arms, Rochester differs both from the authoritarian/authoritative and from the nurturing fathers. He is, and the novel suggests this ever so subtly, the "male mother," whose nurturance, obviously relieved by the caretaking work of servants and governesses, could free Jane to continue her imaginative labor and to write her story. This male mother is the figure Jane chased after in her dreams; this is the parent, the partner fantasized in an adult female family romance. He is both dependent and to be depended upon; he is weak and also strong. He is the embodied father, the vulnerable father, the humble father.

Why, however, is Jane's "firstborn," the only child she mentions in the novel, a boy? Why, like most other nineteenth-century heroines, is Jane unable to reproduce herself? Why does the novel displace a reproduction of daughters?[18] Does the novel still fear the daughter-father bond, a bond always profoundly threatening to both mothers and daughters, and especially so if the father is nurturing as well as powerful? Does Jane fear it because of its seductions, its threats of incest and daughterly exchange? Or does she, like Mrs. Reed, fear it because it would exclude her as a mother from a bond she can never equal for her daughters? Or is it, conversely, that in highlighting the son's mirroring moment with a male rather than a female "mother" ("he could see that the boy had inherited his own eyes, as they once were—large, brilliant and black"), Brontë envisions a "reproduction of fathering" which becomes a "male mothering" and a different masculinity? If this last is true, then the novel even more radically distances itself from St. John's patriarchal Christian imperialist vision, outlined contiguously to it in the text. Linking these two visions of fathering, St. John's paternity and Rochester's male maternity, is Rochester's acknowledgment of a God who had "tempered judgment with mercy" (397) and Jane's happy picture of an extended egalitarian family connected through the sisterhood of Jane, Diana, and Mary, a sisterhood that thrives in the absence of the brother, St. John. This family successfully functions within the law because, as far as the novel reveals, it is not tested: Rochester's son is his "firstborn," but we are not privy to whatever conflict over inheritance and exchange might threaten to reproduce the disastrous familial situations of Jane and Rochester's own families of origin.

It seems, moreover, that although this family romance fantasizes a way of reproducing and changing the father, to the point of casting him as a male mother, it still cannot reproduce female mothering or a female line of transmission. Here it reaches one limit of its radical potential. No legitimate daughter is mentioned in the novel; Adele is

---

[18]Some novels allow the heroine an indirect form of reproduction, through a niece or the child of a friend, but never a direct one. See the little niece Valentine at the end of Sand's *Valentine*, and the little Emma, daughter of Miss Taylor, at the end of Austen's *Emma*.

rather cleverly removed from the family; and Jane never herself adopts a maternal voice. The story she writes, like the pictures she draws, keeps her firmly intricated in her infantile identity and in her own uniqueness and unreproducibility. And although her family romance fantasies do mature to adulthood, they stop short of detailing a vision of herself as a mother who is also a sexual woman and a writer.

If Jane is able to write, if she is able to appropriate from Rochester the access to the symbolic, she may be able do so in spite of being a mother, but she cannot do so *as a mother*. Jane's family romances have transcended the individualist bildungsroman by refiguring masculinity as well as femininity, and by situating individual development in the midst of pressing social, economic, and historical issues of class and empire which shape and reshape the story of *Bildung*. Yet Jane as narrator does remain the separating daughter, the abused and neglected rebel child. It is as daughter and as rebel child, in fact, that she continues to appeal to contemporary feminist readings, whether those readings are celebratory or critical. Although she can envision a male mother who can transmit to his son the contact with the earth and the sky, Brontë is unable to envision a female mother who can write her story in a maternal voice, who can write about the mother and the daughter in the different family romance she fantasizes.[19] Jane's limited ability to adopt the perspective of maternity and adulthood also limits the range of the family romances she can fantasize and enact.

Nor does *Jane Eyre* enable us to step out of the bounds of the familial, and here is where the family romance paradigm reveals both its strengths and its limitations of view. At the end of her plot Jane is firmly based in the new and admittedly renewed family she has forged. The setting of her familial life is inauspicious: Ferndean is Rochester's least attractive property, deemed too damp and unhealthy even to house the mad Bertha. Other than Diana, Mary, and their husbands and children, the Rochesters seem to associate with no one; whatever familial transformation Brontë was able to envision had to remain utopian and limited in scale. Yet the bases of the envisioned transformations also had to remain unexamined. As a new family consolidates itself, it practices its own blindness and exclusions. Adele comes dangerously close to repeating the status of Jane in the Reed household; her removal from the family seems to be rather cruel. Jane's status in her new family is ensured by the financial security she achieves by means of her uncle's colonial possessions, though this source is never

[19]In *Mother-Daughter Plot* I reflect in more detail on the absence of maternal perspectives in women's fiction, expecially in nineteenth-century realism. See esp. chaps. 1–3.

questioned in the space of the text. Rochester's transformation is made possible, however painfully, by Bertha's convenient death and her destruction of their tainted past life. St. John himself, moreover, is excluded from the fold of his metropolitan family and left to absorb the colonial guilt and the civilizing labor which actually facilitate the family's consolidation on both economic and moral grounds. As much as they allow for revision and manipulation, familial fantasies and the family romance paradigm which enables us to analyze them continue to perpetuate structures separating inside from outside which may well be basic to the realist novel. And even as a feminist revision of the family romance allows us to perceive these structures, it does not allow us to step outside them.

Part III
Sites of Critical Practice

9

Philoctetes' Sister: Feminist Literary Criticism and the New Misogyny

NANCY K. MILLER

Feminist critics have a complicated relationship to home. It's a place you might want to visit, but you wouldn't want to live there . . . anymore. The comforts of home (nostalgias about) are bad for politics; they create false intimacies and support hierarchies of domestic violence. In the university, departments can get to seem like home; in some institutions one talks of a home department, the way we had "homerooms" in high school. For some time now I've been without a true departmental home. The last time I had an official one it was the French Department at Columbia (I "belonged" to the "family" by virtue of my degree but was never allowed to grow up there). When I finally left the French Department for the Women's Studies Program at Barnard, I took the first steps toward institutional homelessness. A program, especially an interdisciplinary one, is not a department and is defined by the fact that no one is meant to live there. By the time I joined an English department at CUNY seven years later, my sense of an (intra) institutional home had been radically eroded: add to this the fact that at the Graduate Center I also became a member of the French and Comparative Literature programs (except that at the Graduate Center those programs function as departments), as well as the Women's Studies faculty (which *is* a program), rotating my teaching every semester,

An earlier version of this essay appeared in my book *Getting Personal: Feminist Occasions and Other Autobiographical Acts* (New York: Routledge, 1991), © 1991 by Nancy K. Miller; used here in revised form by permission.

When I wrote the essay that follows for the Conference on Narrative Literature organized by Susan Stanford Friedman and held at Madison, Wisconsin, in April 1989, I was thinking primarily of misogyny practiced by masculinist critics (which did not preclude the possibility of the occasional female honorary man). Writing today, I would need to redefine the field to include egregious examples of "feminist misogyny," building on Susan Gubar's provocative analysis, "Feminist Misogyny: Mary Wollstonecraft and the Paradox of 'It Takes One to Know One,' " forthcoming in *Feminism beside Itself*, ed. Diane Elam and Robyn Wiegman (New York: Routledge). A great deal of feminism in the 90s seems bent on an internal critique indistinguishable in its tactics and vulgarity from the standard masculinist model of rational violence. It is difficult to understand what interests are served by these frontal assaults, if not those of the very misogynists whose discriminatory views engendered the articulation of feminist positions in the first place.

and you start to get the picture. Where did I belong? In an attempt to check my nomadism (I was also expected to change offices every semester), I finally persuaded the powers that be to give me an office . . . in the English Program segment of the corridor of the Grace Building on the fortieth floor. In the tiny office I share (but it has a window!) I have often wondered where I live. (I know I'm in New York because I have a view of the Hudson River.) Once a week I travel to Lehman College in the Bronx, where the office I share has a view of the reservoir; that doesn't feel much like a home either. At CUNY the motto should be: "We are all adjuncts"—or almost; some of us, it's true, travel with tenure.

In this postmodern moment the multiplicity of my sites of teaching seems almost, as they say, de rigueur. I cross departmental borders on a regular basis and have therefore come to wonder whether we ought to be making such a fuss about the permeability of boundaries. In each displacement I'm still bringing whatever it is that I have to offer: as a feminist, as a reader in two languages, as a cultural critic. What does it mean to be a comparatist and a feminist? The answer I have in mind reminds me of the punch line of the old joke that goes something like this: A man crosses the border between France and Italy (or Mexico and the United States) on a daily basis. He does this for years on his bicycle. Finally, the customs official says, "Look, I know you've been taking something across the border. Today's my last day on the job, I'm retiring. Just tell me: What are you smuggling?" And the man tells him: bicycles.

Did Philoctetes Have a Sister?

In "School-Time," the second book of *The Mill on the Floss*, Maggie Tulliver visits her brother Tom, who has been sent away to school for what their father calls "a good eddication: an eddication as'll be a bread to him."[1] What this means to Mr. Tulliver emerges in a conversation he has with Mr. Riley, a gentleman (and auctioneer) who has impressed Tulliver with his learning, and who is advising him in the proper choice of school. To Riley's question about Tom's intelligence, Tulliver replies:

Well, he isn't not to say stupid—he's got a notion o' things out o' door, an' a sort o' commonsense, as he'd lay hold o' things by the right handle.

[1]George Eliot, *The Mill on the Floss* (New York: Penguin, 1979), 56; subsequent references are cited in the text.

But he's slow with his tongue, you see, and he reads but poorly, and can't abide the books, and spells all wrong, they tell me, an' as shy as can be wi' strangers, an' you never hear him say 'cute things like the little wench. Now, what I want is, to send him to a school where they'll make him a bit nimble with his tongue and his pen, and make a smart chap of him. I want my son to be even wi' these fellows as have got the start o' me with having better schooling. (69)

On the first day of Maggie's visit, Tom proves as clumsy laying hold of things by the right handle as with his tongue (moving his lips as he reads his Latin lessons). Trying to impress his sister with his prowess by impersonating the Duke of Wellington, he drops the sword he has been waving about—heroically, he hopes—on his foot and faints dead away from the pain. Tom's accident, which he briefly fears will leave him lame, brings him unexpectedly (and as briefly) closer to his more intellectually gifted schoolmate Philip Wakem. Philip, who reads Greek with pleasure—this impresses Maggie and baffles Tom—has in the past entertained Tom with what Tom calls "fighting stories," and on this occasion he tells Tom and Maggie the story of Philoctetes, "a man who had a very bad wound in his foot, and cried out so dreadfully with the pain, that his friends could bear with him no longer, but put him ashore on a desert island, with nothing but some wonderful poisoned arrows to kill animals with for food" (258–59). Maggie and Tom have different reactions to Philip's narrative about the lame man: Tom claims that *he* didn't roar out with pain; Maggie feels that it is permissible to cry out when injured, but her response to the story is finally less a reaction to the accident itself than to its consequences, the lame man's abandonment on the island. "She wanted to know," Eliot's narrator writes, "if Philoctetes had a sister, and why *she* didn't go with him on the desert island and take care of him" (259). (I will return to Maggie's question.)

In "The Wound and the Bow," Edmund Wilson reflects on the legend of Philoctetes as dramatized by Sophocles. Wilson begins his reflection by observing that the play is "far from being his most popular," and the "myth itself . . . not . . . one of those which have excited the modern imagination." The *Philoctetes*, Wilson argues early in the essay, "assigns itself . . . to a category even more special and less generally appealing [than that of *Le misanthrope*, to which he compares its psychological conflict] through the fact . . . that the conflict is not even allowed to take place between a man and a woman." Commenting on the limited "imprint of the play on literature since the Renaissance," perhaps because of its exclusive focus on the relations between men, Wilson cites the example of a "French dramatist of the seventeenth century, Chateaubrun, [who] found the subject so inconceivable that, in trying to concoct an adaptation which would be acceptable to the taste of his time . . . provided Philoctetes with a daughter named Sophie with whom Neoptolemus was to fall in love and thus bring the drama back to the reliable and eternal formula of Romeo and Juliet and the organizer who loves the factory-owner's daughter."[2]

My concern here is not to determine whether Philoctetes really had a sister, a daughter, or even a mother—though we can, I suppose, feel rather more certain about the last. Nor by my emphasis on Maggie's creation of a woman in the text am I advocating an "ethics of care" (in Carol Gilligan's terms) or a "poetics of need" (in Lawrence Lipking's). I want to suggest instead that, like the feminist critic at the end of the twentieth century, reading against the doxa of indifference and its institutional exclusions, Maggie imagines a sister for Philoctetes and inserts herself in a story otherwise notable, as Wilson points out, for being "devoid of feminine interest" in order to place herself as a subject of cultural narrative. Maggie had already bumped up against the codes of gender in her first visit to Mr. Stelling's school. She had pondered the example in her brother's Latin Grammar of the "astronomer who hated women," wondering whether "all astronomers hated women, or whether it was only this particular astronomer." She concluded without waiting for the teacher's answer: "I suppose it's all astronomers: because you know, they live up in high towers, and if the women came there, they might talk and hinder them from looking at the stars" (220). On the heels of this mournful interpretation, she had heard Mr. Stelling pronounce, to her brother's immense satisfaction, that girls had "a great deal of superficial cleverness," but that "they couldn't go far into anything. They're quick and shallow" (220–21). Maggie, whose father had earlier lamented to Mr. Riley the "topsy-turvy world" which produces "stupid lads and 'cute wenches" (68–69), and who will not be sent away to Mr. Stelling's to learn Latin or Greek, returns home after her visit, reduced to silence by the prospect of "this dreadful destiny" (221).

Feminist critics have for two decades debated the matter of the astronomers and their hatred of women, in particular and in general. Mary Jacobus, in a discussion of the politics of women's writing, has offered an especially rewarding reading of misogyny in these passages and the staging in Eliot's novel of the "question of women's access to knowledge and culture and to the power that goes with them."[3] But

[2]Edmund Wilson, "The Wound and the Bow," in *The Wound and the Bow: Seven Studies in Literature* (New York: Oxford University Press, 1965), 223–24.

[3]Mary Jacobus, "Is There a Woman in This Text?," in *Reading Woman: Essays in Feminist Criticism* (New York: Columbia University Press, 1986), 68.

let us leave the *Mill* and turn now instead to the misogyny of the new astronomers—the Stellings of contemporary literary life in academia. I want to look specifically at the *language* of their reactions to the feminist critics who have pursued in different ways the implications in literature and in culture of the "dreadful destiny" reserved for girls like Maggie Tulliver: the thwarted life and early death—to pick a fable dear to literary feminism—of Shakespeare's sister, famously imagined by Virginia Woolf.

A Report from the Academy, or the New Astronomy

In the fall of 1988 *American Scholar* (the organ of Phi Beta Kappa) published an essay called "Feminist Literary Criticism" (and subtitled "A Report from the Academy"). Its author, Peter Shaw, identified as "the author of the forthcoming *The War against the Intellect: Episodes in the Decline of Discourse*," begins his report with an epigraph from Virginia Woolf: "The greatest writers lay no stress upon sex one way or the other. The critic is not reminded as he reads them that he belongs to the masculine or feminine gender."[4] The choice of epigraph is important, for it appropriates—at the threshold of a hostile review of feminist criticism—the signature of feminist criticism's "foremother," who appears here to authorize the dismissal of one of literary feminism's central questions: the relation of gender to the reading and writing of literature and criticism. Through Woolf the critic both separates himself from the challenge of feminist criticism—having to remember as he reads the effects of a social identity constituted in gender—and universalizes his position through his adherence to the canons: "the greatest writers."

This is not an especially original essay (it is very reminiscent in its basic moves of Denis Donoghue's 1986 attack on feminist criticism: a generic trashing, one might say), but its interest for us here resides precisely in its patronizing familiarity.[5] "Feminist Literary Criticism"

---

[4]Peter Shaw, *The War against the Intellect* (Iowa City: University of Iowa Press, 1989); subsequent references are cited in the text. Although I've consulted several Woolf scholars, I have been unable to locate this quotation, and have begun to wonder whether it has been misremembered, just as the critic converts my phrase "women's writing" to "gender difference." Is this epigraph a transformation of: "It is fatal for any one who writes to think of their sex" (*A Room of One's Own* [New York: Harcourt, Brace, and World, 1967], 108)? Woolf, moreover, tends to use the word *sex*, not *gender*, to mark constructed gendered identities.

[5]The Denis Donoghue piece, "A Criticism of One's Own," originally appeared in the

marks the reincrustation of an updated misogyny—the refusal to acknowledge the epistemological and cultural constructions of sexual difference—within a certain (we're all human) mainstream. I think it's
worth attending to this renewal of discursive misogyny (directed at
feminists on behalf of women!) as part of a general movement of reactionary gestures within a variety of institutional contexts.[6]

The report begins with what its author takes to be the "most troublesome" question within feminist criticism today: "whether or not
women's writing differs in some essential way from men's" (67). Like
Donoghue's, this irascible humanist's difficulty with feminist criticism
is intimately bound up with what he calls, placing it within quotation
marks, "critical theory." "This term," he writes, "which once simply
designated theorizing about literature, has of course come to refer to
the range of French-derived, post-structuralist theories of which the
best known is deconstruction. Feminist critics," he goes on to claim,
"among others, appear to have borrowed the recherché vocabulary of
post-structuralism chiefly as a handy form of certification in today's
theory-ridden academy" (71). In this chronology we are now witnessing
a stage three of "gender theory" which owes its particular tone to its
adoption of "critical theory." He then addresses the "troublesome question" that constitutes the internal failure of this phase of feminist criticism. "The trouble came with the attempt to make a case for an
essential gender difference in the act of writing. For exactly where, they
were forced to ask, can gender be identified as crucial in writing? Does
it manifest itself in plot? In style? In setting?" (71). (It is an intriguing
fact that whenever a critic of feminism wants to criticize feminist theories or practices as being essentialist, she or he—I of course include

---

New Republic and was reprinted in *Men in Feminism,* where I commented on its rhetorical
strategies. See *Men in Feminism,* ed. Alice Jardine and Paul Smith (New York: Routledge,
1987), 146–52, 137–45.

   [6]Other examples that come to mind include Richard Levin's "reading" of feminist
Shakespeareans in the pages of *PMLA* ("Feminist Thematics and Shakespearean Tragedy," *PMLA* 103 [March 1988]: 125–38) and Jeffrey Hart's "Wimmin against Literature,"
National Review, September 30, 1988, 432–33, which also uses Woolf—Mrs. Woolf—against
the "feminist professors" and enlists the "it is fatal for anyone who writes to think of
their sex" against their analyses (44). More recently we have Helen Vendler's "Feminism
and Literature," which appeared in the *New York Review of Books,* May 30, 1990, 19–25. I
should also say for the record that my own feminist criticism, in the form of the essay
"Emphasis Added," comes briefly under (unfriendly) scrutiny in this overview. On the
occasion of the conference at Madison, I included a discussion of those remarks, with
what I hoped sounded like a certain contempt, which I enjoyed reading aloud to a sympathetic audience. It has seemed to me, however, in the time that has elapsed since that
event that the emphasis I want to place in this version of the essay falls less on me—
nothing personal—than on the more general rage against feminist theory and practice.

female critics as well—in turn essentializes the representation by using the terms *essential, essentially.*)

As opposed to the feminist quest for "an essential gender difference in the act of writing" that reads self-consciously *for* the operations of gender in cultural narratives, the humanist defends the old values of transparency: the apprehension of an art outside the pressures of ideology. The critic in that story, a cultivated reader at home in a library of great books, needs to understand of a work only what is self-evidently there; the critic's task is to supply "a satisfactory account of the aesthetic object." The critical elaboration of this account, the argument goes, constitutes a poetics of "moral action," a practice that eschews politics: it is a reading without an agenda, enlisted in the service of art itself. Although such a poiesis is difficult, the failure to share the difficulty of a *beyond politics* as a goal is what shocks in the work of feminist critics. Granted, an "unintended bias" has always accompanied literary criticism; but being "inadvertently influenced by politics" is one thing; to *choose* "subordination to its aims and principles" is a failure of "social morality"—like "cheating at cards."[7] "Feminist critics . . . have repudiated the morality of the aesthetic. . . . Until and unless feminist criticism commits itself to aesthetic value, one can predict, it will continue to turn in on itself, repudiating one stage after another of necessarily inadequate theory" (85). To the extent that feminist criticism is by definition an ethical project, and as such bound to a "morality of the aesthetic" which *includes* aesthetics' ethical contexts (the very sort that Woolf, precisely, understood as integral to a humane apprehension of art), it is difficult to imagine that we stand a chance with our humanist.

But exactly which politics, one might well wonder, have undermined feminist criticism? "Mainstream liberal feminist criticism," we read, "has allowed itself to be taken intellectually hostage by French structuralist biologism, . . . Marxism, white and black lesbianism, and other radical forms of expression" (86). The remaining mainstream, liberal, heterosexual (presumably), bourgeois (white and black, one assumes)

---

[7]On this matter we may well consult the great moralist Trollope, who offers these austere views of the practice in *The Duke's Children* (the conversation is between the Duke and his younger son, Gerald, about his acquaintance, "a so-called gentleman"):

"He should know black from white. It is considered terrible to cheat at cards."
"There was nothing of that, sir."
"The man who plays and cheats has fallen low indeed."
"I understand that, sir."

Anthony Trollope, *The Duke's Children* (New York: Oxford University Press, 1986), 517.

feminists—who have escaped hijacking by these dangerous others, and who are still reading the essay—should renounce their alliances with "political radicals" and rededicate themselves to the arduous apprenticeship of aesthetic value: art for the sake of art.[8] But would that go far enough?

The heart of the matter comes in the final paragraph of the essay, where the promise of the epigraph is fulfilled.

> The one broad avenue to participation in the life of the culture always thought to have been open to women—literature's noble republic of the spirit—is in one way or another effectively denied women by feminist criticism. Yet it was through literature that Mary Ann Evans, writing as George Eliot, could confront her world unfettered by any limitations that might be thought to attach to her as a woman. Through literature Emily Dickinson and Willa Cather were free to write poems and stories in which the "I" who speaks is male rather than female, thereby claiming their privilege to speak for any kind of human being their imaginations were capable of grasping. . . . In a field where women's excellence is incontestable, feminist literary critics, starting out in the conviction that women writers had long suffered at the hands of male critics, have ended up fostering an image of women at least as insulting as any that they set out to protest. (87)

In the celebration of a universal subjectivity in art, the old (we hoped, moribund) tenets of lit. crit.–bashing are resuscitated by an attack on feminist critics cast as a defense of women and culture.[9] Through literature, and more specifically through the use of the male pseudonym and male personae, women writers have been able to liberate themselves and attain a whole human experience.

What is "new" here—but of course misogyny is never really new—is the protection of women from their feminist sisters. By their insistence on the work of gender in culture (Did Philoctetes have a sister? Mary Ann Evans wondered), on exposing the exclusions of women from the "broad avenue to participation in the life of the culture" (George Eliot freed Mary Ann Evans from being read "as a woman"), feminist critics have denied women the subjectivity of their fictional

[8]I owe the image of your "average feminist critic [as the] helpless victim of dangerous lesbian hijackers" to Maaike Meijer, who wonders, sardonically, about Shaw's contradictory defense of "the moral need for an artistic space, where no such thing as morality exists—the ethics of the unethical." Unpublished comments at the conference "Double Trouble," Utrecht, Holland, May 1990.

[9]Donoghue writes in the same spirit: "Indeed, feminist criticism seems at its present stage to me to be a libel upon women" ("A Criticism of One's Own," 151).

"I's" (writing "as a man"). They have also, it seems, denied male critics their fantasy monopoly on human identity.

"Reader, My Story Ends with Freedom"

In the broadside delivered against feminist criticism as a political poetics, the argument assumes that the reading of literary texts can and should be abstracted from the *reminder* of gender, and that writing about them should perform the same forgetting. In the presence of great writing, the reader ideally forgets both the author's sex and his own. I don't know whether the critic of feminist literary politics would go on to make the same argument about black literary feminism and the role played by race in cultural production: the common humanity expressed and transcended through art in a severance from the social. In the attack on feminist criticism I am about to describe, however, the argument connecting gender to race within cultural enactments is made explicitly; and to put that politics of abstraction into bolder relief, I want to begin with a critical reading that, like the text it illuminates, forgets neither gender nor race.

In *Self-Discovery and Authority in Afro-American Narrative,* Valerie Smith argues that the slave narrators of the nineteenth century, like the "protagonist-narrators of certain twentieth-century novels by Afro-American writers affirm and legitimize psychological autonomy by telling the stories of their own lives." Her central point relies on the "paradox" "that by fictionalizing one's life, one bestows a quality of authenticity on it . . . that the processes of plot construction, characterization, and designation of beginnings and endings—in short the process of authorship—provide the narrators with a measure of authority unknown to them in either real or fictional life." In this way, Smith maintains, "narrators not only grant themselves significance and figurative power over their superordinates, but in their manipulation of received literary conventions they also engage with and challenge the dominant ideology."[10]

In her discussion of Harriet Jacobs's autobiographical narrative, *Incidents in the Life of a Slave Girl,* Smith emphasizes the fundamental problem of form that confronts the author of a slave narrative. "When Jacobs asserts that her narrative is no fiction, that her adventures may seem incredible but are nevertheless true . . . that only experience can

[10]Valerie Smith, *Self-Discovery and Authority in Afro-American Narrative* (Cambridge: Harvard University Press, 1987), 2; subsequent references are cited in the text.

reveal the abomination of slavery, she underscores the inability of her form adequately to capture her experience" (40). Jacobs, Smith observes,

> invokes a plot initiated by Richardson's *Pamela*, and recapitulated in nineteenth-century American sentimental novels, in which a persistent male of elevated social rank seeks to seduce a woman of a lower class. Through her resistance and piety, she educates her would-be seducer into an awareness of his own depravity and his capacity for true, honorable love. In the manner of Pamela's Mr. B, the reformed villain rewards the heroine's virtue by marrying her. (41)

The familiar rhetoric of this plot both enables and disables an effective representation of slavery in narrative. On the one hand, the effusive apostrophes to the reader, euphemistic language, and silence about sexual detail create a common reading ground with the white female readers Jacobs must address and persuade; and Jacobs is writing both to "engender additional abolitionist support" and move women readers in the North to action. But at the same time, Smith observes, the insistence on the structural similarity also trivializes the violence that inheres in slave experience. Pamela, after all, can escape to her parents' home, and have her "virtue rewarded" by marrying her master, and "elevating her and their progeny to his position" (37). By definition, or rather by the logic of slavery, the master does not marry his slave, and her posterity becomes another increment to his property.

But as Smith shows, the tension between similarity and difference can produce a gain for narrative. When the reader arrives at the end of the autobiography and is addressed by the apostrophe "Reader, my story ends with freedom; not in the usual way, with marriage," Jacobs "calls attention to the space between the traditional happy ending of the novel of domestic sentiment and the ending of her story" (42). Unlike Jane Eyre, moreover, whose jubilant preclosural address to the reader—"Reader, I married him"—has posed problems for feminist readers, and who, like Pamela, could marry her master and bear his child legitimately, Linda Brent (the pseudonym of Jacob's first-person narrator) ends her story still questing for a "home": "The dream of my life is not yet realized. I do not sit with my children in a home of my own. I still long for a hearthstone of my own." Jacobs's text is constructed, we might say, in the gaps produced by that difference: the irreducible distance between slave reality and sentimental narrative, both of which finally remain authorized by patriarchy.

My account of Smith's argument has emphasized her analysis of the dramatic ways in which narrative commonalities allow us to take the measure of difference in readers: when, for instance, the white female reader who stops over "Reader, my story ends with freedom; not in the usual way, with marriage" perceives the difference race makes—that freedom for one who doesn't own herself comes from being sold, "*sold* at last"—she is reminded of both her gender and her race. Should she as a critic seek to forget this?

In the summer of 1988 Valerie Smith and I participated in a number of events at the School of Criticism and Theory. Smith gave a lecture, "Gender and Afro-Americanist Literary Theory and Criticism," in which she addressed—among other things—the question of oppositional discourses and their relation to institutional contexts and constraints; I presented "Dreaming, Dancing, and the Changing Locations of Feminist Criticism." In his reply to the arguments of this piece, the director of the school, Michael Riffaterre, a well-known semiotician, laid out before an audience of students and colleagues what he took to be the assumptions of my work as a feminist critic. The critique, while necessarily dependent on the existence of my person as a pre-text, identifies itself for the most part as being addressed to what is labeled (by him) in capital letters Feminist Criticism (hereafter FC, by me). In what follows I hope to show how the two takes on FC—the humanist's outcry and the semiotician's lament, which one might not have supposed to interpenetrate—in fact relay each other on a continuum of reaction: the discourse here of universal literary value, which in turn rejoins the earlier call for a "morality of the aesthetic."

Before reviewing the critique, I need to say a word about this mixed mode of autobiography and cultural analysis I call narrative criticism. Although, as I have just suggested, I figure in the story primarily as a convenient metonymy of FC (its Mary Beton, just as the reader may like to imagine the first critic as Woolf's Mr. A., whose phallic "I" casts a long shadow over the pages of his prose, and the second as the angry Professor Von X in *A Room of One's Own*), it is also the case that my account emerges from an institutional performance in which I coincided personally, as it were, with my representativity. My object in returning now to the critical material of that occasion, however, beyond the self-justification that comes with the territory of autobiography,[11] is to il-

---

[11]In his response to the version of this chapter that I read at the Conference on Narrative Literature, D. A. Miller commented, with an edge of misgiving, on the degree to which its writing "finds its source and support in self-vindication . . . shielding the author's very body against (real, remembered, imagined) attack." Perhaps.

luminate the network of theoretical assumptions about literature and literary criticism at the heart of the new astronomy.

The critic moves quickly to his main point, which is to challenge the "insularity of Feminist Criticism." He finds it "strange" that "the same people who would campaign against any form of male-enforced segregation or discrimination against women, or against any discrimination, and rightly so, should become segregationists in Feminist Criticism and discriminate against men as readers." Feminist Critics, he complains, "are not content to define [our] difference, [we] are othering male critics . . . and excommunicating their interpretations." (Feminist critics are addressed through me as "you." I have changed that here to "we.") Explicitly or not, he maintains, we "posit that, being male, they cannot possibly understand or properly read a text that has been written by a woman for women." And, he concludes in the next sentence, "it is obvious that the premises of today's Black Criticism imply the same kind of exclusion."[12]

What is one to make of the scenario that has male critics bodily prevented from reading women's writing and white critics from reading black writing? What feminist beadle has barred their access to the library, banned their books, banished their hermeneutics? Looking out across the cartography of our institutions, one can only wonder: Who left whom on the island? And yet we need now to take a harder look at the language of othering which posits the exclusions and the relations between them. How are Feminist and Black Critics (or, translated into the consecrated phrase of affirmative action, "women and minorities") alike and different? What is going on when feminists are accused of "segregation" in their attitudes toward male critics—a word intimately associated with the history of racism in this country? (More typically in antifeminist rhetoric, feminists are accused of separatism, which is in turn of course a code word for lesbianism.)

The collapsing of distinctions in order to maximize their threat echoes the language of the most reactionary forces at work in the academy today. (It is an emblem of recent political culture.) An example is Jon Wiener's account in the *Nation* of a conference titled "Reclaiming the Academy: Responses to the Radicalization of the University," calling for a "'renewed assertiveness' against feminism, ethnic studies and literary theory." The reporter quotes a spokesperson, Alan Kors, an intellectual historian from the University of Pennsylvania: "The immediate threat to academic freedom comes from antiharassment poli-

---

[12]I am quoting here from the text of Michael Riffaterre's public remarks, which at my request he communicated to me in written form at the close of the meeting.

cies, racial awareness programs and the enshrinement of 'diversity' as a value for the university."[13]

But let us return to the insularity of FC:

> Our duty as critics . . . is to explain and communicate. Furthermore, the only item that needs explaining to others and needs vicarious experiencing by them through the text is precisely the difference, be it gender, or class, or race. Why then, why start by saying that you cannot even succeed unless you own that difference by birthright? . . . Suppose we considered that metalinguistic features depending on gender, race, and class are unlikely ever to be erased, and that criticism by a native from the gender, race, or class under study might facilitate understanding. . . . Even if we were to concede that, the insularity of what I should call native criticism (rather than personal, or gender, or race criticism) would still ignore the very nature of the literary phenomenon, namely that it transcends time, place, and borders.

What would it mean to read *Incidents in the Life of a Slave Girl* as though its project transcended time, place, and borders? Smith's poetics of slave narrative, as we have just seen, focuses on the tensions (and contradictions) between the representational demands of the slave narrative and narrative structures of self-fictionalization. But this attention to formal literary conventions also includes a critical awareness of "the political and economic context in which the texts have been produced." To ignore "the broad context in which [the texts] were written," Smith maintains, "invites misreading and denies their relation to the conditions and the sense of urgency that contributed to their very existence" (6). Does this mean that to read Jacob's text *as* a slave narrative—a female-authored account of that historical experience—is to perform a "native criticism" that by definition "ignore[s] the very nature of the literary phenomenon"? To cite Smith one last time: "The critical work, no less than the artistic, bears the imprint of the conditions under which it was produced and articulates the writer's relation to culture" (7). This belief in cultural context, I would argue, is no more "insular"—you have to be black (a black woman) to "properly read" a black-authored text[14]—than the article of faith that circumscribes the text in order to

---

[13]*Nation*, December 12, 1988, 644. In a letter in the February 6, 1989, issue of the *Nation* (146), Kors complains about being misquoted.

[14]Michael Awkward provides an evenhanded discussion of this complicated issue—do you have to be black to read a black-authored text, and so on—through the work of Clifford Geertz, notably the essay "From the Native's Point of View," in his article "Race, Gender, and the Politics of Reading," *Black American Literature Forum* 22 (Spring 1988): 5–27. It is worth observing, as a participant at the conference on narrative pointed out in

seal its borders. In the case of *Incidents in the Life of a Slave Girl*, for example, if as a critic—black or white, male or female—you failed to explain the inscription of race and gender in the text's structures of address, your "account of the aesthetic object" (to invoke the terms of the argument rehearsed earlier) would by the same token overlook the "metalinguistic features" that give the text its generic specificity.

In other words, rather than adopting a discourse of the monument that rigidly opposes an inside ("the literary phenomenon") to an outside ("time, place, and borders"), we need precisely a revisionary "morality of the aesthetic" that would produce a reading capable of interpreting, for instance, the marks of race and gender in the text as *intrinsic* to literariness itself. This would be another way of understanding the ethical project of feminist aesthetics. The reading model according to which the critic radically divides literature from culture—as though we could ever be sure where to draw the line—seems condemned to the very insularity it seeks to locate outside its operations: to reproducing the politics of its location. Geographically this means not noticing, for instance, that continents are only very large islands.

Lemnos and the Politics of Insularity

Having arrived at this point in my narrative, I find myself wanting to tie up all the loose ends with a novelistic fabrication, a turn or twist of the plot, bringing us all, it all—Maggie, Philoctetes, the conservative backlash—to satisfying, if not sublime closure: marriage or freedom or Troy or home. Reader, I . . . Reader, my story ends with . . . But how does it end? How do I want it to end?

We could return, for instance, to the matter left hanging in Maggie's question about Philoctetes' sister and her conviction that she would have cared for the wounded man left on the island, and have that figure for us a reflection about gendered plots, and specifically about the ways in which universal narratives—what Gayatri Spivak calls "regulative psychobiography"[15]—construct and are constructed by social and political agendas.

We could also observe that these othered male critics would prefer

---

the question period, that in the first case FC is seen as foreign—influenced by France, using recherché words; here, native. In both FC is marked off as different from a transparent, essentialized self-identity: Art, Literature, The Critic, The Text, and so on.

[15]Gayatri Spivak, "The Political Economy of Women as Seen by a Literary Critic," in *Coming to Terms*, ed. Elizabeth Weed (New York: Routledge, 1989), 227.

for feminists to be more like women (like Maggie) and look after their wounded heroes.

We might ponder the current academic debates about the status and effects of oppositional discourses; these are joined issues.

And we might even wonder whether there isn't a way in which, like Philoctetes, feminists have come to love their island and to look with great suspicion on the call (when it is not a demand) for them to return to the fatherland, for this is, I think, what the accusations of insularity, segregation, separatism, and feminist misogyny come down to.

Philoctetes, we recall, was abandoned by Odysseus and their comrades in arms almost ten years before the play begins. They left Philoctetes on the island of Lemnos because they couldn't take the smell of his stinking foot and the howls of pain his wound produced. Now, having learned from a prophecy that Troy can be captured only by Philoctetes' bow—a bow given to him by Heracles—Odysseus and Neoptolemus have come back to get the bow and the man. Philoctetes takes a dim view of rejoining the war at the behest of the man who had so cruelly abandoned him to fend for himself on this deserted island; even though the return to Troy includes the promise of a cure, Philoctetes would rather suffer his pain and find solace on those terms. The crux of the play involves the persuasion of Philoctetes, a decision to leave the island for Troy that is accomplished only through the intervention of a god coming out of the machine: the appearance onstage of Heracles, who commands Philoctetes to pick up his bow and go back to the war.

The *Philoctetes* has attracted a great deal of critical attention and competing interpretations.[16] Following Carola Greengard's emphasis on the play's political dimensions I will recast, for a postmodern feminist theater, the fable of the man on the island as a drama of political positioning.

Suppose, then, that we imagine the lonely Philoctetes on the island multiplied as a collective of feminist critics. They have been put on the island because they have been ruining life on the mainland; they keep complaining about their wound, and that odor di femmina has been overpowering.[17] After the feminist critics have spent a decade of life in

[16]A good summary can be found in P. E. Easterling's "*Philoctetes* and Modern Criticism," *Illinois Classical Studies* 3 (1978): 27–39.

[17]The Lemnian setting, it should be mentioned, "was traditionally associated [both] with the Cybele cult and with myths that center on murderous conflict between men and women or exclusive occupancy of the island by women." Indeed, the "most famous myth is that of the Lemnian women killing all the men on the island in revenge for desertion." It is also possible, following this connection, to interpret, as some scholars have, the "offensive odor of the mythic Lemnian women" as transposed "in Philoctetes's foul

their women's studies community—we can just borrow some pages from Monique Wittig's *Guérillères* to fill in the narrative here—the men (their former colleagues) decide they need them back. They've heard rumors, oracles, that the feminists have unique knowledge that can help them deal with their students: enrollments are down, almost all the graduate students are female and are demanding to read women's and minority writing (even the men want to be in feminism); their publishers are telling them to include women in their articles and their books. They send an emissary—not one of the old guard, of course, but a younger representative (like Neoptolemus), one of the graduate students perhaps, or an assistant professor who does Theory.

Should the women return to save the institution? What faith can they have that promises will be kept? Even if they can forgive past wrongs, can they expect no future ones? It has been painful in the wilderness, but also rewarding. They have forged new identities on the island which challenge the hierarchical conventions of the polis; these might not survive the return to the old war, the rules of a tarnished, virile heroism. In Sophocles' play, we should remember, it takes a god coming out of a machine to force Philoctetes' hand and bring him with his bow to Troy.

After two decades of FC, feminists, black and white, as well as other oppositional groups find themselves both marginalized (put on the island) for reasons of state and accused of insularity, of separatism, even "terrorism;"[18] othered and accused of othering; excluded and taxed with being exclusionary. As we confront the fin de siècle, of which much is being made, the question of the islands and their "natives" becomes more and not less acute.

You will by now have perceived at least one crucial difference between my drama and the legend of the man on the island. The difference is not sexual.[19] It is one of numbers: unlike Philoctetes, we are not alone on our islands. Odysseus, even supported by the gods and their prophecies, can less easily, in this postcolonial moment, make us an offer we can't refuse. We can look from our island not only to the main but peripherally at the other island people and propose what we would now call coalition politics, famously defined by Bernice Reagon as the antithesis of home: "You don't go into coalition because you just *like* it.

---

wound." Carola Greengard, *Theatre in Crisis: Sophocles' Reconstruction of Genre and Politics in Philoctetes* (Amsterdam: Adolph M. Hakkert, 1987), 47–48.

[18]K. K. Ruthven, *Feminist Literary Studies: An Introduction* (Cambridge: Cambridge University Press, 1984), 10.

[19]But, like Philoctetes', our difference—according to the legend—is marked in our bodies.

The only reason you would consider trying to team up with somebody who could possibly kill you, is because that's the only way you can figure you can stay alive."[20] In that spirit we could chant some old radical cries of solidarity like "We are all Lemnians," hoping enough collective historical memory is left to make sense of it. But to end on that note would be to offer a solution that is already nostalgic.

Philoctetes, you recall, had no way to leave Lemnos on his own. As feminist critics we have acquired the freedom to move between the island and the mainland: we can leave and return, and we do.[21] Indeed, the definition of feminist difference has historically been bound up with the movement between identities and locations, with the negotiations between scenes of power. Nonetheless, for us, as for Philoctetes, the stakes of negotiation remain high and require vigilance, since we do not yet set the terms of the discussion. Nor is it clear that the gods are on our side.

Toward the end of "The Wound and the Bow," Wilson reads the *Philoctetes* allegorically: "The victim of a malodorous disease which renders him abhorrent to society and periodically degrades him and makes him helpless is also the master of a superhuman art which everybody has to respect and which the normal man finds he needs" (240). He then identifies the "more general and fundamental idea" of the play to be "the conception of superior strength as inseparable from disability" (235), but more specifically moves on to the "modern" reading that he comes to through Gide's reworking of the legend in his play—"that genius and disease, like strength and mutilation, may be inextricably bound up together." Gide, he remarks, "like the hero of the play, stood at an angle to the morality of society and defended [his] position with stubbornness" (237).

It is finally, I think, these intertwined figures of the wound and the bow, and a stubbornness born of that doubled difference, that we might most usefully retain for now. For through their somatic insistence they

[20]Bernice Johnson Reagon, "Coalition Politics: Turning the Century," in *Home Girls: A Black Feminist Anthology*, ed. Barbara Smith (New York: Kitchen Table Press, 1984), 356–57.

[21]In April 1990 I gave a version of this paper at the Third Annual Conference on Women's Studies at Dubrovnik. As luck would have it, from my room at the hotel I could see the island of Lokrum, a large, beautiful island, thick with trees, which we went to visit one afternoon on a boat ride. After contemplating the island for several days, and making the trip there, I realized I had not sufficiently figured in the ambivalence of perspective that double siting creates: the politics of oscillation. (This could also point to another fable about feminism, the referent, and movements of political liberation, but I will have to leave that for another time.) I thank Myriam Diaz-Diacoretz and Nada Popovich for including me in this event.

mark off the grounds and the position of a necessary resistance to the warriors—"the normal man"—of a very old world.

◇

I wrote "Philoctetes' Sister" in the spring of 1989 following an attack on me—representatively—as a feminist critic the summer before. It was, of course, also an attack on me personally, to which I at the moment did not, could not, reply. The violence left me mute, like Philomela. When two years later I published the essay in *Getting Personal*, a book in which I make the case for an autobiographical criticism, I still was not ready to acknowledge in print the degree to which my troping of insularity was a coded response to the experience of public humiliation. I decided to play the George Eliot card and rise above it.

It seems to me now that this choice left a couple of important things unsaid. The person who trashed me/Feminist Criticism (a cyborg of sorts) had been my dissertation director (another kind of monster) many years earlier. The audience before whom he trashed me was made up, at least in part, of students I was then teaching. In the Charlotte Brontë repertoire this resembled the standard curriculum of sadistic pedagogies: the nightmare of confused identities. And as in a nightmare, the dreamers were paralyzed by the horror of the show. We didn't, as one of my students kept saying afterwards, know what to do. Clearly I didn't either. Not everyone was horrified by the show. Some were entertained, some disappointed: Why didn't I "destroy" him in turn? Oedipal modalities notwithstanding, *I* couldn't have. But in the aftermath of the Clarence Thomas–Anita Hill performances, I have come to think that dignity—which may be too grand a name for my inhibition, not to say fear—is a mistake, even if it has some self-protective value for the moment.

There is nothing new about misogyny in literature or in our social lives. What may be new is an institutionalization of its terms in the best places. The question is: What are we going to do about it?

10

One Must Go Quickly from One Light into Another: Between Ingeborg Bachmann and Jacques Derrida

SABINE I. GÖLZ

We here enter a textual labyrinth panelled with mirrors.
—Jacques Derrida

I am the thought on the bath in the room without mirrors.
—Nadja, as "cited" by André Breton

We have grown used to asserting that "language" somehow contributes to marginalizing some people and centering others. These effects have especially interested feminist critics and theorists working with marginalized ethnic, racial, and colonized groups. Yet the process remains opaque. How can signifying processes make a given symbolic, metaphoric, or linguistic order more habitable to some than to others? To address these issues, let us start with the notion that representational practices are also what makes constructions of knowledge and subjecthood possible in a given symbolic order. Through them we shape ourselves and our world.

To explore these dynamics we must find ways to orient ourselves in the twilight zone of the interference between representations and the practices with which we surround them. Any power of and over representation and the constitution of a "world" derives from the decisions made in that undecidable space. Comparative methodology is indispensable for orientation in this twilight because it allows us to approach this space not in terms of the metaphysical opposition between the original and the copy, the real and the image, but rather by means of a comparison between the various effects that arise out of their interference.

I set the stage here by reading one stanza from a long poem by the Austrian poet Ingeborg Bachmann. The central section of the essay then presents a detailed reading of the first part of Jacques Derrida's essay

"The Double Session,"[1] where I locate the stance of Derridean deconstruction on the map provided by Bachmann's poem. Deconstruction's
practices and choices situate it on a site different from that of Bachmann. The comparison gives relief to the "large trace" of a significant
difference between the stances of these two writers. This difference becomes even clearer when, by way of conclusion, I look at two moments
when each of these writers interacts with another text through *citation*.
This adds the dimension of readerly practice to my considerations. We
end up with a *quadruple* scene of supplementation and differing which
allows us to map divergences between the two stances unperceived by
the deconstructive "double scene."

Ingeborg Bachmann calls for a comparative method of mapping one's
world:

> In a time of large traces,
> one must go quickly from one light
> into another, from one land
> into another, under the rainbow,
> the compass point in the heart,
> the night taken as radius.
> Wide open.[2]

She thus directly addresses the question that interests all of us in this
volume. Her poem further links the necessity for comparison to our
"large-traced" or "overbearing" (*großspurige*) time. She is concerned
with the conditions under which the "large" trace of a whole signifying
apparatus, a predominant practice, can be observed. Central to this ef-

---

[1] Jacques Derrida, "The Double Session," in *Dissemination*, trans. Barbara Johnson (Chicago: University of Chicago Press, 1981), 173–286 (hereafter DS).
[2] "In einer großspurigen Zeit / muß man rasch von einem Licht / ins andre gehen, von
einem Land / ins andre, unterm Regenbogen, / die Zirkelspitze im Herzen, / zum Radius
genommen die Nacht. / Weit offen." Ingeborg Bachmann, "Curriculum Vitae," in *Werke*,
ed. Christine Koschel, Inge von Weidenbaum, and Clemens Münster (Munich: Piper,
1982), 1:101 (hereafter IBW). This poem is quoted with the kind permission of Piper
Verlag, © R. Piper and Co. Verlag, Munich, 1978. The translation is my own. Mark Anderson translates these lines from the sixth stanza: "In an arrogant age / we must rush
from one light / to the next, from one land / into the next, beneath the rainbow, / the
compass points in our heart / and the night as radius. / Wide open." *In the Storm of Roses:
Selected Poems by Ingeborg Bachmann*, trans. Mark Anderson (Princeton: Princeton University Press, 1986), 97. He thus chooses the common meaning of the German *großspurig*
("arrogant") over the more etymological meaning. The choice of the word "rush" and
the multiplication of compass "points" to my mind lose the measured precision of this
line, which corresponds to its geometric metaphorics. Since translations reflect such differences in interpretation, I will be using my own throughout.

fort is the comparative movement across the boundaries delimiting different perspectives and discursive spaces, different lights and lands.

The poem maintains awareness of the observer's irreducible part in constituting the object of observation. It approaches its task not by constructing the "large-traced time" as an object, but by describing procedures for observing it. The only fixed point of the procedure is a compass point placed "in the heart." The gesture piercingly anchors the radius of perception in the observer. The goal of the process, finally, is not comprehensiveness but the production of an opening as "wide" and unlimited as the initial movement was pointed. That opening, however, depends on the poignant precision of the initial gesture.

Only after the procedure has been established can we say what we see: "From the mountains / one sees lakes, in the lakes / mountains (Von den Bergen / sieht man Seen, in den Seen / Berge)." At first glance this chiastic arrangement seems to create a reciprocal relation in which the knowers and the known change places and their difference becomes undecidable. Yet this reciprocity is subtly compromised. Whereas the mountains are a location from which either the lakes or their own reflection in the lakes may be seen, the lakes either reflect or are seen but are never the site of seeing. As the lakes appear and disappear, now object, now mirror, the mountains remain invested with the gaze.

The appearance of complementarity is replaced by a scenario of exclusion as we look (move?) elsewhere: "and in the rack of cloud / swing the bells / of the one world. Whose world / I am forbidden to know (und im Wolkengestühl / schaukeln die Glocken / der einen Welt. Wessen Welt / zu wissen ist mir verboten)." We see "the one" world, *somebody's* world. "One" denotes unification but also has the opposite effect of evoking the shadowy, unnamed possibility of "other" worlds. This reading gains force as the first-person pronoun emerges in the very recognition of its exclusion from knowledge, and as it points to an acoustic dimension ("bells") to which the specular scenario is deaf. If this "I" inhabits a world different from the "one," this world remains unrepresented. We can imagine that the "lakes" where the mountains reassure themselves alternately of their own image and of the objects of their knowledge are inhabited by a gaze which knows itself as forbidden. But the difference of this gaze will appear exclusively in what it sees and hears. Therefore, we will not find it unless we make it our own and begin to see or hear differently ourselves.

The lyrical "I" of Bachmann's poem could be said to position itself in the mirror of representation as what Lacan calls the object *a*. According to Mladen Dolar, the object *a* "is precisely that part of the loss that one cannot see in the mirror, the part of the subject that has no mirror reflection, the nonspecular." Lost is the gaze that *looks back at* the Lacanian subject, as it situates itself on the mountain, founded on both its difference from and self-recognition in a mirror image. That otherworldly gaze out of the lake appears to "the one" subject as uncanny, horrifying and "impossible."[3]

The specular subject and its faith in imaginary unity can be maintained only if the reverse gaze from the mirror remains "lost." But were we to position ourselves (as Bachmann invites us to do) as that missing second gaze, we would begin to perceive a split that is far greater than the founding split between that subject and his mirror image. The missing gaze would appear neither as part of that subject nor as part of his world, but as the gaze of a different kind of subject. This subject, as which we can situate ourselves, must as a founding condition of its existence lose faith in representation, in any image of itself. In order to constitute itself as a subject at all, it must depart from a symbolic space in which it was represented as "nothing," as "impossible." Therefore, it lives in a different "world." The Lacanian subject and *its* world react with horror and abjection to any indication of such an existence, let alone to the idea that it might solidify what it sees into something like "knowledge." Within that space those who look back at this world's subject cannot articulate what they see. To this world, they cannot make themselves understood. Were the lake to betray any "knowledge" of its function, were it to break the surface of the mirror it is and tell the mountain that it is looking back at it, the bells on the cloud rack would turn into a death knell (*glas*).

By way of a solution Bachmann's poems often present themselves as unattributed yet self-conscious scenarios. They map a set of relations without breaking the mirror and assigning positions on this map to anybody. They do not claim to represent any objects other than those that volunteer to identify themselves. Bachmann's writing never "expresses" her. But it maps the arrangement which is responsible for her inability to express herself in the one world. Her texts maintain their difference from the epistemological procedures that engender the overbearing outline of the Western literary and philosophical canon. Thus, they help us recognize its silhouette. They help us see how Jacques Derrida, despite his reputation as a rebel figure, defined by his "difference" from the forces of the literary and philosophical tradition, returns into the fold of the one world.

[3]Mladen Dolar, " 'I Shall Be with You on Your Wedding-Night': Lacan and the Uncanny," *October* 58 (1991): 13, 20.

Because Bachmann's texts thus fail to "contain" or speak what they "know," it is not enough to read *them*. The second half of her work *is* the different look at what it is not. Because a reading of Bachmann takes the strange form of a rereading of, for example, Nietzche or Derrida, it is also no longer simply "her" work. We have to sign for it ourselves. The difficulty of finding a format for such a doubly focused reading continues to beset my own work as a comparatist-feminist. As I reread and write about Derrida, Nietzsche, and Kafka, colleagues and deans remind me that I should be writing the promised "book on Bachmann." What they do not see is that both are part of the same project.

Ever since I began reading Derrida's work, I have felt the need to understand more precisely what appears to me a constitutive reliance of deconstruction on a very gender-specific placement in the intertextual network. That the subject of deconstruction is a male subject has been perceived in general terms, but just what this masculinity consists of remains to be understood.[4]

In this reading of "The Double Session," I approach the gendered site of the subject by focusing on Derrida's performance as a reader (rather than a writer). Two other performers make their way into that text through quotations of texts by Mallarmé (which in turn reach back into an extended textual prehistory). One of them is the ballerina from Mallarmé's "Crayonné au théâtre," who appears in the second part of Derrida's article only to disappear again promptly to make room for a discussion of the "blank" of generalized textual play. The other is the mime from "Mimique," in the same collection, on whose multiple performance Derrida overwhelmingly focuses. The proliferation of discourse around the mime and the ballerina's rapid disappearance signal a choice by which Derrida's discourse situates itself.[5]

What interests me are the discursive configurations that arise around these male and female figures, for they betray certain readerly allegiances which are inflected by gender. These allegiances are neither the expression of an essence nor a mere construction. In them, rather, a dynamic and complex practice takes shape which is responsive to and part of the structure of a signifying space that is thoroughly gendered.

---

[4]Barbara Johnson, for example, calls for analysis of gender issues in Derrida's work, but ambiguously invokes potential "epistemological damage" that might result from attempting to produce "the existence and knowledge of the female subject." See her essay "Gender Theory and the Yale School," in *A World of Difference* (Baltimore: Johns Hopkins University Press, 1987), 40–41.

[5]By contrast, Gayatri Spivak's interest in the functioning of the woman-sign leads her to single out the figure of the ballerina in her critique of Derrida, "Love Me, Love My Ombre, Elle," *Diacritics* 14.4 (Winter 1984): 19–36.

It is significant that the mime is allowed to supply a scenario for the whole project of deconstruction, whereas Derrida self-consciously "arrests" the ballerina's play to turn her figure into a signifier. She becomes the site of inscription for his "knowledge."

Here I concentrate on Derrida's discussion of the male performer-writer figure of the mime and of Mallarmé's strategies in "Mimique." "Mimique" alludes to yet another text, a booklet by and about the mime Paul Margueritte, titled *Pierrot Murderer of His Wife*. In the plot, which persists through these allusions and repetitions, Pierrot, enraged by the infidelity of his wife, decides to tickle her to death. The drama is performed by the mime Margueritte alone: he plays the roles of both murderer and victim, and then writes and publishes a book about his performance. This story paradigmatically allegorizes the murder and exclusion of the "faithless" feminine subject in the history of Western representation. That this could have gone unremarked (until recently noted by Leslie Rabine) is an astonishing token of the reigning blindness to issues of gender in deconstructive discourse.[6]

Margueritte's booklet, object of explicit allusion by Mallarmé, does not close the play of intertextual reference, but rather opens it onto a series of countless precursor versions of the plot whose origin is lost in an extended network of repetitions and replays (DS, 198–205). The complex cross-references, mutual reflections, allusions, and inversions through which the mime's story plays with itself and its parts, the syntactic ambiguites of Mallarmé's text, and finally the relation between the performer-writer and his text all converge in the first part of Derrida's "Double Session" to represent the systematic unmasterability and undecidability of textuality which so fascinates deconstructive discourse.

But there is an element of stability in Derrida's reading: Mallarmé's text remains firmly framed by the reference to Plato's logocentrism. Derrida's reading shuttles between *establishing* the difference between Mallarmé's practice and logocentrism, and *suspending* that difference in allusion, referral, and return. Thus, the reading establishes the "veil" of an "undecidable" relation between Mallarmé's text and the founding text of Western metaphysics. This "veil" both does and does not perform a break with that past and its procedures. The break folds right back into that from which it would break, and it generalizes its own movement: "This redoubling of the mark, which is at once a formal

---

[6]Leslie Wahl Rabine: "The Unhappy Hymen between Feminism and Deconstruction," in *The "Other" Perspective in Gender and Culture: Rewriting Women and the Symbolic*, ed. Juliet Flower MacCannell (New York: Columbia University Press, 1990).

break and a formal generalization, *is exemplified by the text of Mallarmé, and singularly by the 'sheet' you have before your eyes"* (DS, 193–94). Repetition and generalization expand this suspension of difference into "nothing other than the space of writing" (DS, 208): the one (and to Derridean deconstruction *only*) world. The cohesion of this world depends on the break which generalizes it without departing from it and on the "sheet before your eyes" that prevents reading.

Anticipating the suspicion that such continued self-referentiality of a whole tradition might be considered an act of closure, Derrida insists that "such is not the case. A writing that refers back only to itself carries us *at the same time,* indefinitely and systematically, to some other writing. . . . [The] structure is open and closed *at the same time"* (DS, 202). But that "other writing" is also "writing," and thus more of the same. What is denied both existence and "knowledge" is not "other writing" but anything *other than* or exterior to this writing. The hymen "eliminates the exteriority or anteriority, the independence of the imitated, the signified, or the thing" (DS, 210). We are meant to read this "elimination," of course, in the spirit of a resistance to a metaphysics of originary presence which would evade the complexities of language and textuality. Yet this constant turn back to the logocentric paper tiger is as oppressive and confining as logocentrism itself. It colonizes and recontains the space of potential difference. If logocentrism centers on one self-identical presence, deconstruction admits only one difference: the suspended "veil" between itself and logocentrism.

The continuities and discontinuities that create this veil, however, are open to rearrangement. And precisely because "absolute" difference is impossible, we must choose our (dis)continuities carefully. A place where the continuity between the text of metaphysics and that of deconstruction is particularly strong, however, is in the rhetorical function of gender. And in this place I would obviously prefer to introduce discontinuity.

In the pantomime about the Pierrot who tickled his wife to death, the mime plays both gender roles at once, while declaring them indistinguishable and "suspending" their difference. "The crime, the orgasm, is mimed doubly: the mime plays the roles of both Pierrot and Columbine alternately . . . such that in the final analysis what happens is nothing, no violence, no stigmata, no traces; the perfect crime in that it can be confused only with the heights of pleasure [*jouissance*] obtainable from a certain speculation" (DS, 201). But this performance is double in a very limited sense, since there is only a single performer: the white-faced male. Any other performance, including that of Columbine, remains offstage and *hors-texte.* Its very possibility is thus outlawed by the summary dismissal of any exteriority to the space of writing quoted earlier. The trace of the "crime," therefore, consists in this very absence.

But what if one chose to supplement Derrida's text with this "missing" performance? Like Bachmann's "lake," this perspective allows us to discover what it is we are "forbidden to know": that the "nothingness" of the *hors-texte* is also not absolute but perspectival. It is the blind spot that founds the play of writing.

In view of this elimination of otherness by the one world, one must reassess the significance of the two-directional traffic between the double text and its single performer which the story of the mime comes to represent. "Among diverse possibilities, let us take this: The mime does not read his role; he is also read *by* it. Or at least he is both read and reading, written and writing, between the two, in the suspense of the hymen, at once screen and mirror" (DS, 224). We can now no longer regard this scenario of "undecidability" as implying in any way a loss of control for the mime or his readers. Rather, from the vantage point of an absent Columbine-mime who gets to mime no role at all, the back-and-forth between the mime and his two roles presents a scenario that illustrates his control over signification. The performer can participate in writing the script, and the writer can adjust the performance. As long as the mime is read by a scenario that confirms this arrangement, his "subjection" to reading amounts to his acknowledgment (in the Hegelian sense of *Anerkennung*) by the textual tradition. Text and performance fold into each other, occur in terms of each other, in a self-reinforcing loop which creates a protective *antre*/cave/womb. A difference greater than that "between Platonism and itself, Hegelianism and itself" (DS, 207), and thus between the history of male subjectivity and itself, is not allowed to interrupt this circuit.

The mime's scenario, then, illustrates not the elusiveness of a general textual play, but the control over representation and self-representation afforded by the privilege of an undecidable relation between a text and its proper reader. This control is secured by the stable specular exchange between a particular subject and its knowledge, but it also remains confined to the protective space of this "writing."

To mark the fertile juncture where difference is both established and contained, Derrida turns to the metaphorics of the "hymen":

> To repeat: the hymen, the confusion between the present and the nonpresent, along with all the indifferences it entails within the whole series of opposites . . . produces the effect of a medium (a medium as element enveloping both terms at once; a medium located between the two terms). It is an operation that *both* sows confusion *between* opposites *and* stands

between the opposites "at once." . . . But this medium of the *entre* has nothing to do with a center. (DS, 212)

The hymen becomes both divide and envelope, both the mark of difference and the space or union that recuperates it. With this wedding/veil, the deconstructive reversal has produced its own, dissimulated version of a "center."

"Within" that space this play still necessitates the "nothing" that marks the absence of any greater difference. A state of "identity" which lost that trace may be a logocentric subject's chief desire, but it would have disastrous consequences. Were the mime's exchangeability with himself to lose that "nothing" which separates him from himself and enables him to play with himself, he would be incapacitated. The dilemma of a subject deprived of this split or symbolic "castration" is nicely evoked in an epilogue to one of Harold Bloom's books:

At midnight he went down to the lake, to hear the name spoken over
the water, but found no one there to meet him.
So he became two, one to speak the name and one to receive it.
He forgot which one was which.
Both spoke the name, and neither received it.
Then both stood to hear it, but it was not spoken.[7]

"Speech" and "identity" here represent not the plenitude of the speaking subject's masterly self-presence, but rather his predicament in the absence of writing: he cannot mark difference.

This is why the name of woman, the role of Columbine, must remain inscribed in the plot. Her *name* is necessary for the mime to remember "which is which" when he says "I am I." It allows him to distinguish between the two roles he plays *undecidably* as a "subject" in control of self and representation. But he must perform both roles himself to produce "one" subject in the end. Thus the claim of that other name ("woman" or Columbine) to a referent different from, once more, him is denied. Her name becomes the mere mark of suspended (and thus neutralized) difference, the veil itself, and "nothing" beyond.

In the protective space of generalized writing thrives a decentered subject which no longer explicitly insists on its universality. On the contrary: it claims to have *disappeared* at the precise moment when its "universalization" within that space completes itself, since there is no longer anybody else in sight. The combination of the presence of "wom-

[7] "The Name Spoken over the Water," in Harold Bloom, *Kabbalah and Criticism* (New York: Continuum, 1984), 127.

an's" name and the "nothingness" of its referent facilitates the consummation of Narcissus' marriage to the infinite refractions of himself, separating him from and reuniting him with himself:

> "Hymen" . . . is first of all a sign of fusion, the consummation of a marriage, the identification of two beings, the confusion between two. *Between* the two, there is no longer difference but identity. Within this fusion, there is no longer any distance between desire . . . and the fulfillment of presence, between distance and non-distance; there is no longer any difference between desire and satisfaction. It is not only the difference . . . that is abolished, but also the difference between difference and non-difference. . . . By the same token . . . there is no longer any textual difference between the image and the thing, the empty signifier and the full signified, the imitator and the imitated, etc. . . . The confusion or consummation of this hymen eliminates the spatial heterogeneity of the two poles in the "supreme spasm," the moment of dying laughing. (DS, 209)

The logocentric male subject has thus been replaced by the writing subject. Unlike his predecessor, this undecidable performer of his own text no longer bases his "identity" on his difference from "woman." She is dismissed together with the illusion of his substantial self-identity and replaced by the more flexible trace of a gender difference, a veil that spells either difference or union according to need. In the double scene of departure and return, each actor can substitute for the other—Husserl for Hegel for Plato, Derrida for Nietzsche for Mallarmé for Margueritte—as they enjoy the ethereal pleasures of an infinite play with their like(nesse)s. The white noise of a self-supplementing tradition sets the stage for itself, performs itself on it, and watches the play, too. These, however, are the benefits of hegemony, not the unsettling effects of a general absence of reference.

Nevertheless, Derrida expends much energy on the impossibility of tracing any origin in the incessant cross-referencing of Western metaphysics. "One could go on at great length in order to find out where this Pierrot had read the exemplary story of this husband who tickled his wife and thus made her laughingly give up her life. With all the threads provided by the *commedia dell' arte*, one would find oneself caught in an interminable network" (DS, 205). Yes, but one would be engaged in a pointless search. The "origin" is not the problem. The point is not whether Plato, Derrida, or anybody else has "authored" the pernicious mechanism, but rather that this history consists of endless repetitions of the same tired old story. The effort at change must address itself not to a phantasmatic origin but to the exact form taken by, the choices made in, repetition and mimesis.

By situating our reading in the trace left by Columbine's absence, we catch sight of a would-be murderer who theorizes his ability to escape conviction in front of an infinite series of self-portraits or mirrors which mime his movements as he mimes theirs. Like so many Ancient Mariners, they obsessively replay that old story. But the murder is strangely pointless, since its victim is said not even to exist. A clue to this bizarre spectacle may be Derrida's remark that the "difficulty lies in conceiving that what is imitated could be still to come with respect to what imitates, that the image can precede the model, that the double can come before the simple" (DS, 190). If what is imitated is still to come, the mime can never know whether he will have succeeded or not. The future and the elided alterity converge in the "nothing" as which they appear to him, and as which they reside irreducibly in his suspended difference from himself. He is trying to convince himself that we who approach this text now from the angle of this nothing are either dead or not there. But he knows that this is not true, and so do we. He cannot be convicted, then, because the murder *fails*. The unsuccessful "deed" is therefore replaced by the unceasing repetition of this story. And yet— as long as we participate in this repetition and take his representations for "truth," we will indeed be as good as dead.

Since we are not dead, however, his privilege to *represent* himself in the world and to reserve the right to *appear* onstage becomes uncomfortable. He begins to look for ways to transcend his specular captivity in representation. He wishes that he, too, were invisible, a mere nothing, a "blank."[8] The mime's desire to extend his play "infinitely" through the "one world" of writing coincides with the desire to disappear from view. If he succeeds in *being* that world, he becomes invisible.

I argued earlier that the deconstructive reversal does not undo the cohesion produced by the "center," but rather preserves it in a dissimulated version. The logocentric effacement of representation in the name of presence now similarly fails to be undone. The subject of deconstruction, consonant with its desire not to be seen, has developed its own version of effacement. No longer is the trace of representation effaced on behalf of an image of presence, meaning, or the subject. Now, inversely, the undecidable play of textuality is generalized and becomes an imperative emanating from the text as the "image" in which the subject is to be fashioned:

> What Mallarmé *read*, then, in this little book is a prescription that *effaces itself through its very existence*, the order given to the Mime to imitate noth-

---

[8]The "blank" has a completely different meaning for the ballerina. This point I study in greater detail in the unpublished second half of this article.

ing that in any way preexists his operation. . . . It is prescribed . . . to the
Mime that he not let anything be prescribed to him but his own writing,
that he not reproduce by imitation any action . . . or any speech. . . . The
Mime ought only to write himself on the white page he is. (DS, 198)

The reader-performer now lives under the imperative to be nothing but
a spontaneous repetition of his own writing. A "self-effacing" text is
complemented by a reader-performer striving to assimilate himself to
an omnipresent and purportedly untraceable self-recursivity without
origin, conceived in the image of the text, imitating nothing but itself.

The relation between text and mime is "undecidable." What is not
"undecidable," however, is the very specific "meta-mimetic" interaction that binds this textual space and its mime. The readerly activity of
the mime *produces* the undecidability and *brings about* the self-
recursivity of this kind of writing, and finally effaces the mime's role
in doing so. Not any particular image, but the self-recursivity of writing
itself which he thus creates becomes the image in which he models
himself. (What this means concretely will become clearer in the next
section.) The symbiotic interaction between the space of writing and the
specific subject which thrives in and on it, finally, is dissimulated by a
generalization that declares this interaction an impersonal and aper-
spectival process.

Let us have a closer look at the "blankness" of the self-effacing text-
and-mime. Derrida rightly points out that the blank is not simply a
theme. "The 'blank' and the 'fold' cannot in fact be mastered as themes
or as meanings, if it is within the folds and the blankness of a certain
hymen that the very textuality of the text is re-marked" (DS, 245–46).
No "theme" can be stably represented because every representation is
incomplete without the supplement of a reading that re-marks and confirms it. The unsignifiable signification of the blank is that every signifier (including itself) can always be made to mean something
different: "The blank or the whiteness (is) the totality, however infinite,
of the polysemic series, *plus* the carefully spaced-out splitting of the
whole. . . . But for the reasons just enumerated, it is out of the question
that we should erect such a representative . . . into the fundamental signified or signifier in the series" (DS, 252). This "signification" cannot
be confined to one signifier without disappearing.

The substitutions must be *performed* as one subject or meaning is displaced by the next in an open series. The "erasure" that occurs there
is a change in what is read, not an unreadability. And "unreadability"
inversely is a reading. Strictly speaking, there is thus no "blank" at all
except as a theme. The "blank" appears only if we totalize and represent
this process of substitution *in general*. Unreadable is only the "totality"

of those transformations, and the only gaze blinded by this unreadability is the very particular gaze of the old universal subject. Whenever this blindness turns into a privileged "knowledge" which overarches and adjudicates all "local" attempts to read, that universal subject reasserts its hegemony in the space of reading. This strategy as a whole manifests what Nietzsche critiques as the "ascetic" desire rather to "will *nothingness* than *not* will."[9] It wills unreadability rather than allow *somebody else* to read.

When this new subject-in-general is *subject to* reading, a complementary gesture occurs: the mime wears the simulacrum of a blank on his face. "The blank—the other face of this double session here declares its white color—extends between the candid virginity . . . of the white . . . page and the white paint of the pale Pierrot who, by simulacrum, writes in the paste of his own make-up, upon the page he is" (DS, 195). The mime is trying to convince us that he has already erased or "deconstructed" himself, and that we therefore do not have to go to the trouble anymore. He has already returned to the innocence of the white page. Like animal mimicry, the "blank" he wears on/as his face betrays an attempt to blend into an environment and become invisible to potential predators. The white paint, however, is indeed only a simulacrum of nothingness. It betrays his desire to be invisible rather than fulfilling it.

The mime has moved to a stage on which his erasure is imperative—the scene of reading. What he has not left behind are his old signifying habits. He behaves as though erasure could be written, painted, signified. If the "blank" is a representable theme after all, erasure is not. His deeper dilemma is that he cannot erase himself. This is the one thing out of his control. He can only continue to write and to multiply traces which become readable as the effort of the "universal subject" to retain control of the point of his own demise.

What cannot be written are the changing practices and repetitions which representations encounter and undergo. Let me therefore conclude with a look at two citations in Derrida's and Bachmann's works, and at the specific turns they take *as repetitions*. Here, too, the two writers make opposite and complementary choices.

The first citation occurs in one of Derrida's footnotes to "White Mythology." He quotes a text by André Breton, upon which he has, however, "neither the time nor the place to comment":

There is no doubt that I have a "complex" about ties. I detest this incomprehensible ornament of masculine costume. From time to time I reproach

---

[9]Friedrich Nietzsche, *On the Genealogy of Morals*, trans. Walter Kaufmann and R. J. Hollingdale (New York: Vintage, 1969), 163.

myself for surrendering to such an impoverished custom as knotting each morning before a mirror (I am trying to explain to psychoanalysts) a piece of cloth which by means of an attentive little nothing is to augment the already idiotic expression of a morning jacket [*veston à revers*]. Quite simply, it is disconcerting. I am not unaware, from another point of view, and indeed cannot hide from myself, that just as coin operated machines, the sisters of the dynamometer on which Jarry's Supermale practices victoriously ("Come, Madame"), symbolize sexually—the disappearance of the tokens in the slot—and metonymically—the part for the whole—woman, so the tie, and even if only according to Freud, figures the penis "not only because (they) are long dependent objects and peculiar to men, but also because they can be chosen according to taste, a liberty which in the case of the object symbolized, is forbidden by nature."[10]

This passage falls into two parts, between which there occurs a shift in perspective. In the first part an "I" augments the *veston à revers* (the "turncoat" by means of which he is able to switch sides) by an "attentive little nothing" which remains, however, "incomprehensible." In the second part he "cannot hide" from himself "another perspective." There he recognizes the tie he finds himself wearing as a mark of masculinity. The whole monologue addresses itself to "psychoanalysts." Psychoanalysis is meant to close the gap of the attentive nothing of reading with the presence of an analyst who, as we know, functions like a white wall, interpreting nothing, only handing every utterance back to the speaker for interpretation.

Although Derrida does not comment, he does tell us what he sees. Gazing at this text, Derrida sees a "page from the *Vases communicants* on which Breton analyzes an ornament, attending to the rhetorical equivalents of condensation and displacement, and to their economy." He sees both the "page" *and* a man who analyzes its rhetorical displacements, and whom he recognizes as "Breton." Derrida thus vacates his place in front of the mirror of the text in favor of Breton. He folds the text back onto itself *without comment* as the analyst who comes to Breton's rescue and cures his "loss." Effacing his readerly presence, he restitutes Breton to himself as his own destination, his own gaze out of the mirror, and produces the self-recursivity of an authorial subject "in" the text. Now, the space of writerly subjecthood is surrounded by "white walls" which merely fold it back onto itself, "eliminating" every *hors-texte*. But this "folding back" does not happen by itself. It is a

[10]Jacques Derrida, "White Mythology: Metaphor in the Text of Philosophy," in *Margins of Philosophy*, trans. Alan Bass (Chicago: University of Chicago Press, 1982), 222. The quotation in Breton's text is from Freud's "Interpretation of Dreams."

specific readerly supplementation of writing which buttresses the space of male authorship. Derrida himself causes the shortage of a "time" or "place" from which to comment on this space.

This is a miniature model of the stance of deconstruction: it colonizes the open space of reading by returning it to (the subject as) writing. It shrinks the time and space of reading. Thus, the writing subject averts his deconstruction by replacing the self-conscious moment when "I" looks in the mirror with the psychoanalyst's folding back of an unread text. But there is a price to be paid for this strategy: a subject constructed in this way can no longer be "self-conscious" or read at all. "Pierrot returns, and is summoned to testify to his own death: 'I can rejoice no longer in seeing myself'" (DS, 204).[11] This subject rewrites himself as an undecidable play between "blanks." Reading is now a white wall, the text a blank page, and the mime's face white makeup. For fear of encountering the object *a*, his eyes go blank.

In this rewriting a blanket authorial "attentiveness" is installed, masterfully and "omnisciently" presiding over a text that has turned into a mere "page." Text and reader avoid committing themselves to any "content" beyond the specificity of this arrangement. If we grant him this *blanko* awareness of anything that goes on in "his" text, any displacement will have been attended to by the Author Himself. By reading Breton in this way, Derrida "writes himself on the page which he is." But "Himself" can no longer look the "I" in the eye.

As I read this way, however, I repeat Derrida's move. I "see" Derrida reading, when in fact, right now, I myself am doing the reading. Therefore, the question to me as a reader is: Do I, since I clearly have a complex about certain incomprehensible ornaments of masculine costume, want to surrender to the impoverished custom of knotting in front of a mirror? And if I do not want to read so as to reestablish "Himself," what are my other choices?

In my view, Ingeborg Bachmann offers an alternative in "The Writing I" ("Das schreibende Ich"), the third of her five "Frankfurt Lectures on Poetics."[12] There she quotes a passage from the novel *The Unnamable* by Samuel Beckett. She, too, does not "comment" on what she quotes, but merely frames it with a small remark. In Beckett, she writes, there

---

[11]Compare also the atypical modesty with which Nietzsche notes that "the unpleasant thing, and one that nags at my modesty, is that at root *every name in history is I.*" Friedrich Nietzsche to Jakob Burckhardt, January 5, 1889, quoted in Rosalind Krauss, "Bachelors," *October* 52 (Spring 1990): 53–59.

[12]A translation of these lectures into English is being prepared by Karen Achberger and will appear in a series titled "Kritik: German Literary Theory and Cultural Studies," edited by Liliane Weissberg and published by Wayne State University Press.

finally occurs the liquidation of content altogether ("Bei Beckett endlich kommt es zur Liquidation der Inhalte überhaupt" (IBW, 4:235):

> And man, the lectures they gave me on men, before they even began trying to assimilate me to him! What I speak of, what I speak with, all comes from them. It's all the same to me, but it's no good, there's no end to it. It's of me now I must speak, even if I have to do it with their language, it will be a start, a step towards silence and the end of madness, the madness of having to speak and not being able to, except of things that don't concern me, that don't count, that I don't believe, that they have crammed me full of to prevent me from saying who I am, where I am, and from doing what I have to do in the only way that can put an end to it, from doing what I have to do. How they must hate me! Ah a nice state they have me in, but still I'm not their creature, not quite, not yet. To testify to them, until I die, as if there was any dying with that tomfoolery, that's what they've sworn they'll bring me to. Not to be able to open my mouth without proclaiming them, and our fellowship, that's what they imagine they'll have me reduced to. It's a poor trick that consists in ramming a set of words down your gullet on the principle that you can't bring them up without being branded as belonging to their breed. But I'll fix their gibberish for them. I never understood a word of it in any case, not a word of the stories it spews, like gobbets in a vomit. My inability to absorb, my genius for forgetting, are more than they reckoned with. Dear incomprehension, it's thanks to you I'll be myself, in the end. Nothing will remain of all the lies they have glutted me with. And I'll be myself at last, as a starveling belches his odourless wind, before the bliss of coma.[13]

Does this magnificent act of citation need any comment? Bachmann makes this text speak for her more strongly than it could ever have spoken for Beckett because nothing of what it says is the "content" of the text. No author "attended to" this displacement. It happens only as and in the *repetition* of the text in reading. It is therefore only if we, too, read it this way that this citation performs what could not be written without being lost, and what the mimes with the white faces try hard and in vain to simulate in order to prevent it: the usurpation of the speaker's image in the mirror as our reverse gaze takes over the eye/"I." Rather than folding reading back into writing, we thus fold writing out into reading.

There is a hint of a system of justice and judgment in the word *citation*, which goes together with the hesitation on the part of writers

---

[13]*Molloy, Malone Dies, The Unnamable: Three Novels by Samuel Beckett*, trans. Patrick Bowles (New York: Grove Press, 1965), 324–25. Bachmann quotes, of course, a German translation (see IBW, 4:235–36).

such as Breton and Derrida to "commit themselves." Derrida abandons the search for a determinate content, but as we have seen, he ends up walling in the space of writing and committing himself to it as a whole—and so do those who follow him. Nobody who ends up thus imprisoned can plead innocence for their confinement. Nor can those, man or woman, who find themselves inconvenienced by a tie around their neck: "Pierrot's death in Algiers is being announced by Harlequin ('Bah! nothing's surer: his obituary, / On the opening pages of each dictionary, / Is visibly written with paraphs profuse, / Just under a Pierrot attached to a noose')" (DS, 204).

The specific direction taken by my work as a comparatist and a feminist derives from my desire to avoid either of two fates. I do not want to continue "knotting before the mirror" and assimilate myself to "man" and his text by serving as his blind analyst/double. I have nothing to gain from such assimilation, and everything to lose through it. Nor will I commit suicide by responding to murderous interpellations like those of Breton's slot machines. I have to be careful to read, therefore, neither "as a man" nor "as a woman," but as that which both is "lost" in representation and remains "yet to come." I have to look in the mirror of representation and recognize myself not as whatever "face" I see there but exclusively as that which is not represented: the gaze which is, always at this very moment, looking. This gaze cannot be preserved in any representation. But it also cannot be prevented by representation. And without it, without us, all those books would remain inert. This repositioning allows for a reevaluation of the century-long chase for the "object," the "referent," the "truth" from the perspective of that which continued to escape in this process. What thus got away is our life.

Bachmann's may be one of the most carefully theorized works in the consistency with which it maintains this perspective. But it is certainly not alone on the far side of the writerly space of the white-faced mime and his old story. One of the tasks I see for myself is therefore to continue to read for the "large trace" of the kind of difference I have tried to map here. Works such as Bachmann's will remain unreadable in their difference unless we develop new critical strategies and very different readerly skills capable of following the subtler traces of the work done by writers who write without "representing" themselves. Their difference can appear only if we learn to see with different eyes, and to go quickly from one light into another, the compass point in the heart.

11

Dangerous Crossings: Gender and Criticism in Arabic Literary Studies

FEDWA MALTI-DOUGLAS

When the Egyptian writer Naguib Mahfouz was awarded the Nobel Prize for Literature in 1988, it seemed that Arabic literature was at once poised and destined to play an important role in world literature. Visions of Arabic literature in translation flooding the Western reading world danced before the eyes of Arabic specialists, too long consigned to the outer limits of the academy. Places of honor in airport bookshops seemed within easy reach. But, as many specialists of Middle Eastern literature have lamented, this prize has had little effect on the recognition of Arabic literature in the Western literary-critical community. Arabic literature remains foreign, on the far side of a border that few even think about crossing. Taught and read by regional specialists, it is treated essentially as an aid to the practical understanding of a region of the world whose chief exports are oil and terrorism. Recognition of Arabic literature as a significant part of the human cultural heritage and a player in the creation of contemporary world culture is as lacking today as it was a decade ago. Certainly the airport bookstore is as far away as ever!

At the same time, other specialists in the Middle East are actively bemoaning something else; the growth of Western-language translations of feminist women's writings from the Arab world. These are perceived as more dangerous than those of their male compatriots (or even nonfeminist women writers) because more critical. Such works have still not reached the airport bookstores, but their circulation in academic circles has already generated anxiety among specialists in Arabic and Islamic studies.

I write as an Arab and as a woman. My analyses are informed by a variety of critical methodologies. Yet when I cross Arabic literature with gender criticism, trouble emerges. How? Why?

Time was, in the early years of our century, when a writer such as the British scholar R. A. Nicholson could saunter gaily through the field

of medieval Arabic letters isolating one or another author and comparing him to Western writers. The "him" is intended here: scriptors of
the medieval Arabo-Islamic world were generally males.[1] Thus it was
that Ibn Khallikân became the Boswell of the Arabs.[2] This was one way
of domesticating Arabic literature, of denuding it of some of its alterity,
of making it seem familiar and undaunting to the Western reader.

These antiquated forms of comparison are now just that—antiquated.
But if we were once beleaguered by them, we are now beleaguered by
something quite different: objections from many within the field to new
critical methodologies, new analytical approaches, as if labor-filled
years of philological training produced analytical blinders. The faster
the non-Arabic humanities progressed, the more isolated and ingrained
the analysis of the Arabic humanities became. Certainly this has been
the record of the last half century. The solution: imprison the Arabic
text in an ostensibly nonmethodological straitjacket, put an analytical
chastity belt on it, protect it. Academic traditionalists in Arabic studies
call literary criticism a fad, in the obvious hope that if they close their
eyes long enough it will go away. Do these "fads" or "fashions" help
us to understand the text? Do they inform the text? These questions are
not even addressed. How could they be? To counter theory, you need
to use theory.

At the forefront of the battle, and undergoing the most vigorous attack, is gender criticism. Oddly enough, gender unifies political ideo-
logues who seem to disagree on everything *but* how to write (or rather
not to write) Arab feminism. One can oppose feminist work because it is
a species of literary criticism. One can oppose it because it is allegedly
non-Arab in origin. One can oppose it because it is associated with social
movements that threaten entrenched groups in the American academy.

The dilemma of the comparatist Arab feminist is double. Arabic literature, centuries old, needs to enter the canon if that canon is to have
any pretense of universality. "Monoculturalism," to use Lillian S. Robinson's highly loaded term, has become increasingly difficult to defend.[3] I use the term *canon* here as cultural shorthand. Do we need a
fixed, or a slowly evolving, list of "great works?" However one answers
this question, there are at any point in time circuits both intellectual

[1]For a discussion of the gendering of Arabic scriptural traditions, see Fedwa Malti-
Douglas, *Woman's Body, Woman's Word: Gender and Discourse in Arabo-Islamic Writing*
(Princeton: Princeton University Press, 1991).

[2]See, for example, R. A. Nicholson, *A Literary History of the Arabs* (Cambridge: Cambridge University Press, 1969), 452. Nicholson's work was first published in 1907.

[3]Lillian S. Robinson elucidated this point at a public lecture, "Get a Life," at the University of Texas, Austin, September 5, 1990. I am grateful to her for this reference.

and physical: books that are read, books that are taught, books that are bought.

The question is: Through what door does Arabic literature enter these circuits, and what is written on its passport? Third world literature, emergent literature, postcolonial literature: these are categories that elicit much positive response. But to sneak Arabic literature through the door as an emergent literature, to take but one example, is to do it a grave injustice. For the nonspecialist Westerner, Arabic literature is an emergent literature because recently discovered. Yet Arabic literature is far older than literature in any modern European language. To treat the more recent products of this self-conscious tradition as emergent or third world or postcolonial literature is to sever the modern Arabic literary product from its textual heritage. This severing is even more violent now that contemporary Arabic authors are playing intertextual games with their own tradition. Interestingly enough, this is taking place across continents, from the Palestinian Emile Habiby to the Egyptian Jamâl al-Ghîtânî and the Tunisian Mahmûd al-Mis'adî.[4]

The contemporary Arab, even the barely educated one, knows that he or she has a literary heritage, for he or she has lived around the literary and religious classics from an early age. Quotations from the holy book, the Qur'ân, and from the hadîth, the reported actions and sayings of the Prophet Muhammad, are broadcast daily on radio and television. The contemporary Arab moviegoer is not surprised to hear verses from a sixth-century Arabic ode recited on the screen.[5] The sidewalks of Middle Eastern capitals teem with premodern texts, bound editions of the more popular classical works at reasonable prices. Do you have a stomach ailment? Medieval manuals of "Prophetic medicine" are available for your purchase and use. Do you fancy anecdotal literature or homiletics? Here again you will not be disappointed. Or would you prefer erotic manuals from the Middle Ages? You have but to wander the souks of Marrakesh or the West Bank.

That is one problem. A related problem lies precisely in the appeal

[4]See, for example, Fedwa Malti-Douglas, "Mahfouz's Dreams," in *Naguib Mahfouz: From Regional Fame to Global Recognition*, ed. Michael Beard and Adnan Haydar (Syracuse: Syracuse University Press, 1993), 126–43, 183–85. In the case of Egypt, for example, even this model needs to be modified: contemporary novelists and dramatists also exploit Ancient Egyptian materials. See, for example, Fathî Sa'îd, *al-Fallâh al-Fasîh* (Cairo: Al-Hay'a al-Misriyya al-'Amma lil-Kitâb, 1982); Muhammad Mahrân al-Sayyid, *Hikâya Min Wâdî al-Milh* (Cairo: Mu'assasat 'Inân lil-Tibâ'a, 1984); 'Alî Ahmad Bâkathîr, *al-Fallâh al-Fasîh* (Cairo: Maktabat Misr, 1985); Jamâl al-Ghîtânî, "Shakâwâ al-Fallâh al-Fasîh," in *Ard-Ard* (Beirut: Dâr al-Masîra, 1980), 123–43; Yûsuf al-Qa'îd, *Shakâwâ al-Misrî al-Fasîh*, vol. 1 (Beirut: Dâr al-Masîra, 1981); vol. 2 (Cairo: Dâr al-Mustaqbal al-'Arabî, 1983); vol. 3 (Cairo: Dâr al-Mustaqbal al-'Arabî, 1985).

[5]See, for example, Yûsuf Shâhîn's very popular film *al-Ard* (The earth), 1968.

of texts by and on women for the nonspecialist Western audience. It is a vicarious appeal linked to the call of the harem, the exotic, the alien. Yet it is most often the supposedly unmediated testimony that attracts the widest audiences—the interview (whether ethnographic or journalistic), the memoir, or indeed any first-person narrative that is deemed (quite naively in effect) to reflect personal or social realities. Or all of these: the anthology of bite-sized morsels. Like a tourist, the reader thinks he or she is getting the authentic, the peek behind the veil. But we know that there are no unmediated texts. Authenticity is a mirage, as unreal as the tourist's search for the nontourist experience. Analyses are less popular. More demanding, they risk disturbing the Westerner's comfortable righteousness as they highlight patriarchal forms not exclusive to the region.

The woman scriptor is a relatively new phenomenon in the Arabo-Islamic literary tradition. She may be new, but she is not ignorant. Her texts are more often than not informed by the male literary tradition she grew up with. Like her male colleagues, she plays intertextual games, onomastic games, literary-cultural games. She is as deserving of serious study as the male author. To set the Arab woman writer in a category apart is also to sever her from her heritage, in much the same way that Arabic literature is severed when treated as an emergent literature. Yet, studying Arab women's writings in a gender-conscious way is, for some within the field of Middle Eastern studies, increasingly suspect.

October 1992. I travel to the land of colorful trees. Three different settings. The first is a women's studies audience in a big city university; the second, an exclusive seminar in a prestigious Ivy League university; the third, a mixed audience in yet another Ivy League institution. In the first I talk about a prominent Arab feminist's prison memoirs. In the second I talk about a novel by that same feminist. In the third I talk about a prominent woman Islamist. Two Arab female intellectual figures whose politics are radically opposed to each other.

The listeners' responses? From all too many a remarkable convergence of fears. And a remarkable convergence on a single policy: silence. On the one hand, to talk of women is to disempower them—this was said about a leading media personality who is unlikely to be silenced by anything written on this side of the Atlantic. On the other hand, a feminist approach is a threat. By talking about the forbidden, by exposing that which should remain hidden (dare I say behind a veil), am I not exposing Arab society as "pathological"? (I put this word in quotes because it is the very word that surfaced in the discussion.)

The three audiences are peppered with avowed Marxists. Some of them belong to the methodologically most conservative wing of Middle Eastern studies. Philology and Marxism make strange bedfellows. Yet they come together when it is time to close one's eyes to gender issues. Scholars whose considerable intellects are paralyzed by a methodological conservatism bordering on inertia can hide behind a fashionable caricature of Marxism and anti-imperialism. Do not class relations take precedence over gender ones? Does a focus on Arab or Muslim women not betray a species of cultural imperialism? These scruples make useful prophylactics, protecting their wearer from potentially disturbing critical and social issues.

One solution to this pervasive gender problem was actually proposed at the Ivy League seminar: a particularly vehement youngish male full professor from a neighboring, and equally Ivy, institution suggested tracking down the guilty publishers to dissuade them from disseminating these Arab feminist texts in translation. No one around the table objected. The strength of his fear apparently blinded this otherwise intelligent colleague to the utter impracticality of his form of censorship. Another form of severing! I wish I could say that this was an isolated case. The only unusual thing about it was its public frankness. Recommendations of silence are commonly delivered in a friendly tone by well-meaning colleagues.

Methodological obscurantism allies itself with the desire to protect the integrity of Arab civilization. Their point of contact: the idea that it is inappropriate to analyze Arab civilization with foreign (read: Western) intellectual tools. But this mode of protecting Arab civilization is alien to that civilization itself. Medieval Arabo-Islamic culture was, in its finest moments, intellectually open, unafraid, self-confident. And the modern Middle East? There is not a single cultural force or figure in the region, down to the most neotraditionalist of Islamic revivalists, whose thought has not been shaped by contact with the West and its ideas. The notion of a modern Arab culture free of Western taint is as mythical as the unmediated testimony, another touristic dream.

The modern critical dialogue about gender becomes embedded, therefore, in discourses of power and control. Who has the right to speak about the Arab world and about Arab women? At a women's panel that took place not so long ago at the national meeting of the Middle East Studies Association, several Arab women suggested that only Arab women had the right to speak about the Arab woman. History has shown that such identity politics lead ultimately to the defense of existing power groups. Besides, this assertion begs the question of what an Arab woman is. Is she the one living in the Arab world and who knows only Arabic? Is she the one living in North Africa and who is literate only in French? Is she the one living in Europe or America and writing in Arabic? Is she the one living abroad and writing in French or English?

The discourse of power goes deeper. Does the individual who speaks have the right to discuss issues that place the Arabs in a bad light? And primary here is the question of women. After all, why add insult to injury? If the Arabs already have a bad press (and we know that they do),[6] are gender critics not aggravating this problem by raising questions that should better remain dormant?

This argument has clear appeal, and it appeals to many. But why is it that other injustices, like those of wealth and poverty or those of political oppression, can be invoked without fear of adding to the bad name of the Arabs? Why are the most searing of social novels (and social novelists) welcomed by some of the very same people who reject the equally leftist radical feminists? Could it be that attacks on capitalism and imperialism do not threaten academics (a salaried class indeed) the way that those on patriarchy do?

This concern to protect suggests that somehow Arabs should be treated as a category apart because they are supposedly unable to hear criticism of their society or of gender issues. This is the height of cultural arrogance; its result is not to protect but to isolate. No number of Nobel Prizes could then make an impact.

[6]For such an exposé, see, for example, Jack G. Shaheen, *The TV Arab* (Bowling Green, Ohio: Bowling Green State University Popular Press, 1984).

12

Identity Politics as a Comparative Poetics

GRETA GAARD

> This is an intervention. A message from that space in the margin
> that is a site of creativity and power, that inclusive space where
> we recover ourselves, where we move in solidarity to erase the
> category colonized/colonizer. Marginality as site of resistance. En-
> ter that space. Let us meet there. Enter that space. We greet you
> as liberators.
>
> —bell hooks, "marginality as site of resistance"

As notions of diversity and multiculturalism have become central to
most academic discussions, they have raised the related question of
identity politics. I approach this question as a woman, as a white, middle-class lesbian. The question of identity concerns me when I learn
that a male colleague has been assigned a course on women's literature.
I am also concerned when I see that heterosexual women are writing
lesbian feminist criticism. At the same time, I am eager to teach courses
on black women's novels when I learn that there are no such courses
offered at my university, and no black women faculty available to teach
them. Finally, as I work on course proposals for classes in lesbian and
gay literature, and an introduction to queer culture, my authority to
write, teach, or speak as a lesbian is called into question by my community when it learns that I have also chosen men as sexual partners.

In each of these instances I am concerned with developing a politics
of identity which accounts for the particular authority of embodied
subjects, but without falling prey to essentialist notions of identity
which lead one group to excommunicate another. I am interested in a
politics of identity which encourages coalition building across identities
while affirming the uniqueness of each embodied subject. For these
reasons I want to explore the discourse now evolving around the relation of identity politics and bisexuality. As a literary scholar and
teacher, I see the identity of bisexuality as inherently comparative, and
believe this perspective can be used to raise new questions in literary
theory.

Identity politics can be defined as the practice of claiming one's identity as a suitable location from which theory can be made, and as a suitable location for creating a political agenda. The question is: What is identity? How can identity be defined? To answer this question I first briefly survey the essentialism-versus-constructionism debates which have taken place in the lesbian and gay communities. I then offer an alternative theory of bisexuality as a basis for identity politics and a location for comparative criticism. I believe the two have much to offer each other: theories of both comparative literature and bisexuality have arisen from a location of exile, and both are concerned with the problems of translation. Finally, to demonstrate the potential uses of such a theory, I use it to consider Virginia Woolf's *Orlando*.

Within the gay and lesbian communities, essentialism has played an important role. By assuming that all lesbians have something in common, and by extension that all lesbians and gays have something in common, the gay and lesbian community at large has been able to advance important political agendas for improving our conditions.[1] But within the community essentialism has become a kind of police force. Susie Bright, co-founder of the lesbian sex magazine *On Our Backs*, has expressed concern about "the deployment of rigid sexual categories, not only by the Right, but also within our own communities, where investments in the stability, internal coherence, and uniqueness of lesbian identity have not only obscured sexual differences, but generated an active resistance to knowing what we fantasize, desire, do, and think."[2] Similarly, Diana Fuss observes that while "current lesbian theory is less willing to question or to part with the idea of a 'lesbian essence' and an identity politics based on this shared essence," gay male theorists "have been quick to endorse the social constructionist hypothesis and to develop more detailed analyses of the historical construction of sexualities." Her explanation for this difference is persuasive: "If the adherence to essentialism is a measure of the degree to which a particular political group has been culturally oppressed . . . then the stronger lesbian endorsement of identity and identity politics may well indicate that lesbians inhabit a more precarious and less secure subject position than gay men."[3] Whereas gay men have only one

[1] Rebecca Shuster, "Sexuality as a Continuum: The Bisexual Identity," in *Lesbian Psychologies: Explorations and Challenges*, ed. Boston Lesbian Psychologies Collective (Chicago: University of Illinois Press, 1987), 56–71.

[2] Biddy Martin, "Sexual Practice and Changing Lesbian Identities," unpublished ms.

[3] Diana Fuss, *Essentially Speaking: Feminism, Nature, and Difference* (New York: Routledge, Chapman & Hall, 1989), 98.

strike against them (being gay), lesbians have two strikes (being lesbian and being women); the number of strikes increases if the person in question is, for example, differently abled or of color.

The lesbian theorists Monique Wittig and Adrienne Rich refuse to reduce lesbianism to an exclusively sexual, genital act. But the definitions they propose instead seem almost contradictory. For example, in "The Straight Mind," Wittig asserts that "lesbians are not women" but rather a third sex which subverts the false dichotomy between heterosexual and homosexual; conversely, in "Compulsory Heterosexuality and Lesbian Existence," Rich affirms that "all women are lesbians," existing along a continuum that includes "many . . . forms of primary intensity between and among women."[4] As Fuss observes, if Wittig's notion of lesbian identity is too exclusive, Rich's is surely too inclusive. Neither description accounts for specific sexual practices of individual women.

To the question "What is a lesbian?" constructionism seems to provide a more descriptive answer. The earliest description of sexuality as a spectrum, the Kinsey scale, rates sexuality along a continuum with 0 being exclusively heterosexual, 6 being exclusively homosexual, and 3 being equally heterosexual and homosexual.[5] More recently, Michael Shively and John De Cecco define four psychological components of sexual identity, which include biological sex, gender identity (formed by age three), social sex role (comprising masculine or feminine behaviors), and sexual orientation (self-description).[6] Beth Zemsky also uses this scale, adding a fifth component, sexual practices.[7] According to these definitions, a person may be born a woman (biological sex), appear to be feminine (gender identity), but behave in ways considered masculine (social sex role), describe herself as a lesbian (sexual orientation), and have sexual relations with men and women (sexual practice). Which of these components constitutes the "identity" from which to build political strategy? Would the person just described be seen as lesbian or bisexual? The prominence of any one component of sexual identity may depend on the specific political context.

[4]See Monique Wittig, "The Straight Mind," in *Out There: Marginalization and Contemporary Cultures*, ed. Russell Ferguson, Martha Gever, Trinh T. Minh-ha, and Cornel West (New York: New York Museum of Contemporary Art, 1990), 51–58; and Adrienne Rich, "Compulsory Heterosexuality and Lesbian Existence," in *Blood, Bread, and Poetry: Selected Prose, 1979–1985* (New York: Norton, 1986), 23–75.
[5]For a variety of scales defining sexuality, see Loraine Hutchins and Lani Kaahumanu, eds., *Bi Any Other Name: Bisexual People Speak Out* (Boston: Alyson, 1991).
[6]Michael G. Shively and John P. De Cecco, "Components of Sexual Identity," *Journal of Homosexuality*, 3.1 (Fall 1977): 41–48.
[7]Beth Zemsky, "Stonewall Remembered," *GLCAC OutFront* 2.4 (Summer 1991): 1, 3.

The overall purpose, it must be remembered, for defining an identity in such instances is to create a place from which to develop a political agenda, and to specify the position of the theorist. But if constructionism is most helpful in defining identity, essentialism has proven most useful as a political strategy. Amanda Udis-Kessler writes: "While constructionism may represent the better description of human sexuality, the very elements which make lesbian/gay communities strong today—perhaps which make them possible as communities at all—are essentialist."[8] Theories of antiessentialism, by erasing the possibility of essence, also deprive subjects of a platform from which to create political agendas or build coalitions. Defining what counts as a position for building theory becomes immediately a politicized act. In the history of feminism, women have repeatedly defended their authority to speak based on their unique location as women. "The difference between feminists and antifeminists strikes me as precisely this," writes Linda Alcoff, "the affirmation or denial of our right and our ability to construct, and take responsibility for, our gendered identity, our politics, and our choices."[9]

Poststructuralists such as Lacan, Derrida, and Foucault argue, according to Alcoff, that "the self-contained, authentic subject conceived by humanism to be discoverable below a veneer of cultural and ideological overlay is in reality a construct of that very humanist discourse." Lacan uses psychoanalysis, Derrida uses grammar, and Foucault uses the history of discourses to deconstruct our concept of the subject's having an essential identity. Each arrives at the conclusion that there is no essential core: "For the post-structuralist, race, class, and gender are constructs and, therefore, incapable of decisively validating conceptions of justice and truth because underneath there lies no natural core to build on or liberate or maximize. Hence, once again, underneath we are all the same."[10] Such arguments cannot provide a platform for grounding a feminist politics: if there is no "real" difference between women and men, says Alcoff, there can be no basis for an agenda of "women's needs." Teresa de Lauretis agrees: "If 'woman' is a fiction, a locus of pure difference and resistance to logocentric power, and if there are no women as such, then the very issue of women's oppression would appear to be obsolete and feminism itself would have no reason

[8]Amanda Udis-Kessler, "Bisexuality in an Essentialist World: Toward an Understanding of Biphobia," in Bisexuality: A Reader and Sourcebook, ed. Thomas Geller (Hadley, Mass.: Times Change Press, 1990), 51–63.

[9]Linda Alcoff, "Cultural Feminism versus Post-Structuralism: The Identity Crisis in Feminist Theory," Signs 13 (Spring 1988): 432.

[10]Ibid., 415, 432.

to exist (which, it may be noted, is a corollary of poststructuralism and the stated position of those who call themselves 'post-feminists').''[11]

Through arguments such as these, constructionism leads feminists (along with lesbians and bisexuals) to a position of having to defend our very existence. But this is a false position. Shane Phelan writes: "We do not need to prove that we exist, in the manner of metaphysics, which is to prove that we have the right to exist. We do exist. We live our lives, inescapably, with existing others. To justify this by defining, by ontologizing, by tracing descent, is to suggest that our present existence is open to dispute.''[12] Our existence, however, cannot be articulated through an appeal to the body or to our unique experiences, for a variety of reasons. "Bodily experiences may seem self-evident and immediately perceptible but they are always socially mediated," Fuss observes; for this reason "we need to be extremely wary of the temptation to make substantive claims on the basis of the so-called 'authority' of our experiences.''[13] Gayle Rubin reminds us that "we never encounter the body unmediated by the meanings that cultures give to it. . . . It is impossible to think with any clarity about the politics of race or gender as long as these are thought of as biological entities rather than as social constructs. Similarly, sexuality is impervious to political analysis as long as it is primarily conceived as a biological phenomenon or an aspect of individual psychology.''[14] If both essentialism and constructionism are flawed, perhaps the solution lies in a strategy of using essentialist rhetoric while simultaneously problematizing the subject.

Rich, in "Notes toward a Politics of Location," remarks that "perhaps we need a moratorium on saying 'the body.' For it's also possible to abstract 'the' body. When I write 'the body,' I see nothing in particular. To write 'my body' plunges me into lived experience, particularity: I see scars, disfigurements, discolorations, damages, losses, as well as what pleases me." In place of the essentialist, universalizing determiner "the," Rich suggests using the constructionism of the pronoun "my" as a way to locate bodily experiences historically in terms of race, class, gender, and sexuality. As a means of defining identity, then, Rich advises us to ask not "What is a woman?" but rather "Where, when, and

---

[11]Teresa de Lauretis, "Upping the Anti (sic) in Feminist Theory," in *Conflicts in Feminism*, ed. Marianne Hirsch and Evelyn Fox Keller (New York: Routledge, 1990), 255–70.

[12]Shane Phelan, *Identity Politics: Lesbian Feminism and the Limits of Community* (Philadelphia: Temple University Press, 1989), 158.

[13]Fuss, *Essentially Speaking*, 25.

[14]Gayle Rubin, "Thinking Sex: Notes for a Radical Theory of the Politics of Sexuality," in *Pleasure and Danger: Exploring Female Sexuality*, ed. Carole S. Vance (Boston: Routledge & Kegan Paul, 1984), 276–77.

under what conditions have women acted and been acted on, as women?" In posing this question, Rich defines identity politics for women as the "politics of asking women's questions. We are not 'the woman question' asked by somebody else; we are the women who ask the questions."[15]

"Woman" or "lesbian" in this analysis becomes not an essence but a location for the intersection of identities at a given historical moment. In this way, writes Alcoff, "the position that women find themselves in can be actively utilized (rather than transcended) as a location for the construction of meaning, a place from where meaning is constructed, rather than simply the place where a meaning can be discovered (the meaning of femaleness)."[16] Identity becomes not a fixed essence but rather a social construction, a product of the intervening forces of a subject's location in terms of class, color, age, physical ability, gender, sexual orientation, historical moment.

Censorship occurs when only certain locations are authorized as appropriate points for making theory. The issue is not only which theory counts as theory, as knowledge, but more than that, which locations count as sites for the production of theory. As a kind of test case I would offer the earlier question about the role of bisexual practices in defining identity.

Characterized and caricatured as fence-sitters, bisexuals have been seen, and have seen themselves, as having "no place" from which to make theory. Defined as people in the process of moving from one sexual location to another, bisexuals have only recently begun to claim that movement itself as a suitable location for theory. In claiming an identity which is not one of either/or but rather one of both/and, they reject what they see as a patriarchally inscribed dualism, heterosexuality/homosexuality.

Questions of identity group formation often rely on the establishment of boundaries, on defining an identity in opposition to other identity groups. As Andrew Parker and others argue: "National identity is determined not on the basis of its own intrinsic properties but as a function of what it (presumably) is not. . . . But the very fact that such identities depend constitutively on difference means that nations are forever haunted by their various definitional others."[17] Diana Fuss articulates much the same point: "To the extent that identity always con-

[15]Adrienne Rich, "Notes toward a Politics of Location," in *Blood, Bread, and Poetry*, 216.
[16]Alcoff, "Cultural Feminism," 434.
[17]Andrew Parker, Mary Russo, Doris Sommer, and Patricia Yaeger, eds., *Nationalisms and Sexualities* (New York: Routledge, 1992), 5.

tains the specter of non-identity within it, the subject is always divided and identity is always purchased at the price of the exclusion of the Other, the repression or repudiation of non-identity."[18] But feminists have observed that this oppositional way of defining the self as separate is a male gendered trait, whereas defining a self-in-relationship is a female gendered trait.[19] So what are the implications of these gendered processes of identity formation when applied to identity politics? If the two most dominant boundaries of identity are nationalisms and sexualities, as some may claim,[20] what are the implications for a bisexual theory of identity politics? For unlike the clearly delineated boundaries of nationalism, or the hetero-homo divide, in which the identity of self or group is established in clear distinction against a "them" of opposition, the boundaries of bisexual identity formation are everywhere and nowhere. Just as there has been no clear "us," there are also no clear "them"s. Bisexual identity has involved a process of continual repositioning between fixed boundaries of sexualities, a process in which bisexuals are continually made to feel like a "them" no matter where they are located.

The problem is magnified by the fact that both the heterosexual and homosexual communities have a distinct culture, if culture can be defined as having a unique art, literature, music, and theater.[21] I would also add to these language and geographic space, thus underscoring the connections between sexualities and nationalisms. The problem of "seeing bisexual" then becomes the problem of being continually in exile, an outsider in both heterosexual and homosexual cultures.

Bisexuality means more than holding dual citizenship, though many critics of bisexuality, who conceptualize it in this way, censure bisexuals for enjoying undue advantages—the pleasures of homosexuality and the privileges of heterosexuality. The true allegiance of bisexuals is continually called into question; more than exiles, in fact, bisexuals are seen as double agents in a war of dichotomized sexualities. In this way bisexuality is located on the boundaries of sexual discourse and in the margins of lesbian or heterosexual feminist literary criticism. As a marginalized perspective, bisexuality has the potential to be inherently feminist, inherently comparative.

[18]Fuss, *Essentially Speaking*, 103.

[19]See, for example, Nancy Chodorow, *The Reproduction of Mothering: Psychoanalysis and the Sociology of Gender* (Berkeley: University of California Press, 1978); and Carol Gilligan, *In a Different Voice: Psychological Theory and Women's Development* (Cambridge: Harvard University Press, 1982).

[20]See Parker et al., *Nationalisms and Sexualities*.

[21]This definition is offered by Bonnie Zimmerman in *The Safe Sea of Women: Lesbian Fiction, 1969–1989* (Boston: Beacon, 1990).

This form of "dual citizenship" is addressed in terms of color and nationality by Gloria Anzaldúa, who writes of "the New Mestiza" in *Borderlands/La Frontera,* and of the difficulty of "living on borders and in margins, keeping intact one's shifting and multiple identity and integrity." For Anzaldúa identity is defined in opposition to something else: "Borders are set up to define the places that are safe and unsafe, to distinguish *us* from *them.* A border is a dividing line, a narrow strip along a steep edge. A borderland is a vague and undetermined place created by the emotional residue of an unnatural boundary. It is in a constant state of transition. The prohibited and forbidden are its inhabitants."[22] But, like the identity of bisexuals, the identity of the New Mestiza belongs to neither nationality; the New Mestiza is neither "us" nor "them." This position, instead of being a site for erasure and invisibility, may provide possibilities for comparative readings and coalition building across perspectives. Feminists have frequently spoken of the utility of margins and marginalized viewpoints in constructing more inclusive political agendas. It is in the margins that coalition building begins, through the very experiences of the racial, cultural, and/or sexual mestizas.

According to bell hooks, marginality is "much more than a site of deprivation"; it is "the site of radical possibility, a space of resistance." Marginality can be seen as "a central location for the production of a counter hegemonic discourse." But this resistance must be spoken in a language that is not the language of the colonizer: "One can only say no, speak to the voice of resistance, because there exists a counter language. While it may resemble in ways the colonizer's tongue, it has to undergo a transformation."[23] Like the language of the Mestiza, the language of the sexually marginalized appropriates and mixes words to create new meanings. But, as Judy Grahn writes in *Another Mother Tongue,* "there has been no acceptance and exploration of the Gay context that would allow our subterranean slang words to enter the world of dictionaries." Grahn's exploration of gay language reveals "parameters and characteristics of homosexual culture" that are not accessible from a heterosexual perspective.[24] It is, however, precisely because the words are not placed in their gay context that their meaning is inaccessible. Writing about the same problem, Paula Gunn Allen explains that those who attempt to understand Native American cere-

[22]Gloria Anzaldúa, *Borderlands/La Frontera: The New Mestiza* (San Francisco: Spinsters/Aunt Lute, 1987), 2, 3.

[23]bell hooks, "Marginality as Site of Resistance," in Ferguson et al., *Out There,* 341, 342.

[24]Judy Grahn, *Another Mother Tongue: Gay Words, Gay Worlds* (Boston: Beacon, 1984), xiii, xiv.

monial literature apart from its cultural context will be unable to do so.[25] Using a similar rationale, bisexual theorists have begun to reject the very word *bisexual,* arguing that because it originates in the context of heterosexual/homosexual discourse, it retains and embodies an oppressive ideology.

Paula Rust has discovered at least four different ways in which bisexual and lesbian women define bisexuality, all of which remain within the boundaries of the heterosexual/homosexual discourse. Some argue that bisexuality is nonexistent, and women who identify themselves as bisexual are really "confused" or are in transition to becoming lesbians. Others see bisexuality as a combination of heterosexuality and homosexuality, a kind of dual membership in two societies. Relatively few women see sexuality as a continuum, with bisexuality falling somewhere between heterosexual and lesbian sexualities. And finally, still others seem to conceptualize sexuality as a trichotomy, with bisexuality as "a third, distinct sexual orientation." Rust, in "Who Are We and Where Do We Go from Here?" rejects each of these definitions as perpetuating a fundamental homosexual/heterosexual dichotomy, and calls for a new word to contain a new conceptualization: "If we wish to challenge the hegemonic homosexual/heterosexual dichotomy, assert the existence of bisexuality and emphasize the commonality of all people, we must communicate this message in a language that is intelligible and effective in the current political climate. Conceptualizing bisexuality as a qualitatively different form of sexuality . . . offers us the opportunity to do exactly that." Rust rejects the word *bisexual* because it "embodies the negative definition" of bisexuals in that "the emphasis remains on the biological sex characteristics of potential romantic partners. Although we argue that we do not choose our partners based upon their biological sex, we still define ourselves with a word that refers to the biological sex of our partners." Rust, who prefers "to banish the concept of partner sex from our vocabulary of self-identity," suggests "pansensual" as a term that describes an individual's sexual identity in a way that acknowledges sexuality as a wholistic experience more than a merely genital one. Her awareness of the implications of this new description of identity can be seen in her choice of words: she compares the new identity and experience to being in a foreign country, using foreign currency and a foreign language; and she discusses this revised sexual identity in terms of a geographic "territory."[26] Rust's

---

[25]See Paula Gunn Allen, *The Sacred Hoop: Recovering the Feminine in American Indian Traditions* (Boston: Beacon, 1986).

[26]Paula C. Rust, "Who Are We and Where Do We Go from Here? Conceptualizing

definition of sexual identity as a personal characteristic that can no longer be unquestioningly defined in terms of partner sex may be a useful perspective for providing a comparative reading of *Orlando.*

The usefulness of a bisexual (or "pansensual") literary criticism can be seen by examining just one author and one text: Virginia Woolf's *Orlando.*[27] Woolf's sexual identity has been a topic of interest to literary critics for many years. (It is interesting to recall that, just as her sexual identity is difficult to define, so too is her nationality: in *Three Guineas* Woolf writes that as a woman, she has no country.) Whereas Quentin Bell's biography emphasizes the importance of Woolf's relationship with Vita Sackville-West, Louise DeSalvo's study reveals Woolf as a woman severely traumatized by incest and basically incapable of sexual relations of any kind.[28] Although she enjoyed a supportive and enduring relationship with her husband, Woolf's sole sexual relationship was with Vita. As Ellen Rosenman observes, though Woolf lived in an era that equated sexual activity with sexual identity, Woolf made no such equation for herself.[29] The postmodern fragmentation of identity, as in Shively and DeCecco's "Components," along with Rust's definition of the pansensual, may offer a more accurate (though anachronistic) means of describing Woolf's sexual identity as quite distinct from her sexual practices.

But as every literary scholar knows, authors are not to be confused with texts, and Virginia Woolf's sexual identity is not Orlando's. Perhaps the climate of cultural feminism in the 1980's is responsible for the number of literary critics battling to claim *Orlando* as a lesbian text—as if lesbianism were somehow the quintessential state of feminism—and Woolf as the ultimate feminist literary foremother. But, like Woolf herself, or Woolf's friend and lover, Vita, after whom Orlando is modeled, the character cannot be reduced to the binary confines of heterosexuality/homosexuality.

Orlando's identity both transcends and permeates the various locations of gender, sex, and sexuality through which s/he is repositioned. Orlando begins the novel as a "boy" of sixteen (though of ambiguous

---

Bisexuality," in *Closer to Home: Bisexuality and Feminism,* ed. Elizabeth Reba Weise (Seattle: Seal, 1992), 291, 297–301.

[27]Virginia Woolf, *Orlando* (New York: Harcourt Brace, 1928); subsequent references are cited in the text.

[28]Quentin Bell, *Virginia Woolf: A Biography* (New York: Harcourt Brace Jovanovich, 1972); Louise DeSalvo, *Virginia Woolf: The Impact of Childhood Sexual Abuse on Her Life and Work* (Boston: Beacon, 1989).

[29]Ellen Bayuk Rosenman, "Sexual Identity and *A Room of One's Own:* 'Secret Economies' in Virginia Woolf's Feminist Discourse," *Signs* 14 (1989): 648.

gender) who is attracted to Sasha without knowing her biological sex, sex role, gender identity, or sexual orientation: "[Orlando] beheld . . . a figure, which, whether boy's or woman's, for the loose tunic and trousers of the Russian fashion served to disguise the sex, filled him with the highest curiosity. . . . [An] extraordinary seductiveness . . . issued from the whole person" (37). Later, Orlando realizes that what he feels for the Archduchess Harriet is not love but lust (116–17), and he reacts by marrying Rosina Pepita, a Gypsy dancer, then falling into a deep trance, and awakening as a woman when the trumpets blast "The Truth!" (137). Does the call of the trumpets signal that Orlando is "really" a woman, and has "really" been a woman all along? Are we to understand that there is some underlying essence to Orlando? Or is this call for "truth" yet another theatrical shift in the performance of gender?

As the narrator remarks, Orlando's alteration is disturbing only to others. Oblivious to any difficulties associated with this sex change, Orlando departs to live with the Gypsies, but on returning to English society realizes the enormity of the problem caused by this shift in outward identity. In each case the "problem" is related to clothing. In cultures that do not distinguish gender through clothing (the Russian and the Gypsy), Orlando is largely untroubled; in English culture, which insists on such distinctions, both the clothing and the gender roles become restrictive: "It was not until she felt the coil of skirts about her legs and the Captain offered, with the greatest politeness, to have an awning spread for her on deck that she realised with a start the penalties and the privileges of her position" (153). Orlando first delights in gender play, then reviles both gender roles, and finally concludes that she loves Sasha better as a woman because now Orlando understands Sasha's own experiences. Does this section of the narrative mean to imply that homosexual love is preferable to heterosexual since it is based on a more complete way of knowing the beloved? When Orlando returns home and is greeted by her household, it is the animals who best recognize her through her costumery of gender: "No one showed an instant's suspicion that Orlando was not the Orlando they had known. If any doubt there was in the human mind the action of the deer and the dogs would have been enough to dispel it, for the dumb creatures, as is well known, are far better judges both of identity and character than we are" (170). Of course, Orlando is not alone in manipulating the wardrobe of identity: the next day Orlando is visited by the Archduchess Harriet, who reveals herself to be the Archduke Harry.

Orlando's new biological identity has affected her gender: "She was becoming a little more modest, as women are, of her brains, and a little more vain, as women are, of her person" (187). The narrator credits this to the change in clothing—and certainly clothing is the gendered construct of a particular cultural and historical location[30]—speculating that "it is clothes that wear us and not we them . . . they mould our hearts, our brains, our tongues to their liking" (188). But the narrator does not see the culture as controlling Orlando; rather, "clothes are but a symbol of something hid deep beneath. It was a change in Orlando herself that dictated her choice of a woman's dress and of a woman's sex" (188). Not until sex reassignment surgery could such a "choice" be made except in fiction. Would Orlando be better described, then, as a transsexual?

But to ask this question presupposes a unity and uniformity among the components of sexual identity in such a way that they are organized according to a heterosexual paradigm. The narrator suggests something quite the contrary: "In every human being a vacillation from one sex to the other takes place, and often it is only the clothes that keep the male or female likeness, while underneath the sex is the very opposite of what it is above. Of the complications and confusions which thus result every one has had experience" (189). Exasperated with the intellectual life, Orlando cross-dresses—or puts on her own old clothes—and picks up a prostitute. The way the prostitute behaves toward Orlando calls up in her the feelings she had as a man: "To feel her hanging lightly yet like a suppliant on her arm, roused in Orlando all the feelings which become a man. She looked, she felt, and she talked like one" (216–17). Only the biological identity of Orlando is now that of a woman. Does this mean that Orlando is a butch lesbian? A transgendered person? Or simply in drag? Through the prostitute Nell, Orlando meets a whole society of prostitutes, and enjoys their company very much. One might recall Joan Nestle's essay "Lesbians and Prostitutes: An Historical Sisterhood" and wonder if this confirms Orlando's identity as a lesbian.[31] But Orlando's identity cannot be so easily confined. The narrator tells us: "Her sex changed far more frequently than those who have worn only one set of clothing can conceive. . . . From the probity of breeches she turned to the seductiveness of petticoats and enjoyed the love of both sexes equally" (221). What is meant by "sex"? Biological sex? Sex role? Sexual identity? What kind of identity does Orlando assume when enjoying "the love of both sexes equally"? These two series of questions have meaning only within the dominant para-

---

[30]See Marjorie Garber, *Vested Interests: Cross-Dressing and Cultural Anxiety* (New York: Routledge, 1992).

[31]Joan Nestle, "Lesbians and Prostitutes: An Historical Sisterhood," in *A Restricted Country* (Ithaca: Firebrand, 1987), 157–77.

digm of heterosexuality/homosexuality. Because language is created by and serves the dominant class, and because Orlando's identity does not fit the dominant paradigm, there is no language for naming it. In terms of that paradigm Orlando exists outside the boundaries of language as a sexual exile. A modern reader, unless she or he is painfully obtuse, must see this identity as pansensual: Orlando's sexual identity exists independently of her sexual partners.

It is the nineteenth century that puts Orlando firmly in her place as a woman, wanting a wedding ring. Monogamy and heterosexuality—and with these, restrictive gender roles—carry the day. Orlando manages to retain her identity by marrying a woman-manly man, Shel, but her days of gender-bending are over. As a mature woman of thirty-six, Orlando realizes that "nothing is any longer one thing" (305), including herself: "These selves of which we are built up, one on top of another, [are] as plates . . . piled on a waiter's hand. . . . For she had a great variety of selves to call upon, far more than we have been able to find room for, since a biography is considered complete if it merely accounts for six or seven selves, whereas a person may well have as many thousand" (308–9). Orlando's many identities are independent of one another; they can be ordered and reordered like dishes, layered or stacked. To ascribe a single identity or a single sexuality to this character is to resort to simple reductionism. Woolf's novel can be read as nothing so narrow as lesbian, or heterosexual, or even bisexual. The amount of gender play at work here suggests that the most productive critical perspective for reading the text and the character in *Orlando* is the pansensual.

What conclusions can be drawn from using the lens of pansensuality (formerly bisexuality) as a comparative approach? Pansensual identity shows that the two "nations" or discourses of the heterosexual and the homosexual are in fact more alike than not in their shared, bifurcated view of sexuality. Reading *Orlando* from a lesbian or heterosexual feminist perspective fails to account for a multiplicity of meanings which fall outside and move beyond their discourses. A pansensual lens shows, if nothing else, that the borders of sexuality are artificial and arbitrary. Exiled from both heterosexual and lesbian nations, the pansensual feminist perspective uses a comparative approach to reconstitute its own identity, not as androgyny (man/woman) nor as bisexual (hetero/homo), but as a rejection of those very dualistic categories themselves as a meaningful way of organizing discourses of sexual identity.

Identity must be seen not as a stasis but as a movement, a plurality. In this Woolf and queer theorists span the decades of the twentieth century to agree. Ed Cohen writes: "If we can begin to gather together on the basis of constructions that 'we' are constantly and self-consciously in the process of inventing, multiplying, and modifying, then perhaps 'we' can obviate the need for continuing to reiterate the fragmenting oscillations between identity and difference that have been the legacy of post 1960s progressive politics."[32] Ann Ferguson concurs, arguing for the need "to conceive of our goal as international political *movement* building (of interconnected lesbian, gay and feminist movements) rather than *culture* building" because "those who see themselves as building a political movement are more able to tolerate value disagreement than those who see themselves as building a culture."[33] Such a movement, by continually crossing boundaries of nationalisms and sexualities which challenge its exiled status, will be inherently comparative.

[32]Ed Cohen, "Who Are 'We'? Gay 'Identity' as Political (E)motion (A Theoretical Rumination)," in *Inside/Out: Lesbian Theories, Gay Theories,* ed. Diana Fuss (New York: Routledge, 1991), 88.
[33]Ann Ferguson, "Is There a Lesbian Culture?" in *Lesbian Philosophies and Cultures,* ed. Jeffner Allen (New York: State University of New York Press, 1990), 82.

Part IV

Future Engagements

13

Cross Fire and Collaboration among Comparative Literature, Feminism, and the New Historicism

SARAH WEBSTER GOODWIN

Comparative literature as a discipline seems in recent years to have drifted into an uneasy peace. The heyday of comparatist controversy— when scholars from both sides of the Atlantic tossed the word "crisis" back and forth like a football of indeterminate shape—is long gone. Although in this country René Wellek has seemingly won out, and comparatists are supposed to be concerned with "criticism" rather than "history," with defining the literariness of literature and interpreting the canon in the light of weighty abstractions, in practice there is still a lot of source- and influence-hunting going on, a lot of thematology, the kind of literary history that is supposed to be of secondary interest.[1] Much of it has been first-rate, but until the 1990s it remained somewhat overshadowed by giants such as Paul de Man, whose reputations seemed—to switch metaphors—to rise and hover over the discipline of comparative literature, taking on a being and a community of their own. (I do not intend to make them sound quite so much like an angelic host, but the image insistently presents itself.) De Man and his peers belonged to literary criticism and theory more generally, not primarily to comparatists.

But even such absent comparatist giants as they seem to be missing in the 1990s. Feminist literary theory and criticism has an international cast, and feminists are exerting themselves with real intensity to build common models out of disparate cultural materials. Much of the most interesting recent feminist work attempts to mediate between the con-flicting models and assumptions that have brought that field to a crisis of its own.[2] But feminism has remained surprisingly absent from the disciplinary corridors of comparative literature, and the issues and in-

[1] A point made by Henry H. H. Remak, "Comparative Literature: Its Definition and Function," in *Comparative Literature: Method and Perspective*, ed. Newton P. Stallknecht and Horst Frenz (Carbondale: Southern Illinois University Press, 1971), 1–10, 330n.

[2] See, for example, Marianne Hirsch and Evelyn Fox Keller, eds., *Conflicts in Feminism* (New York: Routledge, 1990).

tensities that drive feminist debate seem larger, more pressing, than the problem of defining a distinctly comparatist methodology which so exercised comparatists a generation or two ago. Similarly, the historicist criticism that has come increasingly to occupy center stage in critical discourse goes after the big fish: nothing less is at stake than the relations of culture and politics to literary criticism, both what we write and what we teach. Although the "border disputes" that some of the new historicists have ensnared themselves in may seem petty at times, they also clearly grow out of deeply held beliefs about why literary criticism matters and how it might help bring about a better world. Both feminist and historicist critics define their work as distinct from the aesthetics of formalism. In the context of their politicized rhetoric, matters such as a definition or even a defense of comparative literature seem circumscribed, academic—and as dull as a football game in July. The real skirmishes are elsewhere.

If comparative literature itself has come to seem dull, it is not because dullness inheres in its subject matter. On the contrary. Nothing could be more pertinent to the current climate of cultural criticism than the problems of defining cultures and their exchanges which constitute the natural domain of comparatist work.[3] Furthermore, comparative literature offers the rare example of a feminist critic and scholar—Germaine de Staël—as one of its earliest and most influential theorists. De Staël's contribution makes it clear that feminist, historicist theory lies at the very heart of comparative literature; the work of comparing literary cultures engages that of comparing and constructing genders. Feminism and historicism should come naturally to comparative literature.

Both feminist and historicist thought helped constitute the speculative works that established comparative literature. Both, I would argue, are inherently comparatist in nature, although both have subsided in importance in recent years. There is one major difference between the two, however, and the difference in this case is all. After Germaine de Staël, feminist speculation apparently disappeared entirely from comparatists' methodological debates. In contrast, history in its various guises remained a kind of obsession for comparatists, and retreated in importance only late and briefly, under the pressure of late New Criticism and the work of the Yale school.[4] For this reason, the return of

[3]I am grateful for the insights of Michel-André Bossy in private conversation and in his unpublished paper "Comparative Literature in the 1990s: Notes toward an Axiology." They have contributed much to this argument.
[4]In turn, Marjorie Levinson calls the new historicism "a direct assault upon Yale's

history to the nexus of comparative literature may occur more effort-lessly than that of feminist cultural theory, which has its long absence to account for and overcome.

The reasons for both these disciplinary tendencies within compara-tive literature—an ongoing interest in history, and a resistance to the feminist issues raised by one of its seminal theorists—are not hard to adduce. Because of the historical association between comparative lit-erature and nationalism, because comparatists must incorporate consid-eration of cultural self-definition and boundaries into their work, the discipline has a long-standing and complex relation with the theorizing of politics and history.[5] And because comparative literature, even more than national literatures, traditionally defines its concerns around an elite and exclusively male canon—its sources, influence, branches, and subcanons—it has resisted with particular force the inroads of feminist criticism.

And yet despite these historical differences it seems clear that both feminists and historicists have much to gain from each other. As has become evident in the work of the new historicists, feminist thought has brought significant influence to bear on the categories of historical thought currently in use. At the same time, the larger methodological discussions taking place about the relations between history and liter-ary theory have given feminists a position for debate more potentially central than any other they have occupied in recent history.

The basis for an alliance, however stormy, between historicists and many feminists lies in the conceptions of history and of culture which they are likely to share. For both, "historicizing" the text means reading it in a context to which it is integrally related. History is not a "back-drop," not something of inferior interest from which the text emerges in order to transcend it.[6] Nor is history construed as a unitary world-view or zeitgeist, nor even as explanatory narratives of cause and effect. Rather, history is a problem: fact, causality, cultural unity come into question as the possible creations of hegemonic groups. Text and con-text are alike discursive, and contribute together to cultural self-construction. Literary texts are not privileged over other kinds of texts

---

present-mindedness"; see her essay "The New Historicism: Back to the Future," in *Re-thinking Historicism: Critical Readings in Romantic History*, ed. Marjorie Levinson et al. (Ox-ford: Basil Blackwell 1989), 18–63.

[5]Comparatists who speculate about the nature of their discipline discuss its political dimension, whether or not they consciously foreground it. See, for example, François Jost, *Introduction to Comparative Literature* (Indianapolis: Bobbs-Merrill, 1974), vii.

[6]This sentence paraphrases Carolyn Porter's thoughtful feminist critique of the new historicism, "Are We Being Historical Yet?" *South Atlantic Quarterly* 87 (1988): 770.

except insofar as their representations may be more multifaceted, complex, or self-contradictory. Historicists and feminists share an interest in the ways texts trace the creation, subversion, containment, and conception of power. They also share, in theory, a sense of being themselves historically positioned as readers and writers.[7]

A number of feminists have criticized the new historicism more than they have praised it, but they have not ignored their affinities with its tenets. Judith Lowder Newton has conveniently and sympathetically collated a number of historicists' self-definitions:

> Those engaged in "new historicism," we are told, generally assume that there is no transhistorical or universal human essence and that human subjectivity is constructed by cultural codes which position and limit all of us in various and divided ways. They assume there is no "objectivity," that we experience the "world" in language, and that all our representations of the world, our readings of texts and of the past, are informed by our own historical position, by the values and politics that are rooted in them. They assume, finally, that representation "makes things happen" by "shaping human consciousness" and that as forces acting in history various forms of representation ought to be read in relation to each other and in relation to non-discursive "texts" like "events." . . . There is the notion that "history" is best told as a story of power relations and struggle, a story that is contradictory, heterogeneous, fragmented. There is the (more debated) notion that hegemonic power is part but not all of the story, that "history" is a tale of many voices and forms of power, of power exercised by the weak and the marginal as well as by the dominant and strong.[8]

I quote Newton at some length because this is the best brief definition of the new historicism I know of, although she goes on to argue that there is nothing new or original about any of this, that it is just "history as usual," being practiced by a group of male scholars who fail to ac-

---

[7]This paragraph makes a series of broad generalizations, each of which could entail lengthy debate, qualification, and documentation. Although it offers a basic, probably uncontroversial idea of the now familiar new historicist givens, it assumes a commonality among feminists that is certainly misleading, given both the virulent attacks by some feminists on new historicism and the methodological conflicts among feminists themselves. Still, even as pointed an attack as Carol Thomas Neely's on the "cult-historicists," whose effect she says "has been to oppress women, repress sexuality, and subordinate gender issues," acknowledges the "liberating and regenerative effect" of an approach that also can be seen to provide support for feminist claims that all literature is political; see her essay "Constructing the Subject: Feminist Practice and the New Renaissance Discourses," *English Literary Renaissance* 18 (1988): 7. For more distinctions among historicisms and the critiques of them, see Jonathan Dollimore, "Shakespeare, Cultural Materialism, Feminism, and Marxist Humanism," *New Literary History* 21 (1990): 471–93.

[8]Judith Lowder Newton, "History as Usual? Feminism and the 'New Historicism,'" in *The New Historicism*, ed. H. Aram Veeser (New York: Routledge, 1989), 152.

knowledge their feminist and other predecessors. Nevertheless, we are a long way from the comparatist Paul van Tieghem's assertion in 1931 that "Comparative Literature studies the actions and influences exerted by individuals."[9] No such positivistic concepts as actions and individuals inform the new historicism. None of the familiar historical categories is simply a given: fact, causality, nation, event, objectivity, agency—or meaning.

The result is a kind of criticism pointedly banned by the comparatist Horst Rüdiger as late as the 1966 inaugural issue of *Arcadia: Zeitschrift für Vergleichende Literaturwissenschaft:* Rüdiger outlawed "the discussion of all historical parallels based solely on speculation."[10] For the new historicism, "speculation" is all we have. Rüdiger believes that there are bases for drawing historical parallels to establish homologies between texts that possess factuality or truth-value, but the new historicist would argue that those "bases" for homologies are themselves only texts, subject to interpretation.[11] As Newton points out, the new historicist argument echoes poststructuralist epistemologies that cannot shock anyone, however much they may dismay some who seek a retreat from the alleged hegemony of theory in the academy. The apparent inevitability of the new historicist inquiry in comparative literature follows from the critical developments of the 1970s and 1980s, in which the remnants of positivism have been swept away. It also draws strength from the revelations about de Man's personal history, which have elevated in importance our own historical context as critics. The new historicism thus seems logically unavoidable, even if already ephemeral as a distinct school, precisely because its givens are so familiar.

It is clear that the idea of history sketched here differs significantly from the ways comparatists have understood history in the past. I would also argue that such a renovated view of history, actively integrated into comparatist work, stands to open the borders for feminism in comparative literature—or, to sidestep the chivalric gesture, to put feminists in a better methodological position to storm the checkpoints for themselves. A feminist, historicist criticism is both desirable and possible in comparative literature, despite practical difficulties; it could

---

[9]Quoted in Ulrich Weisstein, *Comparative Literature and Literary Theory: Survey and Introduction* (Bloomington: Indiana University Press, 1973), 4.

[10]Horst Rüdiger, "Zur Einführung," *Arcadia: Zeitschrift für Vergleichende Literaturwissenschaft* 1 (1966): 3.

[11]This is a problem that has received some attention, since much new historicist work proceeds by drawing parallels between disparate texts and then basing a larger cultural claim on those parallels—which themselves at times seem tenuous or fanciful. See Carolyn Porter's critique of Stephen Greenblatt, in Porter, "Are We Being Historical Yet?" 762–63.

indeed reenergize a languishing field. I intend this argument not as a blueprint for silencing controversy, but as one for reviving it. The cross fire and the collaboration we are seeing along the old disciplinary borders are leading us to redraw the maps. Comparative literature can no longer stand by as neutral territory.

Comparative literature's early associations with history as a discipline would seem to have been crucial, if relatively contested. The earliest comparatists thought in terms of historical context. I have already mentioned the importance of Germaine de Staël, the "pioneer comparatist" whose *De l'Allemagne* (1813) is still famous, but who also wrote an early work of what might be called historicist—and also feminist— comparative literature, *De la littérature considérée dans ses rapports avec les institutions sociales* (1800).[12] Although Staël's methodological influence has not yet fully been traced, after her the work of early comparatists remained very closely aligned with that of historians.[13] According to Ulrich Weisstein, the first major conference on comparative literature took place in Paris in 1900 within the context of an international congress of historians, and in both France and Germany comparatists long saw their work as "a branch of literary *history* rather than literary *criticism* or *theory*."[14] There is no need to repeat here the convoluted history of comparatists' attempts to define their discipline; it can be read in any handbook.[15] It is perhaps simply worth noting that the discipline acquired its earliest institutional coherence in France, where Taine and the practice of a positivist history had a long-standing influence on comparatist thought. By later in the century there was also considerable

[12]The phrase "pioneer comparatist" is from A. Owen Aldridge, ed., *Comparative Literature: Matter and Method* (Urbana: University of Illinois Press, 1969), 2. According to Paul van Tieghem, the French comparatist who championed historicist criticism earlier in this century, her work was foundational; see his introduction to Mme. de Staël, *De la littérature considérée dans ses rapports avec les institutions sociales*, ed. Paul van Tieghem (Geneva: Droz, 1959), 1:vii–lxvi. Like most of the male commentators on her groundbreaking essay, he stresses her intuitiveness; unlike them, he also notes the importance of her feminism to her study (xiii, xxvii).

[13]There lies a story to tell in the erasure of Staël's presence. Consistently, histories of the discipline mention her and then drop the subject. Ulrich Weisstein, *Comparative Literature*, calls her book *De l'Allemagne* a "palimpsest" of comparative literature, an overt and unembarrassed metaphor of erasure. More typical is the overture of praise followed by dismissal offered by Hugo Dyserinck: he calls her work decisively influential, then dismisses it for being limited in its point of view; see his *Komparatistik: Eine Einführung* (Bonn: Bouvier, 1977).

[14]Weisstein, *Comparative Literature*, 174–75, 185.

[15]The most lucid example I know of in English is Weisstein's appendix (ibid., 167–252). See also P. Brunel et al., *Qu'est-ce que la littérature comparée?* (Paris: Armand Colin, 1983), 15–30; and Dyserinck, *Komparatistik*, 17–86. Also useful is Remak, "Comparative Literature," which includes an annotated bibliography.

influence from the German hermeneutic tradition, with its historicizing methods. Despite the more ahistorical influence of Goethe and Schlegel in their concepts of *Weltliteratur* and *Universalpoesie*, professional comparatists long had to define their methodology with reference to history.

One way of linking history and literature was to hitch chronologies of literary texts on to the models of historical periodization that history scholars were bent on defining, largely based on monarchs or ruling regimes. Traditional twentieth-century narratives of the discipline's own history point out that the early stages of comparative literature in the nineteenth century are very closely linked to the development of literary history as an idea, but imply that those stages are far behind us, despite the fact that periodization remains the primary organizing feature of both our pedagogy and our professional practice. René Wellek and Austin Warren's *Theory of Literature*, adopting a formalist position, dismisses any idea of comparative literature "conceived . . . on externals," and notes that "the decline of this type of 'comparative literature' in recent decades reflects the general turning away from stress on mere 'facts,' on sources and influences." History, even "literary" history, if construed as "mere facts," seemingly would only distract from the more strictly aesthetic qualities of the texts.[16] We recognize here the terms of the famous crisis in comparative literature of the 1950s and 1960s, in which the "American school" rejected the alleged French obsession with *rapports de fait*, "factual connections," and argued for the importance of "criticism" over "history."[17]

But that one crisis was merely part of the ongoing discussion in comparatist self-definitions about the function of history in comparative literature. Under the influence of Wellek and Warren, for a time history seemed decidedly extrinsic to literary matters. Attempts to define an

[16]René Wellek and Austin Warren, *Theory of Literature*, 3d ed. (New York: Harcourt Brace, 1956), 48. For distinctions among kinds of literary history, see 252–69. As Wellek and Warren point out, the phrase covers a wide range: "Most histories of literature . . . are either social histories, or histories of thought as illustrated in literature, or impressions and judgements on specific works arranged in more or less chronological order" (252). They propose instead an idea of literary history that is based on intrinsically literary qualities, which I discuss later in this essay.

[17]According to the French position in that debate, comparatist literary histories were to be closely modeled on the nineteenth-century elaboration of a positivist history, relying for truth-value on the idea of documentable fact, and for argument on the idea of development and progress. René Wellek and many others called these concepts into question, as do the new historicists, in somewhat different terms. For a well-reasoned account of the crisis, see Dyserinck, *Komparatistik*, 49–64. See also, principally, René Wellek, "The Crisis of Comparative Literature" (1959), in his *Concepts of Criticism* (New Haven: Yale University Press, 1963), 282–95, subsequently cited in the text; and René Étiemble, *Comparaison n'est pas raison: la crise de la littérature comparée* (Paris: Gallimard, 1963).

intrinsically literary history have grown out of formalist criticism, and have involved histories of genres, morphologies, thematic criticism, and the like. Wellek and Warren place this kind of literary history in the section of their book called "The Intrinsic Study of Literature." And yet there has also been a long-standing tradition of comparatist literary history that approaches intellectual and even social history, especially in France and Germany, where the generic boundaries between literature and philosophy have always been more fluidly drawn than in the English tradition. The distinction between extrinsic and intrinsic matters, which now is undergoing redefinition in this country, has never been universally accepted.[18]

If we return to Wellek's 1959 argument for a criticism based on intrinsic matters, we find a position that seems dated, but that also intelligently lays the groundwork for breaking down the very distinctions on which it rests, preparing the way for a new and different historicism in comparatist studies:

> Literary scholarship today . . . must be distinguished from the study of the history of ideas, or religious and political concepts and sentiments which are often suggested as alternatives to literary studies. Many eminent men in literary scholarship and particularly in comparative literature are not really interested in literature at all but in the history of public opinion, the reports of travelers, the ideas about national character—in short, in general cultural history. The concept of literary study is broadened by them so radically that it becomes identical with the whole history of humanity. But literary scholarship will not make any progress, methodologically, unless it determines to study literature as a subject distinct from other activities and products of man. Hence we must face the problem of "literariness," the central issue of aesthetics, the nature of art and literature.
>
> . . . The work of art, I have argued, can be conceived as a stratified structure of signs and meanings which is totally distinct from the mental processes of the author at the time of composition and hence of the influences which may have formed his mind. There is what has been rightly called an "ontological gap" between . . . life and society on the one hand and the aesthetic object. I have called the study of the work of art "intrinsic" and that of its relations to the mind of the author, to society, etc., "extrinsic." (293–94)

---

[18]Basil Munteano took up precisely this issue in "Situation de la littérature comparée: sa portée humaine et sa légitimité," in *Proceedings of the Second Congress of the International Comparative Literature Association,* University of North Carolina Studies in Comparative Literature, 23–24 (1959), 1:124–42. Munteano rejects the distinction between "extrinsic" and "intrinsic" criticism, and argues for a dialectical method.

It would seem hard to draw a more rigorous division between literature and history. And yet, curiously, Wellek goes on to qualify himself in a vein that has been largely ignored: "Still, this distinction cannot mean that genetic relations should be ignored or even despised or that intrinsic study is merely formalism or irrelevant aestheticism. Precisely the carefully worked out concept of a stratified structure of signs and meanings attempts to overcome the old dichotomy of content and form. . . . Nothing would be further from my mind than to . . . erect a barrier between history and formal study" (294). Indeed, it is the vocabulary of "structure," of "signs and meanings," that breaks down the very barrier he has begun to erect. If the work of art consists of such structures, so too might the author's mental processes, the influences on them, the society in which those influences have arisen, and the texts in which we may trace those structures. Inadvertently, Wellek points the way for comparative literature to take as its proper domain precisely a consideration of the interrelationships among such larger structures, specifically in the international context. It is no accident that his essay argues repeatedly for a comparatist criticism that will break down international barriers. He closes it by asserting, heatedly, that "once we conceive of literature not as an argument in the warfare of cultural *prestige,* or as a commodity of foreign trade or even as an indicator of national psychology . . . national vanities will disappear" (295). Wellek's vocabulary here sets up a system of interrelated structures. Psychology—collective and individual—interlocks with metaphors of warfare and trade in a complex system which encompasses literary texts and criticism. The scholar cannot step outside that system, but can evidence greater or lesser awareness of it. Wellek introduces here the very vocabulary of commodity, circulation, and trade which characterizes new historicist analysis. And he does so pointedly in the context of international exchange.

It is that concern with nationalism and with boundaries that makes history a natural subject for comparatists. The relation between national literatures and cultural boundaries lies at the heart of the comparatist enterprise and inevitably raises historical and cultural questions. It is by now no secret that the development of literary studies has followed closely the growth of nationalist sentiment in Western cultures.[19] But this does not mean that the borders of modern nations coincide tidily with those of their cultures, and there are countless borderline areas. It

[19]See, for example, Wellek and Warren, *Theory of Literature,* 51; Albert Guérard, "Comparative Literature?" *Yearbook of Comparative and General Literature* 7 (1958): 1–6; Gerald Graff, *Professing Literature* (Chicago: University of Chicago Press, 1987).

may seem like splitting hairs to question, as Ulrich Weisstein does, whether Heinrich Mann should be considered a German, French, Czech, or American author for the purpose of genuine comparatist work, depending on the respective weight one chooses to lend language, milieu, and citizenship.[20] It is an issue long familiar to English departments in this country, where T. S. Eliot is variously taught in both British and American literature surveys. Does it matter? I would argue that it matters when the decision to cast an author this way or that rests on the political and historical dimensions of his or her affiliations—and that the assumptions behind the choice must themselves be made explicit. In the same discussion Weisstein asks whether it is "comparatist" to compare an East German author with a West German, a question that might in the light of the reorganization of Germany be supplanted by another one: whether a German-language author living in Silesia should be regarded as a Slav or a German. To make the choice is to take sides in a political debate about how "Germany" is to be defined.

What is at stake here is the historical assumption underlying comparative literature as a discipline: that the comparatist's work juxtaposes texts from discrete national literatures. Earlier in his 1959 essay Wellek identifies what he calls a "paradox in the psychological and social motivation of 'comparative literature' " as practiced in this century: a tension between the desire to overcome nationalism and a "strange system of cultural bookkeeping," in which the goal is to accumulate points for one's own nation (287–89). The paradox Wellek locates in comparative literature still stands: it is not just the notorious western Europe–focused ethnocentricity of comparatists that underscores a dominant cultural self-conception, but also their very definitions of what they compare. Like national literature departments, for example, comparatist faculty have traditionally excluded from consideration French, German, or British literatures of non-Continental cultures. And as in those departments, opening the borders to include such literatures is necessarily a political step entailing a historicizing of the curriculum.

If, as I have been suggesting, comparative literature as a discipline inclines toward historical problems, how would the new historicism affect it? One characteristic of the new historicist work is the nature of the contemporary texts it chooses as the context for its readings: political debates, economics, domestic manuals, popular literature, advertising, legal pamphlets—texts that challenge rather than support the

[20]Weisstein, *Comparative Literature*, 11.

hallowed status of the literary. New historicists' concerns are with class, gender, and the shifting representations of power, that elusive Foucauldian force that is exercised only in social contexts and that the literary text may both represent and contest, subvert and contain.

Perhaps the most significant difference between earlier work in what we might call "old" historicist criticism and the new historicism is that identified in an unsympathetic essay by Martin Mueller, published in *Profession 89*. Mueller contrasts what he calls a "hermeneutics of charity," in which the reader is generous to the text, with the notorious "hermeneutics of suspicion" practiced by the new historicists:

> [The New Criticism said:] Read a text or author until you have found the meaning that combines the highest degree of thematic complexity with the highest degree of structural coherence. Now we have an opposite version, which says: Read a text or an author until you have found the meaning that combines the highest degree of ignorance with the highest degree of complicity.[21]

Although this is a caricature, it is not entirely inaccurate: for the new historicist the text is far from sacred. On the contrary, one of the central concerns of scholars such as Stephen Greenblatt, Catherine Gallagher, Laura Brown, and Jerome McGann has been to show the complicity between the literary text and constraining ideologies. Comparative literature came of age as a discipline during the era of charity, when criticism's calling was to celebrate "world" masterpieces. To shift to suspicion means an even more violent rupture for comparatists than for national literature scholars.

This may lead us to some understanding of why the new historicist work has taken place in the context of national literatures, especially English and American, rather than in comparative literature. There are also practical considerations; it is difficult enough to research contemporary documents in one language and culture without multiplying the logistical problems by two or three. Comparative literature is much easier to practice as a formalist criticism: it requires just the reader and the books. In contrast to scholars of English literature, who can often obtain primary sources in this country, comparatists require greater resources and mobility to do historical research. This is not merely a practical issue but one related to a larger problem for comparatists his-

[21]Martin Mueller, "Yellow Stripes and Dead Armadillos," *Profession 89* (1989): 29. Although Mueller does not say so, the phrase "hermeneutics of suspicion" is not his own, but has been used repeatedly and variously attributed by others. It appears to have originated with Paul Ricoeur.

torically: it is very difficult to be fully conversant with a text not just in its literary contexts but also in its cultural, political, social, and economical contexts. The difficulty multiplies with each additional language and culture one approaches. Whatever the difficulties for the comparatist, however, historicist criticism has much to recommend it. It moves away from formalist concerns that enforce a narrow conception of the comparatist canon, and that isolate literature from other aspects of culture. The practice of a historicist criticism is likely also to be coupled with a return to the vexed issue of national and cultural boundaries, this time with fresh critical perspectives.[22]

Because of such theoretically informed and ground-breaking comparatists as Wellek and Warren, de Man, and others, and because American comparatists have been well placed to follow developments in critical theory from the Continent, the discipline has generally not stagnated in this century but has more often been in the avant-garde. For better or worse, the new historicism is the new avant-garde, especially if we consider it more broadly in its affinities with feminism and cultural studies. Claims have been made repeatedly that new historicism is a peculiarly American phenomenon, despite influences from Foucault, the Frankfurt school, and especially British cultural materialists such as Raymond Williams.[23] But it is perfectly possible to do new historicist work without being steeped in Foucault and Adorno: it is striking how little *theory* appears in *Representations,* and Stephen Greenblatt has admitted that in his case the practice comes before the theory.[24] The acknowledged pioneers of the new historicism have come out of English studies, primarily in the Renaissance and Romanticism. Comparatists are having to run to catch up. Should we?

---

[22]No doubt British and German comparatists have already undertaken some of this work, under the influence, respectively, of British cultural materialism and the Frankfurt school. For a German view of comparative literature as a discipline that is integrally historical, despite its inflection of relatively conventional categories of comparatist research, see the essays in Manfred Schmeling, ed., *Vergleichende Literaturwissenschaft: Theorie und Praxis* (Wiesbaden: Athenaion, 1981). The volume makes no mention of feminism or gender criticism.

[23]There is a growing and at times impassioned literature on the differences among new historicisms. See, for example, Dollimore, "Shakespeare"; Lynda Boose, "The Family in Shakespeare Studies; or—Studies in the Family of Shakespeareans; or—The Politics of Politics," *Renaissance Quarterly* 40 (1987): 707–42; Joel Fineman, "The History of the Anecdote: Fiction and Fiction," in Veeser, *New Historicism,* 49–76, esp. 65; and Marlon B. Ross, "Contingent Predilections: The Newest Historicisms and the Question of Method," *Centennial Review* 34 (1990): 485–539.

[24]Stephen Greenblatt, "Towards a Poetics of Culture," in Veeser, *New Historicism,* 1–14. For a discussion of the paucity of theory in the new historicism, see Ross, "Contingent Predilections."

It seems to be precisely this sense of the new historicism as the avant-garde—or the latest trend, to put it less generously—that makes for uneasy relations between historicists and feminists. In fact, I have been writing about the new historicists as though they were a phenomenon almost entirely distinct from feminism. This is clearly not the case. Judith Lowder Newton argues, as we have seen, that feminists have anticipated every important aspect of new historicist work. Newton asserts this as though the historicists had not paid their debts, even though she cites the talk in which Catherine Gallagher credited her own feminism with shaping her critical development and, seemingly, that of other new historicists.[25]

And yet it is true that new historicists, most often men, frequently write as though they had been influenced by feminist thought without, however, citing specific sources. To mention just two examples: Stephen Greenblatt, in a 1990 entry in *Critical Terms for Literary Study*, defines culture as "a particular network of negotiations for the exchange of material goods, ideas, and—through institutions like enslavement, adoption, or marriage—people." His condensed bibliography cites Bakhtin, Benjamin, Elias, Geertz, and Raymond Williams—all men, with no mention of Irigaray, or of others who have written with so much illumination about the symbolic exchange of women. Similarly, in an essay published in a 1989 volume, Joel Fineman claims that the new historicism seems to be peculiarly American in tenor, but he fails to identify American feminism as a contributing factor. He makes no mention that it is American feminist theory that has negotiated the straits between textuality and materialism during the last decade or two, focusing on the construction of gender as its model. In the same volume, Louis Montrose is more generous, citing a long series of ground-breaking feminist works in Renaissance studies, and granting feminist theory real prominence: "In the United States, it is Feminism and the Women's Movement which in recent years have provided the most powerful infusions of intellectual and social energy into the practices of cultural critique."[26] It is an exceptional argument for a male new historicist.

[25]Gallagher's talk, cited in Newton, "History as Usual?" appears as "Marxism and the New Historicism," in Veeser, *New Historicism*, 39–48. Gallagher narrates the development of her critical position in a curious mix of the third-person and first-person plural, though it is not fully clear whom she means to include by her phrase "this generation of critics" (40).

[26]Stephen Greenblatt, "Culture," in *Critical Terms for Literary Study*, ed. Frank Lentricchia and Thomas McLaughlin (Chicago: University of Chicago Press, 1990), 229; Fineman, "History of the Anecdote," 65n; Louis A. Montrose, "Professing the Renaissance: The Poetics and Politics of Culture," in Veeser, *New Historicism*, 26. For various persuasive

These and the other essays in *The New Historicism* may well exemplify the relations generally between feminist and new historicists, reflecting the visibility and vigor of the feminist critiques. In the volume there is a range of positions, with Montrose representing the most deference to feminist theory, and Catherine Gallagher, among the women, representing the least tension between new historicism and feminism. Other essays by women convey downright hostility, the most unequivocal by Jane Marcus, who argues that a " 'feminist' New Historicism is . . . even more limited and dangerous than other varieties of this technique."[27] Both Marcus and Newton assert that new historicist work is less new than it claims to be because it fails to take into full consideration the feminist methodology that has been worked out over recent decades. They thus repeat and elaborate critiques of new historicist work that had been made previously by Lynda Boose, Carol Thomas Neely, Carolyn Porter, and Marguerite Waller.

Newton's key argument in that volume, in her critique of Catherine Gallagher's *Industrial Reformation of English Fiction,* harks back to an old quarrel between feminists and Marxists. Feminists have held that class-centered theories do not suffice to interpret the experience of women, whose class is defined not by their work but through the symbolic exchanges taking place in marriage. As a result, Newton argues, studies that place class rather than gender at the center of their critical readings just do "history as usual," without the genuine change in perspective that comes when gender is placed at the center of the critical method.[28] Thus, she argues, because the new historicism still relies on "male-centered" categories and events, it generally fails to be new, even when it incorporates some critiques of gender ideologies.

The problem is very similar to the one identified and summarized earlier by Catharine A. MacKinnon in her well-known essay in *Signs,* "Feminism, Marxism, Method, and the State: An Agenda for Theory." For MacKinnon, there are seemingly irreconcilable differences between Marxism and feminism, and attempts to reconcile them (surely one of

---

feminist critiques of the way new historicists marginalize women, see Boose, "Family in Shakespeare Studies"; Neely, "Constructing the Subject"; Porter, "Are We Being Historical Yet?"; and Marguerite Waller, "Academic Tootsie: The Denial of Difference and the Difference It Makes," *Diacritics* 17 (1987): 2–20. For the extreme opposite tendency, however, see Richard Levin's attack on new historicism, "Unthinkable Thoughts in the New Historicizing of English Renaissance Drama," *New Literary History* 21 (1990): 433–47. Levin mentions in his first sentence that he is critiquing the new historicists, the cultural materialists, and "a number of feminists associated with them" (as escorts?), although he never names a woman, even when he discusses gender issues.

[27]Jane Marcus, "The Asylums of Antaeus: Women, War, and Madness—Is There a Feminist Fetishism?" in Veeser, *New Historicism,* 138.

[28]Newton, "History as Usual?" 159; subsequent references are cited in the text.

the projects of some new historicist work) inevitably founder. On the one hand, MacKinnon says, Marxists charge feminists with being "bourgeois in theory and practice," with ignoring class differences "in the interest of the ruling class." In return, feminists charge that Marxism is male-centered: "It moves within the world-view and in the interest of men." The problem for MacKinnon, as for Newton, is that class is ineluctably a male-focused category: "Women derive their class position . . . from their associations with men" (7). The position that MacKinnon occupies at the end of her essay is very similar to that of Newton. Their vision is hierarchical, and feminism is at the top. As MacKinnon puts it:

> Feminism stands in relation to marxism as marxism does to classical political economy: its final conclusion and ultimate critique. Compared with marxism, the place of thought and things in method and reality are reversed in a seizure of power that penetrates subject with object and theory with practice. In a dual motion, feminism turns marxism inside out and on its head.[29]

The gesture is triumphant, but is it persuasive?

I think not, on at least two counts. MacKinnon here explicitly aligns feminism with "things" and with "reality," and the triumphant tone of her prose derives in part from her happily physical metaphor, which dares to leave abstraction behind and fight with its hands. But at what cost? The assertion that feminism is more "real" than Marxism is not one that can be defended if proposed outright. Indeed, Marxism itself in many guises tries to lay claim to truth-value via the "real," by locating cultural within material production. As Elaine Scarry has argued at some length, the material body has an ultimate authority in discourse; MacKinnon is trying an old rhetorical tactic in appropriating some of that authority for feminism. The price is high: it returns us to the familiar, meretricious alignment of femininity with the body and of masculinity with the mind. Just as feminist theorists have generally moved away from the "authority of experience," the argument ad feminam, the feminist claim to truth-value cannot lie in the woman's guts.

But this is not the heart of Newton's argument, and she requires a separate and more thoughtful answer.[30] Newton proposes that any

---

[29]Catharine A. MacKinnon, "Feminism, Marxism, Method, and the State: An Agenda for Theory," reprinted in *Feminist Theory: A Critique of Ideology,* ed. Nannerl Keohane et al. (Chicago: University of Chicago Press, 1981), 3, 4, 30.

[30]Newton does conclude her essay with a cautious allusion to the authority of the "real" and to feminism's seemingly privileged relation to it (166). See also Carol Thomas

262 Sarah Webster Goodwin

valid historicist criticism must use gender as one of its central categories, if not its most central one. The phrasing is mine, not hers, and she carefully avoids a vocabulary of validity, of success and failure, and instead addresses what might or might not be new in the new historicism, aligning novelty here with value. (The adjective that does come up, rather than *valid*, is *adequate*—clearly more cautious and positional [166].) The value of novelty for her, of course, is not its routine commodified value but its potential for bringing about change, the one constant and serious challenge Newton's essay makes. Her gravest criticism of the new historicism is that not only does it not contribute to any program of social change, but it undermines the conditions in which change might be brought about.[31]

The key to Newton's argument, and also its crux, is to be found here. She evaluates the three historicist critical texts she considers according to one major criterion: their value for social change. This value emerges from the "political considerations" Newton identifies with an activist feminism that sees "human agency as possible," that makes "gender relations . . . central to history," and that takes material conditions into account (160).

Although I very much sympathize with Newton's sense of an urgent need for social change, I would argue that she presents here what amounts to a narrow prescription for critical practice. Working backwards from her final point, I suggest first of all that effective feminist criticism need not necessarily take "material conditions"—narrowly defined—into account, that the study of a wide and diverse range of texts and materials is essential to working out the full implications of feminism for our history and our culture. Second, it is equally confining to insist that gender relations be the central concern of every study of which they might be a part. This is a large subject by itself, and might best be approached in response to Newton through a defense of Catherine Gallagher's book, in which the analysis of gender issues is effectively situated in the context of other contemporary issues and debates. Newton complains that in Gallagher's book "events or social developments are largely male, and/or are those which have been traditionally seen, and are seen here, in terms of men" (159), as though such

Neely's objection to "the new theoretical discourses" generally: "They go further . . . than most American liberal feminists have done in denying subjectivity, interiority, identity which is continuous across time and not the construct of ideology. Most American feminists have assumed . . . some area of 'femaleness' that . . . makes possible female discourse" ("Constructing the Subject," 7). The relation of "femininity" to the "real" remains an unresolved and painful crux in feminist debate.

[31]Boose makes a similar observation: "Unlike feminism, new historicism is not, meanwhile, an activist politics of social change" ("Family in Shakespeare Studies," 740).

events ought simply to be ignored or always reconstrued from the imagined perspective of women.[32] Not only is this not possible, I doubt it is desirable. Many events in which the principal players have been men have had tremendous impact on women's lives; historical study cannot simply elide the role played by men or omit events traditionally associated with men, but must locate them with respect to women and others whom traditional scholarship has tended to overlook.

Each of these points requires fuller treatment than I can give it here. But I want to turn rapidly to Newton's first and most crucial point, in which she links the possibility of social change to "human agency." The book for which she reserves the highest praise—Mary Poovey's *Uneven Developments: The Ideological Work of Gender in Mid-Victorian England*—is the one that views change as effected by individual agents acting from choice and from conviction. The other two books are more limited, she argues, precisely because they reserve little place for individual agency, for old-fashioned activism. Thus she damns Gallagher's book: "Change . . . emerges to a large degree from logical contradictions in representation itself and from a generalized need for new principles of cohesion. . . . Change does not emerge for the most part from human agents acting out of specific historical positions and with historically determined politics" (160).[33] This view of change in history, for Newton, is "history as usual."

The limits of such a view are striking. To *wish* for the effectiveness of individual agency and to *believe* in it as the major force in history are two very different things, and Newton does not take up the intellectual and abstract argument about the basis of her belief. The debate about the role of the individual willed act in history is an ongoing and complex one, but none of that complexity emerges here. Instead, the critic who engages the innovative and open-minded view is characterized as backward-looking. It is Newton, it seems to me, who is more conservative in her epistemology, who is in fact practicing "history as usual."

These are not just fine points. Newton's is one of the most far-

[32]Neely makes a similar point even more forcefully: "The discursive practices of the cult-historicists would seem to produce, or to reproduce patriarchy. . . . Once again, tragedy and history are the privileged genres. Once again, a focus on power, politics, and history, and especially, the monarch, turns attention away from marriage, sexuality, women, and the masterless" ("Constructing the Subject," 12). The critics Neely has in mind may in fact be guiltier of this than I find Gallagher to be.

[33]Porter, too, notes ruefully that in Greenblatt's work "power has been essentialized so as to absorb all agency" ("Are We Being Historical Yet?" 758). This point is central to Porter's critique of Greenblatt and the new historicism more generally; she gives it a balanced and sophisticated treatment.

reaching feminist critiques of the new historicism. She questions, quite effectively, the feasibility of a feminist criticism that subscribes to the new historicist tenets. The critiques of Newton and others notwith-standing, feminist, new historicist criticism will continue to appear in the years to come. The critical positions are simply too persuasive, the thorny problems too intriguing, the framework for research and anal-ysis too inviting for this new "school"—or critical mode, in both senses—to fail to gain even wider influence.

And yet the very uneasy labels of "school" and mode return us to an issue that we cannot comfortably ignore. When Newton attacks the new historicism primarily on the basis of its fraudulent novelty, she defends an ardently held political position, but she also goes for the jugular. It does call itself the *new* historicism, perhaps in contradistinc-tion to the old historicism of German hermeneutics, but also, doubtless, out of a kind of ground-staking impulse—or, to put it differently, a marketing sense. Never has an academic school been so effectively, if unintentionally, commodified. (The situation is rife with irony.) I take it as a symptom of this that *The New Historicism,* a timely volume in-deed, seems to have represented in it nearly every big name in new historicist studies.[34] The contributors themselves seem repeatedly em-barrassed by the trendiness of their subject. It is telling that even in a volume that marks the emergence of this "school" into an easily acces-sible form, there is such disturbance, such guilt and hostility about the academic marketplace. The stakes are *not* negligible; we all know that the kind of fame a handful of scholars now enjoy brings with it salaries in the six figures, mobility, resources, and above all release time for reading and writing. And almost all of them—all but a handful of those who count themselves "new historicists"—are men.

Nevertheless, the new historicism remains the first major school of literary criticism in this country—aside from feminist criticism itself—that not only has an acknowledged debt to feminism but also routinely embraces feminist positions and analytic practices. At least potentially,

[34]Here are Stephen Greenblatt, Catherine Gallagher, Louis Montrose, Joel Fineman, Jonathan Arac, and even Gayatri Spivak, Hayden White, and Stanley Fish—to name fewer than half the contributors. (Missing are the eminent women doing historicist work, such as Mary Poovey, Nancy Armstrong, Marjorie Levinson, Karen Newman, and Laura Brown, to name just a few.) What is more, I have never seen a volume so hastily edited. At least one of the essays is an untransformed talk, and one is a transcribed telephone conversation—not bad ideas in themselves, but further symptoms of the haste with which the volume was put together. There is no index. Much of the writing badly needs editorial revision, and there are more minor errors of punctuation and the like than I have ever seen in a published book. The reader has the impression altogether of tremendous haste: this volume approaches journalism in its sloppiness.

the new historicism locates the analysis of gender construction at (or near) the very center of its analysis of culture, whether directly, through the study of masculinity and femininity, or more indirectly, through the study of concepts such as public versus private life, domestic culture, the function and theories of representation in varying social domains, and metaphors of value and exchange as they circulate among different groups.

What is the prognosis, finally, for the impact of the new historicism on a feminist comparative literature? Feminism does not yet have much of a history in comparative literature: it is still nearly a blank page. Comparative literature has so far proven a tough Bastille for feminists to storm. The comparatist *Madwoman in the Attic* has yet to be written. The comparatist journals have yet to publish much significant feminist work, and as late as 1990 the annual meeting of the American Comparative Literature Association had a real paucity of sessions on women writers and feminist topics.[35]

An emphasis on historicism, on concepts such as nationalism, the canon, and gender as historical, cultural constructs, may help open up and legitimize feminist areas of research in comparative literature.[36] Despite the practical difficulties of doing comparatist historical research and the danger of slipping into facile generalizations, there is tremendous potential here for a new energy in comparative literature studies. One place to begin rewriting the disciplinary borders might well be with the questions: What are the relations between nations as constructs and cultural models of gender?[37] Are nations exclusively part of a male-centered political world? How do literary texts compare to other cultural documents in the ways they reinforce or undermine national boundaries? How do women and men place themselves with reference

[35]Of forty-seven sessions, only four were organized around topics related to feminism or to women. See *ACLA Newsletter* 21. 2 (1990), conference program. Surveying issues of several comparative literature journals (*Comparative Literature Studies, Arcadia, Comparative Literature,* and the *Canadian Review of Comparative Literature*) from 1986 through 1990, I found only four essays (out of more than a hundred) that could be construed as feminist in method or subject—three of them in *Comparative Literature Studies*—and only two more on women writers.

[36]To some extent this process has begun, with the publication of works such as Margaret Ferguson, Maureen Quilligan, and Nancy Vickers, eds., *Rewriting the Renaissance* (Chicago: University of Chicago Press, 1986), and Constance Jordan, *Renaissance Feminism: Literary Texts and Political Models* (Ithaca: Cornell University Press, 1990).

[37]See, for example, Horst Rüdiger's disingenuous linking of the exotic with the feminine in the context of comparatist criticism: "In the background there is often another force at work. . . . It is the fascination with the Other, the foreign, the exotic, often in the form of the feminine," in "Grenzen und Aufgaben der Vergleichende Literaturwissenschaft," in *Zur Theorie der Vergleichenden Literaturwissenschaft,* ed. Horst Rüdiger (New York: de Gruyter, 1971), 13.

to those processes, and what role do gender constructs play? This is only one set of questions on the table, but it may be one that comparatists in particular should address.

Comparatists might also make significant contributions to the history of print culture and its relation to gender constructs in an international context. What were the contours of *feminine* international literary cultures, in comparison and contradistinction to the masculine cultures which have been well researched? How are the hierarchies of aesthetic value that we have inherited related to the gendering of print cultures? What have been the historical relations between the gendering of commodity culture in market economies and the hierarchies of aesthetic value in the literary marketplaces? Two other specific arenas available for a feminist, historicist comparative literature come to mind: legal codes and wartime culture. What are the relations among laws such as those governing labor, copyright, and property on an international basis? How do literary representations of flight from domestic confinement treat borders between nations, legal codes, and cultures? Jane Marcus, in her essay in *The New Historicism,* has already pointed out some of the ways feminine wartime culture may differ from the masculine. How might such differences be charted in international terms?

These are just a few of the possibilities for a feminist, historicist comparative literature. It is probably not possible to reconceive comparative literature in collaboration with feminism *without* historicizing it—and it is the new historicism we must turn to here, for better or worse, not the history of Taine or of van Tieghem.

14
Talking Shop: A Comparative Feminist Approach to Caribbean Literature by Women

VÈVÈ A. CLARK

Rarely do we examine the relationship between feminist theory and practice as the two arenas converge in pedagogy, particularly in undergraduate courses such as one I have offered at both Tufts University and the University of California. In "Developing Diaspora Literacy and *Marasa* Consciousness," I attempted to chart an innovative theoretical approach to texts beyond the typical dyadic relationships so commonly reproduced in comparative literature studies.[1] Whether confined to texts produced within and defined by national boundaries, genres, and periods, or to intertextual analyses beyond these periods, the prevalent comparative model has indulged in a restrictive one-on-one paradigm. Ultimately, the process creates a vertical hierarchy, reflecting the critic's preference for one text over the other. The *marasa* principle, drawn from traditional Haitian lore, suggests at once a pairing of texts for consideration and a commitment to a creative critical process which illuminates a third or wider field of expression beyond binaries. Following the nature-oriented and mystical philosophies from Asia, Africa, and the Caribbean, this particular theory when applied to comparative literature is based on the notion that $1 + 1 = 3$.

The *marasa* sign clarifies the dynamics of social change, the transformation of cultural oppositions within plantation societies. Movement beyond double-consciousness or the binary nightmare of a psyche divided by memory between Africa and Europe occurred particularly in the development of indigenous religious practices (Vodoun, Santería, Shango, Candomblé), Creole languages and mixed-race identities drawn together rather than apart. Coming to *marasa* consciousness in the late twentieth century means that the structure of analysis is triadic: African/Asian, European, and "New World." This third position looks back at the contradictions of racial definitions of the mixed-blood self

---

[1]The essay appears in *Comparative American Identities: Race, Sex, and Nationality in the Modern Text*, ed. Hortense J. Spillers (New York: Routledge, 1991), 40–61.

as fundamentally black, oppositional stances within colonial educational systems and new letters and liberation movements by commenting on these phenomena in an environment of continuous change. Henry Louis Gates, Jr.'s, successive explications of the Signifying Monkey trope as a hermeneutics of black criticism is a fine example of a fresh approach to comparative literary studies. Gates's interpretations of *Their Eyes Were Watching God, Mumbo Jumbo,* and *The Color Purple* establish contextual and textual relationships beyond binaries among works published over a span of forty-five years by Zora Neale Hurston, Ishmael Reed, and Alice Walker.[2]

The representation of contemporary literary history has assumed a binary, often false, division according to gender. Particularly in African diaspora literary studies, the male (canon) precedes and the women writers follow, as though the two discourses were mutually exclusive. Histories of the New Negro, Indigenist, and Negritude movements of the 1920s and 1930s often portray the period as a male phenomenon of racial consciousness and artistic renewal among writers such as Langston Hughes, Claude McKay, Jacques Roumain, Nicolas Guillén, Léon Damas, Aimé Césaire, and Léopold Senghor. Following a similar paradigm, studies of Caribbean literary history—no matter the language—have separated texts according to a gender-based scheme, or what Roger Abrahams describes as the expressive division between house/yard and road.[3] In other words, we encounter two traditions by women and men that do not seem to merge.

Even as the predominantly male new letters voices of the renaissance materialized in the Caribbean, women novelists such as Suzanne Lacascade and Annie Desroy redefined the male narrative and discursive strategies, inaugurating "la littérature féminine" in the Guadeloupe and Haiti of the 1920s and 1930s. Scholars overlooked these early texts primarily because none of the authors participated in either the Indigenist or the Negritude movements. For over five decades a separate tradition developed, unrecognized as such until Maryse Condé published her study of Antillean novelists, *La parole des femmes* (1979).[4]

---

[2]Henry Louis Gates, Jr., *The Signifying Monkey* (New York: Oxford University Press, 1988).

[3]Roger Abrahams, *The Man-of-Words in the West Indies: Performance and the Emergence of Creole Culture* (Baltimore: Johns Hopkins University Press, 1983). Scholarship devoted to new letters is extensive. For bibliographical references, see Nathan Huggins, *Harlem Renaissance* (New York: Oxford University Press, 1974); Margaret Perry, *Harlem Renaissance: An Annotated Bibliography* (New York: Garland Publishing, 1982); Victor A. Kramer, *Harlem Renaissance Re-Examined* (New York: AMS Press, 1987); Colette V. Michael, *Negritude: An Annotated Bibliography* (West Cornwall, Conn.: Locust Hill Press, 1988).

[4]Maryse Condé, *La parole des femmes* (Paris: L'Harmattan, 1979).

Binaries are barriers to learning, whether the obstacles preventing communication are demographic, socioeconomic, or linguistic. Binary oppositions in the Caribbean mark the borders of power relationships: low/high land; low/high culture; low/high languages. In the last case, rather than embrace New World Creole discourses, authors from the region must confront the long-held value of writing in a metropolitan language and style.[5]

Binary oppositions also inform feminist practice. During the 1980s and 1990s scholarship became a terrain often unsupportive of the wider sociopolitical activism of living writers. Although the historiography of feminist interventions has assumed various stances since the Women's Liberation movement, many scholars of my generation view feminist practice as synonymous with research and publishing—what we do outside the college classroom on our own, usually subsidized, time. Others commit themselves to service benefiting women in general, whether through venues such as on-campus women's centers, editorial boards of journals, and centers for the study of women or committees such as the Modern Language Association's Committee on the Status of Women in the Profession. Essentially, however, all of these endeavors serve an already established network of scholars, whether on or off the tenured track. I would like to suggest another definition of feminist practice in the 1990s which combines scholarship, service to the field, and political action against the contentious intellectual and political climates in which women produce both primary and secondary texts. In my own experience I have noticed a pattern of alternative intervention which, if we acknowledge the binary opposites that maintain stasis and prevent social change, replicates the search for a third principle, or what Haitian peasants understand as *marasa*.

When we support living authors such as Rigoberta Menchú, the Quiché activist from Guatemala, recipient of the Nobel Peace Prize in 1992, or the African American choreographer Katherine Dunham, we enter into a liminal space of activism which they have previously occupied in their works. We engage in solidarity with the texts of their lives. Conceptually we promote feminist practice beyond the boundaries of the academy, often subversively, given the regulation of academic freedom within universities. Such regulatory policies are designed, and rightly so, to restrict political agency within the classroom or the use of the mails (and I assume fax machines) for political purposes. Those

---

[5]The tradition of writing in metropolitan languages as a form of "collective bovarysm" is examined in Jean Price-Mars, *Ainsi parla l'oncle* (Paris: Imprimerie de Compiègne, 1928) and the counter Creole ideology defended in Jean Bernabé et al., *Éloge de la créolité* (Paris: Gallimard, 1989).

of us who brought Rigoberta Menchú to Tufts University in conjunction with her testimony at the United Nations concerning the abuse and torture of Indian activists supported through her honorarium the likelihood that these funds would contribute to direct political action in Guatemala. The organizers of her visit understood the need to serve beyond the binary boundaries of Menchú's existence, namely *altiplano* (mountain villages) versus *finca* (plantations), thereby assisting activists to forge another path—the resistance efforts in towns and villages promoted by nameless Quiché peasants and their supporters. Those of us who had read *I, Rigoberta Menchú* (1983) felt that we knew the author, her family, and the situation she described so painfully in the text.[6] For two hours she responded to innumerable questions about her published oral history and current events in Guatemala. The exchange confirmed our belief in a testimony akin to the slave narratives historically disparaged by readers unwilling to believe the atrocities revealed in the text. Menchú's appearance has led me to teach the text differently; I now expect disbelief, even suspicion of the text's veracity, and chart these responses among Menchú's implied international readership. In this particular case, practice has informed pedagogy at a much deeper level than the text alone might have done.

Testimony as a speech act contains its own limitations. For readers who have never known peasants anywhere in the world, eye contact becomes crucial. They need to see Rigoberta Menchú, the down-and-dirty realities of cane fields, the intrusion of the military. Beyond the dialogics of belief/disbelief, I have found that another territory of reference emerges in screenings of the film *When the Mountains Tremble*, in which Menchú appears. This filmic testimony helps students to visualize the contexts of oppression out of which Rigoberta Menchú's person, commitment, and the text operate.

Similarly, I "met" Katherine Dunham through one of her texts, *Journey to Accompong*, when I was teaching a course, "Folk Cultures of the New World," in the African American Studies Department at the University of California, Berkeley. Later in 1976 she accepted a residency on campus as a visiting professor. I subsequently served for seven summers as her archivist in East St. Louis. Nearly a decade later, President Jean-Bertrand Aristide's daring attempts to establish democratic rule in Haiti renewed Dunham's commitment to Haitian resistance, reflecting her earlier support of President Dumarsais Estimé in 1947.

Dunham's case exemplifies how feminist practice passed from gen-

---

[6] *I, Rigoberta Menchú: An Indian Woman in Guatemala*, ed. Elisabeth Burgos-Debray, trans. Ann Wright (London: Verso, 1984).

eration to generation can intervene as an alternative strategy of response to a crisis constructed within unyielding binary oppositions.
Katherine Dunham, author, scholar, choreographer, and activist, began
a hunger strike in February 1992 to protest the continuing deportation
of Haitian refugees. A three-week fast sent Dunham, at age eighty-two,
in and out of consciousness.[7] An arena of silence entrapped her cause:
the Bush administration refused to acknowledge either her own letter
to the president or the flood of telegrams that supported Dunham's
drastic measures. Subsequently, the media seriously addressed the political environment surrounding the issues of deportation and repression in Haiti, undoubtedly owing to the earlier responses from the
wider community, as well as a series of petitions initiated by activist
scholars in African American studies at the University of California and
in the Los Angeles community. As in the Anita Hill support network
(African American Women in Defense of Ourselves), we petitioned
throughout the country basically to save the life of a woman who had
opened to many of us the fields of Caribbean and African culture during the 1930s and 1940s, whose dance companies toured fifty-two countries for twenty-five years, and who has received highest honors,
including the *légion d'honneur* in Haiti and the Schweitzer and Kennedy
Center awards. As of this writing she continues to live and work in
East St. Louis, Illinois, where she was hospitalized for a month. Katherine Dunham was caught in an opposition between the plight of Haitian refugees and the policies endorsed by the Bush administration. The
petitions circulated nationwide and internationally sought to establish
a road between.[8]

One final example of feminist practice concerns graduate students at
the university. As elsewhere, students devoted to African, African
American, or Caribbean studies find themselves operating dually and
in isolation. Bound to their departments (English, Comparative Literature, Geography, Anthropology), they work against isolation by organizing informal study groups. In 1992, through the African American
Studies Department at U.C. Berkeley, the St. Clair Drake Cultural Studies Forum was initiated as a means to open up an institutional space
for interdisciplinary studies, at once supporting graduate students' research and establishing a community of scholars willing to listen, learn,
and provide models for presenting ideas.[9] Two assistant professors, Sai-

[7]Dunham ended the hunger strike after forty-seven days in March 1992.
[8]The petition was composed by Margaret Preacely of Los Angeles during the evening
of February 20, 1992, and subsequently sent to over fifty individuals, who circulated the
document in churches, among Haitian-American citizens, academics who support the
antideportation efforts, and others who revere Katherine Dunham and her work.
[9]The forum was named for St. Clair Drake, a specialist in social anthropology, who,

diya Hartman and Ula Taylor, and I coordinated this endeavor in feminist practice, intending to provide a landscape, figuratively, for students across the disciplines to negotiate between departmental affiliations and informal study groups under the aegis of Cultural Studies.[10]

For me, the fit between *marasa* theory and practice occurs in intellectual exchanges within the classroom. For the remainder of this essay I refer to examples of feminist pedagogy in my course "*Marasa:* Caribbean Literature by Women." The syllabus sets up dyads among texts by women authors with the expressed intention of exploring and transforming these binaries. Nonetheless, we approach each text on its own merits in interactive discussions before the students write comparatively about the paired or twinned works. The writing in this course progresses from a series of old-style comparisons of two texts to an exam which requires students to apply the *marasa* theory in evaluating at least three works. Throughout the fifteen-week course, the potential for *marasa* analysis accumulates from text to text long before the end-term exam occurs. At Berkeley the students, representing a range of disciplines from biology and English to French and sociology, responded to theory with startling originality.

Marasa is a mythical theory of textual relationships based on the Haitian Vodoun sign for the Divine Twins, the *marasa*. During the research for my dissertation on Haitian folk performance and popular theater, I became interested in the etymologies of certain widely used terms in Haitian folklore, such as *coumbite* and *marasa*.[11] In the case of *marasa*, I traced the term back to ancient Dahomey (present-day Benin) in West Africa, to creation myths among the Fon and Ewe. *Marasa* is a New World deformation of Mawu-Lisa—the female and male gods deriving from the distant but ultimate Creator, Nanabuluku. Mawu-Lisa, according to Fon and Ewe belief systems, generated among others a

---

like Dunham, was trained at the University of Chicago. In the 1970s Drake volunteered for a year's time to participate in a reading group among black graduate students at Berkeley which he ultimately led. On a monthly schedule we read and analyzed texts such as *The Black Jacobins* by C. L. R. James and in essence sat at the feet of one of our master scholars and teachers.

[10]The forum is open to graduate students and faculty working in African, African American, or Caribbean studies. When I characterize the forum as an example of feminist practice, I refer to origins rather than content. During the fall semester of 1991, a number of graduate students who had sought to sit in my undergraduate course in African American studies, "*Marasa:* Caribbean Literature by Women," agreed to participate in a group independent study once a week. These women represented a range of disciplines, including anthropology, English, ethnic studies, folklore, and French. The diversity of their training and interests prompted me to create the forum during the spring of 1992.

[11]VèVè A. Clark, "Fieldhands to Stagehands in Haiti: The Measure of Tradition in Haitian Popular Theatre" (Ph.D. diss., University of California, Berkeley, 1983).

youngest son, Legba, god of fertility and of the crossroads, the chief linguist, who populated the earth. Mawu-Lisa stand at the interstices between divine and human formations of meaning and participate in both. As a feminist I was drawn to these West African myths because of the central role Mawu, a female spirit, performs in concepts of genesis.

The Haitian sign for the *marasa* (appended to the syllabus) plays on uniformity and diversity. I have used this visual tension in my pedagogical approach to writing by Caribbean women from the anglophone, creolophone, francophone, hispanophone, and lusophone regions of the Americas. During the first days of class I invite students to read the *marasa* sign as an intellectual passageway into peasant ways of ordering their largely agrarian realities, a passageway that derives from memories of enslavement and the monocrop culture of plantation economies. The theory is thus based on the peasantry; whether this specific figure drawn from Haitian Creole lore will prove relevant across language and socioeconomic boundaries remains a theoretical tension which we as readers address throughout the course. At this point in my teaching the tension seems more imagined than real, given the common denominator of any number of texts which I have presented over the years. No matter the choices, no matter the historical distance, these texts share memories of plantation economies, cultures, and languages.

Creolization as a process of acculturation and imitation in the Caribbean defines the 1 + 1 = 3 paradigm I proposed earlier.[12] Diversity is a patterned response to combined European and African cultural practices in the New World: to the struggle to survive in a climate rendered hostile by the search for gold (viz. Columbus), to new illnesses which affected Native Indians, Europeans, and Africans differently throughout the sixteenth through the eighteenth centuries, to plantation labor brutal in theory and practice, and finally to colonial education systems imported from the metropole, which engendered forgetfulness among the colonized, ultimately deforming indigenous cultures and the minds of individuals banished to the subjugated categories of humanity. When we theorize diversity in Caribbean life, lore, and literature, we operate on three interconnected planes of articulation which converge in the specifics of Creole culture and language. Beyond the binaries of European and African, European and Native Indian, European Continental and Latin American, Asian and Caribbean, we find that Caribbean cultures and their authors have created sites of difference

---

[12]Edward Brathwaite, *The Development of Creole Society in Jamaica, 1770–1820* (Oxford: Clarendon, 1971).

which challenge our deconstructive notions of the flexible fields of literary theory, practice, and perhaps pedagogy as well.

"*Marasa:* Caribbean Literature by Women" evolved out of a workshop in American Studies at Tufts University sponsored by the National Endowment for The Humanities. In retrospect, one of the participants—the sociologist Susan Ostrander—described our goals thus: "The aim of that workshop was to develop a set of interdisciplinary courses focused on issues of gender that would be cross-listed with home departments and American Studies."[13] The six scholars represented the fields of anthropology, child study, English, psychology, francophone literature, and sociology. I taught the *marasa* course for three semesters at Tufts before offering a revised version in 1991 for African American Studies at Berkeley.

For a number of reasons, my experiences in teaching the course at Berkeley have been the most successful yet. First of all, as I mentioned earlier, my African American studies courses attract a variety of students, including majors in the humanities, social sciences, and sciences, as well as reentry students, some of whom are close to my age. At Berkeley, seven male students enrolled in a class of thirty-one, almost double the number at Tufts. As is typical of Berkeley, the class was truly multicultural, with many African American students, students from multiracial backgrounds, foreign students (from Japan, from Canada by way of Zambia), Asians, Chicana/os, Hispanics, one lone white male, and one lone Jamaican woman. Because of the makeup of the class, diversity was an issue that students were eager to discuss. Additionally, recent translations into English allowed me to pair works more effectively. Moreover, the Berkeley appointment in African American studies enabled me to concentrate on the African diaspora and to roam intellectually among the various language areas defining Caribbean expression, free from my former duties in Romance languages at Tufts, where I taught French conversation and composition, as well as introductions to French literature. The twinning of narratives which I constructed sought to engage students in considering diversity at several levels: according to genre (Hodge/Edgell); to socioeconomic class (Rhys/Ferré and De Jesus/Menchú); and to feminist themes such as mothering, madness, and healing (Schwarz-Bart/Marshall).

Before we actually discussed the major texts, we played with the *marasa* concept in short stories or excerpts collected in the Pamela Mordecai–Elizabeth Wilson anthology *Her True-True Name* (1989), the title

[13]The quotation is from a memo by Susan Ostrander inviting prospective members to join the 1990 workshop.

of which derives from Merle Hodge's *Crick Crack, Monkey* (1970), the first full text we read. With Zee Edgell's *Beka Lamb* (1982), I intended to represent the female novel of formation from the different perspectives of colonial education systems in Trinidad and Belize. With these two works and others on the reading list, through interactive teaching methods, I hoped to draw students to new readings of the texts beyond the facile binary evaluations which, despite significant exceptions, prevail in the critical literature.[14] In their thinking and writing, students tackled one or several areas: themes, characterizations, structure, narrative technique, and language. As the semester progressed, the majority ventured beyond purely thematic analyses—an often frightening terrain for nonliterature majors. For the remainder of this essay I will highlight some of the more revealing close readings that emerged within *marasa* literary practice, and conclude by describing ways in which the students read beyond the twinning relationships which the course design preestablished.

Hodge's *Crick Crack, Monkey* was a wonderful opening for the course because the text is oppositional in theme, characterizations, structure, narrative technique, and language. Essentially, Hodge represents opposed class differences defined as "ordinaryness" and respectability through the protagonist's aunts, Tantie and Aunt Beatrice. In the opening pages of the narrative, the protagonist, Tee, and her brother are orphaned. When their widowed father departs abruptly from Trinidad for England after his wife's funeral, the children are left in a working-class family with a single head of household, riotous Tantie, whose vulgar speech in Creole, working-class wit, and determination dominate the first twelve chapters of the narrative.[15]

Most criticism of the novel focuses on the opposition between the two worlds of Tantie and Beatrice—the bourgeois city dweller and relative to whom Tee is sent for continued education beyond the local primary schools. Using the Caribbean culture's symbolic landscapes—house/yard as sites of expression suggesting women's domains and

[14]The exceptions to which I refer are Simon Gikandi, "Narration in the Post-Colonial Moment: Merle Hodge's *Crick Crack, Monkey*," in *Past the Last Post: Theorizing Post-Colonialism and Post-Modernism*, ed. Ian Adam and Helen Tiffin (Calgary: University of Calgary Press, 1990), 13–22, and Rhonda Cobham's translated essay, "Revisioning our Kumblas: Challenges to Feminist and Nationalist Agendas in the Work of Three Caribbean Women Writers," originally published in German in *Entwicklungen im Karibischen Raum, 1960–1985*, ed. Wolfgang Binder (Erlangen: Universitätsverbund Erlangen-Nürnberg, 1985), 193–210.

[15]Before we approach the text, students learn to hear and read Creole speech by listening to recordings of the poet Paul Keens-Douglas's work, particularly "Tanti Merle and di fire." This piece works well because Tanti Merle's persona so resembles the character Tantie in *Crick Crack, Monkey*.

respectability, as opposed to the road/bridge areas of unbridled male behavior—we examined how these paradigms existed in the narrative, discovering how Hodge expands the landscape of affiliations described in Roger Abrahams's *Man-of-Words in the West Indies* (1983) by including the bush or the mountain refuges of former maroons as part of Tee's legacy.[16] This is the place to which Tee returns for the summer months, to her grandmother Ma, to traditions of storytelling (thus the title of the novel), and to a fading memory, what Zee Edgell's characters refer to as "'befo' time." Deliberately devoting brief space to memories of Tee's summer home Pointe d'Espoir, in chapter 4, Hodge suggests that there is no possible return to communal identity for Tee, even though she resembles her great-great grandmother, called Euphemia by the countryfolk (a process of renaming which occurs as well in Simone Schwarz-Bart's *Bridge of Beyond*). The nickname has replaced Euphemia's "true-true" name, which Ma has trouble remembering: "[Ma] couldn't remember her grandmother's true-true name. But Tee was growing into her grandmother again, her spirit was in me. They'd never bent down her spirit and she would come back and come back and come back: if only she could live to see Tee grow into her tall proud straight grandmother."[17] Nonetheless, references to Pointe d'Espoir, and to the world of Tantie's adopted son Mikey, where unemployed men signify on one another at the bridge, open the narrative to levels of expressive behavior not confined to the glorious and rowdy Creole speech of Tantie or to the repressed anglophile domesticity surrounding Aunt Beatrice. *Marasa* consciousness encourages readers to appreciate a wider range of expression beyond the obvious binary oppositions in the narrative.

Another example of triadic writing surfaces in Jean Rhys's *Wide Sargasso Sea* (1966), which I paired in the course with Rosario Ferré's collection of short stories, *The Youngest Doll* (1976). As a unit these narratives portray indolence and madness among upper-class women in Dominica and Puerto Rico, but more important, they draw the reader into issues of narratology, style, and intertextuality, particularly as *Wide Sargasso Sea* revises Charlotte Brontë's *Jane Eyre* and the topos of the madwoman in the attic on which contemporary feminist thought has concentrated.[18] In brief, *Wide Sargasso Sea* demonstrates conflict at the very level of narrative technique. The novel's three divisions embody divergent perspectives. In part one the child Antoinette reports on changes in her 1830s colonial world as the emancipation of slaves trag-

---

[16] Abrahams, *Man-of-Words*.
[17] Merle Hodge, *Crick Crack, Monkey* (London: Heinemann, 1981).
[18] Sandra Gilbert and Susan Gubar, *The Madwoman in the Attic: The Woman Writer and the Nineteenth-Century Literary Imagination* (New Haven: Yale University Press, 1979).

ically disrupts her *béké* (planter class) environment. The adult Antoinette, of part two, married by convenience to Rochester from *Jane Eyre,* is then seen through his eyes and defined by his voice, uncomfortable, even paranoid, as he lives in a tropical climate new to him with a bride and black household staff he considers insane—a legacy of madness Rhys attributes to the protagonist's mother, Annette. In the final segment, Rochester has transformed Antoinette into "Bertha," and the narrative technique here replicates madness.

Rhys's design in the novel begins with oppositions according to political and socioeconomic difference, gendered perceptions, responses to climate, and language. In the final segment the text confuses point of view intentionally in order to describe the displacement to Britain of a woman whose world is problematically Caribbean—problematic because the central figures over two generations, Annette and Antoinette, rely on a process of creolization through which they participate in black cultural practices such as obeah to alter their situations. Annette is to the servant Christophine as Antoinette is to her playmate Tia, women served and abandoned. In the final section, set in Rochester's mansion, Rhys defines madness in the Caribbean as both cultural and psychological; the ethereal narrative voice constantly changes. There is no center for Antoinette/Bertha Cosway in England, a cautionary tale for the many anglophone Caribbean writers who end their narratives on a note of expectancy: of a better life for colonized subjects in the metropolis. More important, the text invites readers to confront Creole madness from the inside outward, to share Antoinette's confusion, and to enter into "her own where." In other words, Rhys charts a landscape beyond the construct of sanity/madness referenced specifically to women of the *béké*, the dominant Caribbean minority enslaved by the Edward Rochesters within plantation America, themselves disinherited and disoriented in a New World colored environment.[19] Essentially, chapter 3 of *Wide Sargasso Sea* describes the deep-sea spaces of alienation which confine Antoinette/Bertha physically and psychically. Experiencing a negative epistemic break from the flamboyant tropical gardens in the Caribbean of chapters 1 and 2, she is displaced to the gray climate and manicured English gardens that define Jane and Rochester's existence at Thornfield.[20]

[19]See June Jordan's novel in black English, *His Own Where* (New York: Crowell, 1970); Mary Lou Emery, *Jean Rhys at "World's End": Novels of Colonial and Sexual Exile* (Austin: University of Texas Press, 1990); Angelita Reyes, "Christophine, Nanny, and Creole Difference: Reconsidering Jean Rhys's West Indian Landscape and *Wide Sargasso Sea*," in *The Road to Guinea: Essays in Black Comparative Literature,* ed. Edward Ako (London: Heinemann, 1992).

[20]On positive versions of epistemological breaks, consult Sylvia Wynters, "The Ceremony Must Be Found: After Humanism," *Boundary 2* 12.3–13.1 (Spring–Fall 1984): 19–70.

Similar rereadings occurred in our discussions of *Child of the Dark* (1960) by a homeless woman living in the *favelas* of Brazil, in *I, Rigoberta Menchú,* an oral history of the Quiché activist recorded and edited by the Venezuelan anthropologist Elisabeth Burgos-Debray, and in the pairing of Schwarz-Bart's *Bridge of Beyond* (1972) with Paule Marshall's *Praisesong for the Widow* (1983). In facilitating discussion I was aware in advance of the potential for revealing interactions in class, given the many times I have approached these texts from a *marasa* perspective. This time, however, I was amazed at the connections the students made during the exam on the basis of brief quotations I provided in advance from three sources: Laura Neisen de Abruña on bonding, Shoshana Felman on writing and madness, and bell hooks on confession and memory as expressive skills for talking back.[21]

The exams were a delight to read. One student compared nature, community, memory, and ceremony in *The Bridge of Beyond, I, Rigoberta Menchú,* and *Praisesong for the Widow.* Another dealt with the wake as a site of memory in *Beka Lamb, Praisesong, The Youngest Doll,* and *I, Rigoberta Menchú.* In the texts by Hodge, Menchú, and Marshall, another student examined the establishment of critical perspectives on the self. Lisa Ze, a junior, used the Felman quotation to associate madness and the style of narration in the texts by Marshall, Schwarz-Bart, and Menchú. Ze returned to the *marasa* principle in her senior honors thesis, "Crazy Quilt: Movement of the Mulatta in Literary and Personal Discourse," a comparative analysis of theme and narrative technique in texts by Nella Larsen, Michelle Cliff, and Bessie Head—women writing about mixed-race issues over time throughout the African diaspora in the United States, Jamaica, and South Africa. Continuing a pedagogical approach established after the first writing assignment, the week following the exam I asked students to share their subjects orally with their peers. Generally these sessions when readers respond to the paired texts are predictable. Here, however, I was astounded by the connections the students had made over the fifteen weeks—a relatively short time to expect such depths of analysis. I can only attribute their *prix des yeux* (a concept defining the third and highest stage of learning in Haitian Vodoun) to the theoretical framework of the course. In this particular class, *marasa* served as a more creative theoretical concept than I had ever imagined.

---

[21]Laura Niesen de Abruña, "Twentieth-Century Women Writers from the English-Speaking Caribbean," in *Caribbean Women Writers,* ed. Selwyn R. Cudjoe (Wellesley, Mass.: Calaloux Publications, 1990), 90; Shoshana Felman, *Writing and Madness* (Ithaca: Cornell University Press, 1985), 17, 19; bell hooks, *Talking Back: Thinking Feminist, Thinking Black* (Boston: South End Press, 1988), 109–10.

The next generation of this course offered at the graduate level might well compare the ways in which narratives speak to one another beyond gender distinctions. Moving beyond new letters and the construction of Caribbean literary history would, obviously, include the foregoing but would also draw readers to areas of discourse, structure, and genre that represent another principle of interpretation or *marasa*. Holding close to the ground of plantation economies, such a course would examine paradox, cyclicity, repetition, and the bildungsroman in writings by Caribbean women and men, ultimately compelling us as critics to assume another, comparative approach to the dialectic of displacement.

15

Compared to What? Global Feminism, Comparatism, and the Master's Tools

SUSAN SNIADER LANSER

And rain is the very thing that you, just now, do not want, for you are thinking of the hard and cold and dark and long days you spent working in North America (or, worse, Europe), earning some money so that you could stay in this place (Antigua) where the sun always shines and where the climate is deliciously hot and dry . . . and since you are on your holiday, since you are a tourist, the thought of what it might be like for someone who had to live day in, day out in a place that suffers constantly from drought . . . must never cross your mind.

And you leave, and from afar you watch as we do to ourselves the very things you used to do to us. And you might feel that there was more to you than that, you might feel that you had understood the meaning of the Age of Enlightenment (though, as far as I can see, it has done you very little good); you loved knowledge, and wherever you went you made sure to build a school, a library (yes, and in both of these places you distorted or erased my history and glorified your own).

As for what we were like before we met you, I no longer care. No periods of time over which my ancestors held sway, no documentation of complex civilisations, is any comfort to me. Even if I really came from people who were living like monkeys in trees, it was better to be that than what happened to me, what I became after I met you.

—Jamaica Kincaid, *A Small Place*

A few years ago at the lake where I spend my summers, I read Jamaica Kincaid's brilliantly disturbing book *A Small Place*,[1] a pain-filled and searing indictment of racist colonialism and its perpetuation both in postcolonial corruption and in the tourism that brings 10 million people to the Caribbean each year. Since this book began unsettling me, it has attached itself to questions, texts, and topoi that are in various

[1] Jamaica Kincaid, *A Small Place* (New York: Farrar, Straus & Giroux, 1988).

ways comparative, an appropriate consequence since *A Small Place* is "comparative literature" in the most literal sense: a literary work that makes (cultural) comparisons. Although the cover blurbs engage *A Small Place* in a predominantly male canonical intertext (as "Swiftian," as a "jeremiad," as resembling the "Ancient Mariner"), I compare it to writings in which women criticize national and imperial policies: Virginia Woolf's *Three Guineas* (1938), the novels of Christa Wolf (1968–89), Audre Lorde's essay on the invasion of Grenada (1984), *The History of Mary Prince, A West Indian Slave* (1831), and Toni Morrison's *Beloved* (1987). I have wondered about the differences in tone and stance between *A Small Place* and Kincaid's fiction,[2] about the ways in which readers—black and white, male and female, U.S. and Antiguan—have responded to this book, about the different implications conveyed by its publisher's classification (black studies), and by the Library of Congress catalogue (Antigua—Description and travel). *A Small Place* has helped to redirect my thinking about eighteenth-century women writers, to attend to the traces of colonialism in "domestic" fictions such as Isabelle de Charrière's *Lettres de Mistriss Henley* (1784) and Sarah Scott's *Millenium Hall* (1762), to explore the ways in which Françoise de Grafigny's Peruvian princess (1747) reverses the tropes of empire when she names the Europeans "savages" and "barbarians" and the tropes of fiction when she refuses to marry the heroic Frenchman who has befriended her. My research on eighteenth-century women critics has turned toward the relationship between social values and theories of literature as I ask, for example, whether the dismaying conjunction of feminism and racism in Clara Reeve's *Plans of Education* (1792) has any relevance to her conception of the novel in *The Progress of Romance* (1785).

A Small Place has also led me to questions of personal and professional urgency that are less directly textual. I have reexamined real and imagined travel plans. I have asked myself whether there might be resemblances between tourists and comparatists: both "cosmopolitans" who pride ourselves on transcending narrow and parochial interests, who dwell mentally in one or two (usually Western) countries, summer metaphorically in a third, and visit other places for brief interludes. And I continue to struggle with the implications of *A Small Place* for

---

[2]Kincaid has published three books of fiction: the short story collection *At the Bottom of the River* (New York: Farrar, Straus, & Giroux, 1983); *Annie John* (New York: Farrar, Straus, & Giroux, 1985); and *Lucy* (New York: Farrar, Straus, & Giroux, 1990). Both the narrative voices and the political criticisms are far more muted and indirect in these texts than in *A Small Place*. It may not be incidental that all of these fictional works appeared serially in the *New Yorker*, which did not publish *A Small Place*.

my own position as a professional woman privileged to write this essay on a screened porch in the Maine woods ten feet from a lake that overlooks the White Mountains, one of the welcomed but sometimes resented "summer people" in an economically pressed rural community, asking myself what I must not dwell on to be here and what I can return to this small place for the peace and renewal it gives more generously to me than to its own hardworking citizens, few of whom have long summer vacations and houses ten feet from the lake.

These questions that *A Small Place* has raised for me are comparative questions, but they are not by and large the questions with which comparative literature has taught me to concern myself, nor is *A Small Place* the kind of text I have been trained to "compare." I have been a feminist for as long as I have been a comparatist, but my work as a feminist has not had much *formal* assistance from comparative literature as such. For although there has been feminist comparative practice for as long as there have been feminist critics, and although influential feminist theorists from Kate Millett to Gayatri Spivak were trained as comparatists, comparative literature as a self-conscious and self-articulating discipline has remained relatively untouched by feminist scholarship. Even so current a collection as Clayton Koelb and Susan Noakes's *Comparative Perspective on Literature* (1988), which includes three manifestly feminist essays among its twenty-one pieces, does not integrate feminism into its theorizing of the discipline. For what I hope to demonstrate are related reasons, although "East-West" studies have become more common and "third world" literatures are "emerging" into Western syllabi, comparative literature as practiced in the West (and sometimes in the "East") remains, as Koelb and Noakes rightly remark of their own collection, "skewed heavily toward Europe and indeed toward the canonical writers of a few particularly well studied European languages."[3] In comparing white men to white men from white men's vantage points, comparative literature as it is normatively practiced has attached itself in powerfully stubborn ways to what Audre Lorde has called "the master's tools."[4]

Although it is comparative literature and not feminist studies on which this essay concentrates, I acknowledge that feminist criticism has tended to be as insufficiently comparatist as comparative literature has been insufficiently feminist. Whereas Western comparatism has sometimes engaged in feminist practice without significantly disturbing the theoretical foundations of the discipline, academic Western feminism

---

[3]Clayton Koelb and Susan Noakes, eds., *The Comparative Perspective on Literature: Approaches to Theory and Practice* (Ithaca: Cornell University Press, 1988), 4.

[4]Audre Lorde, "The Master's Tools Will Never Dismantle the Master's House," in *Sister/Outsider* (Freedom, Calif.: Crossing Press, 1984), 110.

has, conversely, theorized itself as comparative (that is, as concerned with women across or beyond national and cultural boundaries) without engaging significantly in comparative practices. Feminist criticism has tended to claim as universal what is particular (for example, using "nineteenth-century women" to describe white educated women of England and the United States) or has (increasingly) "included" other literatures without knowing the languages and cultures in which these works originate. This means that neither feminist nor comparatist studies, as generally practiced in U.S. universities, is sufficiently comparative despite each field's commitment virtually by definition to difference as a primary concern. When I criticize both of these fields, I include my own scholarship, which reflects the Eurocentrism of my training and against which I am now struggling, like many others of my generation, to reeducate myself. I have been especially conscious of these limitations in completing my "comparative" study of women writers and narrative voice, which remains restrictively Western even though it "includes" African American literature.

It is not my purpose here to discuss why feminism has been inadequately comparative aside from noting that many U.S. feminist critics are not trained in either "foreign" languages or comparative inquiry (which I distinguish from the inclusion of difference). Rather, it is my intention in this essay to look at comparatism through the lens of (global) feminism in order to ask why comparative literature, which has so often been proudly open and avant-garde, has lagged behind related disciplines in its institutional response to feminist scholarship. I then suggest some premises for transforming the discipline that rely for theoretical support on "borderworks" such as *A Small Place* which are concerned with questions of globalism and nationalism, gender and race, literature and culture, difference and dominance. I hope through this project to make clear why I think comparatism and feminism are necessary not only for each other's institutional and intellectual health but for each one's integrity as a discipline and indeed for the still urgent mission Virginia Woolf framed in the 1930s: how we can "enter the professions and yet remain civilized human beings," human beings who "will teach the young to hate war."[5]

That this volume is the first to raise feminist questions about comparative literature long after other fields have been challenged and reformed already suggests the "small place" feminism has occupied in theorizing the discipline.[6] The lack of pressure feminism has exerted on

---

[5]Virginia Woolf, *Three Guineas* (New York: Harcourt Brace Jovanovich, 1938), 75, 22.

[6]The institutional history of comparative literature in the United States has been manifestly male-dominated. Whereas by my informal count women constitute between 40 and 50 percent of the membership of the American Comparative Literature Association,

comparative literature may in part reflect the discipline's laissez-faire tendencies. The postwar expansion of comparative literature to embrace virtually any study of literature beyond national boundaries has allowed a latitude of practice that may have forestalled a reconceptualization of the discipline. And because the field is vast and its scholars are often dispersed among many departments, comparatists tend to be genial about one another's work without necessarily seeing that work as having implications for their own. But such nonchalance could not fully explain why a computer search of the MLA bibliography for the entire 1980s, a decade when feminist criticism permeated literary scholarship, turned up among scores of entries in the category "Comparative Literature—Professional Topics," only one brief essay focused explicitly on feminism and comparative literature.[7] Certainly it would not explain the virulent response that the feminist comparatist Evelyn Torton Beck received at a 1974 American Comparative Literature Association (ACLA) session when she spoke about gender issues in translation practices. It seems, rather, that comparative literature as it has traditionally been conceived may be incompatible with a global feminist project, that certain thoughts must not cross our consciousness, as they must not cross the Antiguan tourist's consciousness.

I want to press against this disciplinary repression with a large, provocative statement after the fashion of Kincaid: with an intensity that might be related to our institutional vulnerability, comparative literature has been resistant to global feminism because of its intersecting commitments to aestheticism and canonicity, tradition as longevity, theory as Continental philosophy, literature as intertext, and language as the Ur-ground of comparison—all of which reinforce a disciplinary ideology of transcendence and unity. As a result, comparatism has most often been a discourse of sameness even when it purports to be a discourse of difference.

The commitments of which I am speaking are abundantly documented in the comparative theory that built the discipline in Western Europe and the United States. Despite a certain interest in "folk" traditions in the nineteenth and early twentieth centuries, comparative literature has been preoccupied primarily with identifying, studying, and promoting the world's "great" literature. Its sense of authority is reflected, for example, in its traditional undergraduate mission to trans-

---

only three women have numbered among the twelve presidents serving the association since 1960, and only one woman served before 1989.

[7] Amy Vladeck Heinrich, " 'Startling Resonances': Some Comparative Feminist Issues," in *Proceedings of the Tenth Congress of the International Comparative Literature Association*, ed. Anna Balakian et al. (New York: Garland, 1985), 608–13.

mit "the major literary works of the western heritage,"[8] sometimes "enriched" by a few classical "Eastern" texts. These great works are to be viewed, as René Wellek put it, as "monuments" and not "documents,"[9] a position whose troubling underside is implied by Kincaid's observation that colonists build monuments to themselves among the colonized. These literary icons are protected from such disturbing deconstructions because they are read less in a context than in an intertext, since literature is understood to be produced by international literary movements according to universal literary "laws." The predominance of "influence" studies in comparative literature reflects this intertextual commitment most literally by presuming that works are what they are because of the (world) literature that has preceded them. "Minor" works are usually studied in relation to "major" ones—as *A Small Place* is validated by comparison to the "Ancient Mariner"—or in support of a universal textuality. Linguistic and political differences become "artificial . . . barriers" that have "confined the study of literature."[10]

Such an environment easily defines out of greatness writings by women of all races—and men of some—that fail to satisfy white male norms or that lack visible comparative connections with traditional texts. Comparative literature's canons have "included" women primarily by selecting individual works (*The Tale of Genji, La Princesse de Clèves, Emma*) that conform to its aesthetic values and that can be studied without one's having to confront the kinds of questions feminists would ask. Although there has of course been some opening of the comparative canon, signs of anxiety and retrenchment remain. The 1989 ACLA report on undergraduate comparative literature professes (in negative syntax) to "welcome non-Western, women's literature and noncanonical literature" but insists that comparative literature must still ensure "some significant areas of expertise," thereby nullifying both the significance of these fields and the possibility that they are sites of expertise. In pleading that we "not forget also to introduce students to the canonical works upon which are based the prevailing sense of western culture," ACLA's curricular project would ensure that this "prevailing sense" not be challenged by a critique of Western culture such

[8]Robert J. Clements, *Comparative Literature as Academic Discipline: A Statement of Principles, Praxis, Standards* (New York: Modern Language Association, 1978), 24.

[9]René Wellek, "The Name and Nature of Comparative Literature," in *Comparatists at Work: Studies in Comparative Literature*, ed. Stephen G. Nichols, Jr., and Richard B. Vowles (Waltham, Mass.: Blaisdell, 1968), 13.

[10]David Malone, introduction to Werner Friedrich, *The Challenge of Comparative Literature and Other Addresses*, ed. William J. De Sua (Chapel Hill: University of North Carolina Press, 1970), ix–xv.

as *A Small Place*—which would surely also be dismissed as a document, not a monument.[11]

Nor would *A Small Place* be considered "theory" in comparative literature's usual terms. In discussing the engagement with theory that marks the discipline, Koelb and Noakes include only men among the theorists whom comparatists might study alongside the "canonical writers of Western literature": "Marx, Freud, Lacan, Luhmann, Nietzsche, Wölfflin, Adorno, Derrida, Heidegger, Abraham and Torok, Louis Sullivan, and so on."[12] Although surely Kristeva or Irigaray could have been mentioned, this list is disturbingly accurate: comparative literature does still understand "theory" in a Eurocentric and masculinist sense. "Great" theory is defined much like "great" literature: as cosmopolitan, Continental, verbally dense, concerned with what are taken to be "large" and "universal" questions rather than "narrow" or "provincial" ones.[13]

Consonant with its commitment to "great" literature and theory is comparative literature's commitment to long-lived texts, a position in interesting tension with its sense of itself as intellectually avant-garde. The privileging of the traditional has created, for example, what Mary Louise Pratt calls a "selective multinationalism,"[14] by which comparative literature attends to classical Indian works such as the *Mahabharata* but not to the (more politically charged) writings of the colonial and postcolonial periods.[15] This commitment to "traditional" literatures does not, however, override the Eurocentrism of comparatist studies, or courses in the history of criticism would routinely include Bharata's *Natyasastra*, the classic text of Sanskrit aesthetics, alongside Aristotle's *Poetics*. For comparatists the ultimate source of "Western tradition" remains ancient Greece, which at around the same time Goethe first called for a *Weltliteratur* was being reinvented as an Aryan culture against the evidence that its science, art, and philosophy result from "cultural mixtures" created by the Egyptians and Phoenicians who colonized Greece.[16]

[11] American Comparative Literature Association, "Undergraduate Committee Report," *ACLA Newsletter* 20.2 (Spring–Summer 1989): 39–40.

[12] Koelb and Noakes, *Comparative Perspective*, 6.

[13] It seems to me a particularly "comparatist" behavior that the warnings I received from some of my graduate professors about pursuing feminist scholarship argued that such a choice would mean "narrowing" myself.

[14] Mary Louise Pratt, "Comparative Literature as a Cultural Practice," in *Profession 86* (New York: Modern Language Association, 1986), 33.

[15] This is indeed the position Dinesh d'Souza takes in *Illiberal Education: The Politics of Race and Sex on Campus* (New York: Free Press, 1991).

[16] See Martin Bernal, *Black Athena: The Afroasiatic Roots of Classical Civilization*, 2 vols. (New Brunswick: Rutgers University Press, 1987, 1991), 1:2.

Obviously the predilection for "old" works and long-literate cultures implicitly devalues women's writings and "emergent" literatures.[17] Robert Clements, for example, wrote in the late 1970s that although "Black African literature is of course the most visibly lacking component" in comparative literature, this absence is justified "since Africa has contributed fewer literary works that satisfy" the "dual criteria" of "international acclaim and enduring values" so tautologically constructed by comparative literature. On similar grounds "massive areas, like Indonesia with a population of 100 million, would be minimally represented," though as a comparatist good sport Clements allowed "*aficionados* of African or Polynesian literatures . . . of course [to] feature them in theses written for their degrees."[18] Obviously the world's geographic and literary "small places" haven't a chance against such practices by which only what is already deemed important to white men is worthy to be compared.[19]

One reason Clements and other comparatists have given for excluding African or Polynesian literatures is a linguistic one: Africans write in many languages, most of which are not known or taught in Western universities. This argument is easy enough to dismantle both by refusing comparative literature's Eurocentric linguistic hierarchies and by recalling the large body of African literature written in European languages. But it evokes a further reason why comparative literature remains resistant to both the global and the feminist: its insistence on language as the primary site of difference and hence not only the discipline's central basis for "comparison" but the very ground of its disciplinary legitimacy. It is not just that the overwhelmingly dominant languages of comparative literature study—indeed sometimes the only ones that fulfill graduate language requirements—are those of Western Europe or even a restrictive group of these, so that the field's language base is actually rather narrow and most comparatists can enjoy the comfort of having at least one "foreign" language in common. Equally problematic is the fact that the privileging of standard-language difference as the criterion for comparative study risks confusing linguistic knowledge with cultural knowledge and overlooks both cultural differences that are not visibly linguistic and linguistic differences that are

---

[17]Thirty or forty years ago even U.S. literature was commonly considered too new a tradition to be fertile ground for comparatists.

[18]Clements, *Comparative Literature as Academic Discipline*, 31–32. Clements does not mention women or feminism in his book.

[19]Even "small" European literatures are so treated. See Frank J. Warnke, "The Comparatist's Canon: Some Observations," in Koelb and Noakes, *Comparative Perspective*, 48–56.

not phonological. Reinhold Grimm has argued, for example, that in the Nazi period one could point to at least four "German literatures" without including the literatures of non-German countries such as Austria, and surely we would all agree with Walter Cohen that "in no two countries is English the same language."[20] If we go further, we confront ramifications still more charged: the linguistic imperialism by which Janet Frame's New Zealand English is (mis)translated into American by her publishers; the multilingualism of Gloria Anzaldúa, whose eight languages range from Standard English to Standard Spanish to Tex-Mex; Jamaica Kincaid's anger that "the only language I have in which to speak of this crime [of enslavement] is the language of the criminal who committed the crime," which "can explain and express the deed only from the criminal's point of view."[21] Feminist criticism has also raised questions about "women's language" and about the particularly dialogic forms that nonhegemonic writers may adopt to open up or circumvent conventional androcentric languages. In light of these challenges, comparative literature's notions of language have been, like its canon, only narrowly comparative.

It seems plausible to me that one reason why so many of these values have persisted in comparative literature even though similar positions have been dismantled in related disciplines is that institutionally ours remains a beleaguered field, routinely having to justify its existence and its disciplinary integrity. We may feel especially defensive now that theory, once comparative literature's bailiwick, is taught routinely in so many departments of national (and particularly English) literature along with an expanding global curriculum in which works in translation are increasingly routine. It seems to me that challenges to comparative literature often take the form of threats to the field's "virility" not unlike those directed at women's studies: both are deemed deficient in definitive boundaries and methodology, lacking in "rigor" and "precision," professionally impractical. Comparative literature has tended to resist these charges with a manly counterelitism that asserts its superiority to national literary studies on the grounds of a rigorous insistence on the "mastery" of foreign languages and literatures, an engagement with complex Continental theories, a concern with the world's great "monuments," and what Werner Friedrich calls "hard,

[20]Reinhold Grimm, "Identity and Difference: On Comparative Studies within a Single Language," in *Profession 86*, 28–29; Walter Cohen, "The Concept of World Literature," in *Comparative Literature East and West: Traditions and Trends*, ed. Cornelia N. Moore and Raymond A. Moody (Honolulu: University of Hawaii Press, 1989), 6.
[21]See, respectively, Janet Frame, "Departures and Returns," in *Writers in East-West Encounter: New Cultural Bearings*, ed. Guy Amirthanayagam (London: Macmillan, 1982), 91–92; Gloria Anzaldúa, *Borderlands/La Frontera* (San Francisco: Spinsters/Aunt Lute, 1987), 55; and Kincaid, *Small Place*, 31–32.

scholarly principles." A critical aspect of this self-legitimation has been a sometimes vehement dissociation of comparative literature from "general" or "world" literature, which is implied to be an "easy introductory" study of translated works.[22]

But I think there is another, more honorable explanation for the tenacity of the values of universality and transcendence, one that has to do with the political agenda already reflected in early formulations such as those of Goethe and Arnold and especially vigorous when comparative literature was burgeoning earlier in this century. I propose that comparative literature's deep investment in the study of sameness is not only an intellectual agenda but an ideological one, and not only a casualty of cultural solipsism but the unwitting legacy of an urgent need to preserve human dignity and artistic achievement against the real threats of fascism and world war. The investment in sameness is easy to document through decades of apparent dissonance: whether comparative literature has been defined as the study of literature across national boundaries or the study of literature without regard to such boundaries,[23] it has been committed not only intellectually but politically to the notion that literature and aesthetic culture are universal: comparative literature entails "a consciousness of the unity of all literary creation and experience"; "an overall view of literature . . . as inclusive and comprehensive," a focus on "problems that transcend linguistic and national boundaries"; it seeks the "common ground of interest beneath the superficial tangle of differences."[24] François Jost put it most unequivocally in the early 1970s, just when feminist and ethnic studies were emerging in national departments of literature: "The entire globe shares identical literary interests and pursues similar literary goals."[25]

This notion of literature as transcending cultures has an agenda that some comparatists have made explicitly ideological: it is a means for realizing "[our] common humanity"; a way "to consolidate the spiritual unity in our half of the world,"[26] a kind of literary United Nations bent on proving the adage that "it's a small world after all." It is therefore

---

[22]Friedrich, *Challenge of Comparative Literature*, 8.

[23]These positions yield, respectively, what Suzan Bassnett has rightly described as the two different major comparatist projects: the two-text or two-author study that compares, contrasts, or traces influence (literature across national boundaries) and the more general "free-ranging genre study, 'spirit of the age' study, or literary tone study" of the second and more recent type of comparative literature (literature without regard to national boundaries). See Suzan Bassnett, "Comparative Literature and Methodology," *Degrés*, nos. 46–47 (Fall 1986): 1–13.

[24]François Jost, *Introduction to Comparative Literature* (Indianapolis: Bobbs-Merrill, 1974), 29; Malone, introduction to Friedrich, *Challenge of Comparative Literature*, xii.

[25]Jost, *Introduction to Comparative Literature*, 30.

[26]Friedrich, *Challenge of Comparative Literature*, 22.

appropriate that comparative literature's major tasks as they have traditionally been codified—to study influences and analogies; movements and trends; genres and forms; motifs, types, and themes—
encourage us to overlook difference in favor of sameness or to show
the essential similarities beneath surface differences, as A. Owen Aldridge does, for example, in treating Natsume Sōseki's *Kokoro* as a "Japanese Werther."[27] Such a project is made immeasurably easier by the
persistent white male–centeredness of comparative literature's tools
and texts: we are able to define literature, culture, and even "the world"
in terms sufficiently narrow to prove our own claims, while sustaining
an illusion of breadth by reaching out, like open-minded tourists, to
the "finds" among lesser ("folk" and female) cultures and absorbing
them into the established museums of literature.

I have said that there were historically progressive reasons why comparative literature developed this universalizing ideology. Comparatism grew up in an era of imperialist nationalism which some comparatists hoped to combat by affirming a transnational spirit in the
human sciences. This agenda must have seemed especially pressing in
the years when comparative literature was developing in Europe and
the United States, since these were years in which the very countries
collaborating most fully in the comparative project, France and Germany, were bitter enemies. "Rising above" national boundaries and
partisan identities was surely a crucial strategy of resistance, a way to
preserve not simply personal and collegial relations, or even the project
of comparative literary scholarship, but "culture" itself. It is sadly ironic
that this resistance to nationalism ended up constructing an androcentric Continentalism that became its own exclusivity. A sign of the dou-
ble-talk engendered by such a project may be found in a chilling if
well-intentioned passage from Werner Friedrich's 1964 essay "The
Challenge of Comparative Literature." Having proclaimed comparatism to be a "political creed" dedicated to "abjuring all forms of racism"; having lauded the spectrum of European national identities
represented among comparatists teaching in the United States (though
without mentioning Jews, although several of the men he names are
Jewish, and omitting women entirely); having identified the "same in-
spiring wealth" among "the literary figures of America"; and having
unequivocally supported the movement for black civil rights and condemned the violence at Little Rock and Birmingham, Friedrich asks his
listeners to consider, "happily and perhaps a bit proudly, that the voice

---

[27] A. Owen Aldridge, "The Japanese Werther of the Twentieth Century," in Koelb and
Noakes, *Comparative Perspective*, 75–92.

of the Black Man was heard for the first time in history not in Africa, not on the shores of the Congo, but on the shores of the Mississippi— and that it was in ever upward-struggling America that the former slaves . . . were first given a chance to give expression to their hopes and their anguish, to the despair and the vision of a race that is justly aspiring to a respected place on earth."[28] I need not point out the truths of African and American history that are violated in this Eurocentric paean to America for "allowing" black culture to enter its comparative melting pot—as if there had not been centuries of culture in Africa, and as if slavery were now a precondition for literary upward mobility.[29]

Such fictions suggest that comparative literature has embraced "difference" only when it has not visibly entailed dominance, dependence when it has been a matter of indebtedness and not of political power, so that, like Kincaid's tourists, we "needn't let that slightly funny feeling [we] have from time to time about exploitation, oppression, domination develop into full-fledged unease" and ruin not simply our holiday but our livelihood.[30] That comparative literature has preferred not to recognize that "in every cross-cultural encounter there is a dominance, a submission, a merging, or a resistance"[31] might explain its particular resistance to feminism, which sees dominance in difference and for which power relations constitute a theoretical core. *A Small Place* is the kind of text that forces issues of power, though comparative analogies with Coleridge, the Bible, or even Swift might temper the book's contemporary urgency. With its direct interrogation of "you," such a book also asks us to acknowledge, as comparatists rarely do, our own cultural differences—hence our relations of dominance, submission, merging, and resistance—with the cultures we "compare." Since the refusal to confront these imbalances of power is, of course, the privilege of the dominant and of those who align themselves with the dominant, the perspective of the "other" (the woman, the person of color, the colonized—the "borderworker") becomes critical for a fully "comparative" view. In *Three Guineas*, Virginia Woolf distinguishes the England of "educated men" ("so kind to you") from her own, women's England ("so harsh to us") and explains that this is why,

[28]Friedrich, *Challenge of Comparative Literature*, 48–50.
[29]Here indeed is the particularly "American" version of comparative literature, which, as Guy Amirthanayagam says, differs from its British counterpart in seeking actively "to draw from as many cultures as possible in order to build a unique cultural base" but produces from this only a "medley of superficial borrowings" that legitimate a "univeralizing tendency" (*Writers in East-West Encounter*, 5).
[30]Kincaid, *Small Place*, 10.
[31]Frame, "Departures and Returns," 91.

"though we look at the same things, we see them differently."[32] This kind of comparative consciousness counters the disciplinary tradition I have been describing in which comparatists look at different things but see them as the same.

I have dwelled at some length on dissonances between feminism and comparatism in order to begin suggesting both a shape and a rationale for a globally conscious feminist comparative literature. Since I began with a polemical statement about comparative literature as it has traditionally been conceptualized, let me move now toward an equally polemical but positive statement about the kind of comparative literature that seems to me most valuable for addressing contemporary concerns such as those *A Small Place* raised for me. Such a comparatism would understand texts as documents whether or not they are monuments and would expand its notions of both "literature" and "theory" to include an international, multiracial, and sexually inclusive spectrum of verbal practices. It would need to redefine nation, culture, and language in broader and more complicated terms, would value difference at least as much as sameness by exploring works in what I will call a comparative specificity, and, in order to resist reinscribing dominance, would locate both its practices and its practitioners within their own cultural space. Such a comparative literature might, I suggest, realize the visions of earlier comparatists from Goethe to Wellek in ways and on grounds they did not imagine, just as the U.S. Constitution makes possible, as Bernice Reagon points out, the freedoms of people whom the "founding fathers" themselves suppressed or enslaved.[33]

First and most obviously, a feminist comparative literature would need to understand literature as document as well as monument, which also means exploring from an international perspective the processes by which certain documents get transformed into monuments and others do not. Such a project would demand an interrogation of comparative literature's tenacious privileging not simply of *an* aesthetic but of *the* aesthetic, an interrogation that feminist criticism initiated in the 1970s and that Barbara Herrnstein Smith and Pierre Bourdieu have theorized in ways that might speak fruitfully to traditionally trained comparatists.[34]

[32]Woolf, *Three Guineas*, 5.

[33]Bernice Reagon, lecture delivered at Georgetown University, 1986. I do not mean to suggest, nor did Reagon, that these various "fathers" shared a wish for inclusiveness. Indeed, Goethe's conception of *Weltliteratur* ends up subsuming "other" literatures into the literature of the Fatherland.

[34]See Barbara Herrnstein Smith, *Contingencies of Value: Alternative Perspectives for Critical Theory* (Cambridge: Harvard University Press, 1988); and Pierre Bourdieu, *Distinction: A Social Critique of the Judgement of Taste*, trans. Richard Nice (Cambridge: Harvard University Press, 1984). For critiques of the Kantian aesthetic that underpins comparative liter-

Equally urgent, given the ways in which comparative literature now conceives itself as the locus of "theory," is the need for a revised and expanded notion of that term which embraces not only different theorists and different politics but different *discourses*, including those of people whose primary commitments are not academic but activist and for whom "theory" is manifestly not only about ways to think and read but about ways to live. Such an opening of the theoretical canon would have two crucial results. On the one hand, it would challenge some sacred Eurocentric theoretical premises. It is clear, for example, that for feminists, for colonized peoples, and for other silenced groups, conceptions of language, truth, and reality often differ from those held by the avant-garde West. When Mary Prince says the "foreign people" who "say slaves are happy" have "put a cloak about the truth," her discourse requires some belief in a recoverable "truth."[35] Similarly, as postcolonialist narratologists such as Mineke Schipper have made clear, "realism" carries different meanings and imperatives for emerging communities, and the preference for realist fiction that has been associated with various liberation movements cannot be dismissed as retrograde.[36] Likewise, William Walsh contrasts the European distrust of language to the Indian view "that immediate experience and its expression in language are not two wholly different things."[37] A genuinely comparative encounter between such different theoretical positions asks those of us trained in "the master's tools" not to dismiss these dissenting voices as "naive" or "untheoretical." Such an encounter may be possible, however, only when comparative literature is willing to read as theory writings that lie outside its canon of philosophy. To the extent that such a canon represents the thought patterns of a ruling-class minority, we must also entertain the possibility that it reinforces the hegemony of the groups that created it, even when the individual theorist (like the individual comparatist) remains "detached" from matters explicitly political.

On the other hand, different theories and theories in different discourses may also intersect fruitfully. I have found significant similarities (along with equally important differences) between some radical theory by women of color and some poststructuralist theory by whites. I am

ature, see especially Smith, *Contingencies of Value*, 64–72, and Bourdieu, *Distinction*, 486–500.

[35] Mary Prince, *The History of Mary Prince, A West Indian Slave, Related by Herself*, ed. Moira Ferguson (London: Pandora, 1987), 83.

[36] Mineke Schipper, *Beyond the Boundaries: African Literature and Literary Theory* (London: Allison & Busby, 1989).

[37] William Walsh, "The Meeting of Language and Literature and the Indian Example," in Amirthanayagam, *Writers in East-West Encounter*, 108.

struck, for example, by resonances between Audre Lorde's conception
of the relation between poetry and theory in "Poetry Is Not a Luxury"
and Julia Kristeva's conception of the relation between the semiotic and
the symbolic in *Revolution in Poetic Language*.[38] But Kristeva's is the writing that has counted as theory; as bell hooks notes, current academic
practice admits black women to the creative canon but not to the theoretical one, possibly because black women's theories often raise urgent
political issues unbuffered by a generalizing academic terminology.[39] If
Terry Eagleton is right to say that training in literary studies is training
in the ability to manipulate a certain discourse, and that academics are
"allowed" to say anything we wish in this discourse because certain
things simply cannot be said in it,[40] then the encounter of theories that
I am proposing is possible only if we engage a difference in discourse
and not simply a difference in "view." Since comparative literature has
been avant-garde in taking up (and producing) "theory," it would be
appropriate for us now to take a similar role of leadership in expanding
the range of our theoretical competence.

Encounters with antimonumental theories and texts will help—or require—us to redefine nation, culture, and language in new terms.
Woolf's contrasts between "male" and "female" England and Kincaid's
among Antiguan classes and races make clear the need not to rely on assumptions about national or cultural unity but to confront as subjects of
comparison differences within nations and cultures—the differences of
race, sex, ethnicity, religion, sexuality, region, and class that in fact get repressed when nations and cultures define themselves.[41] We can also
study the comparative intersection of various differences, as Selma James
does when she looks through Sir Thomas Bertram's role as a(n Antiguan)
slaveholder at his governance of Mansfield Park. In this process James
shows the value of gender difference to cultural study: "The effect of dis-
missing as unimportant what Jane Austen says women of the slavehold-
ing class had to bear at the hands of the master is to dismiss the attack on
the slaveholder that comes from within his family."[42]

[38]Julia Kristeva, *Revolution in Poetic Language*, trans. Margaret Waller (New York: Columbia University Press, 1984).
[39]See bell hooks, *Talking Back: Thinking Feminist, Thinking Black* (Boston: South End
Press, 1989).
[40]Terry Eagleton, *Literary Theory: An Introduction* (Minneapolis: University of Minnesota
Press, 1983), 203.
[41]On this question, see Homi K. Bhabha, ed., *Nation and Narration* (London: Routledge,
1990), esp. Ernst Renan's historic "What Is a Nation," 8–22. For innovative comparative
work on sexual identity, see Andrew Parker et al., eds., *Nationalisms and Sexualities* (New
York: Routledge, 1991).
[42]Selma James, *The Ladies and the Mammies: Jane Austen and Jean Rhys* (Bristol: Falling
Wall Press, 1983), 41.

Such studies suggest the need for a revision of both the concept and the place of language in comparative literature. We might begin by recognizing that languages embed relations of dominance, as Françoise de Grafigny already understood in 1747 when she accused the French of "according merit to other countries to the extent that their manners imitate our own and their language resembles our idiom."[43] We might then want to "compare" intralingual differences such as dialect and register, or different literatures (Afro-Caribbean and African American, or African American and Jewish American) within "the same" language group. We must also make the crucial distinctions between language and culture that allow comparison, for example, of anglophone African and Indian women writers, or anglophone and Tamil Indian writers, or Jamaica Kincaid's *Annie John* and Annie's "favorite" novel, *Jane Eyre.* In Bharati Mukherjee's *Jasmine* (1989), an Iowan asks the narrator to "come up with a prettier name"—"something in Indian"—for the golf course he imagines building on the family farm. The narrator comments: "I want to say to Darrel, 'You mean in Hindi, not Indian, there's no such thing as Indian,' but . . . he comes from a place where the language you speak is what you are."[44] This passage suggests the importance of distinguishing cultural from linguistic training and creating a comparative literature that embraces both. This does not mean abandoning "foreign language" requirements; on the contrary, at this moment when linguistic imperialism is rising and the study of languages remains in decline, one valuable task the discipline could undertake is to enable students to learn under-studied languages, languages that are primarily oral, and languages of newly literate cultures so that such writings can become part of a fully global literature. This project, in turn, will create a future community of scholars whose linguistic base is immeasurably broader than that of my generation of comparatists.

Such a linguistic reformation would facilitate a deconstruction of the political and cultural hierarchies which, in its efforts at transcendence, comparative literature has tended to reproduce. We would be avoiding what John Dorsey calls a "cultural wealth-of-nations outlook,"[45] the position whereby the "best" literatures, or those most worth studying, are those with the most exports. (Feminist criticism, my own work by

[43]Françoise de Grafigny, *Lettres d'une péruvienne* (1747), in *Lettres portugaises, Lettres d'une péruvienne et autres romans d'amour par lettres,* ed. Bernard Bray and Isabelle Landy-Houillon (Paris: Flammarion, 1983), 249.

[44]Bharati Mukherjee, *Jasmine* (New York: Grove Weidenfeld, 1989), 10–11.

[45]John T. Dorsey, "National and Comparative Literature in Japan," in Moore and Moody, *Comparative Literature East and West,* 184.

no means excepted, has already reproduced such dominance in its overconcentration on British, French, and U.S. works.) This means resisting a superpower comparatism by which smaller literatures (including literatures by women) are overlooked by or swallowed up in larger ones. In fact, one fertile field for comparative study is precisely the relationship between the production (and reception) of literature and various forms of global power—political, linguistic, economic, cultural. Comparative literature could help to rebalance the cultural map by studying the literal and metaphoric "small places" we have traditionally overlooked. If we value linguistic difference and richness, then let us follow Albert Wendt's call to explore the literatures of Oceania, with its 1,200 indigenous languages in addition to English, French, Hindi, Spanish, and various forms of pidgin, which give this region, Wendt argues, a potential to be the most creative in the world.[46] Let us explore complex relations between gender and colonialism which Edna Manlapaz queries, for example, when she explains that it was the overthrow of Spanish imperialism in the Philippines by its American counterpart that gave Philippine women the equivocal gift of a university education to write literature in a foreign tongue within a British-American intertext.[47] And let us acknowledge that much of the globe—including Europe—is becoming what Ulf Hannerz calls "creolized," so that even to speak of individual nations or continents, or "East" and "West," is becoming culturally inaccurate.[48]

A new comparative practice might also entail redefining or replacing those traditional modes for organizing literary study which have encouraged homogeneity. Joan Kelly's now classic argument that women did not have a Renaissance reminds us that most literary periodizations suit only the productions of European men.[49] Kincaid writes that "to the people in a small place, the division of Time into the Past, the Present, and the Future does not exist."[50] Women have likewise written about gendered differences in understandings of time.[51] It may become

---

[46]Albert Wendt, "Toward a New Oceania," in Amirthanayagam, *Writers in East-West Encounter*, 212.

[47]See Edna Zapanta-Manlapaz, "Our Mothers, Our Selves: A Literary Genealogy of Filipino Women Poets Writing in English, 1905–1950," *Philippine Studies* 39 (1991): 321–36.

[48]See Ulf Hannerz, "The World in Creolisation," *Africa* 57.4 (1987): 546–57. Hannerz's view is to my mind rather too sanguine and does not sufficiently allow for relations of dominance. Of course "East" and "West" have always been Eurocentric inaccuracies on a planet that is spherical.

[49]See Joan Kelly, "Did Women Have a Renaissance?" in *Women, History, and Theory* (Chicago: University of Chicago Press, 1984).

[50]Kincaid, *Small Place*, 54.

[51]See, for example, Angelika Bammer, *Partial Visions: Feminisms and Utopianism in the*

more fruitful to supplement the notion of chronological period by identifying movements or impulses that occur at different times in different places but have similar consequences, so that, for example, one might identify moments in which there seems to be an insertion of anticolonialism or feminism into a culture's discourses. Genre theory would likewise need deconstruction, given the ways in which marginalized literatures have either been omitted from genre studies or have themselves rejected conventional generic forms. And "influence" would surely have to be redefined to account for the nonsalutary as well as the benevolent: the influence of England on Antigua, the related influence of *Jane Eyre* or *The Tempest* on Caribbean writers, the subtler influences of hegemonies (male, white, European) that "outsider" writers have both accommodated and resisted in complex ways. Obviously, notions of "tradition" would have to be revised as we interrogate the restrictive and selective uses to which the concept has been put and the values and agendas served by the legitimation that the word provides.

All these practices imply a conception of the comparative that is grounded in the assumption of difference as a premise at least equal to the assumption of similarity. Such a position opens infinitely more complicated ways to understand textual relations as racial, sexual, regional, or colonial and to recognize that a considerable share of the world's literature is "borderwork." Those of us trained as traditional comparatists would have to resist our easy reach for the similar. Now that I have learned, for example, that Kincaid acknowledges Alain Robbe-Grillet to be a major influence,[52] I would have to temper my wish to turn her uses of the you-as-protagonist into a simple replication of *nouveau roman* strategies.

The key to such a revised practice seems to me to lie in the idea of what I call a *comparative specificity*, which would embrace both difference and similarity but would never simply dissolve a text, idea, writer, group, or movement into a safe and homogeneous whole. Angelika Bammer's study of feminism and utopianism in the 1970s models such specificity by understanding feminism as a multinational movement of nationally situated politics.[53] What happens when such understanding

---

1970s (London: Routledge, 1991); Frieda Johles Forman, ed., *Taking Our Time: Feminist Perspectives on Temporality* (Oxford: Pergamon, 1989); and, of course, Julia Kristeva's widely anthologized "Women's Time," in *The Kristeva Reader*, ed. Toril Moi (New York: Columbia University Press, 1986), 187–213.

[52]Selwyn R. Cudjoe, "An Interview with Jamaica Kincaid," *Callaloo* 12.2 (Spring 1989): 396–411.

[53]See Bammer, *Partial Visions*.

is absent is dramatically illustrated in Kelly Cherry's review of *A Small Place*, which lambastes Kincaid's book precisely for its specificity:

> It is not that the author is wrong to be so furious but that she truncates the reader's sympathy for her emotion by denying . . . that there are other sources of rage, rage as deep as hers.
>   . . . Every one of us *is* an island, "a small place" harboring the humiliations and despairs of a history of abuse, racial or sexual, political or economic, personal or professional.[54]

When Cherry turns Kincaid's "small place" into a metaphor, she erases the particular pain of slavery and colonialist racism beneath a fiction of universal and presumably equal suffering. Isabelle de Charrière's *Lettres écrites de Lausanne* (1785) enacts a similar universalizing gesture when Cécile finds herself pitying a "poor Negro" sold into slavery and now dying alone in Geneva, but then "corrects" herself by commenting that it doesn't really matter whether one is a slave or a king since both will die: "The King of France will be like this slave one day."[55] I am suggesting that comparative literature at this historical moment needs to allow the slave a specificity that is dissolved in this analogy with the King of France as in the metaphorizing of Antigua as an island of generic pain. The slave narrator Mary Prince reveals the danger of such idealist slippages when she talks of Christianity's messages to slaves that "the truth will make me free" when in fact it was not "the truth" but white colonizers who had that power.[56]

Finally, a global feminist comparative literature would have to acknowledge that comparatists are individuals constituted in culture—in nation, gender, class, race, ethnicity, religion, ideology, sexuality. To "compare" would mean neither a denial of these specificities nor an imprisonment within them, but a dialectical engagement of what Adrienne Rich calls a "politics of location" with what Virginia Woolf calls a "freedom from unreal loyalties" which together would allow one—paradoxically and probably always only partially—to stand "outside" the very culture in which one also locates oneself and one's work. We would first need to accept Rich's recognition that "as a woman [comparatist] I have a country; as a woman [comparatist] I cannot divest myself of that country merely by condemning its government [or by

---

[54]Kelly Cherry, review of *A Small Place* in *American Book Review* 11 (September–October 1989): 19.
[55]Isabelle de Charrière, *Oeuvres complètes*, vol. 8 (Geneva: Slatkine, 1980), 187.
[56]Prince, *History of Mary Prince*, 83.

styling myself a 'world citizen'].''[57] Although comparatists may not live in our culture of origin, none of us is a culture-free globe dweller, and most are white, European, and middle-class in ethnic origin, training, or outlook. We have proceeded as if these identities, and the differences both among ourselves and between ourselves and the cultures we are studying, did not exist. Comparative literature has, in effect, echoed Virginia Woolf's claim that "as a woman I have no country. As a woman I want no country. As a woman my country is the whole world" without recognizing as Woolf did the need first to divest oneself of one's "unreal loyalties," the seductions that stem from "pride of nationality . . . religious pride, college pride, school pride, family pride, sex pride" in order to see from a critical comparative vantage point.[58]

Indeed, Woolf's strategy for achieving this balance between location and distance was precisely through comparative studies; she asked her woman reader to "compar[e] French historians with English; German with French; the testimony of the ruled—the Indians or the Irish, say— with the claims made by their rulers," and then if there remained "some 'patriotic' emotion, some ingrained belief in the intellectual superiority of her own country over other countries," to "compare English painting with French painting; English music with German music; English literature with Greek literature, for translations abound. When all these comparisons have been faithfully made by the use of reason, the outsider will find herself in possession of very good reasons for her indifference."[59] Woolf's suggestion that women and other outsiders might have a particular critical perspective on their "own" culture seems to me amply supported by the revision I have been engaging here, which was made possible by the thinking of women such as Woolf and Rich, Lorde and Kincaid, Mukherjee and Grafigny, who refuse to engage in "unreal loyalties" yet who locate their own comparative practices within the framework of their sex, race, sexuality, and nationality instead of pretending to proceed, as the 1979 ICLA (International Comparative Literature Association) defined the comparative project, from "an international point of view."

I conclude with the utopian suggestion that this kind of specific and located cross-cultural comparative practice might help to fulfill the desires of the earlier comparatists for a just and harmonious world, goals

[57]Adrienne Rich, "Notes toward a Politics of Location," in *Blood, Bread, and Poetry: Selected Prose, 1979–1985* (New York: Norton, 1986), 212.
[58]Woolf, *Three Guineas*, 109, 80.
[59]Ibid., 108.

that I believe can be achieved not by denying relations of power and difference but only by confronting and dismantling them. Comparative literature's future may well lie in those texts it has ignored and marginalized and in a new generation of scholars from around the world who will take the discipline, as *A Small Place* has taken me, into the places of discomfort that are so often the places of growth.

16

Bringing African Women into the Classroom: Rethinking Pedagogy and Epistemology

OBIOMA NNAEMEKA

Nothing so sentimental (or arrogant) as ignoring differences, nor so cowardly (or lazy) as overemphasizing them.
—Robin Morgan

Knowledge leads no more to openings than to closures. . . . Between knowledge and power, there is room for knowledge at rest . . . "the end of myths, the erosion of utopia, the rigor of taut patience."
—Trinh T. Minh-ha

Borders are imaginary lines.
—Anonymous

Explorations into the character, possibilities, and survival of feminism and sisterhood on a global scale have led me to revisit the evolution of feminism in the West, especially in the United States, since the 1960s and to examine the question of identity in structuring and destructuring alliances. The crisis in the feminist movement in the United States is a microcosm of the problems that militate against women forming alliances across continents. The troubled history of second-wave feminism in the United States chronicles the movement from the radicalism and sexual politics of the 1960s to the theorizing and feminist politics of the late 1970s and early 1980s to the narcissism and identity politics of the 1980s. A study of this evolution raises some epistemological and pedagogical questions: How do the ways in which we construct, teach, and disseminate knowledge of the Other undermine or promote alliances between women?

As feminists take stock of years of concerted struggle, some suddenly realize that their shared experiences are expressed and articulated in a language they no longer understand. The theorizing of feminism created structures of power in the feminist movement analogous to those for which patriarchy is attacked. As positions of margin and center became delineated, the resistance of the marginalized to the imperious hegemony of that center became more apparent. Not opposed to recognizing differences, the resistance instead has challenged the creation of a hierarchical paradigm in which these differences are placed and interpreted. The theorizing and the subsequent ideologizing of feminism have culminated in the legitimation of the subject/object, self/other, center/margin dyads within the feminist movement itself. Such strategies of exclusion intensify group identification and loyalties which could ultimately fragment the movement. Identity politics or "home politics" should be not an end in itself but the means to an end, providing the initial building blocks for constructing social change. Nonetheless, the security that identity politics can offer may insulate us from forming the alliances necessary for political action. Bonnie Zimmerman cautions that a fine line separates autonomy from fragmentation: "There is a price to pay for a politics rooted so strongly in consciousness and identity. The power of diversity has as its mirror image and companion, the powerlessness of fragmentation. Small autonomous groups can also be ineffectual groups."[1]

In a television interview on December 31, 1979, Tom Wolfe characterized the decade that was closing as the "Me Decade." Feminists were part of the "Me Decade," too, and the identity question that simmered in the late 1970s intensified as the 1980s wore on. Symbols of commonality, oppression, and sisterhood, for example, through which the feminist movement sought to forge solidarity, became increasingly questioned as women began to assess these symbols in all their complexity. As oppression took on a human face, thus raising questions about difference, the issue of sisterhood, especially global sisterhood, assumed wider implications, transcending biology and genealogy. The belief that "sisterhood is global"[2] became a political matter.

Some feminist scholars continue to have faith in feminist scholarship because of, not in spite of, the fissures within it—fissures that enhance its vibrancy and relevance. Our faith, however, should not deter us from examining the sources of these fissures, and from working to prevent them from deepening and destroying women's ability to form and maintain alliances. We must therefore thoroughly scrutinize the theoretical and epistemological issues, the methodological procedures,

[1]Bonnie Zimmerman, "The Politics of Transliteration: *Lesbian Personal Narratives*," in *The Lesbian Issue: Essays from Signs*, ed. Estelle B. Freedman et al. (Chicago: University of Chicago Press, 1985), 268.
[2]This is also the title of the book edited by Robin Morgan, *Sisterhood Is Global: The International Women's Movement Anthology* (New York: Anchor Press, 1984).

and pedagogical questions in feminist scholarship as it addresses marginalized women, particularly African women.

In this day and age of "multiculturalism" and "pluralism," we find a corresponding shift in feminist scholarship from the theorizing of difference to theorizing diversity. Skeptics and cynics (often with good reason) might scream, "Hell, no! Let diversity be!" Theorizing diversity is a risky business; when diversity comes eyeball to eyeball with theory, it is diversity that blinks! Difficult questions remain: How can we theorize diversity without falling into the trap of erecting hierarchies, upholding difference, and legitimating exclusions? How can we save the dynamism of diversity from the hegemonic grip of theory? Trinh T. Minh-ha brilliantly articulates the danger in the use of what Amilcar Cabral calls "the weapon of theory"[3]:

> Indeed, theory no longer is theoretical when it loses sight of its own conditional nature, takes no risk in speculation, and circulates as a form of administrative inquisition. Theory oppresses, when it wills or perpetuates existing power relations, when it presents itself as a means to exert authority—the Voice of Knowledge . . . Difference needs not be suppressed in the name of Theory. And theory as a tool of survival needs to be rethought in relation to gender in discursive practice.[4]

The tension between theory and diversity motivates Susan Griffin's claim that any theory in which "the knowledge of oppression remains mute" will begin to destroy as it is transformed into ideology. I do not believe in theory as a purely innocuous formulation "born of genuine feeling of a sense of reality." Because many theories evolve from the distortion and manipulation of reality, we cannot totally absolve theory from the hegemony that taints ideology. I agree with Griffin when she asserts that ideology "is a martinet."[5] But isn't theory also a "martinet" in its own way? Theoretical frames also border and exclude. Our concern should be less with what is framed in and more with what is framed out, with what is silenced. In feminist scholarship, as we charge ourselves to listen to silences, particularly in women's writing, we must, with equal enthusiasm, listen to the silences imposed by theory. We must interrogate the history/histories of theory/theoretical frameworks and in so doing bring to the fore the human agency implicated in their

---

[3]"The Weapon of Theory" is the title of chapter 14 in *Unity and Struggle: Speeches and Writings of Amilcar Cabral* (New York: Monthly Review Press, 1979), 119–37.

[4]Trinh T. Minh-ha, *Woman, Native, Other: Writing Postcoloniality and Feminism* (Bloomington: Indiana University Press, 1989), 42–43.

[5]See Susan Griffin, "The Way of All Ideology," *Signs* 7 (1982): 647.

formulation, suspecting the smoke screen of objectivity which obscures the ever-manipulative human agency. The smoke screen's illusion undermines us all.

The fundamental dissimilarity between the theorizing of difference and theorizing diversity is that the latter emphasizes the centrality of contiguity. The focus on contiguity which simultaneously recognizes difference and the possibility and/or reality of connection reminds me of a quilt. The quilt, separate patches revealing different and connected geographies and histories, suggests a lesson in possibilities, particularly the possibility of creating harmony out of contradictions. The quilt's beauty transcends aesthetics; the quilt is beautiful because it is also a powerfully political act and art. A theology of nearness—genuine connections, mutually empowering intersections, and fruitful interpenetration—must nurture the theorizing of diversity. Here lie the difficulties and the risk. Feminist theorizing and praxis must be rooted in *genuine* feminist ethics. The troubling contradictions between what we preach and write and what we do fuel the frustrations felt by many who continue to value and practice feminist scholarship.

In the last decade or so feminist scholars have bandied around the word *intersection*. For considerations of intersection to be meaningful, however, we must not embrace the term arbitrarily. Intersection must be allowed to assume its full meaning and range. We cannot talk about the intersections of class, race, gender, ethnicity, and sexual preference without carefully considering the intersection of theory and practice, without recognizing the intersections of world systems, particularly as the world gets smaller owing to technological advances that shrink distances.

We must interrogate feminist scholarship not only on theoretical but also on epistemological grounds. Instead of making the usual philosophical wanderings into epistemology, we must reframe questions about epistemology. Instead of perpetually constructing and renegotiating the so-called standpoint epistemologies, we must take a stand against epistemological inventions and manipulations. In short, we must ask fundamental questions about the manipulation of knowledge, about information management; the politics of publishing must be investigated and interrogated. Information management feeds partial or possibly distorted knowledge, which in turn undermines the intersections we theorize.

In 1980 Zed Press (London) published Nawal El Saadawi's *Hidden Face of Eve*. This edition's preface remains one of the best analyses of the Iranian revolution and of the relation between imperialism and Islam, outlining its effect on women in the Arab world. Saadawi categorically states in the preface that to understand and explain fully the condition of women in the Arab world, one must take into account foreign, particularly American, intervention in the region. This important preface, which establishes a connection between imperialism and the rise of Islamic fundamentalism, with the attendant repression of women, did not appear in the American edition published by Beacon Press, an omission that prompted a strong reaction from Saadawi:

> Yes, and here is a very subtle form of exploitation practiced, unfortunately, by feminists—so-called progressive feminists. Gloria Steinem of *Ms* magazine writes me a letter in Cairo and asks me for an article about clitoridectomy. So I write her an article setting forth the political, social and historical analysis, along with comments about my personal experience. She cuts the political, social and historical analysis and publishes only the personal statements, which put me in a very awkward position. People asked, how could Nawal write such a thing? She has such a global perspective on clitoridectomy, how could she write such a thing? They didn't know Steinem had cut the article. The second example is Beacon Press in Boston. I gave my book, *The Hidden Face of Eve*, to the publisher in London; he published all of the book—the preface, introduction, everything. The preface, which is a long preface, is crucial and important to the book. Beacon Press cut it without my permission, making me feel that I have been exploited and my ideas distorted. Without the preface, it appears that I am separating the sexual from the political, which I never do. To me, women who think they are liberated but who are obsessed with sexuality are not liberated. They are living a new slavery. They are obsessed by not having men around just as they were obsessed with having them around. It is the other side of the same coin.[6]

Although *The Hidden Face of Eve* has been widely read in the United States, the American audience, reading an incomplete version, is denied this powerful book's full impact. As readers of Saadawi in North America lead their war against physical excisions made on Arab girls, they should with equal enthusiasm challenge the type of excision Saadawi claims was performed on her book. Such manipulations of information have grave implications for our theorizing and praxis.

How can we theorize difference or diversity, and what are the pitfalls in such theorizing? How do we gather information about the Other? How do we organize, order, and disseminate that information? In short, how does information management contribute to our construction of a notion of self and at the same time alienate us from the Other? These

[6]Quoted in Tiffany Patterson and Angela Gillam, "Out of Egypt: A Talk With Nawal El Saadawi," *Freedomways* 23 (1983): 190–91.

are crucial questions that we, as students and teachers, confront in varying degrees. These and other related issues have led me to explore the subject in my essay titled "Bringing African Women into the Classroom." While working on this essay, I got a call from a colleague. During our conversation I told him about my topic. "Eh! Bringing African Women into the Classroom!" he sneered. "What do you mean by 'bringing'? Can't they walk? How do you bring them?" he asked. I replied, "You bring them on a leash." Although my response was meant to be a joke, in retrospect I believe I accurately described the profound objectification of African women in classrooms in the West. And as we consider the commodification of African women in Western classrooms, we must also address the issue of tokenism. Quite often the work of an African woman writer is thrown into a course syllabus in order to take care of race, gender, ethnicity, and class issues in one fell swoop, thereby creating a "multicultural course" which will in turn produce "multicultural students."

To study a culture presupposes in some ways that one is outside it. Can we teach as outsiders? Oh, yes, we can. The pertinent question, however, remains: How do we learn and teach as outsiders? In studying and teaching another culture, the teacher finds himself or herself situated at the congruence of different and often contradictory cultural currents. This point of convergence where the teacher stands has its privileges and rewards, but it is also fraught with danger. To survive at this precarious position requires a large dose of humility. Issues involved in researching, writing, and teaching about other cultures are inextricably linked to survival. Can we cross cultural boundaries and still survive? And the notion of crossing cultural boundaries is in itself problematic. What do we mean by "crossing"? Do we mean moving from one point to another, in the process abandoning one set of realities for another? It seems to me that a cross-cultural pedagogy entails not a "crossover" but a transgression whose partial enactment denies the finality implicit in a "crossover."

As students and teachers we discover that our explorations into understanding other peoples and cultures place us in an ambiguous site where we will never accomplish a "crossover" but rather stand astride cultures: our culture and other cultures. It seems to me that crossing cultural boundaries means standing at the crossroads of cultures. In other words, we must see that we enter other cultures with our own cultural baggage. The extent to which we allow narcissism and notions of self to mediate our analysis will determine the degree of distortion in our conclusions. As we learn and teach about other cultures, two fundamental questions should be asked: (1) Why do we want to learn and teach other cultures? (2) How can we learn and teach other cultures?

The first question raises the issue of intention. Charges of concern with economic advancement and professional upward mobility have been levied against some scholars, ranging from historians and social anthropologists to feminists and cultural critics, who proclaim themselves experts on Africa in general and African women in particular.[7] The same could be said about studies of other minorities in which insiders and outsiders to the minority cultures collaborate to advance themselves economically and professionally by means of distortions they invent about the minority cultures, distortions that run against the sacred nature of these cultures. As Ward Churchill writes:

> The past 20 years have seen the birth of a new growth industry in the United States. Known as "American Indian Spiritualism," this profitable enterprise apparently began with a number of literary hoaxes undertaken by non-Indians such as Carlos Castaneda, Jay Marks (AKA "Jamake Highwater," author of *The Primal Mind*, etc.) and Ruth Beebe Hill (of *Hanta Yo* notoriety). A few Indians such as Alonzo Blacksmith . . . and Hyemeyohsts Storm . . . also cashed in, writing bad distortions and outright lies about indigenous spirituality for consumption in the mass market. The authors grew rich peddling their trash, while real Indians starved to death, out of the sight and mind of America.[8]

An issue related to the methodological concerns that the second question raises is that of perspective, equally crucial to evaluating how we learn and teach other cultures. Perspective, distance, objectivity. Perspective implies possibilities, alternatives, choice. How can we choose an appropriate location to situate ourselves? How far or close should we stand vis-à-vis the subject of our analysis? In a 1961 lecture in Japan, Simone de Beauvoir affirmed that in a war situation the privileged and probably the most objective position is that of the person on the sideline, the war correspondent, who witnesses the battle but is not embroiled in the fighting.[9] Richard Wright brilliantly articulated the problematic of perspective: "Perspective is that part of a poem, novel, or play which a writer never puts directly upon paper. It is that fixed point in intellectual space where a writer stands to view the struggles, hopes and sufferings of his people. There are times when he may stand

[7]Ifi Amadiume, preface to *Male Daughters, Female Husbands: Gender and Sex in an African Society* (London: Zed Press, 1987).

[8]Ward Churchill, "Spiritual Hucksterism," *Z Magazine* (December 1990): 94.

[9]Simone de Beauvoir, "Women and Creativity," in *French Feminist Thought: A Reader*, ed. Toril Moi (Oxford: Basil Blackwell, 1987), 27.

too close and the result is blurred vision. Or he may stand too far away and the result is a neglect of important things."[10] In our study and teaching of other cultures, balance and humility must mediate our choice of perspective.

Different problems arise depending on whether one teaches a culture as an insider or an outsider. As I mentioned earlier, one can teach as an outsider, but to do so requires the humility that is grounded in knowledge. Unfortunately, when teaching about Africa and African women, many outsiders prove too impatient to claim expertise. A three-week whirlwind tour of Africa does not an expert on Africa make; speed-reading two or three African novels cannot produce an expert on African literature. Sadly enough, schools in the West sustain tremendous institutional tolerance and encouragement of such expertise. As the academy provides a breeding ground for such experts on Africa and African women, it puts in place stiff requirements for the teaching of Western cultures and literatures. In such areas expertise must be proven through transcripts, graduate degrees, and teaching experience. Trivializing other cultures encourages the type of miseducation that leads to further trivializing of such cultures.

Teaching as an insider poses its own set of problems. Overidentification with one's culture leads to the type of romanticization that produces other levels of distortions. Good examples surface in some Negritude writings. The romanticization of Africa and the subsequent oversimplification of issues have led to much of the negative reaction against the Negritude movement. Furthermore, insiders can also be alienated from their own culture. A Western-educated African who teaches African culture also speaks from a position of alienation which may not necessarily be as profound as that of the outsider. Whether one teaches as an insider or an outsider, the issue of distance is crucial. It is Chinua Achebe's recognition of the interplay of identification and distance that sets him apart as one of Africa's foremost writers. With Achebe we experience a rare moment in literature where the writer balances himself or herself strategically. In spite of his Western education, Achebe remains a true son of Igboland, what the Igbos would call "a son of the soil." Immersed in his cultural and social milieu but possessing a critical eye, he simultaneously identifies with and maintains a distance from his environment. In his works Achebe narrates with charm his profound identification with and love for his environment while at the same time he recognizes its flaws, particularly those

---

[10]Richard Wright, "Blueprint for Negro Writing," in *The Black Aesthetics*, ed. Addison Gayle, Jr. (New York: Doubleday, 1971), 341.

generated by foreign interventions.[11] Achebe demonstrates that a post-colonial subject can maintain a balanced view of the postcolonial condition.

The issue of balance is neglected in the one-dimensional Western constructions of the African woman—usually poor and powerless. We African women have witnessed repeatedly the activities of our over-zealous foreign sisters, mostly feminists who appropriate our wars in the name of fighting the oppression of women in the so-called third world. We watch with chagrin and in painful sisterhood these avatars of the proverbial mourner who wails more than the owners of the corpse.[12] In their enthusiasm, our sisters usurp our wars and fight them badly—very badly. The arrogance that declares African women "problems" objectifies us and undercuts the agency necessary for forging true global sisterhood. African women are not problems to be solved. Like women everywhere, African women *have* problems. More important, they have provided solutions to these problems. We are the only ones who can set our priorities and agenda. Anyone who wishes to participate in our struggles must do so in the context of our agenda. In the same way, African women who wish to contribute to global struggles (and many do) should do so with a deep respect for the paradigms and strategies that people of those areas have established. In our enthusiasm to liberate others, we must not be blind to our own enslavement. Activities of women globally should be mutually liberating.

During the Gulf War the biggest issues in the U.S. media were Saddam Hussein and Saudi women. I will leave Saddam Hussein to George Bush. I was, however, intrigued by the numerous stories about Saudi women. American pronouncements regarding Saudi women suggest prevalent attitudes about other peoples and cultures. One remarkable example comes to mind. On December 27, 1990, the television show *Inside Edition* carried a segment on Saudi women, focusing less on Saudi women and more on the veil—supposedly the ultimate symbol of oppression. The first part of the segment showed us faceless Saudi women shrouded in ample yardage of black cloth. They did not speak. They were not made to speak. They moved against a powerful male presence: the male reporter who commented on their lives of abject subjugation.

---

[11]See in particular Chinua Achebe, *Things Fall Apart* (London: Heinemann, 1958), and *Arrow of God* (London: Heinemann, 1960). Equally pertinent is Achebe's critique of the West in his books of essays, *Morning Yet on Creation Day* (London: Heinemann, 1977), and *Hopes and Impediments* (New York: Doubleday, 1988), as well as his critique of post-independence Africa, in particular Nigeria, in *A Man of the People* and *The Trouble with Nigeria* (Enugu: Fourth Dimension Publishers, 1985).

[12]An Igbo proverb.

Halfway through the tedious, patronizing commentary another Saudi woman appeared, a college student in Jordan. She wore Western clothes (symbols of freedom!) and perched on a red convertible (another symbol of freedom!), ready to speed away into the limitless unknown. This "liberated" Saudi woman spoke; she deserved to speak because she was "free."

At the end of the segment another male presence was installed. Bill O'Reilly appeared on the screen. With an evasive look in his eyes and a dubious smile on his lips, he asked the viewers, specifically the female viewers: "Aren't you lucky to be here?" A program designed to teach us about Saudi women turned out to be a lesson on how lucky and free American women are. After watching that program, I found that my concern was not for Saudi women, since the program gave me no meaningful information about them. My concern was for the millions of American women who went to bed that night believing Bill O'Reilly and his assurances. My concern is about the naïveté and arrogance that such assurances nurture. Many who teach African women writers in classrooms in the West are no different from Bill O'Reilly. As we look at other cultures, relativist arguments and arrogant feelings of superiority numb us to the realities of our own predicament. We need to be conscious of our own oppression in order to collaborate with those who are similarly oppressed.

In the classrooms where we teach and learn about other cultures, three important elements continuously interact: the text, the teacher, and the student. Each takes enormous risks in being there. The text is at risk primarily because it cannot defend itself against use, misuse, and abuse. But the essential question we should ask is this: Why do certain texts and not others on the same subject (in this case, African women) find their way into classrooms? What factors determine our choice of texts, films, and other teaching materials? Does one attribute such choices to a teacher's ignorance (the teacher does not know any better) or to the fact that particular texts and films confirm and legitimize the teacher's prejudices about other cultures and peoples? As we study and teach other cultures, do we enter into meaningful dialogue with the materials we have chosen? In order to unearth the prejudices and assumptions inherent in the materials we use, we should ceaselessly ask questions such as: Where is the writer in the text? Where is the filmmaker in the film? In short, we cannot meaningfully communicate information without first of all asking serious questions about the construction of knowledge. We should examine not only what the texts say but, more important, how the information and data in the texts came into being and are articulated. Concern with epistemological and methodological issues is therefore crucial if we are to save the text. A course syllabus not only demonstrates how much the teacher knows but also betrays the teacher's limitations and prejudices. The same could be said for compilers of anthologies, particularly those designed for use in world literature classes.

Often, token gestures of inclusion are extended to women and so-called third world writers. In such quasi-invisible inclusions, the relevance of a token contribution to the entire anthology or syllabus receives little attention. On a couple of occasions colleagues have asked me to name an African woman writer for inclusion in their course. The appropriate thing would have been for them to tell me the focus of the course and the required texts already on the syllabus. This information would determine whether I recommend the work(s) of Bessie Head, Aminata Sow Fall, Tsitsi Dangarembga, Flora Nwapa, or any other woman writer from Africa. My point here is that, contrary to current thinking and practice, African women writers are not easily interchangeable. It is not so important that Bessie Head's work appears on a syllabus as that it relates and speaks to other chosen materials. Such intertextual considerations help us derive optimal benefit from even the token inclusion we make. I once saw a literature syllabus that lumped Chinua Achebe together with *Robinson Crusoe* and Saint-Exupéry. Evidently the several missions that Saint-Exupéry flew over North Africa and the Sahara earned him the spot beside Achebe! It seems to me that Chinua Achebe and Joseph Conrad would have made a better combination.[13]

Students who flock to courses on African women do so probably for as many reasons as they take other courses, ranging from the desire to learn about African women because it is in vogue—the right thing to do in this day and age of cultural literacy and pluralism—to the possibility that other courses are filled and the students have nowhere else to go for credits. Nonetheless, many non-African (particularly Western) students who walk into courses on African women fall into a different category; almost all of them come in with expectations pretty much defined and entrenched in their minds. The teacher is, therefore, expected to teach those expectations. The teacher who teaches otherwise risks, among other things, receiving uncomplimentary evaluations for his or her unpardonable deviancy. And when African students take courses on African women, they are often called on to validate the

[13]Joseph Conrad's *Heart of Darkness* could be taught in conjunction with Chinua Achebe's *Things Fall Apart* and "An Image of Africa: Racism in Conrad's *Heart of Darkness*," in Achebe, *Hopes and Impediments*, 1–20.

pervasive distortions of African women's lives in texts and films. If the African students dare to think or argue otherwise, they are accused of overreacting. Tension builds up, creating a potentially explosive situation that impedes learning and understanding. Not merely an individual who disseminates information, the teacher who survives must also be a diplomat and psychologist.

Not too long ago I taught a course, "Women in Developing Areas: Power, Politics, and Culture," in a small Midwestern liberal arts college. We started by reading materials written by Judith van Allen and some African women scholars, Ifi Amadiume, Bolanle Awe, and Kamene Okonjo.[14] At the end of two weeks of intense reading, one of my students informed me that she was not getting anything out of the course. Her complaint surprised me since a few other students had mentioned to me that there was too much information to absorb. After a long discussion with the student, it dawned on me that her problem lay more with the nature of the materials we were reading, which discussed primarily the powerful positions that women occupy in indigenous African social and political formations. My student was basically asking, "Where are those excised/circumcised African women in marriages arranged by families who eventually shipped them off to be victimized by heavy-handed polygynists?" I told the student to exercise patience. Circumcision, arranged marriage, and polygyny would be discussed during the seventh and eighth weeks of class; she had only five short weeks to go! Our preconceived notions can be so strong that they get in the way of our learning about cultures and other peoples whose lives and realities transcend our cultural boundaries. As teachers we can overcome this difficulty by painstakingly and judiciously selecting materials that build a balanced syllabus.

The teaching of cultural studies often focuses on exposing differences between cultures. It seems to me, however, that we could accomplish much by teaching similarities and connections as well as differences. It makes sense politically that women, as teachers, teach connections, thereby reducing the distance between the student and the foreign culture and increasing points of interaction and identification. It is the teacher's responsibility to delineate the differences and commonalities

---

[14]The recommended readings were: Ifi Amadiume, preface and introduction to *Male Daughters, Female Husbands;* Bolanle Awe, "The Iyalode in the Traditional Yoruba Political System," in *Sexual Stratification,* ed. Alice Schlegal (New York: Columbia University Press, 1977), 144–59; Kamene Okonjo, "The Dual-Sex Political System in Operation: Igbo Women and Community Politics in Midwestern Nigeria," in *Women in Africa,* ed. Nancy Hafkin and Edna Bay (Palo Alto: Stanford University Press, 1976), 45–58; Judith Van Allen, " 'Sitting on a Man': Colonialism and the Lost Political Institutions of Igbo Women," *Canadian Journal of African Studies* 6 (1972): 165–81.

between the student's culture and the foreign culture, without unduly establishing facile universalism and untenable connections. This methodology which I call teaching connections has been helpful to me in my teaching of African women to a Western audience, especially in teaching the three most discussed issues about African women—clitoridectomy, polygyny, and arranged marriage.

The pervasive sensationalization of clitoridectomy in Western media and scholarship leads to the equally pervasive belief in the incompleteness of most African women, a belief that basically questions our humanity. From the West an intense war led by Fran Hoskens, the guru of clitoridectomy, has raged against this "barbaric act" perpetrated against helpless African and Arab women. Women within Africa and the Arab world have equally condemned the practice. There is disagreement, however, about how to wage the war.[15] Our Western sisters have seen clitoridectomy primarily as an issue of sexuality, and the fixation with sexuality in the West helps explain the intensity of their intrusion. They denounce clitoridectomy because, according to them, it prevents African women from enjoying sex. But then, wasn't clitoridectomy initiated in part precisely to prevent women from going around and enjoying sex? This unmitigated advocacy of the enjoyment of sex most often leads to a stricter imposition of certain customs on African and Arab women. Foreigners, however well-meaning they may be, must not fail to see how they contribute to the intensification of oppressive patriarchal practices in Africa and the Arab world. The upsurge of religious fundamentalism in the Middle East and other parts of the Arab world occurs as a sign of resistance to imperialism and other forms of foreign intervention. The return to the veil arises not by accident. In the name of resisting foreign interventionism, patriarchal societies resort to rigid and heavy-handed enforcement of old ways—tradition, religious fundamentalism—which often oppress women. So by fighting our wars badly, our Western sisters inadvertently collaborate in tightening the noose around our necks.

Clitoridectomy goes beyond sexuality. It raises questions with profound social, political, and economic implications.[16] Any meaningful fight against this practice must coordinate with other battles against the political, social, and economic conditions that generated and continue to perpetuate such a practice. We must consider an issue such as this

[15]See AAWORD, "A Statement on Genital Mutilation," in *Third World: Second Sex*, ed. Miranda Davies (London: Zed Press, 1983), 217–20.

[16]See Nawal El Saadawi, preface to the English edition of *The Hidden Face of Eve: Women in the Arab World* (London: Zed Press, 1980).

in all its complexities. We must establish linkages, teach connections. Furthermore, we must acknowledge the history and global nature of circumcision and clitoridectomy in order to situate the debate where it duly belongs. As Nawal El Saadawi rightly points out, the issue is not barbaric Africa and oppressive Islam. The issue is patriarchy:

> In Copenhagen, we had a lot of disagreement, we women from Africa and the Third World, with her [Fran Hoskens]. In our workshop, we argued that clitoridectomy has nothing to do with Africa or with any religion, Islam or Christianity. It is known in history that it was performed in Europe and America, Asia, and Africa. It has to do with patriarchy and monogamy. When patriarchy was established, monogamy was forced on women so that fatherhood could be known. Women's sexuality was attenuated so as to fit within the monogamous system. But she doesn't want to hear any of this.[17]

There are other aspects of teaching connections which I apply to my teaching of clitoridectomy. I teach clitoridectomy in tandem with teaching abuses of the female body in other cultures: forms of plastic surgery in the West and foot-binding in China, for example. For a Western audience I bring the issue home by comparing breast reduction surgery and clitoridectomy. We must not be distracted by the arrogance that names one procedure breast *reduction* and the other sexual *mutilation*, with all the attached connotations of barbarism. In both instances some part of the female body is excised.

Some women undergo breast reduction for some of the reasons that some young girls undergo clitoridectomy—to be more attractive, desirable, and acceptable. For the women in areas where clitoridectomy is performed, beauty is inextricably linked with chastity and motherhood. The crucial questions we must ask are: For whom are these operations undertaken? For whom must these women be desirable and acceptable? Women's inability to control their bodies is not country-specific. Abuse of the female body is global and should be studied and interpreted within the context of oppressive conditions under patriarchy. Teaching connections radically shifts the grounds for debate from racial and national particularism and idiosyncrasies to comparisons of women's oppression under patriarchy. In the American classroom I have observed that this shift interrogates and modifies the notion of self among the students, particularly the female students. They go from

[17]Quoted in Patterson and Gillam, "Out of Egypt," 90–91.

thinking nationality (American) to thinking simultaneously nationality, sex, and gender (American women).

Polygyny has been condemned in the West as one of the worst symbols of African women's oppression without any assessment of the advantages the practice accords women: sharing child care, emotional and economic support, sisterhood, companionship, and so on. Our Western sisters who pity us for having to share our husbands with other women forget that husband-sharing was perfected and elevated to an art form in the West. Polygyny comes from two Greek words: *poly* (many) and *gyne* (woman or wife). *Polygyny* has, therefore, two possible meanings—"many women," or "many wives." The English dictionary sanctifies only one of the two possibilities, "many wives," a limitation to which no one seems to object. I remember that the first English dictionary I used in the colonial school was written by one Michael West, a man. I gather that men still write dictionaries—English dictionaries!

Polygyny as "many women" places the Western man with one wife and one or more mistresses in the same category as the African man who legitimates his relationship with more than one woman. We must not also forget the brand of polygyny euphemistically called serial monogamy in the West. The need to qualify monogamy in this instance is suspect. As a matter of fact, an African woman in a polygamous relationship seems to be a step or two ahead of her Western counterpart living under the illusion that she is not sharing her husband: the African woman knows who else her husband is with. In teaching and understanding polygyny, the issue is not uncivilized Africa but men.

Arranged marriage is another issue used to illustrate the enslavement of African women. As I teach connections, I point out practices in the West similar to the arranged marriage for which African and Asian societies have been ridiculed. One wonders if the dating services mushrooming all over the United States do not engage in some similar arranging! I have watched with amazement the facility of arrangements conducted on the television show "Love Connection." On a couple of occasions I have witnessed the triumphant return of a "connected" couple to the show: the woman walks out jubilantly with a baby in her arms, and the man, now her husband, follows a few steps behind with a conspiratorial grin on his face. A family is established before our eyes, and we applaud. Again, in the issue of arranged marriage, it seems to me that African women are better off: they do not pay for the services for which their American counterparts pay exorbitantly. My American feminist friend has argued vehemently in favor of dating services because, according to her, the issue of choice is crucial. With a dating service a woman can decide to choose or not choose a particular "allocation." Incidentally, the day my friend argued her strong case, I saw sticking out of her bookshelf a book titled *Smart Women/Foolish Choices*. She must have bought the book in a moment of doubt.

At stake in our divergent views is the issue of cultural difference. In order to teach difference, we must thoroughly examine how difference comes into being. Can we distinguish between constructed and actual difference? Ideology thrives on differences; ideology actually constructs differences, thus hiding similarities and actual differences. Concerning African women in the classroom, what we see in most classrooms in the West is not the study of *African women* but rather the study of the *African woman*, in whatever way we choose to invent the myth. Usually the invented African woman carries a heavy load on her head and a baby strapped to her back, and holds two kids, with about four more in tow. Of course she lives in a village. She is the myth. The problem with myths is not what they reveal but what they conceal. In order to understand African peoples and appreciate the rich diversity of Africa, we must put a human face on the African continent. In teaching African peoples, an observer notes, "we need to breathe life into our classroom."[18] Distortions in the study and teaching of African concerns stem from imperialism's refusal to historicize and differentiate African space and peoples. We Africans must realize that our survival depends to a large extent on our ability to reclaim our history. As bell hooks correctly notes, "Our struggle is also the struggle of memory against forgetting."[19]

The understanding and mutual respect which can emanate from teaching connections are necessary tools for revisiting global sisterhood and reconceptualizing marginality. Sisterhood is not an abstraction which all women can claim simply on the basis of commonality of sex; it flourishes only through hard work. True sisterhood is a political act, a commonality rooted in knowledge, understanding, and mutual respect. For true sisterhood to emerge, women must realize the intersections of their personal and collective histories and recognize how and where their liminal histories touch. These points of intersection and convergence constitute sites of energy, power, and agency, sites where we can name ourselves or refuse to be named as we center our marginality. Only in full recognition of the possibilities of the marginal site

[18]Donna Blacker, "On Student-Centered Education," unpublished manuscript, 11.
[19]bell hooks, *Yearning: Race, Gender, and Cultural Politics* (Boston: South End Press, 1990), 148. This quote is taken from the ANC Freedom Charter.

may we begin to see it not as a position of loss and disenfranchisement but rather as a location of contestation, gain, and empowerment.

The epistemological issues raised here clearly indicate that knowledge must ground the teaching of connections. The battle flaring in the academy over issues of diversity and multiculturalism is more than a struggle over power and turf. The bitter fight to protect the sanctity of the canon and to exclude "marginal discourses" betrays an anti-intellectualism that I call the new illiteracy: the refusal of literate people to read, to learn, and consequently to know and grow.

The current debate over transforming the academy reveals that the issue of knowledge entails risks, both institutional and personal. Institutions may engage in the diversity business to give a polite nod to change and pluralism. They set out to burn a tree but find that they have set the forest ablaze. What ensues is the panic control we find in a crisis. Crisis management during a panic leads to the dangerous vacillation of one step forward, two steps back.

In response to this situation, I renew the call for a thorough examination of the relationship between sisterhood and knowledge. Susan Lanser's essay in this volume offers a fertile terrain for understanding and analyzing this relationship. True sisterhood grounded in knowledge (of self and others) will shield us from the alienation and disconnectedness of the voyeur-tourist in Lanser's study of *A Small Place*.

In order to teach our sisters, we must know them, not assume knowledge of them. Teaching connections makes great demands on our energy, time, and dedication. It compels us to retool ourselves through knowledge. Instead of using pluralism and multiculturalism as excuses for creating superficial and irrelevant visibility of peoples and issues that have for so long been relegated to the margins of scholarship, we should use them as modes of production for bringing about personal and societal transformation through knowledge. When I teach Mariama Bâ, I do not make territorial claims to the entire field of knowledge and experience contained in her work simply because, like the author, I am an African woman. Mariama Bâ's work grew out of an African tradition with which I am familiar, but it also evolved from an Islamic tradition with which I was totally unfamiliar. Her work required me to retool myself. I read the Koran and familiarized myself with Islamic culture, particularly the status of women in that culture.

The personal risks involved in teaching connections are great. The courses that are designed to teach inclusiveness and diversity stand as mirrors in which we as teachers see ourselves as well as the other alien cultural fields and cartographies of pain that come under our purview.

As we all know, self-knowledge can be frightening and humbling, but it is also necessary, healthy, and empowering. Equipped with proper and adequate knowledge, we can no longer walk though our sisters' "small place" as voyeur-tourists, but rather we become true sisters who are aware of how we and the institutions of which we are a part are implicated in creating our sisters' "small place."

What Lanser calls "unreal loyalties" may blind us to the full extent of our complicity and shield us from engaging in positive action informed by the transforming powers of knowledge. "Home politics" can be meaningful not only in terms of understanding and legitimating our "home" but also, and more important, in terms of understanding how our "homes" connect to and affect other "homes." Teaching connections requires that we grasp and teach sameness and difference simultaneously.

Notes on Contributors

Bella Brodzki is a member of the Literature Faculty at Sarah Lawrence College. With Celeste Schenck she coedited *Life/Lines: Theorizing Women's Autobiography* (1988). In addition to her work in women's autobiography, she has published articles on Borges and on feminist theory and deconstruction. Her current project is a study of slavery and the politics of subjectivity in francophone women's writing.

Vèvè A. Clark is Associate Professor of African and Caribbean Literatures in the African American Studies and Comparative Literature Departments at the University of California, Berkeley. She has published numerous articles on Caribbean literature and theater and African American dance. Clark is coeditor of *The Legend of Maya Deren: A Documentary Biography.*

Chris Cullens is an independent scholar living in San Francisco. Her book *Female Difficulties: Novels by English and German Women, 1752–1814* is forthcoming from Stanford University Press.

Greta Gaard is an Assistant Professor of Composition at the University of Minnesota, Duluth. She has published *Ecofeminism: Women, Animals, Nature* (1992).

Sabine I. Gölz, Assistant Professor of Comparative Literature and German at the University of Iowa, has published articles on Ingeborg Bachmann and Jurek Becker. Her collection of essays *The Split Scene of Reading: Nietzsche, Derrida, Kafka, and Bachmann* is forthcoming from Humanities Press.

Sarah Webster Goodwin, Associate Professor of English at Skidmore College, is author of *Kitsch and Culture: The Dance of Death in Nineteenth-*

Century Literature and Graphic Arts. She has also coedited *Feminism, Utopia, and Narrative* and *Death and Representation.*

Margaret R. Higonnet, Professor of English and Comparative Literature at the University of Connecticut, is the author of *Horn of Oberon: Jean Paul Richter's "School for Aesthetics."* She edited *The Sense of Sex: Feminist Perspectives on Hardy* (1992) and several volumes of the journal *Children's Literature;* she also coedited *Behind the Lines: Gender and the Two World Wars* (1987) and *The Representation of Women in Fiction* (1983).

Marianne Hirsch is Dartmouth Professor of French and Comparative Literature at Dartmouth College, where she helped found the Women's Studies Program. She is the author of *Beyond the Single Vision: Henry James, Michel Butor, and Uwe Johnson* and *The Mother-Daughter Plot: Narrative, Psychoanalysis, Feminism.* Currently she is working on a new project titled "Family Pictures: Photography and Narratives of Loss."

Susan Sniader Lanser is Professor of Comparative Literature, English, and Women's Studies at the University of Maryland, where she directs the Comparative Literature Program. She is the author of two books, *The Narrative Act: Point of View in Prose Fiction* (1981) and *Fictions of Authority: Women Writers and Narrative Voice* (1992). Her essays on women's studies, literary theory, and narrative poetics have appeared in *Feminist Studies, Style, Semeia,* and *Eighteenth-Century Life.* She is coediting an anthology of eighteenth-century women critics and preparing a study of social ideology and literary theory in their work.

Françoise Lionnet teaches French and comparative literature at Northwestern University. She held a Rockefeller fellowship at the Center for Advanced Feminist Studies at the University of Minnesota (1991–92). She is the author of *Autobiographical Voices: Race, Gender, Self-Portraiture* (1989) and *Spiralling Tensions: Authenticity, Universality, and Postcolonial Women Writers* (forthcoming from Cornell University Press) and the coeditor of a two-volume issue of *Yale French Studies* on postcolonial literature (1992).

Fedwa Malti-Douglas is Professor of Arabic, Semiotics, and Women's Studies and Chairperson of the Department of Near Eastern Languages and Cultures at Indiana University. She has published extensively in Arabic, French, and English on classical and modern Arabic literature and Islamic civilization. Her latest books are *Blindness and Autobiography* (1988); *Woman's Body, Woman's Word* (1991); and *Men, Women, and God(s): Nawal El Saadawi Writes Arab Feminism* (1994) .

Lore Metzger, Charles Howard Candler Professor Emeritus of English and Comparative Literature at Emory University, is the author of *One Foot in Eden: Modes of Pastoral in Romantic Poetry* (1986), and contributing editor to the *Marginalia,* volume 12 (in five parts) of the *Collected Works of S. T. Coleridge* (Princeton University Press, 1980–). She has also published articles on English and German Romantic poets and critics and is completing a book on issues of genre, gender, and ideology in Goethe's *Faust* and works of English Romanticism.

Nancy K. Miller is Distinguished Professor of English at Lehman College and The Graduate Center, CUNY. She is the author of *The Heroine's Text: Readings in the French and English Novel, 1722–1782* (1980), *Subject to Change: Reading Feminist Writing* (1988), and *Getting Personal: Feminist Occasions and Other Autobiographical Acts* (1991). She is the editor of *The Poetics of Gender* (1986) and coeditor with Joan DeJean of *Displacements: Women, Tradition, Literatures in French* (1990).

Obioma Nnaemeka is Associate Professor of French and Women's Studies at Indiana University, Indianapolis. She was a Rockefeller Humanist-in-Residence at the University of Minnesota and a visiting Edith Kreeger-Wolf Professor at Northwestern University in 1991–92. Her publications have appeared in *Signs, Feminist Issues,* and *International Third World Studies.* Her books *Agrippa D'Aubigné: The Poetics of Power and Change; Marginality: Orality, Writing, and the African Woman Writer;* and an edited volume, *Sisterhood, Feminisms, and Power,* are forthcoming.

Rajeswari Sunder Rajan has taught in both India and the United States. She has published a book of essays, *Real and Imagined Women: Gender, Culture, and Postcolonialism* (1993), and has edited *Lie of the Land: English Literary Studies in India* (1992). Her essays in cultural critique and Victorian studies have appeared in *Signs,* the *Yale Journal of Criticism, Social Scientist,* and collections. She is preparing a critical study of Dickens, "The Novel Subject: Subalternity and Realism in Dickens's Fiction."

Anca Vlasopolos, Associate Professor of English at Wayne State University, has directed the Program in Women's Studies. Her areas of specialty are feminist studies, comparative drama and poetry, especially British and French, contemporary world literature, and film. She is the author of *The Symbolic Method of Coleridge, Baudelaire, and Yeats* and of articles on Mary Wollstonecraft, *Frankenstein,* Virginia Woolf, Shakespeare, Yeats, Tennessee Williams, and the "woman's" film. She has also published a poetry chapbook, *The Evidence of Spring,* and poems in *Interim, Seneca Review, Wascana Review,* and *Moving Out.*

Index

Abel, Elizabeth, 27, 38n
Abrahams, Roger, 268, 276
academia: feminist power structures in, 301–2; financial incentives in, 264, 307–8; misogyny in, 12, 189–206, 284, 294
Accad, Evelyne, 23
Accused, The (film), 61, 75
Achebe, Chinua, 308–9, 311
ACLA (American Comparative Literature Association), 3, 4, 265, 284–86
aesthetics, in literary criticism, 195, 199, 202, 247–48, 253, 284–86, 289, 292–93
Africa: diasporic literature from, 9, 47–48, 267–79; female excision in, 21–23, 305, 312–14; internal slave market in, 48, 55–56; literature of, 10, 29–41, 42–60, 150–52, 287, 291, 301–18. *See also* African American literature
African American literature, 8, 46n, 197, 200, 268, 278; gender differences in canon acceptance of, 268, 294. *See also* slave narratives
African American Women in Defense of Ourselves, 271
Age of Sensibility, 101
Agnes von Lilien (Wolzogen), 104–7
Ahalya (Hindu legendary figure), 65, 77
Ahmad, Aijaz, 78n
Akhmatova, Anna, 147
Alcoff, Linda, 233, 235
Aldington, Richard, 152
Aldridge, A. Owen, 290
Alexinsky, Tatiana, 150, 156
Allen, Paula Gunn, 237–38
Alverdes, Paul, 149
Amadiume, Ifi, 312
American Comparative Literature Association (ACLA), 3, 4, 265, 284–86
American Scholar, 193

Amirthanayagam, Guy, 291n
Anderson, Mark, 208n
Andrade, Susan, 51, 57n
Andrews, William, 44, 57
Angelou, Maya, 61, 72, 73, 76
Annie John (Kincaid), 295
Another Mother Tongue (Grahn), 237
antiethnocentrism, 20. *See also* multiculturalism
Antigua, 280–82, 294, 297, 298
antitheater, 120–43
Anzaldúa, Gloria, 1, 237, 288
Arabic literature, 22–23, 27–28, 29–41, 224–29, 304–5, 314
Arabic women, 309–10, 313. *See also* Saadawi, Nawal El
Arac, Jonathan, 264n
Arcadia: Zeitschrift für Vergleichende Literaturwissenschaft, 251
al-Ard (film), 226n
Aristide, Jean-Bertrand, 270
Aristotle, 123, 125, 126, 130, 131, 134n, 136, 286
Armstrong, Nancy, 115, 164, 264n
Arnim, Bettina von, 108
Arnold, Matthew, 289
artists: depiction of, 96–98, 102, 144–45; and maternity, 162–85. *See also* literary production
audience. *See* drama; readers
Austen, Jane, 117, 172, 175n, 285, 294
authenticity, of authorial voice, 47, 102. *See also* authority
authority, 230, 233, 235, 261; Menchú's, 270
autobiography, 31, 32, 44–45, 83, 197. *See also* slave narratives
Awakening, The (Chopin), 173n
Awe, Bolanle, 312
Awkward, Michael, 201n

Geschichte des Fräuleins von Sternheim (La
Roche), 111
Getting Personal (Miller), 206
al-Ghîtânî, Jamâl, 226
Gide, André, 205
Gilbert, Sandra, 148, 152n, 164
Gilligan, Carol, 192
Gilman, Sander, 130–31
Girard, René, 127–29
Godzich, Wlad, 50n
Goethe, Johann, 103; and ballad form, 9,
85, 87–93; as comparatist, 253, 286, 289,
292; and German women's novels,
104–6, 111
Goldman, Dorothy, 148
Goll, Claire Studer, 150, 156
Gölz, Sabine, 11, 207–23
Goodwin, Sarah Webster, 12, 247–66
Gordimer, Nadine, 41
Gosse, Edmund, 152
gothic genre, 98n, 103, 106, 113
governesses, 178–79, 183
Grafigny, Françoise de, 281, 295, 299
Grahn, Judy, 237
Greece (ancient), 286. See also Aristotle;
Philoctetes, Plato
Greenblatt, Stephen, 257, 258, 259, 264n
Greengard, Carola, 203
Griffin, Susan, 303
Griffith, Elizabeth, 113
Grimm, Reinhold, 288
Gruber, William, 125
Guatemala, 15, 269–70
Gubar, Susan, 164
Guérillères (Wittig), 204
Guillén, Claudio, 1n, 81, 82
Guillén, Nicolas, 268
Gunew, Sneja, 30

Habiby, Emile, 226
Hager, Philip, 148
Hahn, Elisa, 112
Haiti, 267, 268, 270–71
Hall, Radclyffe, 150
Hamilton, Elizabeth, 113
Hannerz, Ulf, 296
Hardy, Thomas, 71
Harlem Renaissance, 268
Harrison, Regina, 7
Hart, Jeffrey, 194n
Hartman, Saidiya, 272
Harvest, The (Serao), 153, 160
Hays, Mary, 113
Haywood, Eliza, 111
Hazlitt, William, 96
H.D., 149

Head, Bessie, 278, 311
Hedda Gabler (Ibsen), 123, 134, 136, 141–42
"Heidenröslein" (Goethe), 90
Herder, Johann, 87
Hernadi, Paul, 82
hero: in antigeneric plays, 135–37, 142;
Aristotle on, 125
heroine, 136. See also hero
Her True-True Name (Mordecai and
Wilson), 274
heterosexuality, 168, 171–72, 235–43. See
also bisexual theory; sexuality
Hidden Face of Eve, The (Saadawi, Nawal
El), 22–23, 29–30, 36, 38, 304–5
Higonnet, Margaret, 1–16, 144–61
Highwater, Jamake, 307
Hill, Anita, 206, 271
Hill, Ruth Beebe, 307
Hinduism, 61–70
Hippel, Theodor von, 109
Hirsch, Marianne, 9–10, 20n, 162–85
history. See also cultural differences;
"new historicism"; periodization
History of Mary Prince, A West Indian
Slave, 281, 293, 298
Hodge, Merle, 274, 275–76
home: in Incidents in the Life of a Slave
Girl, 198; as metaphor, 157, 189, 318; in
The Slave Girl, 51. See also domestic
violence; exile
home front, 145, 152, 153–61
Hommes passèrent, Des (Capy), 153, 157
homosexuality. See bisexual theory;
lesbian texts; sexuality
hooks, bell, 230, 237, 278, 294, 316
Horen, Die, 104
Hoskens, Fran, 313, 314
Huber, Therese, 112–13
Hughes, Langston, 268
Hurston, Zora Neale, 144, 268
husband worship, 65
hymen, 214–16
Hynes, Samuel, 145, 148, 149, 152
"Hypocrisy Unveiled, and Calumny
Detected" (anonymous pamphlet), 88

Ibn Khallikân, 225
Ibsen, Henrik, 141–42
identity: female, 51, 69–72; individual, 8–
9, 55, 59, 298–99, 306–7; linguistic, 7; of
mixedbloods, 237, 267, 278; national,
6–7, 10, 42, 43–44, 59n; oppositional,
236, 237; politics of, 12, 46, 230–43,
301–2; racial, 46. See also bisexual
theory; female subject; gender; male
subject

Reading Women Writing

A SERIES EDITED BY
Shari Benstock and Celeste Schenck

Tainted Souls and Painted Faces: The Rhetoric of Fallenness in Victorian Culture
by Amanda Anderson
Greatness Engendered: George Eliot and Virginia Woolf
by Alison Booth
Talking Back: Toward a Latin American Feminist Literary Criticism
by Debra A. Castillo
Articulate Silences: Hisaye Yamamoto, Maxine Hong Kingston, Joy Kogawa
by King-Kok Cheung
H.D.'s Freudian Poetics: Psychoanalysis in Translation
by Dianne Chisholm
From Mastery to Analysis: Theories of Gender in Psychoanalytic Feminism
by Patricia Elliot
Feminist Theory, Women's Writing
by Laurie A. Finke
Colette and the Fantom Subject of Autobiography
by Jerry Aline Flieger
Autobiographics: A Feminist Theory of Women's Self-Representation
by Leigh Gilmore
*Cartesian Women: Versions and Subversions of Rational
Discourse in the Old Regime*
by Erica Harth
Borderwork: Feminist Engagements with Comparative Literature
edited by Margaret R. Higonnet
*Narrative Transvestism: Rhetoric and Gender in the
Eighteenth-Century English Novel*
by Madeleine Kahn
The Unspeakable Mother: Forbidden Discourse in Jean Rhys and H.D.
by Deborah Kelly Kloepfer
*Recasting Autobiography: Women's Counterfictions in Contemporary
German Literature and Film*
by Barbara Kosta
Women and Romance: The Consolations of Gender in the English Novel
by Laurie Langbauer
Penelope Voyages: Women and Travel in the British Literary Tradition
by Karen R. Lawrence